NEW PERSPECTIVES ON
the French Revolution:
READINGS IN HISTORICAL SOCIOLOGY

NEW PERSPECTIVES ON
the French Revolution:
READINGS IN HISTORICAL SOCIOLOGY

❧❦❧

JEFFRY KAPLOW

Assistant Professor of History
Columbia University

JOHN WILEY & SONS, INC.
New York   London   Sydney

Library of Congress Catalog Card Number: 65-24292
Printed in the United States of America

PREFACE

Anyone who has taught a course in the history of the French Revolution to undergraduates knows how difficult it is to surmount the language barrier. It is true that many of the older and classic works have been translated, but the current research is published largely in French and not usually translated. Because too many students do not have sufficiently developed linguistic abilities, they are unaware of these new developments, except for information they may glean from lectures.

This book was conceived as an attempt to fill the communications gap. It is a project in translation, but it is also an attempt to introduce students to new fields and methods of research. I have added a rather long introduction in an attempt to situate for the student the work of the contributors in the long-run context of French revolutionary historiography.

The choice of selections is more or less arbitrary, a reflection of what I consider to be the most fruitful approaches to the subject. I can only hope that my choice will prove, if not comprehensive, at least useful to both undergraduate and graduate students.

I should like to thank all those who have cooperated in making this book possible, and a list of specific acknowledgements is included.

JEFFRY KAPLOW

Paris
June, 1965

61280

ACKNOWLEDGMENTS

Acknowledgment is hereby made to the authors and publishers for permission to reprint the following articles, which originally appeared in their respective publications:

To the Comité des Travaux Historiques for:

M. Vovelle and D. Roche, "Bourgeois, rentiers, propriétaires: Eléments pour la définition d'une catégorie sociale à la fin du XVIIIe siècle," in Ministère de l'Education Nationale, Comité des Travaux Historiques et Scientifiques, *Actes du Quatre-Vingt-Quatrième Congrès National des Sociétés Savantes (Dijon, 1959), Section d'Histoire Moderne et Contemporaine* (Paris, 1960), pp. 419–452.

M. Vovelle, "De la mendicité au brigandage. Les errants en Beauce sous la Révolution française," Ministère de l'Education Nationale, Comité des Travaux Historiques et Scientifiques, *Actes du Quatre-Vingt-Sixième Congrès National des Sociétés Savantes (Montpellier, 1961), Section d'Histoire Moderne et Contemporaine* (Paris, 1962), pp. 483–512.

To the Société des Etudes Robespierristes for:

A. Soboul, "Problèmes du travail en l'an II," *Annales Historiques de la Révolution Française* (1956), pp. 236–259.

A. Soboul, "Sentiment religieux et cultes populaires pendant la Révolution: Saintes patriotes et martyrs de la liberté," AHRF (1957), pp. 195–213.

J. Egret, "La prérévolution en Provence," AHRF (1954), pp. 97–126.

G. Rudé, "La taxation populaire de mai 1775 à Paris et dans la région parisienne," AHRF (1956), pp. 139–179.

To the Revue Historique for:

J. Egret, "Les origines de la Révolution en Bretagne (1788–1789)," *Revue Historique*, CCXIII (1955), pp. 189–215.

G. Rudé and R. Cobb, "Le dernier mouvement populaire de la Révolution

à Paris: Les 'Journées' de Germinal et de Prairial an III," *Revue Historique*, CCXIV (1955), pp. 250–281.
To the Annales: Economies, Sociétés, Civilisations for:

F. Furet, C. Mazauric and Louis Bergeron, "Les sans-culottes et la Révolution française," *Annales: Economies, Sociétés, Civilisations*, XVIII (1963), pp. 1098–1127.
To the Société d'Histoire Moderne for:

R. Cobb, "Quelques aspects de la mentalité révolutionnaire (avril 1793–thermidor an II)," *Revue d'Histoire Moderne et Contemporaine*, VI (1959), pp. 81–120.

L. Trenard, "La crise sociale lyonnaise à la veille de la Révolution," *Revue d'Histoire Moderne et Contemporaine*, II (1955), pp. 5–45.
To the Commission d'Histoire Economique et Sociale de la Révolution Française for:

Y. Lemoigne, "Population et Subsistances à Strasbourg au XVIIIe siècle," in Commission d'Histoire Economique et Sociale de la Révolution Française, *Mémoires et Documents*, XIV, *Contributions à l'Histoire Démographique de la Révolution Française* (Paris, 1962), pp. 13–44.
To the Presses Universitaires de France for:

G. Lefebvre, "Foules révolutionnaires," in his *Etudes sur la Révolution Française* (Paris, 1954), pp. 271–287.

G. Lefebvre, "Le meurtre du comte de Dampierre," *Ibid.*, pp. 288–297.

G. Lefebvre, "Le mouvement des prix et les origines de la Révolution française," pp. 138–169.

Greatful acknowledgment is hereby made to Mrs. Orest Ranum and to Professor Robert Wagoner, Department of Humanities, State University of New York for their English translations of these articles.

CONTENTS

Introduction, 1

I. Social Structure at the End of the Eighteenth Century, 23

   M. *Vovelle and D. Roche*, Bourgeois, Rentiers, and Property Owners:
   Elements for Defining a Social Category at the End of the
   Eighteenth Century, 25

   Y. *Lemoigne*, Population and Provisions in Strasbourg in the Eighteenth Century, 47

   L. *Trénard*, The Social Crisis in Lyons on the Eve of the French Revolution, 68

II. The Beginnings of the Revolution, 101

   G. *Lefebvre*, The Movement of Prices and the Origins of the French
   Revolution, 103

   J. *Egret*, The Origins of the Revolution in Brittany (1788–1789), 136

   J. *Egret*, The Pre-Revolution in Provence (1787–1789), 153

III. The Popular Movement in the French Revolution, 171

   THE URBAN MOVEMENT, 173

G. *Lefebvre*, Revolutionary Crowds, **173**

G. *Rudé*, The Bread Riots of May 1775 in Paris and the Paris Region, **191**

A. *Soboul*, Problems of Work in Year II, **211**

F. *Furet*, C. *Mazauric*, and L. *Bergeron*, The Sans-Culottes and the French Revolution, **226**

R. *Cobb and* G. *Rudé*, The Last Popular Movement of the Revolution in Paris: The "Journées" of Germinal and of Prairial of Year III, **254**

THE RURAL MOVEMENT, **277**

G. *Lefebvre*, The Murder of the Comte de Dampierre (June 22, 1791), **277**

M. *Vovelle*, From Beggary to Brigandage: The Wanderers in the Beauce During the French Revolution, **287**

COLLECTIVE MENTALITIES, **305**

R. *Cobb*, Some Aspects of the Revolutionary Mentality (April 1793—Thermidor, Year II), **305**

A. *Soboul*, Religious Sentiment and Popular Cults During the Revolution: Patriot Saints and Martyrs of Liberty, **338**

Bibliography, **351**

NEW PERSPECTIVES ON
the French Revolution:
READINGS IN HISTORICAL SOCIOLOGY

INTRODUCTION

Because history is a constant questioning of the past by the present, it can be said that no historical epoch, no important set of historical incidents need ever lose its interest. Indeed there are always historians who devote themselves to the study of the ancient world and the Middle Ages and who find in them matter relevant to our current experience. This present-mindedness, although it has often been criticized and may, if ill used, lead to curious misinterpretations, is nonetheless the key to the writing of significant history. Without it, historical study runs the risk of becoming antiquarian, that is, of collecting facts for their own sake.

When this has been said, it becomes clear that certain periods of history are more likely to attract continuing interest than others precisely because of the connections men see between them and their own times. In the United States one such era is the Civil War and the controversy over slavery that preceded it. In France, and a good many other parts of the world, the French Revolution has stirred men's imaginations for 175 years.

No subject of historical discourse has been more controversial than the French Revolution. We have only to name a few of its many historians— Thiers, Tocqueville, Taine, Juarès, Mathiez, Lefebvre—to realize how true this statement is. It has even been maintained, not without truth, that the attitude assumed toward the French Revolution still constitutes in contemporary France the point of departure for all other political and social options.

1

The reasons for this are not far to seek. They lie in the nature of the Revolution itself. The French Revolution changed the world. It overthrew the monarchy, destroyed the widespread privileges of a parasitic aristocracy, introduced a certain amount of democracy into parliamentary government, opened careers to talented individuals, created the conditions for the generation of new wealth and a class of *nouveaux riches*, and then, through the twin agencies of propaganda and the revolutionary armies, proceeded to spread these innovations to the rest of Europe and the world. Even in areas where the specific accomplishments of the Revolution never took hold or were later destroyed, society would never again be the same, if only because revolution had now become a political fact, a threat constantly to be reckoned with. Never before had a revolution in Europe or America reached down to all strata of the population, invoked their participation and changed their lives at the ordinary, commonplace, everyday level. To put it in a positive light, the French Revolution was the first to raise what nineteenth-century Europeans liked to call the "social question" concerning the role the "lower classes" ought to play in the community.

The reactions of contemporaries to the French Revolution were many and varied. At the start there was a wide consensus of opinion that all was not well with the old regime and that certain changes were in order. The resistance to monarchical despotism, as it was called, was started by the nobility as early as 1787. When the Estates General were called in 1789, numerous liberal nobles and a large part of the clergy, including some bishops, joined with the third estate to pass reform measures and to demand a constitution. The initiative passed very early to the bourgeoisie, whose spokesmen were found among a highly articulate group of lawyers and professional men. But even at the beginning the peasants who burned the feudal records and the chateaux that contained them, the shopkeepers and artisans who rioted in the cities were already playing a central role in the revolutionary process.

But this consensus was more apparent than real. If everyone—or almost everyone—agreed that some change was necessary, they were not in agreement as to the nature of that change. Should feudal dues be destroyed outright or only redeemed by cash payments? Should the Parlements and the provincial estates be retained or abolished? Should there be a democratic suffrage, or one based on property? Should the corporate regime be abolished? What should be done with the Church? How far ought the government to go in setting prices and wages? Should the monarchy be overthrown and a republic set up in its place? What ought the French to do to defend the Revolution in the face of universal hostility? In a word, how revolutionary was the Revolution to be.

These were the problems that caused splits in the ranks of the revolutionaries as time went on. It may be said that there were four distinct phases in the Revolution, and each of them was marked by the defection of some who had been revolutionaries. The first phase (1787–1789), often called the prerevolution, was marked by aristocratic opposition to royal plans for reform. The second (1789–1791) was the truly bourgeois phase in which middle-class parliamentarians, with the aid of liberal nobles, carried out their program. There were already certain notorious defections at this time. The King's brothers, the Comte d'Artois and the Comte de Provence, emigrated in 1789. More important still, men like Mounier, a lawyer and important revolutionary leader from the Dauphiné, withdrew from political life, because he felt that popular sovereignty had already become a threat. In the third period (1791–1794), characterized by an increased participation of the *sans-culottes* in an effort to push the Revolution in a more democratic direction, emigration began on a mass scale, and it was by no means limited to members of the nobility, just as victims of the Terror came from all classes of society. This phase witnessed the beginning of a deep and lasting split within the bourgeoisie. Some bourgeois, the Montagnards in particular, assumed the leadership of the popular movements, while others passed over to the opposition. The triumph of that opposition after the fall of Robespierre (1794–1799) constitutes the last phase of the Revolution before the accession of Napoleon. The Thermidorean Reaction and the Directory which succeeded it marked an attempt by the bourgeoisie to consolidate its power within the framework of the reforms of 1789–1791. This time it was the men of the Left who found themselves deprived of power.

The Revolution was, then, many things to many people. As reality fell out with their dreams, they were faced with the necessity of making a choice. They had either to accept that reality or to battle against it. Those who chose the latter course were of several sorts.

There were, first of all, those who may be called the pure reactionaries, those to whom all change was suspect, if not evil by definition. The Comte d'Artois, the future Charles X, was such. The very idea of an Estates General seeking to dictate policy to the king was repugnant to him, and so he left the country in order to rally counter-revolutionary forces. He was simply defending his power and authority, just as surely as the domestics who accompanied him did so in order to go on making a wage.

The cases of others who deserted the revolutionary cause are not quite so simple. There were those who despised democracy and were convinced that nothing but anarchy could come of it. There were those whose grievances were of a religious nature. Some were hostile to a government that attempted to regulate the economy and thus flew in the face of common sense and the laws of nature and/or society. Still others were shocked by what they felt to be the brutality of the Reign of Terror. It can be argued that all these reactions are explicable only in relation to the social position of the interested parties. But to maintain that there was a one to one relationship between these options and the social class of those who held to them is to overlook a thousand nuances. The reaction of a given individual is ultimately explicable only in biographical terms. And that is why it is incorrect to argue that the defection of one or a whole series of bourgeois must necessarily challenge the concept of the bourgeois nature of the French Revolution. In other words, the analysis of a group's action remains valid even though it can be shown that some members of the group had motives different from those of the whole for acting as they did. It is a matter of precision, not contradiction.

But this is to go off on another track. The point here is simply that contemporary reactions have been carried on across time in the historiography of the Revolution. An essay on this subject would run to a fair-sized book and thus cannot be attempted here. A few pages about the different schools of interpretation are nonetheless necessary in order to situate the work of the scholars represented in this book.

The first distinction that must be drawn is between historians who are prorevolutionary and those on the counter-revolutionary side. Taking them in chronological order, the former include Thiers, Guizot, Michelet, Aulard, Jaurès, Mathiez, and Lefebvre, and the latter, Taine, Cochin, Funck-Brentano, and Gaxotte. The list is not complete, but it represents the major tendencies. Most notable by its absence is the name of Tocqueville, not so easily classifiable in either group.

Adolphe Thiers (1797–1877)[1] and François Guizot (1787–1874)[2] were both active politicians in the second and third quarters of the nineteenth century. Both held high ministerial office, Guizot being identified primarily with the July Monarchy, while he served as Prime Minister, while Thiers went on to play a most important role as the first President of the Third Republic. Although they often opposed one another in politics, they shared a common view of the Revolution and, indeed, of the evolution of European society since the Middle Ages. For them, the motive force of the previous several centuries had been the bourgeoisie. That class had had to struggle against all sorts of obstacles set up by kings and aristocrats in order to free itself from oppression and to take its rightful place of authority within the French nation. The Revolution was its crowning achievement. If it was regrettable that certain of the more radical elements of the third estate, that is, those without property, had succeeded in pushing the Revolution to the left and into the Terror, the whole process was nonetheless justified because it resulted in the accession of the bourgeoisie to power.

In Thiers and Guizot, we find representatives of a bourgeoisie not yet afraid to admit its revolutionary origins. It would be a mistake to look at them as callous, because they lacked sympathy with popular aspirations and failed to take sufficient account of the popular movement in the Revolution. They followed the nineteenth-century liberal program in both their history and their politics. Guizot's reply to those who argued that the Revolution had done nothing for the dispossessed is typical. "Get rich," he said. He meant that one ought to take advantage of the unbounded oppor-

[1] Adolphe Thiers, *Histoire de la Révolution française* (Paris, 1823–1827, ten volumes).
[2] François Guizot, *Histoire de la civilisation en France* (Paris, 2nd edition, 1840, four volumes)

tunities for economic expansion in midnineteenth-century France. Progress was the order of the day, and anyone might participate in it if only he would make the effort.

It was perhaps in reaction to this point of view that Jules Michelet (1798–1874) wrote his *Histoire de la Révolution Française.*[3] Michelet was the first academic historian to deal with the subject. He was at the same time a stylist of a high order in the Romantic tradition, who exercised great influence over several generations of Frenchmen. He found ecstatic accents to celebrate the Revolution, which was to him the work of the "people," whom he defined as synonymous with the French nation. "One thing that must be said to everyone . . . is that the human and benevolent epoch of our Revolution [that is, before the Terror] was the work of the people itself, the whole people, everyone. And the epoch of violence, the epoch of sanguinary acts into which danger later pushed it was the work of a minimal, infinitely small number of men," he wrote.[4] The people, from the honest worker to the "charitable and compassionate" prostitute, incarnated wisdom and goodness. In its most glorious moments, the Revolution had been the expression of that people, whom nothing separated from the bourgeoisie. There had been no classes, only individuals full of devotion to the common good. How noble and glorious was this struggle for human emancipation, a struggle over ideas, not inspired by mundane material considerations, like the need for bread. Those who, like Louis Blanc,[5] dared to suggest that famine might have had something to do with it were false friends of the Revolution.[6]

If one thing characterizes Michelet's history, it is his generosity of spirit. He was striving—quite deliberately, I think—to forge the various classes of French society into a single whole, despite their differences. He would even deny that those differences existed. Writing in 1868 of the Revolution he had lived through twenty years earlier, he spoke of it, correctly, as a struggle between "the diverse children of the Revolution." But he added: "We exaggerated the differences that divided us."[7] Nothing could have been further from the truth in 1848 and subsequently. Michelet's failure to recognize this fact or perhaps his semiconscious wish to avoid this recognition made it difficult for him to see the diversity of forces at work in the Revolution of 1789. His *History* consequently suffered and fell victim to his moral options. Today we read his works more as documents of the state of mind of a midnineteenth-century French intellectual than for their historical value.

After 1870 the conflict between historians of the French Revolution

[3] Jules Michelet, *Histoire de la Révolution française* (Paris, 1847–1853, seven volumes). The edition cited was edited by Gerard Walter and published by Gallimard in the Bibliothèque de la Pléiade, 1952 (two volumes).

[4] Michelet, *Révolution*, I, 7.

[5] Louis Blanc, *Histoire de la Révolution française* (Paris, 1847–1862, twelve volumes).

[6] Michelet, *op. cit.*, I, 81, 228–29, 293.

[7] *Ibid.*, I, 10.

became one between republicans and antirepublicans. Now, the republican parties in France have always ranged over a broad spectrum of political choices. They have in common only their acceptance of the Republic as a framework for action. The Revolution founded the Republic and was thus part of its heritage. It was clear that it ought to be defended. But how, in what sense? The way was still open for numerous disagreements.

Alphonse Aulard (1849–1928) held the first chair of history of the Revolution established by the city of Paris in 1886 in the Sorbonne. He was a Radical-Socialist, that is, a member of the party most closely allied to the Jacobin tradition. The party's ideal was a France of small landowners and small industrial and commercial entrepreneurs, whose hold on property would be justified by their working for a living alongside their employees. And the assumption was that the employees might someday raise themselves up to the same level. If the Revolution had not completely succeeded in establishing such a society, it had gone a long way toward the goal. Perhaps there was still room for reform, but the essential of nineteenth-century progress was already an accomplished fact—France was a democratic state in which the influence of the Church was on the wane.

Aulard considered the Revolution from this point of view. To him it was essentially a political movement and he neglected to study its social, economic, and cultural aspects in depth. It has indeed been justly remarked that his *Histoire Politique de la Révolution Française* (1901) [8] is no more than a history of republican ideas between 1789 and 1799. The neglect of certain areas of study resulted in something of a disfiguration of revolutionary history. But Aulard's great contribution—and his outstanding merit— was his defense of the Republic against those who looked upon it as *la Gueuse*, the fallen woman, the root of all contemporary evil.

The chief hero of the Radical-Socialist school of historians was Danton. Jacobins though they were, they distrusted Robespierre and the Terror. Above all, they found them embarrassing. All too often they accepted the version of the Terror presented by right-wing writers. They did not understand that the Terror was a necessary instrument of political action in a country faced with internal conspiracies and the external threat of the European coalition. To Robespierre, who accepted the responsibility for the Terror although he did not create it singlehandedly, they preferred the calmer, more deliberate action of Danton. It may also be that their lack of sympathy for the "Incorruptible" was due to his economic program, the general maximum in particular.

The quarrel between defenders of Danton and Robespierre was, in reality, based on a much more fundamental difference of opinion. It marks the emergence of a new, radical school of historians led by Jaurès, Mathiez, and Lefebvre.

First of all, these historians turned their attention to social and economic,

[8] Aulard's work has been translated into English under the title, *The French Revolution: A Political History* (New York, 1910, four volumes).

rather than exclusively political, questions. Much influenced by Marx, they could no longer be content to view the Revolution as only a debate over politics carried through by a kind of united anti-monarchical front. Further, their sympathy for the popular movement led them to rehabilitate Robespierre, who had hitherto been viewed as a demagogue and dictator.

Jean Jaurès (1859–1914), whose work as a historian was only a sideline to his major activity as the leader of French socialism, published his *Histoire Socialiste de la Révolution Française* in 1901–1904.[9] The most important thing about the book is the author's instinctive sympathy for his characters. Perhaps it was because of his own political experience that Jaurès was able to cast so much light on the strivings of the *sans-culottes*. In his hands, the popular movement began to take on a certain consistency and texture. It would be left to others to flesh in the portrait, and all historians who have carried on in this way acknowledge the debt they owe Jaurès. His suggestions for further research are even now far from being exhausted.

Albert Mathiez (1874–1932), who succeeded Aulard at the Sorbonne at the end of World War I, was responsible more than any other man for the apotheosis of Robespierre. Spurred on by the pressure of the popular movement—proof of whose independent existence Mathiez also helped to establish—the Montagnards were willing to mobilize the country against counter-revolution. This entailed regulation of the economy, creation of a military establishment, and political purges. Terror became a necessity when they met with resistance. Robespierre was willing to assume the grave responsibility implied by the application of this policy. He knew that, to borrow a phrase from Jaurès, the future of his country, of generations yet unborn depended on his actions and so he "called upon death to create around him the unanimity of opinion of which he had need."

Mathiez' contribution [10] to our knowledge was enormous. It would be most unjust to paint him in the colors of a simple hero worshipper. But because he did not fully understand the desires of the *menu peuple*, he concluded, somewhat ironically given his declared left-wing sympathies, that everything to the left of Robespierre was not only ephemeral but somehow undesirable.

Georges Lefebvre (1874–1959),[11] it may be said, carried on where Mathiez left off. His own major work had to do with the peasants during the Revolution. But he encouraged more intensive research on social structures and the activity of the *sans-culottes* which has resulted in new interpretations of the Montagnards and the Revolutionary Government being put forth. Robespierre, for all his greatness, was caught in an insoluble dilemma. Be-

[9] There is a second edition edited by Mathiez (Paris, 1922–1924, eight volumes).
[10] A. Mathiez, *La Révolution française* (Paris, 1922–1924, three volumes). Mathiez was extraordinarily prolific, and it would be impossible to cite all his works here. Particular attention should, however, be paid to his *La Vie chère et le mouvement populaire sous la Terreur* (Paris, 1927).
[11] See, in particular, his *La Révolution française* (Paris, 1957, third edition).

lieving in the Jacobin ideal, he was forced by circumstance to establish a controlled economy. This he considered a temporary expedient, to be used judiciously. However well disposed he may have been personally toward the demands of the *sans-culottes* for bread and work, he had to reckon with his political supporters, many of them proprietors not at all happy with the legislation on price limitation, the maximum. He thus was forced to adopt the policy of a blow to the left for every blow struck at the right, and he intensified the Terror. Consequently, he had no one to appeal to when his former supporters turned against him. At the same time, the *sans-culottes*, who did not constitute a social class but only a political group of petit bourgeois shopkeepers, master artisans, and wage earners, acted only under the pressure of immediate misery. They were too divided among themselves, too much a part of the eighteenth-century status system, to resist success-fully either Robespierre or the much more oppressive policy of the Thermi-dorean Reaction that followed him. Lacking the cohesion of a social class, they could not generate their own leadership and a common program that alone would have allowed them to survive as a political force.

For all their quarrels, the Republican historians form a single group when compared to those who stand on the other, counter-revolutionary side. In-deed, there have been few right-wing historians who have made important contributions to our knowledge of the Revolution. Is this because they have been too busy denouncing it? Perhaps. It may also be that their lack of sympathy for its accomplishments keeps them from understanding it.

There are, even so, different schools of interpretation among the counter-revolutionaries. Some, like Funck-Brentano [12] and Gaxotte,[13] are content to recall eighteenth-century comforts and to deplore their loss. The argument implicit in this sort of work is that all that is despicable and corrupt in present-day society might have been avoided but for the Revolution. These books have an enormous public in France, but they are more tracts for the times than serious works of historical scholarship.

More important is the argument of Hippolyte Taine (1828–1893) who published his *Origines de la France Contemporaine* between 1875 and 1893. Taine's opposition to the Revolution was, no doubt, at least partially inspired by his fear of contemporary upheavals. He had lived through the Paris Commune of 1871, which was for him a kind of anarchy in which all kinds of injurious passions had been allowed to run wild. The year 1871 was only the fulfillment, the logical consequence of 1789. What, precisely, had happened?

For Taine all members of a society are cells of a single social organism for whom the primary need is the conservation of the whole. The task of conservation constitutes a duty to the community that has nourished and protected the individual since childhood. A kind of contract may be said to

[12] Fr. Funck-Brentano, *La Révolution*, volume V of *l'Histoire de France racontée à tous*, ed. L. Madelin (Paris, 1911).
[13] P. Gaxotte, *La Révolution française* (Paris, 1928).

exist which must be preserved. To achieve this, there is a need for authority to be placed in the most capable hands. The law ought to serve neither the majority nor the minority, but the entire community. No one has a right to change this order of things, because the "commonweal" belongs to the past, present, and future. "Each generation is only the temporary administrator of a precious and glorious patrimony that it has received from the preceding one with the injunction to transmit it to the following one." [14] Taine put the argument more strikingly when he noted that "in the matter of history, it is better to continue than to begin again." [15]

This was perhaps the primary fault of the men of 1789. Their movement "was not a revolution, but a dissolution" of all tradition.[16] That the old regime was in many ways unjust and inadequate Taine readily admitted. The city crowds were moved by hunger, and they can hardly be blamed. But essentially all France needed were two reforms: equal taxation and a new form of control over the state treasury. "It was enough; for a human society, like a living body, falls into convulsions when one performs overly large operations upon it; and the two reforms referred to, although limited, were probably all that France could bear in 1789." [17]

But if the old regime fell of its own weight as it were, the causes of the Revolution are to be found elsewhere—in the philosophy of the Enlightenment.

Visibly a new ferment had entered into the ignorant and boorish mass, and the new ideas had their effect. It had been a long time since they had filtered imperceptibly from one stratum to another, and after having won over the aristocracy, and the entire literate part of the third estate, the men of the law, the schools, all the youth, they had insinuated themselves drop by drop and through a thousand cracks into the class that lived by the work of its hands. the *grands seigneurs*, while dressing, had scoffed at christianity and affirmed the rights of man in front of their valets, their wigmakers, their suppliers, and all their servants. The men of letters, the lawyers and solicitors had repeated, in a rougher tone, the same diatribes and the same theories in the cafés, in the restaurants, on the promenades, and in all public places. Men had spoken before the people as if they were not there, and, from this eloquence spread about without care, spatterings had reached into and taken hold of the brains of the artisan, the tavernkeeper, the messenger, the woman dealing in second-hand goods, and the soldiers." [18]

Because it had good reason to be discontent, the multitude was ready to accept these ideas. These ideas released in them a political passion that would soon destroy everything in its path.

[14] Taine, *Origines*, III, 217ff.
[15] *Ibid.*, I, 41.
[16] Taine, *Origines*, III, 3–4.
[17] *Ibid.*, III, 216.
[18] Taine, *Origines*, III, 40–41.

But what was wrong with the ideas in question? They were too simple, and reduced everything to the single dimension of reason, while denying the authority of religion and tradition. When this happens, only one result is possible: anarchy followed by despotism. The bourgeoisie, by spreading these ideas, had called forth the people, "a blind and frightened brute." Had there been conspiracy? Not necessarily, although it was certain that "the Machiavellis of public places and evil haunts had stirred up the men of the gutter and the women of the streets." [19] Left without restraint, the people acted basely and brutishly, eventually even throwing over those who had urged them on. The ravages of unlimited violence comes to an end only with the rise of a military dictator who constructs "philosophical barracks," [20] institutes the omnipotence of the state, destroys private initiative, and suppresses the moral qualities of human nature. Napoleon is thus seen as the logical, the necessary consequence of the Revolution, and the France of 1870 is seen as his heir.

No doubt the ablest representative of conservative historiography in the period just before World War I was Augustin Cochin, although his principal book was not published until 1925, several years after his death.[21] In the tradition of Taine he undertook to show how the upholders of Enlightenment ideas had in fact influenced the outbreak of the Revolution. He argued that a group of men, whom we might today call the intelligentsia, drawn from both the nobility and the bourgeoisie, had conspired to destroy the monarchy. Organized in what he labeled "sociétés de pensée" or "thinking societies," ranging from salons to provincial academies and from reading rooms to Masonic lodges, these men were as fertile in ideas as they were far removed from reality. Because the monarchy was weak and indecisive, they were able to grasp the opportunity offered them by the agitation of 1787–1789 and by the convocation of the Estates General to influence public opinion. Men of the pen, they were masters of propaganda. Respected and powerful in their communities, they were able to control the elections and the drawing of the cahiers, even when their wishes did not correspond to the demands of their constituents, as was particularly true in peasant communities. And finally, when they got to Paris they organized themselves into clubs, the better to be able to control the deliberations of the Estates.

There is no doubt a grain of truth in the above interpretations. It is doubtful that the ideas of the Enlightenment had any direct influence on the outbreak of the Revolution. On the other hand, numerous revolutionary leaders had in fact been active in provincial learned societies, had become accustomed to questioning the accepted standards of the day. And if the Revolution was not *caused* by ideas, it was nonetheless a battle between holders of diametrically opposed ideologies.

[19] *Ibid.*, III, 153.
[20] *Ibid.*, VIII, 430–31.
[21] Augustin Cochin, *Les Sociétés de pensée et la Révolution en Bretagne*, 1788–1789 (Paris, 1925, two volumes).

It is a long way, however, from this recognition to the statement that the revolutionary leaders acted out of allegiance to abstract formulae. It is further still to the thesis that they directly controlled, or at least influenced, the popular outbreaks of 1789. To argue in addition that a conspiracy actually existed is to venture into a no man's land from which all evidence is absent.

A word remains to be said about Alexis de Tocqueville (1805–1859), an historian who cannot be easily classified in either of the above categories. The scion of a Norman family of the *petite noblesse*, he was born in 1805 and so grew up in the new regime. By the time he turned to the study of the Revolution, he was already well known as a political analyst for *Democracy in America* published in 1836. He had been in politics, a member of the Chamber of Deputies during the July Monarchy, and had been forced into retirement by the advent of the Second Empire in 1851. An aristocrat to the manner born, he probably felt that monarchy was the best system of government. But he was not unfriendly to parliamentary institutions. It was a question now of making the best of the heritage of the Revolution. Blind reaction, a desperate hanging on to the status quo would not do. It was far better to recognize the necessities of the hour and yield —partially—to them. Only in that way could a certain freedom of action be preserved. Reform could prevent revolution.

In *The Old Regime and the Revolution*,[22] Tocqueville viewed 1789 as the result of the irresponsible action of the monarchy on all fronts. Ever since Louis XIV, the French crown had been striving for absolute power. It had downgraded the aristocracy, prevented the bourgeoisie from taking a legitimate part in government, and oppressed the masses. But at the same time it had driven a wedge among the several classes. When each reacted to monarchical pretentions—and circumstances willed that these reactions should be simultaneous—the result was the destruction of the old regime. The mutual hatreds created by royal tactics of division and conquest made the creation of a stable system of government practically impossible. And so France had been, and was likely to continue, in a state of turmoil.

Tocqueville's analysis suffered from the weakness of being based on the assumption that social conflict could have been avoided, had the monarchy been of a different sort. On the other hand, it accepted conflict, however regrettable, as a *fait accompli*. Therein, together with its emphasis on real social divisions and insistence on research, lies its strength. That is why we can continue to read Tocqueville today with profit although not always with confidence, for further research had invalidated many of his conclusions.

A very brief background of present-day studies of the French Revolution has been sketched here. They have lost none of their passion, although the tone is at once more erudite and less polemical than it once was. This book

---

[22] A. de Tocqueville, *L'ancien régime et la Révolution* (Paris, 1856). The best edition is printed as volume II of Tocqueville's *Oeuvres Complètes* (Paris, 1956), edited by J. P. Mayer with an introduction by Georges Lefebvre. The currently available English translation (New York: Anchor Books, 1955) is not always reliable.

is intended to illustrate some of the new questions being asked and the new approaches being used to resolve them.

Every book, even a collection of readings as this is, has a thesis or, if you will, a moral. In this case it is to argue against ivory-tower history, the accumulation of facts for facts' sake. Frenchmen who have studied their Revolution have always approached the subject with questions suggested by concern with the contemporary world. The results have been salutary, constantly opening new perspectives onto the past. Without this consciousness, what we write will be the hollowest sort of acadamic exercise, without passion and without significance. Our obligation is never knowingly to distort the facts, but any other "objectivity" is excluded by the very nature of the historian's task, the ordering of evidence according to criteria of what is and what is not important, that is, according to assumptions of how society develops. If we accept this way of proceeding, the prospects for the study of the French Revolution will remain bright. The events of our own time will see to it that its history continues to be fascinating. It is up to us to keep it significant.

The readings in this book deal with three basic topics: social structure at the end of the old regime, the beginnings of the Revolution, and the popular movement. This selection does not by any means exhaust the possible topics. A section on the influence of the Enlightenment, studies of the counterrevolution (an increasingly popular field of research) might have been included, to name only two possibilities. I have chosen these three subjects, not only because I think them important, but also because enough work has already been done on them to permit us to draw up a statement of preliminary results.

In recent years, two different but complementary types of research have come to the fore in the study of the Revolution. Under the direction of Professor Labrousse of the Sorbonne, a large group of scholars is using the latest in statistical and computer techniques to analyze notarial archives (wills, marriage contracts, property transfers, and so on) and fiscal records to get an accurate picture of French social structure on the eve of the Revolution. It is no longer satisfactory merely to generalize about the nature of this or that class, we must know them at first hand in all their complexity. The notion of class is still considered basic, but it is no longer assumed that belonging to a given class breeds ideology and political action in a one to one ratio. Each class contained many groups distinguished from one another according to levels of wealth, occupation, access to authority, social contacts, geographical location, to name only a few criteria, and they are often in conflict with one another. The close and rigorous study of social relationships at the local level—in so far as they can be isolated within the society as a whole—will pave the way for a new synthesis.

The popular movement in the Revolution, in the provinces as well as in

Paris, has also been studied through the use of similar techniques. In an age of revolutionary upheaval, we are increasingly concerned with the motives of mass discontent and the way in which that discontent is mobilized in politics. In the case of the French Revolution, this concern has led to a renewed interest in economic history, for it has been shown that there was a direct correlation between popular outbreaks and the price of bread.

There is, however, a missing link. People grumble under stress of economic hardship, but it does not automatically lead them to take revolutionary action. Obviously, they interpret their situation within the framework of preconceived notions and inherited ideas. If this is true, then there can be no task more imperative for the historian than to find out how men's minds operated in the past. Without this there can be no real understanding, unless, of course, we assume that men's minds always operate in the same way, which is only to ring the changes on the old theme of an unchanging human nature now so justly discredited.

The urgent need for this kind of study will perhaps become clear when we note that by the "operation of men's minds" we do not mean formal logic and the teachings of philosophers. We mean, rather, the symbols that were significant to specific groups, their value systems, traditions, amusements, family relationships. All this and more make up "collective mentalities." The techniques of psychoanalysis applied to dead individuals can at best secure only speculative, or presumptive, knowledge. The study of collective mentalities can, by exploiting as sources the artifacts of everyday life as well as the cultural representations thereof, get to the heart of past society. Happily, more and more work is being done in this field of historical psychology.

Let us look now at the results the application of these research techniques to the history of the French Revolution have achieved. As we go along we will also note some of the problems that remain to be solved.

The French Revolution has generally been seen as a bourgeois revolution, and all of the historians represented in this book agree on this point. It is true that this has not been a universally shared point of view. Only recently, Professor Alfred Cobban of the University of London has been at pains to prove its inadequacy.[23] Although, in my view, he has not succeeded, he has raised some points that merit consideration.

If the Revolution can be qualified as bourgeois, it is because the bourgeoisie initiated it and emerged triumphant from it. That this triumph may not have been complete and that the bourgeoisie was later obliged to exercise its power in collaboration with survivors of the old-regime nobility or by calling upon a man on horseback does not alter the argument. Nor does the knowledge that other classes collaborated in the making of the Revolution and came close to pushing it in the direction they desired

[23] A. Cobban, *The Social Interpretation of the French Revolution* (London, 1964). See also his *Myth of the French Revolution* (London, 1955) and my review of his latest work to be published in the *American Historical Review*, July 1965.

alter it. On the other hand, it is most relevant to ask exactly who were the bourgeois, that is, did a bourgeoisie really exist. If it did not, then the whole argument falls to the ground.

The problem, then, is to define the bourgeoisie. Clearly what we have come to call the bourgeoisie in the nineteenth century did not yet exist in the eighteenth. There was, prior to the Revolution, no class of industrialists owning the means of production and operating within a capitalist model. The existence of such a class was a result rather than a cause of the French Revolution, although it had already begun to develop before that. But does that mean that there was no bourgeoisie at all? I think not. What of all those who occupied the middle ranks of society between the nobility on the one side and the "people" on the other? They did have distinguishing characteristics. They were set apart from the nobility by legal privileges and disabilities. They were excluded from the command posts of the state, at least on the national level. Many of them engaged in economic activities that the nobility disdained or was restrained from participating in by considerations of tradition and prestige. Those who did not directly engage in commerce or industry were often tied to these activities by family origins or marriage. In the professions—the army, the Church, the law—they were assigned certain roles which nobles did not care to play. At the same time, they were set apart from the "people" by their wealth, their contacts, their access to local political power. They were beginning to become conscious of themselves as a class and shared a definite set of values.

In my view, all this is enough to constitute a separate class. It is, to be sure, a class constantly in the process of *becoming*, not yet fully formed, still open to penetration from below, still lacking the essential element of a fully formed class consciousness. Certainly, it did not have the unity or consistency of its nineteenth-century successor, which could only develop as the road was cleared for the acquisition of new forms of wealth. There were great differences between a *négociant* in Paris and a small-town provincial lawyer, between the resident of a commercial town and one whose city was dominated by the presence of a Parlement. They would react differently to the same stimuli. But they had in common their exclusion from the consecrated power structure, their favorable disposition toward change, their potential revolutionism.

What we know about the eighteenth-century bourgeoisie is extremely limited. The reading by MM. Vovelle and Roche printed here is enough to show the great material differences that existed between one section of the bourgeoisie of Chartres and that of one Parisian quarter. Not only must this kind of study be extended to other areas and to include other bourgeois elements, but we must also begin to study other aspects of the bourgeoisie —its recruitment and its style of life. The subject is not an easy one, for the sources are sometimes sparse and always difficult to work with. Literary evidence is available, but it cannot be relied on exclusively. Still, there do exist tax rolls, marriage contracts, records of property transfers, inventories of possessions, wills, statements of bankruptcies, and, less frequently, account books, and records of purchase of offices that are invaluable for the study of material conditions. An elementary knowledge of accounting, of eighteenth-century legal and financial procedures is prerequisite to their use. Handwriting has its peculiarities, but it is not a major problem.

Still more difficult to carry to a successful conclusion is the study of the bourgeois mentality. There are only occasional memoirs and diaries still in existence. We are more likely to find good source material in administrative correspondence (letters of town officials to ministers, for instance) and in the pleadings of the lawyers. Of course, the proceedings of academies and debating clubs and lists of the contents of private libraries are not to be overlooked.

With the next reading we turn to the problem of studying the "lower classes." It should be noted immediately that the plural is justified, for we are not dealing with a proletariat in the modern sense. Such a class did not exist in the eighteenth century. Rather, we are dealing with what the French like to call *le menu peuple*, the little people, meaning all those who worked with their hands, were poor, and/or occupied a marginal position in the struggle for survival. They cover a wide range of social groups, from the master artisan in the food or clothing trades working alone or with the help of an employee or two (often an apprentice) and increasingly subject to the control of a large-scale merchant, to the fruit seller, street merchant, messenger, domestic, agricultural laborer forced to seek urban employment, and beggar. They run the gamut from the well-established, if poor, shopkeeper to the wanderer in search of a job or subsistence. The differences among the various categories are infinite and, once again, have not been sufficiently studied. They have in common, however, a living made by the work of their hands and the constant threat of loss of their already limited means of survival.

The reading by M. Lemoigne serves to introduce us to some of their problems. The author argues that in the period after 1750 there was an increasing imbalance between demographic growth and the food supply. No longer do we have a situation in which famines and epidemics kill off great numbers of people suddenly and without warning. Rather, more people survive to maturity than previously. But they live on a marginal level of subsistence, constantly threatened. In other words, the eighteenth-century economy did not absorb them, but neither did it destroy them. The consequences of this state of affairs are not far to seek. Poverty in the midst of plenty creates tensions for which there is no resolution within the system. There must be increasing discontent. But what form did it assume? Must it necessarily lead to the development of a political consciousness and thence to revolution? These are questions which still remain to be answered.

Lemoigne takes Strasbourg and the Alsatian hinterland as his field of study. We have now to carry on from there, to use his suggestions in extending the analysis to the rest of the country. The development or degeneration of material conditions needs to attract our attention. In addition to the questions of recruitment and style of life which are always basic to a study of class divisions, we need microcosmic analysis of diverse professional groups. We must try to gain some understanding of the mental sets of these people. We want to know about the role of the guilds in setting the conditions of the work process. We ought to investigate the way in which eighteenth-century charitable institutions worked, perhaps constituting a kind of safety valve for popular discontent. We want to know about crime, both amateur and professional, as an outlet for frustration. The study of other manifestations of social disorganization (alcoholism, prostitution, insanity, suicide, and so on) may enable us better to comprehend the people who were later to become part of the revolutionary crowd and the *sans-culottes* movement.

Once again the problem is how to go about getting at source material. We are dealing with people who were largely illiterate and inarticulate. On the other hand, certain kinds of evidence are available. There are population statistics issued by government agencies and recorded by private observers. They are not always reliable and must be used with great care. If they do not give us precise indications, they can furnish orders of magnitude. In many areas registers of baptism, marriages, and deaths survive that can be used as a clue to demographic developments. The parish registers often include information on family relationships that are invaluable.

Another bias by which the study of the "lower classes" can be approached is that of the food supply. Price lists and, to a lesser extent, wage records can be consulted. The administrative correspondence is abundant, particularly in times of shortage and crisis. Material on beggary and plans for doing something about it are found scattered throughout the archives. Guild records are available. Hospital and prison archives add to our knowledge of crime and mores. Finally, the multiplicity of administrations that overlapped one another in the eighteenth century has left us reports that are goldmines of social history—the interrogations of persons accused of crime is only one example.

The last reading in this section deals with Lyons, France's second city. It is an excellent illustration of social conflict before the Revolution, but it also shows what forces were at work to keep social conflict from coming into the open. It shows that eighteenth-century institutions, the guilds in particular, impeded the conversion to industrial capitalism. Perhaps even more important, we learn that all parts of the *Grande Fabrique*—merchants, master craftsmen, journeymen, and apprentices—had become so accustomed to things as they were, so morally (and economically) committed to the maintenance of the old system that they opposed this changeover. This is paradoxical in light of the fact that the textile industry, of which Lyons was one of the major centers, was no doubt the most highly developed, the most economically modern of all French enterprises at this time. This made for special problems, for it implied the existence of a strong commercial bourgeoisie and an increasing polarization between it and other elements of the population. We can already see in the reactions of the master craftsmen in 1789 that drive for political democracy and for the maintenance of economic traditionalism which was to characterize the *sans-culottes*. Furthermore, the exceptional situation of this great urban center is the beginning of an explanation of its turn toward counter-revolution in 1793.

When we consider the outbreak of the Revolution, we come smack up against an old cliché: revolutions only take place in times of severe economic misery. Indeed, this was the assumption of most writers before Tocqueville, if they thought at all about economic conditions. Tocqueville then showed that France was indeed in the midst of a great expansionary cycle in 1789, and he reasoned from there that revolution came about at a point when people had made enough progress to begin to realize the unlimited opportunities that lay before them, if only certain noneconomic restraints could be removed. There is little doubt that he was right—in part. The growth of productivity, of foreign trade, the development of new industries (metallurgy, for example), the extension of the road and canal network all mark the possibility of an increased accumulation of wealth. And economic growth had a political impact in that it stimulated the bourgeoisie to think of itself as the only productive, and therefore desirable, part of the French nation. But—and it is a big but—1789 was also a time of economic recession. The researches of Professor Labrousse [24] have demonstrated the mechanisms of this crisis: poor harvests, rise in agricultural prices, the closing of the internal market for manufactured goods, competition between town and country laborers for a smaller number of jobs. The crisis may have been made still more serious, as the contemporaries liked to argue, by the application of the Anglo-French Commercial Treaty of 1786.

The Revolution was, then, the result of both growth and decay. The paradox is more apparent than real. Simply stated, it is a fact that economic growth in a nascent capitalist system does not proceed in a linear fashion. There are, rather, cycles of upward thrust and retrenchment alternating with one another. The balance over the long run is indisputably positive, but men react to short-term economic influences rather than to charts showing progress over an eighty-year period. If, as has already been stated, growth had insensibly brought about a change of outlook within the bourgeoisie, hardship urged them on to the work of renovation. For a great part of the peasantry and the urban mass, the rise in the price of bread was the last in a long series of grievances and the one responsible for stirring them to revolutionary action. The selection by Georges Lefebvre undertakes to sum up the work of Professor Labrousse and to place it in the theoretical context offered by François Simiand.

Whatever the economic and social pressures that eventuated in the out-

[24] Ernest Labrousse, *La Crise de l'économie française à la fin de l'ancien régime et au début de la Révolution* (Paris, 1944). See also his *Esquisse du mouvement des prix et des revenus en France au XVIIIe siècle* (Paris, 1933, two volumes).

break of the Revolution, it is nonetheless true that the government had already been weakened by opposition to its plans on the part of the aristocracy. It is customary now to speak of the years 1787 to 1789 as the period of the prerevolution. Professor Egret, two of whose articles are reprinted here, has devoted his career to the study of this phenomenon and has, more than any one man, been responsible for our current conception of it. In the case of each province studied, resistance to the royal will was, in the first instance, proclaimed by the nobility of the robe. They were soon joined by what may be called the bourgeoisie of the robe, that is, persons in legal occupations who did not hold high judicial office and were members of the third estate. Later still, other bourgeois—and sometimes popular—elements entered the scene. New questions arose over the form and proportion of the representation of the third estate and its share in the power structure. Invariably the initiative passed more or less quickly from the parliamentary nobles to their bourgeois partners, who soon became their enemies. The bourgeois had more or less radical programs in proportion as they saw their future linked up with the maintenance or destruction of traditional institutions, particularly judicial institutions. The legal bourgeoisie and the representatives of the privileged towns were, in turn, often replaced by persons whom no vested interest linked to the preservation of the status quo.

When we speak of the Parlements and their role in creating the political preconditions of revolution, certain questions immediately spring to mind as to their role in the eighteenth-century community. The Parlements claimed that, by refusing to follow the King's orders, they were resisting monarchial despotism. And popular crowds seem to have responded to this argument by rallying to the parliamentary cause on a whole variety of issues, in the struggle over the Jesuits in the 1750s, in the controversy over Maupeou's reforms of 1771–1774, and for the last time in 1787–1788. But why and how were the parliaments able to assume this leadership? Who precisely responded to their appeals? Did these incidents constitute a kind of united front in which the partners had one thing and one thing only in common, that is, opposition to the crown? Or is the alliance more than accidental? Is there some parallel here to the London crowds urged on from above by the men of the City, as George Rudé has described them? [25] We do not as yet know, and this remains an open field for research.

This leads us directly into the study of the popular movement during the Revolution, of which the crowd was the primary manifestation. But what precisely is a crowd? Is it a heterogeneous aggregate of individuals, or is the whole larger than the sum of its parts? Why and how does it form and act? What are its motives? These are some of the questions to which Georges Lefebvre addresses himself in the next selection. It results

[25] G. Rudé, *Wilkes and Liberty* (Oxford, 1962).

from his work that there are in fact several different kinds of groups that we normally lump together under the generic term "crowd." These range from the aggregate to the (potentially revolutionary) assembly, and the development of the latter from the former is dependent on the formation of a collective mentality. The variety and extent of these gatherings make it incumbent upon us to study each of them individually and to pay attention to the specific circumstances of their formation.

Georges Lefebvre wrote this essay in 1931, but significant research in the field began only after World War II. George Rudé, Richard Cobb, and Albert Soboul have been most prominent in carrying on the work. Rudé's book *The Crowd in the French Revolution* [26] is by now a classic and ought to be read by all serious students. As it is generally available in college and university libraries and will soon be published in paperback, I have refrained from using any part of it in this book. Instead, I have chosen two readings, one on the bread riots of 1775 and the other on the popular stirrings of Germainal and Prairial year III done in collaboration with Richard Cobb.

The first is a study of a spontaneous movement provoked by high prices and *fear* of famine. It is important to note the italicized word. We must never, of course, neglect the actual effects of famine upon human beings even to the point of physical degenerescence. But there is an added dimension of a psychosomatic nature. The people who revolted had more to fear than fear itself, but that does not negate the influence of fright upon them. To neglect this factor is to make it impossible to explain why the high point of eighteenth-century bread riots came in 1775, while the cyclical maximum of bread prices between 1709 and 1787 was reached seven years earlier, in 1768.

The crowds in the Parisian region in 1775 participated in what was uniquely a bread riot. The *sans-culottes* of the Faubourg Saint-Antoine in 1795 were fighting against political oppression. But were their motives so very different? The year III was a time of profound famine. Shortages and the repeal of the maximum had had disastrous effects. The men and women of the *faubourg* wanted to eat as much as had their fathers. There is, however, a difference. First of all, the *sans-culottes* had been politicized. They knew, however imperfectly, that the question of bread was tied to other considerations, and that they could, if organized, exert pressure on the government. Consider the simple syllogism of one of their number: "Under Robespierre, blood flowed and we had bread. Now the blood has ceased to flow, and we have no bread. Blood must flow in order for us to have bread." And upon the other side stood the Thermidorean bourgeoisie also moved by fear—this time, of the *sans-culottes*. All of this combined to create an explosive situation. Yet it is true that the movement of 1795 was less successful than its simpler forerunner of twenty

[26] Oxford, 1959.

years before. Germinal and Prairial were revolts of despair. The people
who made them were actually, not just potentially, haunted by starvation.
They had reached the end of their rope, and their action here was a
paroxysm just before they let go and fell away into the dark hole of absolute indigence. They were tired, perhaps biologically, certainly mentally.
That is why they gave in so easily to the troops of the Convention and
failed to ignite the cannon they had bracketed on their adversaries.

Some indication of the nature of the popular movement has been given
in the last paragraphs. The next two selections treat the matter with much
greater precision. Albert Soboul tells us about the organization of work in
revolutionary Paris and its implications for that highly hybrid category,
the *sans-culottes*. Furet, Mazauric, and Bergeron summarize the evidence
of Soboul's great thesis on *Les Sans-culottes parisiens en l'an II* [27] and of
Tonneson's work on *La Défaite des sans-culottes en l'an III*.[28] The basic
propositions to be noted are those concerning the political nature of the
sans-culottes, that they were not a social class. Contrary to the argument
put forth by Daniel Guérin,[29] they did not constitute a proletariat. They
were therefore an ephemeral group that would fall away into their component parts as the Revolution came to an end. There was nothing to
unify them beyond temporary political needs. Even at the height of their
influence in the year II, their leadership came from the independent
artisans, that is, those closest to the bourgeoisie. Thus, what we have come
to call the *sans-culottes* movement only imperfectly reflected the desires
of the *sans-culottes*. Our present knowledge is the jumping off point for
research both backward and forward in time. We want to know what forces
were at work on the eve of the Revolution to shape an incoherent mass
into a politically conscious group, and we must see what became of the
sans-culottes after the defeat of the year III, especially in the period up to
the Revolution of 1830.

Alongside the urban popular movement, there was a wave of peasant
uprisings. Without them, the remnants of feudalism, especially seigneurial
dues, that existed in 1789 would not have been destroyed so rapidly and
so thoroughly as they were. The National Assembly, in its famous decree
of August 4, 1789, went only a short way toward complete abolition, and
provided for money payments to redeem dues that had not originated
in personal subjection but represented rather a kind of economic rent. Only
the action of the peasants themselves in 1789 and 1793, in particular, forced
the legislators to give *de jure* recognition to the *de facto* end of seigneurial
collections.

The word "peasant" is often misleading in that it makes us think of a

[27] Paris, 1958. A partial translation into English is available: *The Parisian Sans-Culottes
and the French Revolution* (Oxford, 1964).
[28] Oslo and Paris, 1959.
[29] D. Guérin, *La Lutte des classes sous la première république: bourgeois et "bras nus"*
(1793–1797) (Paris, 1946, two volumes).

socially undifferentiated agricultural class. This is quite the opposite of reality. The peasantry in 1789 was already divided by considerations of wealth, agricultural technique, extent of holdings, and legal status. The number of serfs was certainly not more than one million, but the condition of most agriculturalists was not any the more enviable for that. The differences cited were, if anything, further developed in the course of the Revolution by the sale of national lands and the abolition of common rights.

Our knowledge of the peasantry still leaves much to be desired. Georges Lefebvre's monumental thesis on *Les Paysans du Nord pendant la Révolution française* [30] is the model for the work that must still be done in other regions of France. But it can already be said that we have gotten away from two once prevailing myths about the peasants: that they were a united body with common goals and that their actions in the course of the Revolution were the result of a blind and animalistic desire for revenge. Lefebvre's essay on the murder of the Comte de Dampierre admirably demonstrates the second point.

The Great Fear described by Lefebvre in yet another major work [31] was not uniquely a rural phenomenon, but peasants, less organized than the *menu peuple* of the cities, were probably more subject to it than anyone else. It was the belief that first appeared in the early summer of 1789 to the effect that brigands were wandering through the countryside with the double intent of committing all sorts of heinous crimes and putting an end to the Revolution. Worries over personal security and the supply of food were its principal foci. It turned out to be a kind of self-fulfilling prophecy, for, instead of waiting for the arrival of the brigands, the peasants undertook preventive action. They revolted against their lords, burned archives and chateaux, raided convoys of grain destined for shipment to other areas. In so doing, they were motivated not only by material need, but by fear of a conspiracy to deprive them of life and liberty. They thought in terms of the so-called *pacte de famine* of 1775, but their action was more significant because of the new, revolutionary context in which it took place.

A community in which the only source of contact with the outside world is oral communication is always subject to the upsetting effects of rumor, especially when that community is constantly threatened by the absence of elementary material needs. The amount of beggary at the end of the old regime was enormous in both town and country and constituted a continuing administrative headache. No adequate means had been found to cope with it before the Revolution, and the economic troubles of 1792 and after only added to the problem. Desperation turned many an established beggar into a thief and a bandit, while swelling the ranks with newcomers. Those who engaged in this activity were outside the mainstream of

[30] Originally published in Paris, 1924. A new edition without the footnotes was published at Bari by Laterza in 1959.
[31] G. Lefebvre, *La Grande peur* (Paris, 1932).

revolutionary action. Indeed, they were a pool of potential counter-revolutionaries. Vovelle's study of the Beauce is the first to undertake an investigation of this group. It is to be hoped that it will be followed by numerous others.

We come now to two articles dealing with what we have previously called collective mentalities. This most fascinating subject of historical investigation is still in an underdeveloped state, although it is now attracting more and more attention. Richard Cobb, in addressing himself to the study of the revolutionary mentality, raises several important questions. First of all, what makes a man a revolutionary? This is more than merely asking what makes a man revolt. Beyond that, what makes him take an active part in a section or a club? What leads the normally tranquil individual to risk his life or to engage in violence? Why can a man applaud, or contribute to, an execution or, exceptionally, a massacre, and still return home immediately afterward to play tenderly with his children and pets? On the other hand, what was it about his state of mind that destroyed the typical *sans-culottes'* revolutionary propensities?

To argue that the study of collective mentalities is of prime importance is not to neglect the material circumstances that prompt individual or group behavior. The fault lies as much in the stars as in ourselves. But what happens in the external world filters through our perceptions before we act upon that stimulus—and to neglect the process of filtration is to lose one dimension of historical understanding.

Consider the case of religious belief as a political framework. Soboul's study shows how popular Catholicism could be deformed to serve as a vehicle for revolutionary action. The liturgy and forms of thought that had been implanted over the centuries now took on a new meaning. This was neither the first nor the last instance of this phenomenon in European history. However limited the perspective of protest within the rhetoric of religion may have been, however much it was necessary that the religion give way to secular concerns, who can afford to ignore the impact it had in shaping the consciousness of large masses of people? [32] Traditional Catholicism, the new cults of reason and the Supreme Being, the numerous festivals all contributed to the making and maintenance of revolutionaries. They must, therefore, be studied, if we are to get the complete picture.

To sum up is difficult. This introduction has provided some idea of the development French revolutionary studies have undergone up to now, and it has indicated some new directions for research. If some readers, university students and others, are induced to undertake this sort of historical study, I shall be more than justly rewarded. If a majority or significant minority, as I may more rationally hope, becomes aware of the issues and methods involved and henceforth pays more than passing attention to the new work in the field, that, too, will be sufficient.

[32] On this point see E. J. Hobsbawm, *Primitive Rebels* (Manchester, 1959 and New York, 1963), and Vittorio Lanternari, *The Religions of the Oppressed* (New York, 1963).

PART *I*

Social Structure at the End
of the Eighteenth Century

BOURGEOIS, RENTIERS, AND PROPERTY OWNERS

Elements for Defining a Social Category at the End of the Eighteenth Century

By M. Vovelle and D. Roche

Our economic and historical vocabulary has given a precise meaning to the word "bourgeois."

Since the rise of the liberal economic system in the nineteenth century, the bourgeoisie has held control of the means of production, the income of which derives essentially from industrial and financial capital. In this modern view, the bourgeois appears as an active personage or, as he has been called, "the conqueror."

Against this modern conception it is possible to compare the original definition of "bourgeois," taken in its broadest sense, as the inhabitant of a "bourg," a town or city. For the historian of the Middle Ages a bourgeois was an artisan, a tradesman, even a wage earner, provided he lived within the walls of a city.

Between these two types we would like to place a third "bourgeois," the one in the eighteenth century. In the popular sense of the word, this bourgeois was no longer the same as he had been in the Middle Ages. Every

25

city dweller was no longer *ipso facto* a bourgeois. The bourgeois remained a commoner as opposed to the nobility and the privileged classes. But within the urban population the term was restricted to nonactive categories. Legal documents of the day speak of bourgeois "living like the nobility." The bourgeois had become a man without an occupation, living on the interest from his investments, receiving an income independent of any trade or profession.

Within this definition, the eighteenth-century bourgeois was also unlike the modern-day bourgeois to the extent that his mode of living, as well as his income, was tied to a feudal system, the term conceived in its broadest sense. Income from real estate or income from government bonds was the principal source of his revenue.

The French Revolution dealt a mortal blow to this social class. Just as it replaced the tillage farmer with the agriculturalist and royal government officials with civil servants, so it substituted for the "bourgeois" the property owner, *le propriétaire,* and the *rentier* [the individual living on income or interest from property or securities]. The term "bourgeois" was to be given a new meaning in the nineteenth century, both in the writings of economists and in popular parlance.

This study is therefore, from the outset, a study in social terminology. By considering two examples—a provincial city: Chartres and a district of Paris: *le Marais*—we will endeavor to define the meaning of the term "bourgeoisie" at the close of the Old Regime with respect to it recruitment, its way of life, and its sources of revenue. Our study will attempt to determine in what ways the term and the category itself disappeared during the Revolution to be replaced by the *propriétaires,* property owners, and their collateral group, the *rentiers.* In this manner, pivoting on a question of semantics, an effort will be made to sketch one of the processes whereby a France of property owners and a France of Notables came into being during the first half of the nineteenth century.

From a strictly legal standpoint a "bourgeois" of the seventeenth and eighteenth centuries differed little from a "bourgeois" of the Middle Ages. Loyseau in his *Traité des ordres et dignités* (1678) and Nicolas Delamare in his *Traité de police* (1722) designated as "bourgeois de Paris" anyone who had lived in Paris for a year and a day, who was not employed as a domestic, who did not live in rented lodgings, and who shared in the common assessments (the tax on boundary markers and street lamps).

There was no such specific definition of a bourgeois in a provincial city like Chartres. Indeed the title was not as much sought after and esteemed as that of "bourgeois de Paris." Did not Delamare declare "the status of 'bourgeois de Paris' occupies first place in the common law of cities"? Now the title was not without its advantages since it entailed for the bourgeois exemption from *la taille,* the right to acquire fiefs anywhere in the kingdom without having to pay the duty of *franc fief,* exemption from the *ban* and the *arrière-ban,* exemption from having to quarter troops on one's premises, not to mention such enviable social privileges as conducting legal matters only under Parisian jurisdiction, being able to have a debtor arrested by the king's authorities, and to sell wheat, grains, wines, and ales duty free.

Without being as enviable as the status of a Parisian bourgeois, membership in the bourgeoisie of many provincial cities was not a privilege to be scorned. In Chartres, as in many other cities exempt from *la taille*, it lightened the burden of government taxes. In reality, if any city dweller, fulfilling certain residential and minimal financial requirements, could call himself a bourgeois, we note, nevertheless, that toward the close of the Old Regime the term was limited to certain highly restricted categories. In Chartres, as in Paris, only certain people were called "bourgeois," namely, those who were no longer active in any trade or profession or engaged in any private or immediately productive activity. It is likely that the rest of the urban population did not insist on this title any longer since its advantages had merged with the common rights of all.

Along with anachronistic definitions in treatises, a new practice was born. The term "bourgeois," taken in its restrictive sense, was approved in Paris for use in deeds executed and authenticated by a notary. They constitute our principal source of information in this matter. Elsewhere the term can be verified in political or fiscal sources such as the roster of taxpayers. In Chartres, for example, the lists of inhabitants summoned in 1766 to take part in the election of Notables included a special category for the "bourgeois of the city of Chartres." At the time of the elections for the Estates General these bourgeois found themselves grouped with the other members of the Third Estate in Chartres, those who belonged to no community (largely rural and suburban) for the purpose of electing two special deputies.

Hence, in the eyes of their contemporaries, those bourgeois "living like nobility" formed a separate and very limited category among the urban population.

In the case of Paris, the importance of the Parisian bourgeoisie with respect to the population as a whole varied according to the age group under consideration and the sources at our disposal: marriage contracts or last wills and testaments with their inventories, liquidations, and property settlements. As for marriage contracts, a sampling over a 5-year period (1750–1755) disclosed twenty-eight "bourgeois de Paris" in 359 official records, while in the matter of property inventories, there were thirty-two out of 491. The importance of the category varied in accordance with the age group, and the percentage, by comparison with the total population, fluctuated between 7 and 15 per cent. The increase at the time of death reveals a greater number and variety of "bourgeois" and may well indicate a greater measure of their social importance. In studying people at their entry into the normal activities of social life, we omitted such groups as retired persons, widows, and young women who had come of legal age, but they are found once again at the time of death. Taking into account the relativity of these percentages (the margin of individuals not included in our sources and the limited bases of our statistics—a 5-year span in five different notarial offices), the category includes between 10,000 and 17,000 persons out of a population of approximately 110,000. These figures represent no more than probable conjectures in view of the many problems entailed in evaluating the population of Paris.

In this apparently fluid category what elements do we find? Property inventories give us the general composition, and marriage contracts allow us to refine our observations. Of the eighty-two "bourgeois" encountered at time of death, 27 per cent were *rentières* [women living on interest from some sort of property], widows or young women legally of age; 22 per cent were retired males, former officials or businessmen; and 51 per cent were "bourgeois de Paris" who had held this title since the moment they had become a part of the social life of Paris. Thus we are dealing with a category slightly less than half of which consisted of women or retired persons. Accordingly, the "bourgeoisie" was not only an age group but represented a complex social situation.

Out of twenty-eight marriage contracts only seven were drawn up for sons of bourgeois. The role of bourgeois heredity was consequently limited (28 per cent). If we look at the social origins of the remaining 72 per cent, two groups stand out—rural people (32 per cent) and members of the liberal professions (28 per cent)—minor officials, law clerks, attorneys, and so on. The importance of rural origins (farmers and vine growers) reveals the newly bourgeois nature of this category. It was an acquired status. The percentage of hereditary bourgeois and of various officials establishes the category in the middle bourgeoisie. The weakness of the contribution of commercial and artisanal strata to the formation of this class is noteworthy.

It is interesting to compare the social status of the male bourgeois with that of his father-in-law. The proportions are in inverse ratio: 31 per cent married daughters of Parisian bourgeois; 28 per cent married daughters of tradesmen. Note the disappearance of rural people (one case), and the relatively few marriages with persons of the working class and the Parisian liberal professions. Through his marriage a bourgeois acquired full status in Parisian bourgeois society. The typical status of this category is much clearer if we note the very real social distinction between a Parisian notary or attorney and his provincial counterpart. Unity was achieved between the commercial bourgeoisie, a portion of the liberal professions, and the bourgeois of Paris. The legal title was not acquired by age and consequently was already a symbol of social status. This fact is confirmed if we examine the records of the known heirs of Parisian bourgeois. We find the same mixing of classes, the rights of inheritance on the part of a third, with business and liberal professions making up the remainder. The few instances of marriage between bourgeois and nobility scarcely altered the picture. The category became deeply rooted in Parisian society, and the rural elements disappeared. The geographical situation confirms these tendencies. Out of twenty-eight marriages only 28 per cent were made by sons of Parisians. The others came from regions around Paris. As for the status of in-laws, the proportion was reversed. Sixty-seven per cent were Parisians. The bourgeoisie of the Marais district was an open social group, relatively young, a partial reflection of the attraction of the city to outsiders.

◆∽§∌◆

As for Chartres, the problem of determining the make-up of the bourgeois class at the close of the Old Régime can be approached from several angles. Unlike Paris, there are statistical sources available, both fiscal and political, that permit us to give figures on the size of this group. There is a per capita list of taxpayers assessed for the support of the needy, and there are lists of eligible voters for the election of Notables in 1766. Unfortunately, the latter figures include only male members of the population.

In a population of slightly over 10,000 (3000 households), there were approximately 250 men and women with the title of "bourgeois" listed among those required to pay the poor tax, a figure representing 567 persons if we take into account their families and dependents. This was 8.3 per cent of the number of households and 5.6 per cent of the total population. The distribution according to sex among the members of the bourgeoisie reveals a marked degree of imbalance. There were in Chartres only about sixty men (forty-eight to fifty-eight according to the respective sources) who called themselves "bourgeois" as against three times that figure for the number of women in the same category. This disparity can be easily explained. The status of *rentière* is much more common in a society where women do not work except among the lower classes and in a society where the notion of retirement is applied only to restricted categories of the male population.

Just who were these members of the bourgeoisie? Clearly, they cannot be confused with all retired persons or with all retired commoners. As a matter of fact, the lists mention, alongside the bourgeois, unemployed commoners (*roturiers*), who had no right to the title of "bourgeois." There were retired workers, for instance, designated by their former profession. By the same token, all unemployed women were not bourgeoises. There is mention of widows and adult females in the lower categories. Therefore, the category was not merely an age group. It presupposed a certain measure of affluence. Not just anyone could be a bourgeois. If that is so, can we say then that members of the bourgeoisie constituted a kind of nobility among commoners—a marginal type of nobility, a kind of caste system that was hereditary and transmissible? We think not. There is another source of information that enables us to follow the fortunes of this classified group at different stages of its development, namely, the legal records of notaries.

Marriage contracts (examined over a five-year period) disclose only a very tiny percentage of "bourgeois" in the social composition of Chartres: 1 per cent or three out of 300 in the 5-year survey. There can be no doubt that it was an acquired title that put a seal of approval, at the close of their career, on the social success of a portion of the members of the active, local bourgeoisie.

The lists of bourgeois in Chartres, drawn up in 1766 as eligible to participate in the election of Notables, are sufficiently explicit to enable us to classify the different social groups that came to be included in this classification. Out of sixty *bourgeois de Chartres*, there is no indication of the social origins of one-third (nineteen); one-third (eighteen) were retired tradesmen; one-fourth (fifteen) were former lawyers or government officials. Only four were former artisans; three were wealthy farmers who had retired to Chartres. However limited our statistical base may be, it seems to us sufficient to offer a summary view of the constituent elements within the category, its two principal sources being businessmen and members of the liberal professions, with workers accounting for only a very small fraction of the group. Concurrently, a few rural individuals, retired farmers, were added to the category. It would appear that only a small percentage of its membership was recruited from the city itself. Only 35 per cent of these bourgeois were originally from Chartres. The remainder were equally distributed over adjacent rural areas and the rest of France. The provincial city had become at that time the place to which a portion of the rural bourgeoisie retired, whether coming from the open country or from tiny villages—market places of the Beauce—which were like so many relay stations linking the urban center with the rural areas.

The provincial bourgeoisie at the close of the Old Régime appears, in this instance at any rate, as a class group based on age. It was rare for the title to be transmitted by heredity. There existed a whole series of exchanges among members of the bourgeoisie in business, in official functions, and in the liberal professions. In the case of Chartres it appears that only a few dozen families succeeded in acquiring hereditary rights to the title thereby achieving a status similar to nobility. They are easily identified from the fact that, added to their own name, there appears the name of their lands and properties, a current practice in a society in which a Pétion called himself Pétion de Villeneuve or Pétion de la Bâte. The Brissots called themselves Brissot de Warville. As a general rule the bourgeois of Chartres formed an element comprising the typical urban bourgeoisie in which businessmen, officials, and those living on independent means were linked together by countless ties, including family connections among others.

Two investigations into two separate urban societies therefore present images of the *bourgeois* at the end of the Ancien Régime which are quite dissimilar. The point in common, apart from the fundamental unity of their way of life, was doubtless the very title and status of these bourgeois in urban society. They differed from the nobility by their position as commoners (*roturiers*), with all their ties linking them to the rank and file of the local bourgeoisie in business, official functions, and the liberal professions. From father to son, from son-in-law to father-in-law, a steady stream of exchanges tied them to the active bourgeoisie.

But against this common background two social types are delineated. First, we have the provincial type of bourgeois for whom the title was often merely confirmation of a certain degree of affluence acquired in the practice of a profession. Except for a few families, it seems there was scarcely any hereditary bourgeoisie. This situation, most probably, arose because the very title of "bourgeois" was less meaningful, less significant, and consequently less attractive in a provincial town than it was in Paris. The Parisian bourgeois was a more complex individual. Sometimes he was a retired businessman or a retired member of the liberal professions. Sometimes he was a person from the provinces who had come to enjoy living as a *rentier*, as a person with an independent source of income, in the French capital. But it was also possible for the term "bourgeois" to mean more than just a title. It could mean a definite social status. Some were bourgeois at birth. Some became such by marriage. And some passed the title on from father to son. More than a distinction by age group, it could, in these instances, be regarded as a sort of caste system, though an open one, to be sure. Can we say that the Parisian bourgeoisie constituted an authentic class of "noble commoners" at the close of the Old Régime? In order to explore the problem more fully, let us abandon the formal study of the sources from which its members were recruited to probe more deeply into a social analysis as revealed by a study of bourgeois wealth and income.

❧❧❧

Of the total wealth of the Marais district, as reported in the inventories sampled, the "bourgeoisie" controlled only 4.4 per cent. This percentage assumes its full significance if compared with the percentages of other social classes: 73.4 per cent for the nobility, 10.8 per cent for the liberal professions, 8.9 per cent for merchants and tradesmen, and 1.1 per cent for the working classes. Thus from 7 to 15 per cent of the population controlled 4.4 per cent of the wealth, a rather substantial figure if we keep in mind that workers possessed only 1.1 per cent while representing more than 17 per cent of the population, and tradesmen accounted for 8.9 per cent of the wealth for 15 per cent of the population. If we compare the bourgeois share in the two principal kinds of wealth, we can see the typical situation more clearly: 7 per cent of the total amount of personal property and barely 4 per cent of the total holdings in real property and real estate. Thus the bourgeoisie controlled a rather sizable share of personal property and a rather small portion of the wealth in real estate. Its wealth was grouped among those individuals depending more on income from *rentes* than on income from real estate. Its position in the Parisian bourgeoisie placed it very close to business and liberal professions, far above the workers and wage earners, alongside the nobility and the upper bourgeoisie. The bourgeois of Paris were in a unique position as a study of the structure and distribution of their wealth reveals.

If we consult only the records of marriage contracts, we would be inclined to conclude that there was very little wealth held in the form of real estate. Only three records mention wealth in this category. On the other hand, inventories of estates reveal that 32 per cent of the bourgeois made legal declarations claiming ownership of land, a house, or part-ownership of a house in Paris or elsewhere. They were of middling value, never exceeding 20,000 livres for real estate and 40,000 for improved property (*propriété bâtie*), and never less than 500 or 1000 livres. The typical situation was generally in the range of 1000 to 10,000 livres. Revenues from urban rentals did not exceed 2000 livres per annum. As for income from rural leases, these were nonexistent. As the real estate was located near Paris in Gonesse, Satory, Versailles, Montlhéry, in the Beauce region or in Brie, and as the bourgeois of Paris did not lease out these properties, they constituted a second residence. And finally, this real estate was generally inherited rather than purchased. If we consider its place in the total wealth of the bourgeoisie, it constituted only 9 per cent and was concentrated among a few people. The corresponding average for inheritances in personal property indicates a rather affluent level. The bourgeoisie of the Marais district must not be judged on the basis of its wealth in real estate but on the basis of its fortune in personal property.

It is personal property that allows us to reconstruct the economic hierarchy of the bourgeoisie. Our study, based on the issuance of marriage contracts, reveals two principal groupings: one ranging from 1000 to 1500 livres of dowry, the other from 3000 to 4000 livres. The total discloses a very representative breakdown of bourgeois wealth since only 32 per cent of young married couples had more than 10,000 pounds at their disposal. The curve based on the dowry (a customary legal figure) confirms this evaluation. The spread of bourgeois wealth at the outset remains very fluid, from 300 to 30,000 pounds. But the classification based on the figures for marriage contracts is too sketchy. It does not list in detail the husband's wealth. We know only that this personal property consisted of *rentes* and household furniture (*meubles meublants*:movable goods) for the more economically privileged, and in movable goods and clothing among the poorer bourgeois. Liquid capital is a sign of wealth. Real income is still unknown.

Inventories made upon the settlement of an estate reverse this situation. Personal property valued at less than 10,000 livres no longer dominates the picture. Thirty-seven per cent of the bourgeois and adult females (*filles majeures*) possessed at the time of death more than 20,000 livres in transmissible assets. And in this higher bracket among the Marais bourgeoisie, we find 50 per cent with fortunes in excess of 50,000 livres and four large estates greater than 100,000. The wealthier bourgeois approached the economic level of the nobility. The fortune of the bourgeois was comparable most commonly to that of a tradesman or member of the liberal professions. In its lower categories, the bourgeois was still better off than the average artisan or the upper level of wage earners.

The difference between the economic cross sections at the time of marriage and at the time of death reflects, of course, the difference in social and economic status. But this differentiation is also noted in the general economic upswing of the eighteenth century. The bourgeoisie became wealthy. The comparison of figures on inheritances with those indicating the amount of money brought into a marriage reflects the evolution of the wealth of an entire generation and reveals the consolidation of that wealth. The two curves show the contrast: fortunes in excess of 10,000 pounds are predominant at the time of death, while the opposite holds true at the time of marriage. Economic and social failures were fewer than economic and social successes. A study of the structure of bourgeois wealth underlines the principal factors.

The bourgeoisie of the Marais district of Paris had more than 70 per cent of its wealth in *rentes*. The remainder was distributed among household furnishings (and movable goods) and wearing apparel (65 per cent); negotiable instruments, stock certificates, and letters of exchange (9.3 per cent); miscellaneous items, jewelry, and personal funds (6 per cent); promissory notes (4 per cent); and offices (3 per cent). Since real estate was limited to the wealthy bourgeois, the distribution of the various economic assets varied from one end of the social category to the other. We note a level less than 500 livres in which the only assets were furniture and clothing. Before the figure reaches 1000 livres we discover silverware and sums of cash. Between 1000 and 5000 livres we find negotiable instruments appearing with still very few *rentes*. Above 10,000 livres, *rentes* are foremost with personal property seldom exceeding 1000 livres. Finally, in fortunes above 20,000 pounds, *rentes* account for more than 70 per cent of the wealth with stocks, offices, finer furnishings, jewelry, and cash on hand making up the balance.

The social status of a bourgeois, retired or not, can be defined by the possession of *rentes*, for the most part backed by excise taxes (*les aides et gabelles*), occasionally by the clergy or the provincial estates, but more rarely by private individuals. Two thirds of these *rentes* were perpetual. The effects of economic crises under the Old Regime find a new echo in this context. The mass of *rentiers*, large or small, could not fail to become apprehensive over crises. The slight variations in kinds of wealth were like a façade concealing a uniform outlook on life and vanished in the face of a common bourgeois mode of living.

We may speak of bourgeois comfort, but we rarely find evidence of luxury. The value of household furnishings seldom exceeded 2000 livres, and the external signs of wealth in the Old Regime—paintings, art objects, horses, carriages, and retinue—were rare among the bourgeoisie. The distinguishing mark of an above-average bourgeois was perhaps his ownership of two residences. The Marais bourgeois did not own luxurious mansions (*hôtels urbains*). They lived in apartments. In sixty-six cases most families were modestly housed, sometimes in extremely simple lodgings even when economically well off. If we try to compare the number of beds per family with the number of people in the family, we discover that the majority were satisfied with little more than a bare minimum of comfort. Only 25 percent had domestic help and never, with two exceptions, more than one domestic. It was a modest way of life with no excessive luxury but with the advantages of just enough comfort to set the bourgeoisie apart from the masses or the working classes who often lived under deplorable conditions. The degree of comfort, however, was not enough to distinguish the bourgeois from a tradesman or a member of the liberal professions. Bourgeois unity was realized in a common way of life just as it expressed itself in a common pattern of alliances and fortunes.

As a group, the bourgeoisie of Chartres occupied a position considerably more important than its actual size in numbers. Fiscal sources, the capitation tax in particular, reveal a preponderance of bourgeois and *rentiers* in the highest tax brackets. Out of 151 tax assessments exceeding 40 livres in 1774, 63, or 40 per cent, were among bourgeois and bourgeoises. This proportion is significantly smaller in the lower tax brackets. Among commoners (*roturiers*) members of the bourgeoisie were numbered among the wealthiest, or at least among those paying the heaviest taxes, for noblemen and officials were tax-exempt.

Accordingly, it would be interesting to move from this fiscal index to more reliable sources, notarized documents or documents legally registered. This study can only be roughly sketched here. A sampling of statistics concerning the distribution of inheritances as found in the public registers of Chartres (*le bureau du contrôle des actes*) during the last 25 years of the Old Régime reveals that at least 7.5 per cent of total inheritances occurred in this social category. This was a limited proportion, to be sure, compared with 18 per cent occurring among the nobility and 26 per cent among government officials. Nevertheless, figures and percentages help to establish the position of bourgeois income within the over-all income of the urban population. It was lower by more than half, both as an absolute figure and as an average, by comparison with the nobility and government officials (*officiers royaux*). Average values approximated those of tradesmen and lawyers. Here again we are thus able to define more accurately the status of this *bourgeoisie roturière* (bourgeois commoners) in the complex of the urban middle bourgeoisie.

The truth is that if the income of the bourgeois commoner remained far below the level of the nobleman or government official, we cannot say that this revenue was appreciably different in nature from that of the privileged classes. In the framework of a provincial city like Chartres at the end of the Old Regime, income from real estate (*rente foncière*) remained the most reliable and important form of wealth.

In dealing with the Old Regime, it was not found possible to study on a statistical basis the distribution of income among the bourgeoisie. Estate inventories or property settlements, following the death of a bourgeois, indicate however the continual primacy of income from real estate over income from personal property. The total value of personal property was always far less than the value of real estate. In the case, for example, of the bourgeois Guillaume Brissot, the father of the member of the National Convention, personal property accounted for only one-sixth of the total fortune he possessed. As for another bourgeois, a woman in comfortable circumstances, it represented a net worth of 3000 livres out of an estate valued at 23,000—13 per cent of the total. This is the percentage generally encountered.

Apparently, this category of provincial bourgeoisie at the close of the Old Regime had not really discovered the value of transferable securities (*placements mobiliers*). The latter were widely known only in certain very restricted quarters, among notaries or those in legal professions in the broad sense of the term. To the extent that the bourgeois owned stocks or annuities (*titres et rentes*), their nature reveals the retarded character of this provincial group. The major kinds of income within this group—perpetual incomes or life annuities—were on private individuals. The families of Chartres were linked together by many interdependent financial ties. Often the debtor was also a rural person, a farmer of an urban bourgeois. That was one of the principal links between urban and rural societies. Moreover, these fixed annuities (*rentes constituées*) were far less numerous than short-term loans, simple credit accounts. Government bonds or corporate bonds were much rarer. In the inventories we find annuities on the *taille*, on the salt tax, or on ecclesiastical property. A bourgeoise at the time of her death had 13,000 livres of capital at her disposal, half of it consisting of government bonds on *tailles*, 25 per cent in bonds on the *aides et gabelles*, and the remainder in *rentes* on the clergy and the tanners.

The local community offered, as a matter of fact, several possibilities for investments. By taking public loans, guilds gave members of the bourgeoisie the opportunity to invest their money safely. But these opportunities were quite limited in the city proper according to figures disclosed by a study of guilds in Chartres in 1755.

Between income from personal property, which was not very sizable and showed little diversification, and income from real estate there was a transitional kind of income—*rente foncière*: perpetual income deriving from a piece of real estate. This kind of income was extremely common in this provincial society at the end of the Old Régime. There was hardly an inheritance, however modest, that did not include one or two such titles— limited revenues since they usually ranged from 15 to 50 livres a year, but nevertheless, very reliable sources of income.

Unquestionably, we come back to real estate as the most important source of revenue. It took various forms, but it was always present one way or another. Improved urban property was monopolized to an important degree by this class, the "passive" bourgeoisie. The first land tax register in the city of Chartres (1791) reveals that nearly 30 per cent of the income from real estate was in the hands of citizens who had no profession (*sans état*). This figure includes former noblemen whose share we must deduct. Nevertheless, it appears that the former bourgeois commoners (*la bourgeoisie roturière*) must have received from 15 to 20 percent of the income from improved property. This investment was a source of revenue: the average per owner was about two houses (1.64). Accordingly, these bourgeois had tenants. The basis for our income is thus once again landed property. Varying in size, according to the inventories and allotments, it was never negligible. An adult female of modest means owned at least a dozen *hectares* (about 30 acres) which provided the main source of her income. The average bourgeois, like Guillaume Brissot, owned about 100 hectares (approximately 250 acres) in the Beauce region, in four or five lots.

We can discern two general kinds of property holdings: nearby property, one the one hand—a vineyard in the suburbs or around the country house; and remote property, on the other hand, in plots of ground or even in small patches of land suitable for cultivation. Dual households were characteristic of the Chartres bourgeois, who generally had a house in town and one in the country. The social hierarchy within the bourgeoisie was established in terms of one's holdings in real estate far more than in terms of one's movable goods or personal property.

The bourgeois class was indeed extremely diversified from the highest to the lowest tax brackets. Perhaps one-third of them payed over 50 livres, the figure which, according to our sampling, corresponds to the average well-to-do provincial bourgeois (*le bon bourgeois*) owning a fortune of 60,000 to 100,000 livres deriving from real estate averaging 50 to 100 *hectares* (125 to 250 acres). Below this category we find the mass of *petits bourgeois*, and particularly women, widows, or young women (*filles majeures*) living on extremely modest incomes. Nearly half of this group paid a capitation tax of less than 10 livres. Hence this category appears as one of the least homogeneous in urban society, a fact that should not be surprising in view of its make-up, a reflection of urban society which, by its very nature, is quite differentiated. Between one bourgeois and another there was the gulf that may separate a baker from a royal councilor.

This is not to say that there was not a certain unity among the bourgeoisie. It was present in their way of life and, as such, was the basis for the social unity of the class. These bourgeois had their own home, generally three to four rooms, often simply furnished but with a measure of discrimination that set them apart from ordinary working people. They owned their own home. They had a domestic, usually a maid. Toward the close of the Ancien Régime there was scarcely any wife of a bourgeois who did not have a servant woman (100 domestics for 150 bourgeoises, approximately). The bourgeois had his vineyard and his country house. He planted and cared for his own vines. If he was one of those wishing to enhance his social status, he added to his own name the place name of his property, and thus he gave himself the airs of nobility.

But the bourgeois way of life was unlike that of the city's *noblesse*. In the first place it was usually much less resplendent; his house was generally quite small and shabby in comparison with the mansions of the Chartres nobility, and he had far fewer servants. Also the bourgeois was unlike the nobleman in terms of the original definition of his status. The bourgeois was primarily a city dweller. The nobleman, likewise, had dual residences but in an opposite sense from the bourgeois. A nobleman's principal residence was his country château, while his town house was of secondary importance.

From the standpoint of incomes, the analysis of the two types of "bourgeois" we have sketched confirms the dissimilarities suggested by the breakdown of our classification. In Paris the bourgeois was above all a *rentier* who derived his principal income from annuities (*rentes*), primarily in government bonds. Only the rare exceptions owned real estate, and these were among the wealthiest members of the bourgeoisie. They accounted for a very limited share of the total bourgeois income. The Marais bourgeois appears to have enjoyed a modest degree of affluence in his mode of living. His life was centered in the apartment he occupied. Only rarely did he have any means of escape to a country house.

In the provincial town of Chartres the same term denoted a rather different condition. Seldom a *rentier*, the bourgeois of Chartres was primarily a property owner. Income from real estate was his main source of revenue whether it came from tenant farmers (*fermages*) or various forms of ground rent (*rente foncière*). This bourgeoisie generally had nothing to do with negotiable securities (*placements mobiliers*). Investments of this sort played only a secondary role. Oriented toward a rural milieu by the very nature of its income, the bourgeoisie of Chartres was likewise rural minded in its way of life. Double domicile was not uncommon. And even within the urban framework, the Chartres bourgeois appears very often to have enjoyed a greater measure of affluence than his Parisian counterpart. This appearance may perhaps have been due only to the lesser spread of the provincial social hierarchy.

The Revolution saw the disappearance of the bourgeois. In ten years the term vanished from legal documents and from fiscal or electoral registers. It was replaced by the words *propriétaires* (property owners) and *rentiers*. Not, of course, that the transition was an abrupt one. Age-old habits are not changed overnight. The term "bourgeois" remained in the vocabulary. In Chartres, in 1818, where more than 400 heads of families called themselves *propriétaires* and about 100 referred to themselves as *rentiers*, there still remained twenty-nine inhabitants who clung to the title of bourgeois. In popular speech, unlike the language of census reports, it is probable that the term was even more widely used. However, the legal change was clear and unmistakable. Voter eligibility lists and fiscal records no longer referred to the bourgeoisie during the first years of the Revolution. In 1791 and down to the time of the Directory (fiscal registers of the Year IV) we find no mention of the new classification. Legal documents were content simply to identify citizens by name with no mention of status or business. It was beginning with the Consulate (1799–1804), in civic records of the year IX and in lists of taxpayers in the year X, that the new term *propriétaire* forced itself into popular acceptance. It was to reappear soon afterward in all the lists of Napoleonic Notables.

The new term was as ambiguous as the old one. Who, under the Old Régime, could not call himself a "bourgeois" in the broadest sense of the word? And who, in 1800, however small his possessions might be, was not entitled to call himself a *propriétaire*, a property owner? The vague term was to acquire a more specific meaning. Just as "bourgeois" had come to mean more than merely an individual living on private sources of income, so the term *propriétaire* was to apply in time to the individual who had at his disposal enough real property to be able to live on its income; and likewise, the term *rentier* would refer to one whose various securities permitted him to live without working.

The new term filled a need in the changed social conditions. As the abolition of titles and castes had removed the barrier between the bourgeoisie and the nobility, it was necessary to regroup them under a new classification. The category of *propriétaires* was to be much more inclusive than the old one of *bourgeois*. But behind this semantic revolution was there not a deeper social revolution? Of all social classes the bourgeoisie was to be one of those most drastically affected by the Revolution. Sometimes gaining certain advantages and at other times losing them, the bourgeoisie experienced rather violent dislocations. During the Revolution bourgeois wealth in both real estate and personal property was substantially reduced. Farm rents were difficult to collect during the Revolution. Several letters written by bourgeois in Chartres at that time express grave concern and anxiety over the situation. In any event, the property itself generally remained intact.

It was not the same with income from securities. Established *rentes* and credit accounts emerged from the social upheaval greatly reduced in value. The fall of the assignat enabled many debtors to liquidate their obligations advantageously. New legislation authorized the redemption of perpetual annuities such as *rentes foncières*. The Revolution witnessed the almost complete disappearance of this type of investment which had been very much sought after under the Old Regime by the provincial bourgeoisie, such as the bourgeoisie of Chartres, because of its safe returns. Whereas even the most modest fortune included under the Old Regime a few securities in real estate (*titres de rente foncière*), practically none are encountered at the close of the Empire period. The phenomenon has been studied in the case of several rural parishes around Limoges. We have been able to verify the statistics in the case of Chartres. Of limited occurrence until 1793, amortization of *rentes* became important in 1793 and in the Year II to reach a fever pitch in the Year III: 250 legal acts of amortization for four notarial offices of Chartres, indicating a total of 1000 for the entire city. It seems that at the turning point of Year III there was an unusually large number of liquidations of *rentes:* income from bonds of one kind or another, income from real estate, and various types of securities, reaching their maximum number in the spring of the year. After the Year III the movement stopped as quickly as it had begun.

What were the actual consequences of this pressure on urban revenues in the Year III? They were probably limited because of the relatively unimportant role played by transferable securities and personal property in the economic wealth of the bourgeoisie. The abolition of seigniorial *rentes*, the drop in value of government bonds, the redemption of *rentes* from real estate, and more generally the redemption of personal *rentes* (*rentes constituées*) were just so many phenomena whose cumulative effect does not seem to have compromised the firmly established economic status of the provincial bourgeoisie. A parallel study among Parisian *rentiers* would very likely disclose far greater economic dislocations there than among non-Parisian bourgeois.

The most reliable evidence of this drop in income among provincial bourgeois was once again reflected in their way of life, their standard of living, which underwent as drastic a change as any social group in Chartres. Among Chartres property owners the number of domestics dropped from 252 to 191, the loss being most noticeable in the lower fringe of the category. In 1791 almost 100 widows could afford to keep a maid. In the year X this luxury was enjoyed by scarcely ten of them. It appears, however, that well-established families did not abandon their former way of life even if they had to make temporary adjustments and economies.

In any event, the situation was a temporary one. By the end of the Empire the bourgeois standard of living had returned to an economic level comparable to the one enjoyed at the end of the Ancien Régime. While losing in one sector of the economy, the bourgeoisie of Chartres made gains in other areas and consolidated its position through the purchase of real estate. It was one of the chief beneficiaries from the sale of national land. With the beginning of sales in 1791, members of the bourgeoisie were to be found in the forefront of urban buyers, alongside the élite of local society: big businessmen, lawyers, government officials, and members of the nobility as well. Numerically, their percentage was not large: one-tenth of the buyers in 1791, a ratio that was to continue throughout the Revolutionary era despite a falling off in the year II.

On the other hand, the size of their acquisitions placed them among the biggest property owners. Entire farms, units of exploitation issuing from the liquidation of Church property, passed into the hands of those who already possessed sufficient funds and assets; members of the bourgeoisie were at the top of the list. Out of twenty-six bourgeois purchasers of national property in 1791, 10 bought very large amounts. The acquisition might consist of several houses, of entire farms, or of land units exceeding 100 *hectares* (approximately 250 acres). In this manner one bourgeois family of Chartres, the Coubrés, with connections among government officials on one side of the family and with merchants on the other side, appears to have purchased through its several members some 400 to 500 *hectares* in 1791 in the form of four farms, formerly the property of the cathedral chapter, and several pieces of real estate, the largest of which was not less than 85 hectares. This was, perhaps, the most unusual example of bourgeois participation in the purchase of national lands.

In order fully to appreciate the significance of the example we have given, it is necessary to bear in mind that the class itself was not stable at the time. The bourgeoisie was in process of being expanded under the very pressures of the social upheaval. Members of the bourgeoisie were buying land. But the rush on the part of certain active members of the urban bourgeoisie to acquire available property very often induced businessmen and lawyers to take advantage of an early retirement to enjoy their new income. It was for this reason, in the year II, during the food crises, that we find the city government deliberating as to whether it should allow a butcher, who had made his fortune through the purchase of national lands, to retire at the risk of depriving the public of a necessary service.

This was not an isolated case. In the records of the forced loan in the Year IV to which we have had access, we find an investigation made concerning the disposition and status of the larger fortunes during the Revolution. There is frequent mention, with respect to lawyers and businessmen, of the importance in their overall income of revenue accruing from recent acquisitions of real estate. And we note that more than one business is described as in process of liquidation because its owner was living primarily on his *rentes*.

Accordingly, this problem merges directly with the question of the nature of the new class that came into being during the Revolutionary years, the class designated as *propriétaires*, property owners. Just as it was subject to many economic hazards regarding its wealth and income, this social category was equally overhauled in respect to the recruitment of its membership. The *propriétaires* of the year X, as listed in the tax records of persons paying personal property taxes, were no longer the "bourgeois" of the Ancien Régime. Of 420 property owners counted in the census, only fifty-three (one-eighth) were classified as "bourgeois" in 1789. There is nothing unusual in this. The classification was an old one that had undergone a profound change in 12 years. More than 25 per cent of the *propriétaires* of the year X were former tradesmen who had retired during the Revolution. Ten per cent were former members of the liberal professions (notaries, solicitors, men of the law in general).

This normal renewal of the category would not suffice to explain the total strength of the Chartres *propriétaires* in the year X. We must add to it the number of families of the nobility, nearly 100, who no longer had the right to a separate classification, as well as the number of newcomers: former government officials—sixty-seven (one-sixth of the total)—who generally gave up their positions during the Revolution and lived on their *rentes*.

Consequently, this new social category of *propriétaires* which came into being was much more open and unrestricted than the former limited group of bourgeois of the Old Regime since we find it augmented by former members of the nobility and the socially important group of former government officials. The components of the new category corresponded roughly to the cumulative membership of these three groups under the Old Regime.

Having thus observed the birth of this new class of *propriétaires*, we must now take note of the way in which it lived during the early years of the Restoration when the France of Notables, forged during the Revolution and the Empire, acquired its definitive form.

In the microcosm of Chartres, in which we see the reflection of this France of Notables, the historian's task is made easier by the existence of an important collection of source materials dealing with the years in question: the first city-wide census, the lists of qualified voters, and fiscal records (the personal property taxes paid in 1816). The picture has been completed by consulting the records of the *Enregistrement*, the registry office [with the records of wills and probates].

In Chartres, a city of 13,000, there were about 600 families living without working. If we include their domestics, these families numbered more than 2000 persons, approximately one-sixth of the entire population. Let us look at them in terms of the classification they gave themselves. First there were the *rentiers* (97) to whom we may add those designated as *retired* (70), for the most part in 1818 officers, unattached or on half pay. The principal group consisted of *propriétaires*, property owners (417). The title of "bourgeois" had not disappeared, but it was used by scarcely thirty inhabitants (29). From all indications it was a hold-over from the Old Regime, an anachronism, for it is difficult to discover any real difference between a *bourgeois* and a *propriétaire*.

Accordingly, the two basic categories were the *propriétaires* on the one hand and the *rentiers* on the other. These two terms were not interchangeable, and each designated a very restricted group according to the nature of its income. In this connection, it is already interesting to note that there were four times as many *propriétaires* as *rentiers*, an indication of the permanent nature of revenue derived from real estate. A sampling among the bourgeoisie of a larger city might produce a different ratio between the two groups.

Let us try to see what social elements were included under these two classifications. First, there were members of the nobility, about fifty families in all, fewer certainly than under the Old Regime but larger than during the Revolution and the Empire. It appears that, beginning with the Restoration (1815), noblemen of the Beauce region began leaving their town houses to take up residence in their country châteaux. Alongside them were former royal officials who had entered upon full retirement. These *propriétaires* with hereditary titles hardly constituted more than a hundred families in the aggregate.

The majority within this category consisted of former tradesmen or retired members of the liberal professions as is indicated by the higher age brackets for the group as a whole. Very few *propriétaires* were under 45 years of age. A large number were between 45 and 50 years, which would correspond to the retirement age of the different members of the urban bourgeoisie, while the largest thrust occurs in the 60 to 65 age group, the time when the majority of small businessmen and artisans normally retired. The coupling of higher age groups alongside *propriétaires* with hereditary titles, noblemen, and former government officials, reveals another element which seems to characterize this social category—the premature retirements (at age 45) of members of the active bourgeoisie.

It was not the same with respect to women, who comprised the third source of recruitment for this classification. More numerous than the male *propriétaires*, these female *propriétaires* or *rentières* were frequently older which corresponds to the recruitment of widows of tradesmen or notaries. In these figures we also find younger unmarried women and spinsters living on their *rentes*.

It was in this manner that the new social class drew sustenance from the different branches of urban society. But it would be useful to add a geographical study to this analysis of its formation. The renewal of this social category during the events of the Revolution was of no small magnitude. In 1818 the portion made up of *rentiers, propriétaires,* bourgeois, noblemen, and former government officials born in Chartres had not reached 50 per cent of the total. The local Notables comprised a social group geographically less stable than adjacent categories, less stable than rural people, more than 75 per cent of whom were born and remained in the same locality, and less stable than artisans, 51 per cent. Only tradesmen, 30 per cent of whom were native to Chartres, and also civil servants, also about 30 per cent, were more mobile than the *propriétaires*. Moreover, this instability varied with the various elements within the group.

The largest percentage of people residing in Chartres who had come originally from somewhere else were semi-retired people or retired civil servants. The nobility itself presents an interesting case of renewal. Only 42 per cent were attached to the old aristocracy. Of fifty-six cases, twenty-seven noblemen had settled during the Revolution and the imperial period. Was that a permanent or temporary characteristic of a nobility

affected by Revolutionary events, leaving rural residences to establish themselves in the city? Some who came from Nantes, Paris, or the West Indian
Islands settled there permanently. Others were to return to the country, a
fact that leads us to regard the phenomenon as transitional rather than
permanent. And finally, among the *rentiers* and *propriétaires* themselves,
only half were members of old families. The others were persons who,
having made their fortunes, had come to spend their years of retirement in
the city. The geographical origins of the group of Notables reflects simultaneously the process of their taking root in the community and the temporary mixing with other social groups.

Its composition much changed, the new class of *propriétaires* also appeared in a rather different light with regard to income, way of life, and
standard of living. The expansion of the classification to include the entire
inactive urban population explains the increased importance of its revenue
within the total urban income: 46.5 per cent of all personal property, 62
per cent of all landed property according to a 5-year cross section of the
settlement of estates and the distribution of property among heirs. In this
provincial city at the start of the Restoration period, *propriétaires* enjoyed
an indisputable economic pre-eminence.

But the type of income enjoyed by inactive members of the bourgeoisie
had not changed appreciably. At the start of the Restoration, the nonproductive bourgeoisie (*la bourgeoisie passive*) still lived primarily on income
from real estate. Estimates as to the ratio of income from personal property
and transferable securities compared with income from real estate within
the overall wealth of this category indicate that it did not exceed one-sixth
of the total (as against one-fourth among those in business and the liberal
professions). A study of real estate holdings in this category, as reflected in
an inventory of inheritance allotments over a 10-year period (1810–1820),
indicates that ownership of real estate was always just as substantial.

The least affluent group of *propriétaires* in Chartres lived on revenues
from merely a few plots of land, from 10 to 25 *hectares* (25 to 62 acres) on
the average. The well-to-do bourgeoisie, on the other hand, which now
included noblemen, former government officials, and wealthy businessmen,
generally owned more than 50 *hectares* and often more than 100 *hectares*
(250 acres), in two or three farms in the Beauce country. A few of the
nobility had fortunes well in excess of these average figures, some as high as
1000 to 1500 *hectares*.

The kinds of personal property held by the *propriétaires* confirm the fact
they were a rather unenlightened, backward, provincial group. A 5-year
study of estate inventories reveals that their wealth in personal property
consisted of 28 per cent furniture and movable goods, 16 per cent cash on
hand, 51 per cent—more than half—in active credits (*créances actives*) as
against only 4 per cent in fixed annuities and securities (*rentes constituées*).
These figures alone are virtually conclusive evidence. Forty-five per cent was
in furniture and ready cash, that is, nearly half of their personal property

was in a sterile, unproductive form of wealth; and 51 per cent was in active credits (short-term loans) while only 4 per cent was in income-yielding securities. This indicates how seldom modern-type investments were to be found in provincial society. The *propriétaire* continued to be the short-term lender at high interest rates. He rarely derived any income from investments, and such *rentes* as he did have were generally arranged with a private individual [rather than a corporation or governmental agency]. By the very structure of their incomes the *propriétaires* were, for the most part, the direct heirs of the former bourgeoisie under the Old Regime.

This thread of continuity was also reflected in their mode and standard of living. They lived in the same houses, the same streets, and the same sections of town formerly occupied by the bourgeoisie. Even now, in our own day and age, whoever strolls along the streets adjacent to the cathedral of Chartres can still feel, behind the walls of these dwellings, the ever present stability of fortunes established generations ago. The possession of domestics remained an index of their unaltered way of life. Almost to the exact figure, the total number of servants in the employ of these new masters equaled the collective number of those employed by noblemen, government officials, and bourgeois of the Old Regime. After stormy times and events, the bourgeois had recovered their maids and housekeepers.

Can we say then that nothing had changed? No, indeed. It would be adopting a very mechanical view to maintain that the *propriétaires* were the direct descendants of the social elements that comprised this new category. For one thing, idleness had been democratized—600 *rentiers* and *propriétaires*, more than 15 per cent of the urban population, is substantially larger than the total members of the groups that had merged into it. And this process of democratization produced an appreciable diversification within the new category. Alongside the old established families who kept their mansions and their former way of life, there were changes primarily among the lower economic groups. Male and female *rentiers*, widows and young women, were more numerous than before the Revolution. There is an abyss between them and the great proprietors. The average value of inheritances was about 14,000 francs among the proprietors and ten times less among small *rentiers* (1358 francs). The extremes vary between 200 francs and more than 100,000 francs. A graphic representation shows one mode situated between 1000 and 2000 francs, another for the inheritances of more than 10,000 francs. The two modal upswings correspond rather well to the cleavage which set the great proprietor in opposition to the small *rentier* in this provincial society.

Consequently, behind certain permanent factors—their way of life and their sources of income—the new class acquired certain distinctive characteristics, notably, its appreciable increase in size and its greater diversification. The increasingly pronounced contrasts within the social category itself were due to its heterogeneous nature since it included more diverse elements than had comprised the former bourgeoisie. The question of its expanded size presents a more difficult problem to analyze. However, it seems certain that among a large segment of urban society, the French Revolution hastened the process, already of frequent occurrence in the Old Regime, of a steady movement into the class of the *bourgeoisie rentière*. The sale and liquidation of government properties induced many a lawyer and businessman to retire at an early age. Under such circumstances is there any reason to be surprised at the appreciable expansion in the ranks of the independent bourgeoisie living on its *rentes?* It only replaced, from a numerical point of view, the former privileged groups: monasteries and chapters, so important at the close of the Old Regime. (There were more than 500 members in Chartres.) Together with a democratization of idleness, we may speak of its secularization within the framework of this small provincial society.

In concluding this study of the bourgeoisie as a social group, we have been able to perceive certain permanent characteristics and others that were only temporary. At the close of the Old Regime, its true nature was revealed in spite of the anachronisms of various legalistic definitions. Over and beyond any broad generalizations we may make, there appears a specific kind of behavior common to the group as a whole. The bourgeois of Chartres and the bourgeois of Paris perhaps resembled each other much more than appears on first examination. On the title of "bourgeois," laden with advantages, the real role of this class superimposed itself. The bourgeois way of life received the practical sanction of fiscal controls and the consent and approval of judicial acts. But in the two examples we have studied, we have seen two different faces of the bourgeoisie.

In his attitude toward wealth, the bourgeois in the large market town behaved differently from the bourgeois in the capital. In the former, everything oriented him toward a rural milieu. His wealth was in land ownership, and even his *rentes* derived from real estate. In Paris, on the other hand, a more highly developed city, directly affected by the great economic movements of the century, everything induced the bourgeois to participate in more modern forms of economic activity. His investments were in securities and his *rentes* were in government bonds. In both cases, a common pattern of social recruitment and a common mode of living placed the bourgeois *rentier* in the middle of the urban bourgeoisie. Their many mutual ties, family interrelationships, and social connections placed the bourgeoisie on the level of tradesmen and members of the liberal professions, above the wage-earning classes, equally removed from both poles of the social hierarchy—the nobility at one end and the wage earner at the other. This basic class unity was exemplified in the simplicity of a way of life in which the elements of comfort and well being reflected no abrupt changes or sharp dissimilarities. The differences between the provincial *petits bour-*

geois and the Parisian bourgeoisie were perhaps due to the profoundly different possibilities offered by their respective environments. In contrast to the narrow, self-contained provincial milieu stood the French capital, alert to changes and quick to respond to them. The evolution of the bourgeoisie of independent means (*la bourgeoisie rentière*) in Chartres under scores its social continuity outside of and nothwithstanding the fundamental changes brought about by the Revolution and the Empire. Expanded and incorporating elements from new social and geographical horizons, the class of *propriétaires* reflected the extension of a way of life, the way of life shared by *rentiers* and Notables.

There can be no doubt that the very limited bases for the starting point of our study have not gone unnoticed—a single district in the French capital and one fair-sized market town. Would it not therefore be deemed hasty and premature to formulate any sort of generalization? The large provincial cities directly affected by the economic activity of an expanding capitalist economy—Nantes, Bordeaux, Rouen—permit us no glimpse of their bourgeoisie. Of a more typical and representative nature perhaps, but just as important for understanding the social reaction of France as a whole, the large regional cities with a more parochial outlook than Paris, cities like Grenoble or Orléans, likewise remain silent on the subject of their bourgeoisie.

In view of these limitations, just how many members of this social group remain outside the narrow confines of our statistical probe? However limited our figures may be, they have, nevertheless, the advantage of being statistically reliable within their scope, and have permitted the most thorough possible study of a few typical examples. We would like to compare the Parisian *rentier* at the beginning of the nineteenth century with the Notables of Chartres, who were partial heirs to the bourgeoisie of the Old Regime. We cannot help feeling that we would discover a stable provincial society, even during times of change, in marked contrast to a Parisian society much more affected by the economic and social evolution that took place during the Revolution and the Empire.

POPULATION AND PROVISIONS IN STRASBOURG IN THE EIGHTEENTH CENTURY

☙ By Yves Lemoigne

"Everyone should thank Providence for a long succession of happy years which are multiplying production, prolonging life, sheltering it from infirmities . . . and giving daily employment through progress and the consumption of manufactured goods." Messance thus acknowledged that the entire economic system of the eighteenth century was governed by the long- or short-term movements of grain prices. Strasbourg is no exception to the rule. A very marked growth in the population made the population-provisions balance increasingly fragile, and it was frequently broken by more or less deadly crises. After 1770 and 1771 the economic and social uneasiness spread through the entire city. Underemployment and mendicity became major preoccupations for the *Magistrat* of Strasbourg. Relief measures went hand in hand with police activity.

Population and Consumption

"Ist die jetzige Bevölkerung grösser oder geringer als in den vorigen Zeiten?" (Is the current population superior to or inferior to that of previous periods?) This pertinent question was asked in 1776 by an editor of the

47

Bürgerfreund. His demonstration is concise, documented; allusions to recent French or foreign works alternate with theoretical discussions over the various manners of evaluating the Strasbourgeois population. His answer is categorical: the population has increased. This demographic increase parallels that of Alsace; it even results from it. In a century the population of Alsace doubled. Here are the statistics of the stages in this evolution keeping in mind that we must "interpret absolute figures as if they were relative ones, expressing a movement rather than a level."

Year	Population
1697	257,000 inhabitants
1700	245,000
1709	347,976
1745	415,736
1750	385,783
1760	445,000
1784	624,000
1787	576,000
1789	655,000

Toward 1780, Alsace was classed among the regions with high birthrates: 1200 births per 1000 deaths. Moheau in 1778 ranked it seventh in population density: a little less than 1700 inhabitants per square league, or 77 per square kilometer. The foothills of the Vosges and the areas near major transportation routes had densities superior to 100 inhabitants per square kilometer, as did the cities.

The Population of Strasbourg

In the eighteenth century Strasbourg was considered a major city in its surface area and its population. It would now be appropriate to study the causes and to delineate the results of this demographic development.

ITS EVOLUTION. Documentation is relatively abundant but often contradictory. Here is what the different sources reveal to us:

Dates	Census Figures	Estimated Figures
1697	26,481	28,065
1709	32,510	—
1720	—	45,598
1726	36,456	—
1730	35,974	42,780
1734	—	39,000
1745	76,425[1]	36,425 (?)
1750	—	49,870
1767	—	40,780
1771	33,113	—
1774	35,400	—
1776	—	43,000
1784	—	46,000
1789	49,948	

After this collation, the difficulties begin. What are these results worth? The first and last censuses (1697 and 1789) were very carefully carried out. The former was carried out by a royal administration desiring to know exactly the ability of a recently conquered city to pay taxes; the latter by a man accustomed to manipulating large numbers—Hermann, Secretary of the *Chambre des* XV. "We are very careful, on the one hand, to make no omissions, and on the other, to avoid using the same figure twice," he affirmed, but his system of classification does not permit us to verify any details. Did he include the clergy, estimated in 1785 at 914 persons, including domestic servants? Undoubtedly, for he refers to them in a note; ecclesiastics would therefore be listed under the heading "bourgeois and others" and their servants divided among at least four different categories.

By contrast, some of the intermediate numbers are debatable, overestimates (1720, 1745, and 1750) alternating with underestimates.

We are still far from having answered all aspects of the question. "The statesman who wishes to know the number of a country's population needs only approximate figures," declared Moheau. Thus contemporaries forged a whole arsenal of techniques to use in such estimates. The *feu* [household] is the most classic but also the one which has given rise to the most violent criticisms. Schoepflin used the coefficient 5, Hermann 4.7, Boersch 4. The error lies in preferring any one of these three authorities and of consistently applying the selected coefficient from 1700 to 1800. This coefficient should vary along with the population.

"Domiciliary accumulation" can give some results. In 1709 there were thirteen inhabitants per house in Strasbourg. In 1783 there were 3514 houses. This totals 45,682 inhabitants, a number very close to that proposed by Necker. Is this a valid calculation? Everything depends upon one postulate: can we go from 1709 to 1783 without making any adjustment?

Other methods were also put to use in the eighteenth century; such as the multiplication of the number of marriages, of baptisms, and of deaths by a certain coefficient. Here are two examples for Strasbourg:

	Expilly: 1763–1767			Bürgerfreund: 1776		
	Number	Coef.	Total	Number	Coef.	Total
Feux	8156	5	40,780	9100	4.5	40,950
Baptisms	1560	30	46,800	1538	29	44,602
Deaths				1550	28	43,400
Marriages				380	111	42,180

[1] This figure refers not to the city alone but to the city and subdelegation of Strasbourg (seventeen *bailliages*). As the author points out, estimates and census figures vary as to their reliability. For instance, the figures for 1771 and 1774 are probably too low. Lemoigne thinks that the figure for 1771 should be 38,205–42,450, depending on whether one adopts the coefficient of 4.5 or 5. For 1774 the figure should be between 37,642 and 41,825. Why these underestimates? Because of the desire of the Strasbourgeois authorities to escape the fiscal burden imposed by the monarchy. They thought they could do so by exaggerating the evil effects of the crisis of 1770–1771,

At ten years' interval, the same method is applied differently. Expilly seems to use coefficients found in general works. The editor of *Bürgerfreund* seems to show a better understanding of the local environment. Though he multiplies the number of Lutheran baptisms by twenty-eight, he uses the coefficient thirty for the Catholics; in our table we use twenty-nine. This detail would prove that the Catholics produce less children than the Lutherans (one baptism for every thirty inhabitants as compared with one for every twenty-eight Lutherans). By varying his coefficients, and by discussing each figure, the author applies a difficult method in a serious manner.

Father Mols has clearly shown the dangers of such speculation: "to reconstitute the figures of the absolute population, on the basis of nothing but data concerning the birth rate, and by applying a uniform coefficient for every period, involves serious risks of error; this is also true if one wishes to rely upon a retroactive calculation of the marriage or death rates." Boersch (1836) has clearly shown the variation of these coefficients according to the decades. Here are several examples:

Decades	*Marriages*	*Births*	*Deaths*
1728–1737	1 per 98 inhabitants (0.0102)	1 per 25.6 inhabitants (0.0390)	1 per 22.4 inhabitants (0.0446)
1758–1767	1 per 101 inhabitants (0.0099)	1 per 27.3 inhabitants (0.0366)	1 per 25.5 inhabitants (0.0392)
1768–1777	1 per 111 inhabitants (0.0090)	1 per 26.7 inhabitants (0.0378)	1 per 26.2 inhabitants (0.0381)
1778–1787	1 per 125 inhabitants (0.0080)	1 per 29.1 inhabitants (0.0343)	1 per 27.2 inhabitants (0.0367)

In conclusion, we can say that the population of Strasbourg went from 30,000 inhabitants in 1700–1705 to 40,000 in 1760–1765 to 50,000 in 1789. The increase thus stands at 66 per cent. It took sixty years to go from 30,000 to 40,000 (33 per cent) but only twenty to jump from 40,000 to 50,000 (25 per cent), after about 1774. What are the causes of this increase and, if possible, of this varying rhythm?

CAUSES OF THE DEMOGRAPHIC INCREASE. "More people are dying than are being born in Strasbourg, but we must not conclude that the population of the city is decreasing," declared our anonymous editor of 1776. Migratory movement makes up for the deficit in natural movement.

Natural Movement. The demographic deficit prevailed, but it weakened progressively until 1789. The break occurred in the 60's. The negative balances of 1735 (−1054) and of 1743 (−605) have no equivalent after 1760; the maximum is found in 1772 (−335). We should refer these numbers to the total number of the population in order to see their relative importance. The deficit of 1735 affects a population of about 36,000 inhabitants and represents a loss of 3.7 per cent. That of 1772 is spread among some 40,000 inhabitants and represents a loss of less than 1 per cent.

❧❦❧

Until 1760 the demographic surpluses remain slight—eleven years of surplus, the maximum occurring in 1754: +229; fifteen years of surplus after 1760, for a shorter period, with the maximum being reached in 1766: +370. A marked improvement can thus be seen from the 60's on.

Mortality Decreases. From 1728 to 1737 the rate is .0446, from 1777 to 1790, .0367. But the infant death rate remains high. We have calculated that for the period 1760–1789, it remains well above 50 per cent of the total number of deaths. This is confirmed by a remark of Moheau's: "In its first years almost half the population dies."

The birth rate increased slightly. There were fewer marriages after 1768; the rate went from .009 (1768–1777) to .008 (1778–1787). In absolute figures, the total number of marriages rarely was above 400 after 1769. But the fertility of marriages increased, as a result of the reduction, small though it was, in infant mortality. Here are some details of Boersch's research: the number of births per 100 marriages:

$$
\begin{aligned}
&1728\text{–}1732: && 100 - 370 \\
&1738\text{–}1747: && 100 - 380 \\
&1768\text{–}1777: && 100 - 410 \\
&1778\text{–}1787: && 100 - 430
\end{aligned}
$$

The editor of the *Bürgerfreund* declared that four children should be born of a marriage and observed that in Strasbourg the average fertility did not measure up to that norm. The figures contradict his pessimism. But births still did not make up for deaths. From 1728 to 1758, there were 100 for 110 deaths. From 1759 to 1790, there were 100 for 102 deaths. Actually, it is really a question of baptisms; the number of births has therefore been slightly underestimated. For 1789, Des Pommelles gave the city of Strasbourg 450 births per 100 marriages and 105 births per 100 deaths.

The average age increased. Boersch estimated that from 1728 to 1757, it was 24 years; and for the period 1758–1787, it was 27 years. As a group, the population remained youthful. In 1789, children (up to age sixteen) accounted for 39 per cent of it.

All these factors partly explain the demographic growth of Strasbourg, especially after 1770. These factors themselves have various causes.

An Increase in Healthfulness. The "demographers" of the eighteenth century attached a great deal of importance to the "physical" improvement of the cities. They listed it among the causes favorable to demographic growth. The Blondel plan (1765) corresponded to this ideal: widening, paving, and better orientation of streets. Police *ordonnances* concerning the cleanliness of the streets laid down very strict rules about the removal of rubbish and the sweeping of public squares. These efforts, accompanied by better personal hygiene, perhaps formed a serious obstacle to the spread of epidemics, whose number and violence decreased after the hecatombs of 1735 and 1744.

Medical Reasons. The increase in the birth rate can be credited to the activity of J. J. Fried and of his followers. Fried (1689–1769) became *accoucheur* for the city in 1727 and, in 1728, master of the midwives. He reorganized this profession, initiated a new technique in delivery (podalic version), and provided an annual theoretical course of instruction followed by an examination. After 1733 all complaints about "charlatans" ceased, and the prestige of the profession increased as a result of the efficacy of its methods. In the hospital in which his practice was located Fried trained specialists who went as far as Russia. Pregnant and postpartum women were carefully observed, and as early as 1727 Fried declared that he would treat the poor without charge, even outside the hospital. How many deaths this action must have avoided! Fried's work was unquestionably successful, for by 1750–1760 he had trained a generation of students capable of applying his methods, though these results cannot be expressed by means of figures.

All these reasons are not sufficient to explain an increase of 66 per cent in ninety years. We must look elsewhere.

The Migratory Movement. "It is in the nature of cities to do their recruiting in the rural areas and to suck up their population without there being any spirit of reciprocity," observed Moheau. A general phenomenon which we also encounter at Strasbourg. The editor of 1776 spoke of a "very great influx of foreigners." By foreigner he meant anyone not a Strasbourgeois by birth. It is, however, difficult to follow this migratory movement in both directions.

Departures. A text of 1773 speaks of an exodus of 275 families in 1750 and 1770, most of whom settled at Kehl, across the Rhine from Strasbourg, having been attracted by the advantages they found there; but this text arouses suspicion. Among the bourgeoisie departures were rare. From 1781 to 1783, there were nine such departures. The obligation to pay the city government a compensation estimated at one-tenth of one's possessions, probably made one weigh such a step carefully. In reality, these departures were those of the common people, *manants* or *habitants*, anonymous in history, whose names were not even honored by appearing in the registers of the bourgeoisie.

Arrivals. The discontinuation of the Book of the Bourgeoisie in 1736, and the absence of such a book for *manants*, hinder us from forming an idea of the general picture. The few statistical documents available allow us to form only partial conclusions. From 1741 to 1761, the *Magistrat* recorded the arrival of 1590 *manants* (heads of families), or a yearly average of eighty. In 1774, the number of bourgeois admitted was 165; and from 1781 to 1784, the number was 449, including 284 naturalized citizens, for an annual average of 112. It would be imprudent to draw any conclusions from such sketchy documentation. One last point: the rural areas of Alsace were overflowing with people. While Strasbourg counted 105 births for 100 deaths, the rural areas had a total of 137. This surplus poured into Strasbourg, which formed a very strong magnetic pole. A royal city, it attracted civil servants and office workers of all sorts. A fortified city, with no service required in the militia, it attracted that segment of rural population that desired to escape such service. A labor market, whose corporative system was integrated with that of Germany, it attracted journeymen from beyond the Rhine who came to perfect the technique of their craft and who frequently settled there.

Results of This Growth

"The city has considerably increased in population and consequently in poor people."

The increase mainly involved *manant* families. Their number increased by 69 per cent (1506–2548) as compared with 20 per cent for the bourgeoisie (5629–6858), from 1709 to 1789. The *droit de manance* was from 50 to 70 per cent lower than those paid by the bourgeoisie. In 1784 there were 26,000 bourgeois. At the same date the population of Strasbourg was 46,000 persons. That left 20,000 *manants* and *habitants*. The new element of the population was made up of people who were not very well off, even poor.

This increase in population was especially to the advantage of the Catholics. In a period of 80 years they caught up with the Protestants, going from 5119 (1697) to 23,700 (1789). After 1740 the total number of their marriages was always superior to that of the Lutherans. The Catholics were in a minority within the bourgeoisie, accounting for a third of it. But they formed the major part of the *manants* (two-thirds) and undoubtedly of the *habitants* as well. Catholics, *manants, habitants* are categories that overlapped. With a few exceptions, Catholics in eighteenth-century Strasbourg had the reputation of being poor. The population therefore increased on its lower levels. Strasbourg was inundated by a mass of persons who were not well off financially, who were burdened with a brood of children, and who were the sure victims of a rise in grain prices. And the *Magistrat*, the majority of whom were Lutherans, always begrudgingly gave alms and relief to the poor, who were largely Catholic.

The Garrison

It forms a group just as complex as the civilian population and just as difficult to study, considering its mobility—certain groups being stationed there only three or four months, just enough time to bring the troops to their full force—and the extreme variability of the number of troops, according to the units or types of weapons being considered. Two conclusions, however, are certain. During the eighteenth century the total number and types of troops varied. Until 1769, the garrison of Strasbourg always numbered 7000 to 8000 men. This number was proportionate to the role that Strasbourg played in the Monarchy's continental wars. The regiments did not stop long at Strasbourg, which was a strategic halting place. After 1760, the number of men in the garrison was stabilized at about 5000. The names of the same corps reappear periodically. Strasbourg became a garrison city. Troops of French origin predominated until 1760. There was a military reason for this: Strasbourg, a crossroads city, watched the entire French army march by as it was constantly being called into action. There was also a political reason: in a city still reticent about the royal regime, would it not be imprudent to implant regiments of German origin? After 1760 "German" regiments were installed in the city, now won over to the regime.

It was a fortunate coincidence that the number of troops decreased at the precise moment when the demographic growth of the civilian population increased. The large garrisons of 1730 to 1760 increased the demand for grain at a time when the agriculture of Alsace was regaining its strength. The reduced garrisons of 1760 to 1789 alleviated the situation. The civilian population could thus profit from the agricultural surpluses to a greater degree.

CONSUMPTION

It is difficult to follow the development of food consumption in detail. Documentation is fragmentary. It is nevertheless possible to advance several conclusions. For those grains used in bread, there was a marked increase between 1720 and 1789: from 110 to 160,000 *rézaux* (a *rézal* was on the average worth three-quarters of a Parisian *setier*), or an increase of 45 per cent. But these grain entries do not necessarily correspond to the total consumption of Strasbourg. Flour is not mentioned, and the city could have been consuming flour two or three years old. In addition, all the grains traded were not immediately milled.

Did the grain supplies parallel the demographic growth? That is the problem. In 1743 "it has been clearly verified that the annual food supplies never go beyond 90,000 sacks," not including the garrison. This estimate is valuable to us. According to Moheau, the annual consumption per person was two *setiers*, or 2.77 *rézaux*. At this rate, the population of Strasbourg would be 32,500 persons, a result that corrects Orry's estimate (1745) in a satisfactory manner. The food supplies of the 50,000 inhabitants of 1789 would require some 140,000 sacks. The accounts of 1788 indicate 147,000 sacks. A surplus? Not in the least! The ration of the garrison was included in this number: 6000 persons, or 17,000 sacks. Of this number we must deduct the grain destined for storage. Without exaggeration we can speak of a deficit of 20,000 sacks. Incoming shipments no longer met the demand; grain and bread were expensive.

The Movement of Prices and of the Population

It would be desirable if we could discover whether the most abundant years for the fruits of the earth are also those for the production of human beings. . . . We have compared the years of high mortality with the years of scarcity, and although some authors have thought they found some analogies between them, we have observed that there is none.

This was Moheau's opinion. Does Strasbourg bear it out?

PRICES AND MORTALITY. The comparison of the percentages of the increase in cereal prices (as compared with a previous minimum) and of the death rate is informative.

Years	Wheat	Rye	Death rate
1735	35%	40%	77%
1760	60	79	30
1771–1772	120	167	38

The effects of prices upon the death rate decreased in the course of the century, despite quite marked increases in prices. Until 1750 to 1760, scarcity was accompanied by epidemics which ravaged the population to a terrible degree, and which had consequences across the years through the phenomenon of the *classes creuses* [that is, of gaps in population and therefore in the reproductive cycle]. One example: 1756 was a year of cyclical minimum and still it was marked by a serious demographic deficit. There are three possible hypotheses:

—an epidemic? Boersch does not mention one.

—an excessive military death rate? This was the beginning of the Seven Years War and 9000 soldiers poured into Strasbourg. Such troop movements are always accompanied by deaths, but in what proportion?

—an excessive infant mortality rate? The children born about 1735 were the sons and daughters of underfed persons (crisis of 1735–1736) and were undernourished themselves (latent crisis of 1741–1747). Could they not have given birth, toward 1756, to especially feeble children, who were carried off like wisps of straw, or even stillborn?

To a certain degree Moheau was right. In his work, he always chose examples from 1763 to 1775. This is precisely the period in which "the price wave begins to no longer be followed by such great demographic declines, and in which cyclical accident loses its virulence." And according to Mr. Meuvret, "the wheat market plays its part, but it did not kill at once, as in the seventeenth century, nor everyone at once; it wore them down slowly."

Prices and Marriages

Here we find that 1765 to 1770 again marked a division. Until that date, marriages followed the cyclical movement of prices. This is a classic demographic phenomenon. After scarcity, there is a rash of marriages. Between 30 and 48 per cent more are celebrated than in the preceding years. The population, in a frenzy of activity, seems to wish to make-up as quickly as possible for the losses it has undergone. Marriages also multiplied during the cyclical minima. During the 1763–1767 period, which the generation of 1770 was to look upon as "the good old days," more than 450 marriages a year were celebrated, a record which would never be beaten until 1789.

After 1770, the marriage curve stabilized at the level of 350–400. This phenomenon is paradoxical, considering the marked increase in the population. There are several possible explanations. One is the effect of the *clases creuses*: There were fewer marriages in about 1780 because the period 1758–1763, itself having been determined by the period of 1735–1743, was not very prolific. Or perhaps the newcomers to Strasbourg were already married. Or else, they were marrying less or later, because they had become aware of the increasing difficulty in assuring the basic food supplies for a family. The number of illegitimate children consequently increased.

Death and birth rates are often related to the price of wheat, but crises no longer succeeded in containing the rising tide of the population.

THE FOOD CRISES AT STRASBOURG

The crises, by their periodicity, are so many "privileged" moments if not for the consumer, at least for the historian. In general, contemporaries give us a detailed account which completes the dry enumeration of the lists of market prices. The entire life of the city was upset for a moment. Owing to prices, the population and the grain supply met face to face, and the city government tried to reconcile the extremes and reduce the ill effects. This was a major confrontation, in which diverse elements intervene. But with the development of these elements, the crises themselves also change in character. We have been able to distinguish between two types of crises.

CRISES WITH DEMOGRAPHIC CONSEQUENCES

"Through the different researches which have been done, we have found proof that the years in which wheat was the most expensive were at the same time those in which mortality was highest and illnesses most widespread. . . ."

The High Prices of 1735–1736

Our only sources are the market price lists and the annual population records. No administrative or literary document completes these two categories of information. We can only present hypotheses on the causes of this crisis. Undoubtedly it was due to a poor harvest.

A Difficult Period between Harvests. *The Increase of the Winter of 1733–1734.* From December to March, the grain prices rose considerably: 24 per cent for wheat, and 31 per cent for rye, when compared with August 1733.

The Plateau of the Spring and Summer of 1734. Prices were stabilized at about 11 *livres* (wheat) and 7 *livres* (rye). This fits the pattern of seasonal fluctuations.

The Increase of Autumn 1734. A poor harvest, with the fears, grounded or not, which it aroused, undoubtedly provoked a sharp rise. Wheat was at its maximum price in November (15 *livres*, 4 *sols*) and rye in December (10 livres, 12 sols), respective increases of 58 and 78 per cent when compared with August 1733.

The Maintenance of High Prices until November 1735. Wheat cost 12 to 13 livres, rye 9 to 10 livres.

The Abrupt Drop: Late 1735–Early 1736. The decrease began in November 1735. By spring 1736 prices had returned to their level of autumn 1733.

Demographic Consequences. The record year of the eighteenth century for deaths in Strasbourg was 1735. There were 2322, or about 7 per cent of a population estimated at 35,000. Epidemics accompanied the food shortage. Undernourishment, by increasing the illness rate, at the same time increased the death rate. In 1734, there was "an invasion of a new malady, but one which from this time on became endemic: the military ailment." J. G. Saltzmann described its symptoms (chills, labored breathing, dizziness, heavy perspiration . . .) and blamed the floods of the Rhine and the excessive humidity resulting from the heavy rainfalls of the summer of 1734. "It mainly attacked mature individuals, sparing children and old people. . . ." Parish registers seem to bear out this observation. The infant death rate was not at all excessive (for the period); 45 per cent of the total deaths. We will see much higher rates, in 1765, for example; 60 per cent.

Prolonged High Prices: 1741–1747

Like a large part of the kingdom, Strasbourg was affected by the crisis of 1741. But the cyclical minimum that followed was not as ample as that of the "national" curve of Mr. Labrousse. It cannot even claim to be called by such a name. Prices decreased slightly, but they remained at an elevated level. It was a latent crisis which in reality continued until 1750.

The Physiognomy of Prices. *The Plateau of August 1742 to June 1744.* Wheat prices remained stationary at about 11 to 12 livres. But the situation was not at all alarming; public and private granaries were still well supplied.

The Recrudescence of August 1744 to February 1745. It affected only wheat, whose price climbed 30 per cent as compared with June 1744.

A Year of High Prices: August 1745–September 1746. Until 1749, the alimentary situation of Strasbourg and the province remained precarious. In November 1748, the Intendant forbade the exportation of potatoes by wagon and on December 29, 1749, De Vanolles forbade bakers and private citizens of Alsace to "sell bread to foreigners . . . ."

The Causes. *Military Purchases.* They multiplied during this period of war. Alsace provided the supplies for a great part of the royal army; prices at Strasbourg were affected. *Préteur royal* Klingen recalled in 1750 that "food supplies for the city were disrupted for a certain period for the King's service, then were decreased by the extraordinarily high consumption owing to the great influx of people occasioned by the presence and sojourn of His Majesty's armies in the areas about the city . . . ." A convoy of 80,000 sacks was even sent from Strasbourg to Lyons in 1748. Under these conditions, the granaries of the city were never full, and the *Magistrat* could only play its regulatory role with difficulty.

The Pandours (Hungarian Soldiers). Their brief stay aggravated an already difficult situation. During the summer of 1744 they spread out in the plain of Basse-Alsace (the northern half of the province) and plundered the harvests. At Strasbourg there was "an unaccountable flood of refugees from the hinterland which for some time occupied and filled even the streets of the city day and night." As the peasants were in the city, the shipment of supplies into Strasbourg was momentarily interrupted. The *Magistrat* kept the city alive on the reserves which had already been badly reduced, and it encountered serious difficulties owing to "all the public assistance we had to give to those from the hinterland in the form of grain and bread." From 1744 to 1749, the *Magistrat* threw upon the market 7500 sacks of grain, including 4000 sacks of rye. It was only in 1750 that normal reserves would be rebuilt (16,000 sacks) and that optimism would return.

The Festivities Offered to the Inhabitants by the Magistrat on October 5, 1744, on the Occasion of the King's Arrival. They reassured the population which was momentarily being threatened with a siege and created a diversion in the midst of high prices, by the free distribution of bread, wine, and meat. This popular feasting, though it left a pleasant memory, only cheated hunger for a short time. The population of Strasbourg paid dearly for this long period of scarcity.

The Consequences. Once more scarcity and epidemics combined their murderous effects. From 1742 to 1744, the mortality rate continued to increase: 1910, 1993, 2154 deaths; the normal rate fluctuated between 1400 and 1500. Children's deaths increased: 48 per cent of the total number in 1743, 62 per cent in 1746. A new epidemic of catarrh, coming from Germany, descended upon France from 1742 to 1745. Sauvage christened it the *"grippe."* "It is doubtless to it that we must attribute the increase in mortality of the years 1742–1744," asserted Boersch. Its virulence can only be explained because it encountered an undernourished population, stripped of all protective elements. In April 1746, the Intendant received twelve boxes of pharmaceutical supplies, with 4236 "rations of medicines" prepared especially for the provinces by Mr. Helvetius. Was the shipment too late or the remedies not efficacious? The toll of 1746 was high: 1862 deaths.

These crises were typical. They were still connected with those of the seventeenth century. The increase in the prices of cereals had immediate deadly effects, accentuated even more by the action of epidemics. The principal victims were adults. But, as Boersch nicely stated, in the eighteenth century we witness a new transformation "in the type of epidemic . . . as we move to the end of the century, epidemics change their character and eruptive illnesses (measles, small pox) replace catarrh-type epidemics (quinsy, peri-pneumonias) . . . ." The chief victims of these were children, since on

April 27, 1772, the *Magistrat* of Strasbourg had forbidden the small-pox vaccination, "for the method of inoculating, by increasing the poison of the small pox matter in the air, increases the number of illnesses." The number of adults surviving therefore increased, as a result of the temporary increase in infant mortality and as a result of immigration. Food crises assumed another form. "The mortal crisis was replaced by the venial crisis, the crisis which spares life but postpones problems by accumulating the population." That of 1770 and 1771 was the first of a long series.

CRISES WITH SOCIAL CONSEQUENCES: THE CRISIS OF 1770-1771

Though we find the same haunting fears in the collective psychology in 1744 and in 1770, the consequences of these two crises were very different. In 1744 as in 1770, it was said that "granaries are flying away like butter-flies." For the "physician of the city," and the rationalists of the period, the matter was simple: "the larvae of the wheat moth or phalaena, hide between the lobes of the grain, rip the bran in order to enter, empty it, and spin a cocoon. Towards June or July, various hatchings of them come out of the granaries. They are present in such great number that the entire pile seems to be moving." This was the result of the improper upkeep of the granaries. It is significant, however, that the people only observed the infestation, which appears to have been a common one, during a period of high prices. The collective mentality, deformed by the psychosis of scarcity, was made sensitive to anything which represented a "loss of grain." To it, high costs became a calamity, accompanied by "supernatural phenomena." But the comparison between 1744 and 1771 stops there. The crisis of 1771 was not accompanied by a hecatomb. It multiplied the number of beggars, of "economically weak" persons. "Poverty thus became a sort of meteorological accident." Were contemporaries aware of this change? It so happens that the crisis of 1770–1771 is exceptionally well documented; there are reports of each market addressed to *Préteur* Baron d'Autigny by Acarie, *Receveur* of the municipal granary, or by Zorn and Lemp, Directors of the same granary. A recapitulatory memorandum was even drawn up.

The Development of the Crisis

A DIFFICULT PERIOD BETWEEN HARVESTS. The harvest of 1769 had been insufficient. By autumn, the customary seasonal depression gave way to a slight increase in prices. On December 27, 1769, forseeing future difficulties, the *Préteur* ordered experiments on a potato bread which lasted until March 1770. The aim of these experiments was limited. It was a matter of making a cheap bread for the prisoners in the *Maison de Force*. But they constituted a precedent which in the near future would be remembered by the *Magistrat*, especially since by January 1770 the technique and recipes had already been perfected.

In May 1770, prices rose. Was it a seasonal change or the threat of a crisis? Despite the public rejoicing which accompanied the passage of Marie Antoinette through the city, the population must have foreseen the imminent crisis. Madame d'Oberkirch asserted she had seen "bread trampled under foot without the poor even bothering to pick it up." This is a report of dubious value, in which we can see an aristocrat's prejudices that "the populace" is responsible for its own misfortune. At Strasbourg, wheat was at 17 livres. This price quotation already was at an alarming level, for the bourgeois as well as for the *manants*.

In June and July came catastrophe. Bakers became restless; their shops were searched; they were forbidden to bake cakes (June 15). In July the average price of wheat reached 24 livres, 15 sols. On July 6, the *Magistrat* announced to the bakers that "whatever the price of grain, the fixed price of bread will not be raised," but promised that it would itself supply them with the necessary items. Thus it avoided granting a price increase which would correspond to the average price of 23 livres.

In August, prices were stabilized at around 23 livres a *rézal*, because of the combined action of the *Magistrat*, which distributed 350 sacks of rye to the bakers at 15 livres (the average price was 16 livres, 6 sols), and of the *Préteur*, who went before the group of bakers and threatened them with the closing of their shops for a month if they did not buy this grain.

The gap was a difficult one to bridge. From the moment it was applied, the new price of bread established in March 1770 was submitted to a rugged test. It was never regularly enforced. In order to keep the price of bread low, the *Magistrat* did not respect the price ruling. But all this was only a dress rehearsal.

THE NEW PRICE OFFENSIVE: AUTUMN-WINTER 1770. The *Etat général des Récoltes* (general summary of harvests) of September 1770 was alarming. The subdelegation of Strasbourg announced that the harvest of wheat and rye had been only two-thirds of an "ordinary year," as a result of snows in April and dampness in July. Faced with this situation, the appropriate authorities re-established price regulations. On July 14, 1770, Terray suppressed the exportation of grain. The *Magistrat* of Strasbourg took identical measures within its jurisdiction and restricted all transactions of cereals to the markets alone.

By September, fears were justified; wheat rose to 25 livres a *rézal*; rye was at 20 livres, 6 sols. Until the beginning of January 1771, wheat remained at 24 livres, but in February prices began to rise again.

THE EXTREME POINT: MARCH 1771. On March 27, 1771, wheat reached its peak price: 29 livres, 12 sols and rye stood at 20 livres. This was a respective increase of 117 and 129 per cent as compared with August 1769. On April 4, the official price of bread rose to 28 livres.

CONTINUING SCARCITY: APRIL-JULY 1771. During this period the 1800 sacks a week necessary for the city's needs rarely appeared on the market. Thus the *Magistrat* decided to put some of its stored grains on the market. Six hundred sacks (400 wheat, 200 rye) were put on the market on April 19, at the price of 24 livres and 18 livres, a step which made the average price of wheat drop 2 livres. By this means, and despite the protests of the bakers who bought at high prices in order to make the official price of bread rise, the *Magistrat* succeeded in gradually reducing the fixed price to 25 livres. To quiet the bakers who were "inclined to disparage the city's grain," Maréchal de Contades, Governor of Strasbourg, threatened to have four or five of them hanged as examples. In July the average price of wheat fell to 22 livres.

THE PRICE COLLAPSE: AUGUST 1771. "The market of August 9 was so fine that it astonished all observers, and the great abundance ended all these difficulties." The peasants brought in 1800 sacks of grain, and the city stopped putting its grain on the market. The average price of wheat decreased 4 livres (from 21 livres to 17 livres). In September, prices once more became "normal" (15–16 livres).

We have observed the *Magistrat* at work throughout the crisis. Let us look more closely at its role during this period of scarcity.

The *Magistrat* in Action: The Struggle Against Scarcity

THE MAGISTRAT SEEKING INFORMATION: MAY-JUNE 1770. Did the period between harvests present such problems everywhere? This is the theme of the correspondence among the *Magistrats* of Landau, Wissembourg, Sélestat, Colmar, and Belfort from May to June 1770. On the basis of their grain quotations, the cities consulted replied that the scarcity was a generalized one. By July, the inquiry became more widespread. Information about the quality of bread and about the means of controlling prices was requested of the authorities of Nancy, Metz, Rouen, Bordeaux, and Lyons. Pessimism reigned everywhere.

THE MAGISTRAT REPLENISHING ITS RESERVES: AUGUST 1770–MARCH 1771. In 1770, the municipal granary was almost empty. The *Magistrat* borrowed 50,000 livres from [religious] foundations and began a policy of large-scale buying. One solution was eliminated: shipping in grain from Marseilles, for the costs would be too high. That left the northern countries. The *Magistrat* looked over the entire Rhine valley. It exchanged copious correspondence with brokers, merchants, and diplomatic representatives established in Germany. Until September, it was largely preoccupied with the net costs of grain, shipping costs included. By October, its main concern was buying grain.

Cappaux, a member of the *Magistrat* of Strasbourg, surveyed the Frakenthal region (South West of Worms). He found 1500 sacks of wheat at 16 livres. But the affair dragged on until January 1771. He could not obtain the necessary export visas, for the Elector Palatine had forbidden all exports under penalty of death. In order "not to find himself in a vexatious position," on June 22, 1771, he sold the grain he had been buying for the past 8 months.

Sieur Odunne, French envoy to the Court of Mannheim, was contacted by the *Magistrat* as early as September 14, 1770. But the few grain purchases he made were blocked along the Rhine; they had to be sold in June 1771.

In September 1770, the *Magistrat* began negotiations with Barozzi, Resident of the French Court at Frankfurt. By October the latter was advising it "to resort to Holland if the Palatinate does not give something," and for this purpose he sent the *Magistrat* the price quotations of the Grain Exchange of Amsterdam. On December 16, 1770, he returned the 100 louis which the *Préteur royal* had advanced him to make purchases.

Did this mean that the *Magistrat* had lost the "grain race?" No. It nevertheless succeeded in obtaining from the Grand Chapter of the Cathedral and from the Jewish merchant, Cerf Berr, 5126 sacks of wheat for 125,460 livres (an average price of 24 livres, 6 sols) and 407 sacks of rye for 7643 livres (an average price of 18 livres, 15 sols). In the beginning of April 1771, the *Magistrat* had available a working amount of 13,500 sacks, consisting of the grain received as annual revenue in kind, which it had carefully preserved; the grain from the religious foundations; and the grains purchased. It could intervene in the grain market.

THE MAGISTRAT PROVIDING SUPPLIES FOR THE MARKET: APRIL–AUGUST 1771. The *Magistrat* very early strove to curb the waste of grain. On July 28, 1770, it forbade starchmakers to buy more than two sacks of wheat a week. This measure "saved" about 2000 sacks of grain during the 1771–1772 period.

On April 19, 1771, the *Magistrat* decided to intervene. It planned to distribute to each market 300 sacks of wheat and fifty of rye until October 4, or a total of 7200 sacks. Its grain reserve made this possible. It was not so much a question of selling as of influencing the prices and of imposing them upon the peasants by simulating abundance. The operation was highly successful. In all, the *Magistrat* sold, either in the markets or directly to the bakers, 3622 sacks of wheat and 1119 of rye. It admitted, shamelessly, that it was in this way able to get rid of all the grain it had received as annual revenue in kind, "the inferior grain," in order to empty its granaries. The operation nevertheless involved a loss of 20,000 livres, but "we have done a really good deed for the bourgeoisie and above all for the poor, we have stopped public complaints, we have satisfied the generals, and we believe that the loss suffered by the city had been amply compensated for by the tranquillity which the city and we ourselves now enjoy."

THE MAGISTRAT SUPPORTING THE CONSUMER. Assuring the supplies of bakers was only the first step. The consumer still had to be protected. The *Magistrat* worked at this faithfully. It fixed the official price of bread at the lowest possible level, without respecting the bakers' rights. If prices of grain rose, they would only alter the official price three or four weeks later. Bread consistently cost less than the legal price.

Despite this "trituration" of the controlled price, bread remained the principal problem. Even with a manipulated price, it was still too expensive for a large part of the population. From October 20, 1770, on, the *Magistrat* ordered the *Receveur* of the poorhouse to make potato bread (one-third wheat, one-third rye, one-third potato). On March 6, 1771, the Intendant encouraged this step by forbidding "the use of potatoes in the fabrication of any distilled spirits." The experiments of late 1769 thus were applied on a large scale. From October 23, 1770, to June 11, 1771, the *Receveur* carried out 193 "bread bakings" and delivered 29,591 round 3-pound loaves costing 4 *sols*, 6 *deniers*. The same loaf of household bread (half rye, half wheat) at the official price of 21 *livres*, cost 6 *sols*, 6 *deniers*.

The *Magistrat* also tried to educate the consumer by distributing a printed prospectus with the recipe for an "economical rice to aid the poor in this period of high prices." With a base of rice, potatoes, and turnips, a cauldronful "produces 418 to 425 pounds of nourishment; this ready-cooked rice costs only 1 *sol* a pound and each portion is sufficient to nourish one person; it is also suitable for children." This measure was not exceptional. In distributing its recipe, the *Magistrat* used for its own advantage a measure first taken by the Crown, which during the same period was distributing rice to those provinces suffering from scarcity.

Despite these efforts, the excessively high prices of 1771 haunted the memories of Strasbourgeois because of their grave consequences.

The Consequences of the Crisis

DEMOGRAPHIC. In the collective mentality, scarcity and epidemic were indissolubly connected. After the price increase of Autumn 1770, the most alarming sort of rumors began to circulate through the city: "plague in Moldavia, in Poland . . . ." Anxiety reigned until December 1771.

The mortality rate resulting from the crisis of 1770–1771 was not at all comparable with those of 1735 or 1744. The year 1771 had what might be called a normal number of deaths: 1542. The year 1772 was more murderous: 1830 deaths, and the death-birth ratio was a negative one: —335. The effect of the crisis was postponed, and 57 per cent of the deaths were among children. "The sinister triad, historically linked, of hunger, plague, and war was impaired and broken up."

SOCIAL. *Emigration.* After having forbidden the export of grain (July 14, 1770), Terray had also forbidden the exit of men (September 24, 1770). Now, at Strasbourg the edict appeared difficult to enforce. Maréchal de Contades complained to the *Magistrat* about "the mania for emigrating" observed at Strasbourg. Emigration was a means of escaping high costs. A number of Strasbourgeois discovered its effectiveness for themselves. Some went as far as Hungary and returned after unfortunate experiences. A few returned, but how many definitive departures, not listed in the police reports, were there?

Mendicity. Those who hesitated to leave, and for whom even potato bread was too expensive, became charges of the city. The years 1770–1771 were record years: the hospitals were filled to overflowing, the Alms Chamber showed a deficit for the first time and had to dip into its reserves. In 1770–1771, nearly 3000 persons were aided, as compared with a little over 1000 in 1760. The Hospice of the Poor, created in 1767, had 287 pensioners in 1768, a total of 512 in 1770, and 483 in 1771. The expenditures of the Alms Chamber fluctuated from 1764 to 1767 between 9 and 10,000 livres; they rose to 24,000 livres in 1770 and to 26,000 livres in 1771. Another document even mentions 35,000 livres.

The crisis of 1770 and 1771 staggered Strasbourg, as it did a great part of France. It marked the rupture in the balance between population and supplies. After this "commotion" things were seen in a different light. Harvest conditions were followed attentively. At the least sign of trouble, the *Magistrat* without waiting threw several hundred sacks of grain upon the market in order to maintain prices at a moderate level. It had become aware of the fragility of its wheat-supply system, caught in an inexorable set of circumstances: a long-term price increase. From 1771 to 1789, the crisis was constantly present, in a latent form. With the least increase in prices, even though slight in absolute figures, tension again became extreme. The death rate rose a few points. "Deadly epidemics of purple fever due to the uncleanliness of the grain . . ." were mentioned just about everywhere. What happened to those who had survived the crisis?

"THE LOUIS XVI CONJUNCTURE" AT STRASBOURG
UNDER-EMPLOYMENT AND MENDICITY

The price increase was to a certain degree the result of the demographic increase. The demand exceeded the supply. But the food crisis unleashed an economic recession in the economic system of the Ancien Régime. The search for work and for bread became the dominant preoccupation of a population that was becoming proletarian. Numerous immigrants had invaded Strasbourg, in the hope of finding work there. This expectation was very often disappointed, and by 1765 the *Magistrat* was zealously attacking the problem of mendicity.

Contraction of the Labor Market

The *Magistrat*, a product of the guild system, did nothing to encourage the implantation of new forms of business. Latent underemployment reigned in numerous guilds, and salaries felt its effects.

UNDEREMPLOYMENT. The industry most typical of Strasbourg was the manufacture of tobacco, "the nourishing leaf of the city." In this field, we can observe in all its breadth what Labrousse has called "the cyclical contrairiness of the movements of grains and industrial production." The manufacture of tobacco was extremely sensitive to the cyclical movement of grain prices. Here are several examples:

1734	65,000 *quintaux* worked	1769	37,704 *quintaux* worked
1735	45,042 *quintaux* worked	1770	36,744 *quintaux* worked
1736	70,704 *quintaux* worked	1771	41,742 *quintaux* worked
1768	42,174 *quintaux* worked	1772	59,874 *quintaux* worked

The guilds also were affected, especially the luxury trades: starchmakers and wigmakers, whose ranks had been inflated during the prosperous period of the first half of the century, constituted a real danger after 1771. Even a traditional trade such as the boatmen did not escape the crisis. Their guild was divided into two groups that worked alternately, a procedure that thus avoided the total unemployment of a part of its members and assured everyone half-time employment. "Full employment in under-employment . . . ."

In order to mitigate this deficiency in the labor market, many attempts were made (projects to create a vermicelli factory, 1749; a sailcloth factory, 1758; a hat factory, 1771; a hemp-spinning mill, 1774; a cloth manufacture, 1782). They always met with opposition, and even hostility, on the part of the *Magistrat*. It was an atmosphere of "economic Malthusianism." Affected by underemployment, the guilds took refuge behind the literal application of their by-laws. The guild system closed it ranks in order to assure its members a minimum salary.

SALARIES. The study of salaries is a delicate matter. The very fragmentary documentation does not permit us to chart their evolution. The rare data we possess concern only municipal employees who were often given room and board. Between 1770 and 1780, the stonecutter earned 24 sols a day, the mason 20 sols, the laborer 16 sols. While passing through Strasbourg, Arthur Young pointed out that the salary of the agricultural day-laborer was 20 to 24 sols in summer and 16 sols in winter.

Between 1770 and 1789, we can assert without much risk of error, that a daily salary of 1 livre (20 sols) was common. The year only included 260 working days, so a number of heads of household only earned 260 *livres* a year.

What was the purchasing power of these 260 livres? According to eighteenth-century economists, "men do not consume, on the average, more than two *setiers* of wheat, Paris measure, in a year." Ten *setiers* were therefore needed for a family of five, or 13.85 *rézaux*, Strasbourg measure. At 20 3/10 livres a *rézal* in 1770, one needed no less than 281 livres for what was considered a normal supply. In 1786 (a cyclical minimum) this still came to 164 livres. Bread alone used up almost the entire salary. If one wished, in addition, to buy clothes or fuel, it was tragic.

Lavoisier estimated the minimum subsistence salary for a family of five as 38 sols a day (410 livres). Outside the guilds (that is, the bourgeoisie), this situation must not have been common in Strasbourg. The increase in the number of children per family, that is to say of persons of an "economically dependent" age, which was noticeable after 1770, made the salary-bread problem insoluble. Women and children went out to seek supplementary wages. But the guilds refused to admit them. Children met "at the theater ticket office" to beg. Their parents resigned themselves to accepting private charity or the public relief assistance of the *Magistrat*.

Mendicity in Strasbourg

Aware of the social danger which the proliferation of mendicity constituted, the *Magistrat* attempted to count and to isolate the beggers and the poor, and to neutralize their potential injuriousness by work; in short, to "make of these dangerous classes, working classes."

During the eighteenth century, Strasbourg had improved its hospitals. The traditional facilities were composed of the Bourgeois Hospital, rich (100,000 livres income in 1784), receiving a good amount of income in kind (5000 *rézaux* of grain), and with a capacity of 523 beds; the Orphans' Hospital, which sheltered up to 250 children; and the Almonry of Saint Mark, which granted subsidies in products and in cash to an increasing number of heads of household (610 persons were aided in 1782, and 991 in 1784). After 1771, this institution continually worked at a deficit.

These establishments were intended only for the bourgeoisie. The principal contributors, they were also the beneficiaries of a system of public aid established by the *Magistrat* which went back to the Middle Ages. But in the eighteenth century, the bourgeoisie formed only half the population. Under these conditions, the other half (*manants, habitants*) benefited from no form of legal aid. Excluded from political life, they had no right to the "municipal manna." Urged by the Court and obliged by the urgency brought on by existing conditions, the *Magistrat* undertook the creation of new public assistance groups, such as the Foundling Home, founded in 1748 and enlarged in 1763 at great cost. It received 530 children in 1782 as compared with fifty-nine in 1749. Also the Poor House was founded in 1767 and entrusted with the care of poor *manants*. The nourishment provided, which represented perhaps the "physiological minimum", came to 4 sols a day (76 livres a year). The total upkeep came to 106 livres a year per pauper. This sum represents the barest "essential minimum" between 1770 and 1789.

The various relief foundations thus had more than 400,000 *livres* annual income in about 1781. The *Magistrat* was proud of possessing such ample facilities.

Once lodged, the beggars had to work in order to compensate for the expense of their upkeep: spinning and weaving for the Poor House, work in woolen textiles for the Foundlings. Despite its efforts, in 1783 the *Magistrat* was forced to admit that mendicity was still on the increase. In 1783, there were 2800 persons cared for in the hospitals or assisted by the foundations. In 1784, there were 9094 poor (almost one-fifth of the population), including 6356 Catholics and 2738 Protestants.

Such were the results of the increase in grain prices. One inhabitant out of five was indigent, one Catholic out of four, one Protestant out of nine. The demographic increase had been too great. With the guilds refusing to enlarge their membership, all the *Magistrat's* new creations were only ephemeral palliatives. The population-supply balance, which so many times before had been threatened, had been permanently disrupted.

THE SOCIAL CRISIS IN LYONS ON THE EVE OF THE FRENCH REVOLUTION

 By L. Trénard

"Nowhere more than in this city," wrote Michelet, "have there been utopian dreamers. Nowhere has the wounded, broken heart searched more anxiously for new solutions to the problem of human destinies." A precocious maturity, a passionate discussion of proposed remedies, and a zealous, crusading spirit characterize the originality of Lyonnais social thought. It had already appeared at the time of the prerevolutionary crises. More or less consciously the members of the *Fabrique* [the guild of silk workers], accustomed to thinking about these agonizing questions on which the very existence of their families depended, laid down the guidelines for other workers to follow and, in a France predominantly made up of peasants, artisans, and shopkeepers, launched movements that presaged nineteenth-century developments.

"The city of Lyons encloses within its walls a population of workers: the most interesting and most numerous are those employed in the manufacture of silk products;" so begins a memorandum written in 1788. The community also benefited from other activities—the hat trade, the building trade, and the printing industry . . . . Nevertheless, it owed "its affluence and its fame to the *Grande Fabrique*" which gave life and nourishment to all business enterprises.

68

At the time of the long "splendid reign of Louis XV" the silk industry set the pace for commerce, stimulated banking, and was responsible for the four annual fairs . . . . The years 1774 to 1778 marked the last great wave of prosperity. When the crest of the wave broke, an ebb tide began. Already in 1772 the *syndics* (trustees), who were the *gardes jurés* (the sworn guardians) of the *Fabrique*, had addressed an urgent appeal to the Intendant of Commerce: "Prompt assistance has become an absolute necessity, failing which, the few remaining workers will soon be ruined, and this great industry, which has always deserved the full protection of the sovereign, will be completely destroyed." After 1778 well-established enterprises were affected and many of them failed. When Brissot de Warville came to Lyons in 1782, all the notables of the city—the mayor, Tolozan de Montfort, the attorney general, Joseph Servan, and the former administrator of the East Indies Company, Pierre Poivre, confirmed for him the state of economic recession. The celebrated Girondist even claimed "that there were not four families who were untouched by bankruptcy." He added: "Wherefore it is possible to declare bankruptcy without difficulty . . . public opinion has become indulgent of bad faith . . . ." And he noted this detail: "In the Town Hall portraits of all the city magistrates are on display. When they file bankruptcy, the portraits are turned to face the wall, and a large number are now facing the wall."

When a slight improvement occurred in 1787 in certain sectors of the French economy, the sensitive mechanism of Lyonnais industry did not profit from it and a depression ensued at once. "An excessive scarcity of money and a decline of monetary reserves" followed the Assembly of Notables, banker Guillaume Couderc wrote to his uncle in Geneva. "At last there is a great crisis, but it will prove salutary," he concluded, for it will hasten the return of Necker to power. The drop in the exchange rate was accompanied by a cessation of textile manufacture. "The silk harvest has failed everywhere," the *Secret Memoirs* noted. "The manufacturers have stopped work because of exorbitant costs. More than 4000 looms are idle. The number increases daily. Workers are already protesting to the Consulate. But how can one support 40,000 to 50,000 workers? A large number of them have asked permission to leave the country but passports have been denied them."

The markets closed down in turn: "At the moment when the high cost and scarcity of silk became apparent, the factories witnessed the withdrawal of all the commissions they normally had. The troubles in Holland and the war in Russia soon deprived them of those outlets. They were reduced to French consumption alone; but the latter decreased owing to events that had occurred the year before and to the introduction of foreign textiles authorized by the treaty with England, the terms of which are so ruinous for business." The intermediary Commission of the Provincial Association accused "the sumptuary laws of Prussia, Sweden, and the Empire, the Russian war with Turkey, the lack of orders from the Levant, the factories in Italy and those of Valencia in Spain, and the radical fashion changes in the capital which have long been detrimental to the industry." Textiles piled up in the warehouses. The unemployed were selling their furniture and sometimes their looms as well, thus adding to the difficulties of an eventual business recovery.

That was one of the worst aspects of the situation. Distributing their samples among the principal European centers, sales representatives often unveiled new styles and fashions. Foreign courts, taking advantage of the plight of the *canuts* (silk workers) and even of the designers, lured them away with advantageous offers. They thus established enterprises to rival those of Lyons. Unlike the rural exodus which enriched those who remained behind, the migration of silk workers, whether spontaneous or provoked, only increased the distress in Lyons. Pierre Bertholon, analyzing the causes of their decline for an academic competition, showed how the revocation of the Edict of Nantes and internal divisions and crises, by driving away the workers, favored the rise of rival firms in Suze, Harlem, The Hague, Berlin, Vienna, Mannheim, and Talavera de la Reina. The designer and manufacturer, Paulet of Nîmes, also reproached the Lyonnais merchants for having let their ablest weavers get away. "Too harsh treatment made them decide to take their skills and talents elsewhere. . . ." These expatriate technicians created factories in neighboring countries.

Accordingly, the danger of migration among the workers became, rather tardily, a source of anxiety to the merchants. For an entire year in 1785 they did not hesitate to multiply their demands to the Comptroller General of Finance and the Intendant of Commerce to obtain permission for a man from Lyons, pursued by his creditors and established in Turin, to return to France provided with a safe conduct pass. And he was permitted to draw an annual bonus on the pretext that he was the only artist capable of making with requisite skill the irons used in making velvet and the steel combs used in producing other materials! They hastened to address petitions to Vergennes and Devin de Gallande, for they were afraid this worker would let himself be seduced by the government of the Piedmont. The danger lay in the good market for Italian, Spanish, or English textiles and in the greater flexibility of this young industry. It adapted itself to the whims of its customers while the Lyonnais *Fabrique*, proud of its past, clung to its reputation as the arbiter of taste and the defender of tradition. The Eden treaty [with England] aggravated this rivalry. The Lyonnais community protested mainly because it had not been consulted, but various reports indicted this freedom of enterprise with every kind of misdeed: "The fantastic, unpatriotic, and disorderly preference for English textiles spread with frightening rapidity."

The "decline of Louis XVI" was becoming general. A report drawn up by order of the city officials mentioned more than 5400 looms unoccupied, half the total in Lyons, and a memorandum of 1788 estimated that 2000 workshops were destroyed: "At least 40,000 workers have left our city. It will take ten years to repair our losses." The figures may be questionable but not the seriousness of the crisis. It was felt all the more keenly for coming on the heels of a period of prosperity. People become quickly adjusted to living comfortably and to a state of business prosperity. The crisis was all the more fearful for having affected an even larger population which owed its size partially to the well-earned reputation of the Lyonnais weavers. Lyons and its suburbs had risen to 143,000 inhabitants. Three-sevenths of that number belonged to the *Fabrique*. Thirty houses possessing 2700 looms made *passementerie* (braid and trim); about twenty had specialized in *tirage d'or* (gold trimming); embroidery work employed 6000; hatmaking, which even had customers in the United States, provided employment for 8000 workers in shops located throughout Lyons. This large number, which was unusual at that time, impressed contemporaries.

Its prosperity seemed fragile and extremely sensitive even to the slightest influences. Business flourished or weakened, like all luxury industries, in direct ratio to the state of the economy. Economic anxieties could tighten credit, halt trade, and paralyze industry. Inclement weather ruining the grape harvest or the wheat crop caused a drop in purchase orders by reducing ground rent and income from agricultural products. Worse yet, the death of a prince could deprive Lyons of its best customers. "Mournings over deaths at Court," said a report in 1784, "which are reflected in the rest of France through vanity and etiquette, are as disastrous for our industry as hail is to our wheatfields; the latter destroys a harvest; the former destroys all the textiles for an entire season." The Lyonnais economy thus found itself dependent on deliveries of raw silk, on the whims of fashion, and on foreign competition. A wise observer noted:

With your luxury trade you cannot guarantee your workers two days' livelihood. Today they are employed, but tomorrow a harvest fails, the consumers' tastes change, a prolonged period of mourning at Court bans the use of your products, another manufacturer captures public preference, a war breaks out, your looms are idle, your workers are without bread. In any crisis the first economy a citizen makes is to cut back on expenses for pomp and pleasure and ostentation. What becomes of your workers? When the cost of living rises and they need a wage increase, it is then they are out of work.

The merchants were doubly threatened: in their wealth by the business stagnation, and in their prestige by the poverty and attendant dangers of social agitation that they had been unable to avert. Undismayed, they explored every possible means of reviving the economy. They appealed to the skill of the designers to produce textiles noted for their finish and their decorations, and to renew inceasingly the themes and designs that their brocades and figured materials were noted for. They encouraged technicians, convinced that a better developed mechanical process would produce more goods and reduce the number of workers, especially women engaged as cord pullers and men employed as shuttle throwers. This in turn would reduce production costs. The latter depended primarily on production methods. The manufacturers were most concerned with methods. Improvement in the purchasing power of a worker's wages would result from greater productivity. There could be no economic development without perfecting the craft. In this age of the *Encyclopédie* the burgeoning middle class could not imagine that a machine might escape its creator, dominate, and eventually subjugate him. Essentially optimistic, the bourgeoisie did not realize that technical success leads to social progress only if the forces thus liberated are rationally utilized.

The opinions of "the bourgeoisie of talents" were solicited. In 1774 the Academy proposed this question for one of its competitions: "What are the simplest and least complicated ways of employing in the mechanical arts, or in any other manner, workers in the weaving industry at a time when that industry is confronted with a work stoppage?" Soon thereafter the abbé Raynal offered a prize for the best dissertation on a similar theme. There remained the supreme hope—recourse to the King. Merchants frequently intervened at Versailles to secure orders. In 1780 the officials of the *Grande Fabrique* declared in a petition that the mourning in which all Europe was participating over the death of "Her Imperial Majesty, the Queen of Hungary," was going to reduce more than 30,000 workers to utter poverty. They begged the King to modify national customs. To revive the *Fabrique* without changing its structure, that was the businessmen's dream. For them the prerevolutionary stagnation in industry was limited to its economics. But in a more general sense the problem affected the very structure of Lyonnais society.

ఆంర్ఆ

Alone among the Lyonnais corporations the *Grande Fabrique* presented a complicated hierarchy. Like all forms of industrial production, the textile industry was under the thumb of the great merchants [négociants]. The master merchants or manufacturers, without possessing establishments, held the capital, furnished the silk and the designs to the master craftsmen, and bought back the finished product. Their only role was that of distributing and collecting the piece work. The master craftsman, a free artisan who also called himself a manufacturer, worked with his wife, a journeyman, an apprentice, two assistants, and three or four looms which he owned. The unit was thus made up of a master weaver who supervised five workers. For the most part they were specialists. Some worked on solid cloth, others on figured material and brocade, while still others made gauze, handkerchiefs, or stockings. Accordingly, the master body of the corporation consisted of two groups: the merchants and the craftsmen. The latter employed the bulk of the journeymen and apprentices to whom were added countless assistants: readers-in, mounters, reelers, and warpers . . . . On the eve of the Revolution the *Fabrique* was composed of 400 merchants, 6000 master craftsmen, and perhaps 30,000 journeymen, apprentices, and assistants. But it appeared more complex than any other corporation since it included four separate groups with differentiated specialties within each.

The entire personnel and the nature of their products were subject to strict rules and regulations. The Lyonnese thought that only Colbert's policy could insure stable values for their fabrics. It was another codification of rules which the officials demanded of the Intendant of Commerce whenever their corporation was in trouble.

The disorders which have arisen for lack of laws applicable to the manufacture of textiles and the supervision of standards have not been unimportant in contributing to the ruinous decline of the industry . . . the clerks are often inexperienced, lazy, and sometimes dishonest. . . . . Nothing can do more to satisfy the majority of the workers in this corporation than the law requested for more than twelve years and which, by restoring order and tranquility, will surely bring back part of the business which has gone elsewhere because of suspicion and distrust.

The governors of the industry thus linked the economic recession to the decline of the corporate regime. They were endeavoring to maintain rigid rules and standards for their product. In 1775 there were still decrees regarding "the width, texture, and selvage" of cloth called Batavia as well as the use of spangles of different sizes . . . . With a suspicious vigilance, the *Community* undertook frequent inspections to prevent the use of false gilding, various deceptive practices, and above all the theft of raw materials. The *piquage d'once* [the theft of raw materials by the workers] was discrediting "our manufacturers abroad through defects in the materials and the color of textiles made with re-dyed silks not uniform in weight and quality."

Unfortunately, this legislation deprived the *Fabrique* of the elasticity and flexibility required to overcome the serious difficulties which the industry periodically encountered. The *Community* prescribed working conditions, technical processes, and the length of the materials. These detailed specifications, originally intended to insure a perfect product, precluded innovations, encouraged routine practices, and prevented the industry from changing and adapting itself to new conditions. The long training period —five years as an apprentice and five years as a journeyman—guaranteed excellent professional skill but did not allow for regulating recruitment according to industrial needs. In times of prosperity there was a lack of journeymen. In times of recession these skilled artisans maintained they were incapable of performing any other trade. The Consulate set forth their plight in a note addressed to the King in March 1788:

The sedentary life of these individuals, the poor quality and sometimes the shortage of food, and their often over-burdened work loads, reduce them to a state of physical weakness. The children of this class of men, born of frail fathers, come into the world for the most part unhealthy and suffering from rickets. From the cradle on they learn nothing except how to handle silk and then to make cloth, and for any other profession they have no strength or skill.

In any event, proud of his knowledge and skill, the silk weaver would have felt humiliated to have to weave any other material. By reinforcing this state of mind, the guild was moving toward an economic Malthusianism within a self-contained society which reserved for itself, after a long period of training, the right to work silk.

Turgot hoped to encourage the economy by liberalizing the laws. He abolished guilds that did not permit "the poor man to earn a livelihood from his work," which forced "the poor to obey the laws of the wealthy" and were becoming instruments of monopoly. Following the edict of 1776 the *Fabrique* became indignant and addressed protests to the King and notes to Turgot, Necker, and Maurepas. The Bureau wrote to the Comptroller General asking him to retain its regulations and to exempt the *Fabrique* from the abolition of the *jurandes* [guilds]. Turgot was asked to support this request. The *maîtres gardes* (master guards) advised the Consulate to intervene with His Majesty to show him how indispensable it was to retain the Bureau and a central regulatory body. Without transitional measures, the corporate statutes, certainly often bothersome and abusive but also often protective and well-founded, were giving way to an unlimited freedom which risked dangers of abuse. The workers and the merchants were moving toward an open clash. The controversy aroused the emotions of enlightened groups. While the merchant patriciate protested firmly against the plans of the Comptroller General, liberal members of the nobility and the bourgeoisie, who were imbued with ideas of the philosophic movement, applauded the proposed reforms.

Turgot's fall from favor brought about the condemnation of his work. His successor, Clugny, restored the guilds (in Paris first) according to a simplified organization with reduced entrance fee. "The faithful subjects of both classes united," comprising the Lyonnais *Fabrique*, requested "in view of the fact they had more goods than debts and that their only property, called the Bureau of Assembly, was an absolute necessity, to be allowed to participate in the benefits of the restoration edict." Their wishes were granted in January 1777. Among the forty-one guilds, which greatly resembled the old ones, "the art of silk" comprised five specialties: merchants, workers, thread makers, silk throwers, and pressers. The law gave each guild the right to set its own rules. Sixteen commissioners selected from both classes were named to revive this archaic institution.

❦

From then on, the *Fabrique* was beset by more and more problems. Children and widows of master weavers complained of losing their privileges; sons left the country, and "the daughters having no other dowry for the most part, languished in poverty or increased the rather large number of unfortunate women who trouble and corrupt society." The edict of 1782 partially restored their rights. Then it became necessary to sell the building that housed their governing body, the archives, and the museum. The eight "master guards," responsible for policing and administering the business, were recruited half from the merchants, half from the workers. The merchants disliked this equal representation and complained about the new regime. The King's attorney noted that the interested parties showed no eagerness to sign up. It was necessary to remind the master merchants, journeymen, and apprentices that they were supposed to be accredited, pay a contribution, and make formal registration. There were several deferments granted until the year 1784. The guild could no longer find experienced guards because of this abstention.

In 1779 the decree of Marly authorized complete freedom of manufacture. But it failed to end the disputes because material conforming to the old rules received a special mark from the bureau of the *Garde jurée* [the inspection office]. The new regime provoked recriminations. An anonymous report denounced this freedom: "The permits which some merchants have obtained to make textiles, unauthorized by wise regulations," have resulted in frauds with respect to raw materials, weights, and dyes. Prospective buyers, fearful of being cheated, have by-passed Lyons. "A good set of regulations having the force of law would put an end to many abuses by severely punishing anyone found guilty of dishonesty." To learn about this ruinous situation at the *Fabrique*, "one need only write to the master guards of the guild and to each class separately so that each might answer freely without fear of constraint." Otherwise the reports would be "dictated by the interests of the most powerful."

In this undermined economy middle-class businessmen jealously guarded their rights. As soon as they gained a certain freedom, they tried to deny the same to their competitors. As soon as they enjoyed a certain privilege, they wanted to make it a monopoly. When the new guild authorized master weavers to establish shops in the outlying districts of the capital, it aroused opposition. Already in 1780 a report had been drawn up opposing the opening of a factory in the village of Cuire in the province of Franc-Lyonnais. A similar dispute arose in 1786 when the King authorized each worker to possess an unlimited number of looms. The Consulate interpreted the law to mean that the looms must be in the master weaver's own domicile and not in scattered locations, otherwise, a master might employ nonaccredited workers for his own benefit in various workshops.

The same anxiety was apparent when an effort was made to admit women into the guild. Immediately there was a protest because the men feared competition for their jobs. "To limit women's pretentions is not to reduce them to a disadvantageous and non-lucrative position . . . . Those fresh from the country, often inept, begin by arranging the cords on the looms . . . . The more intelligent ones move on to other jobs: they work the shuttles, unwind the silk threads . . ." When the edict of September 3, 1786 admitted women workers, the *Grande Fabrique* subjected them to the same training as was required of male apprentices and journeymen. Another symptomatic debate took place in 1786. There was talk of admitting Protestants into the *Fabrique*. Immediately the merchants protested. "They do not know anything yet about silk manufacture and will know only what they learn from Catholics. As for their money, we can get along without it. Catholics are not short of funds. As for the number of workers, they have continued to increase thanks to progress in manufacturing techniques." This is a curious document: Protestants controlled the bank of Lyons. But businessmen gave as their reason: "Would we not have to fear that Protestants might move our industry abroad where they have more intimate ties?" They would thus succeed in depriving Lyons of orders from Germany and the northern countries, one of the sources of Lyonnais wealth.

To make a long story short, a report in 1784 noted that the guilds "are in the most dreadful state of anarchy since the revolution of 1777," and that "a spirit of independence is rising rapidly among workers in every category." In this feverish period of debate and discussion, a proposal by the master craftsmen of the *Grande Fabrique* is significant. In 1785 they asked for a separation of the two classes whose interests were at variance—the merchants and the workers. The former had the backing of the Consulate. They controlled the common funds and thus exercised "a kind of despotism over the impoverished workers." The latter could not use the money to defend themselves and to obtain legal counsel. "This denial of pecuniary resources is the principal cause for the oppression in which our class has languished for so long." The guild should have two separate treasuries. The mayor, Tolozan de Montfort, rejected such a suggestion which would have done much to revive the guild. He explained to the Indendant of Commerce, Devin de Gallande, that this measure would be harmful to the harmonious workings of the industry, that the master merchants are more sensible and solvent, and that their control over the corporation's resources maintained the proper degree of subordination of the workers.

By this time the corporation yoke was growing heavy and was being condemned by enlightened members of the bourgeoisie. Intendant Terray himself did not fail to express his disapproval when obliged to execute a decision safeguarding the guild's monopoly. "The exclusion of women is a custom contrary to natural law . . . . It is desirable for business and for the welfare of the State in general that the industry's practices should be free of any pecuniary tax, that conditions for admission to the profession should be reduced to include only those which truly guarantee the necessary knowledge, talent, and industry of the person seeking admission." During this difficult phase the corporate framework was no longer adaptable to circumstances. Criticism increased. The *Société d'agriculture de Lyon* proposed to study the question "whether it would be advantageous in the principal cities to abolish the bakers' guilds and *jurandes*." Roland de la Platière thought that the unrestricted right to work would bring about an improvement in the workers plight and a revival in Lyons' industry. Especially in economic matters he had specific ideas which he had thought about for a long time and which he resolutely defended. In 1787 he stood firm against corporate tyranny. "We no longer live in an era when the mother's wedding gown is handed down to her daughter and in turn to her grandchildren. Nowadays people want colors of every description and shades of every color. One must change clothes every season and not fall back on what has already appeared." Rules that fix unchangeable models banish all originality. "The merchant's or manufacturer's desire for profit is like thirst to a drunkard." It has erected corporate barriers which torment one's rivals and favor one's relatives. The abbé Pierre Bertholon, who seems moreover to have understood the principles of industrial liberalism, protested in 1788 against the multiplicity of rules and regulations. Since certain rules were contradictory, he admitted that manufacturers observed only the most useful ones. "The violation or abolition of certain less advantageous regulations has greatly contributed to the prosperity of the city of Lyons."

A neighboring example serves as an illustration: the municipality of Villefranche asked the chancellor of the Duke of Orléans to include the city among the towns free of corporations or enjoying a special regime with reduced entrance fees. It was partially successful. At the time of the meeting of the States General only nine guilds out of twenty still existed. The report from the Seneschal's jurisdiction in Beaujolais asked for the abrogation of Clugny's edict and a concession of greater freedom for artisanal industry. It would accept, if necessary, the maintenance of corporate bodies, and their control provided that it entailed no taxation. No doubt this adherence to a certain type of economic liberalism was due to the influence of the Duke of Orléans, of Roland de la Platière, and the pressure of new industrial cadres which were fighting against the *Fabrique* of Lyons and for whom freedom of action was advantageous.

Lyons did not accept these views so easily. The lists of grievances [*cahiers de doléances*] indicate that opinion was far from unanimous. The Lyonnais nobility wanted above all freedom of trade. It went on record in favor of abolishing the *jurandes* except those having jurisdiction over apothecaries, locksmiths, goldsmiths, and gold washers, and "except for prescribing simple, precise rules for the manufacture of silk cloth, hats, and bakery goods which, because of their importance and the large numbers employed in these trades in the principal cities, may require a special kind of discipline." As for the delegates of the guild, they did not propose the abolition of the *maîtrises* and *jurandes*. They merely asked the States General

to ponder carefully whether by establishing rules to guarantee the authenticity of materials and the quality of textiles, not generally visible to the naked eye, it would not be wiser to leave such decisions to the industry which is continually increasing its resources, without imposing on manufacturers oppressive restrictions which, far from favoring business, almost always serve to hinder its progress.

Consequently, the campaign conducted by talented people in favor of free enterprise did not achieve complete success. The nobility and the middle class remained attached to traditional procedures. The populace showed itself hostile to a freedom which opened the road to capitalism, to the concentration of business activities, and which left common people at the mercy of the merchant class.

❧⚬❧

Economic difficulties and discussions about working conditions gradually prompted the workers to give attention to their situation. Eighteenth-century prosperity had enriched the middle-class businessman. He had profited from the rise in agricultural prices thanks to real-estate holdings in Forez or Bas-Dauphiné. Inflation in the price of precious metals had permitted these businessmen to expand their enterprises. Hard working, cautious, economical, they controlled the leading industrial region in France. With their business orders they governed virtually two-thirds of the population of Lyons. They held a large part of the city's wealth. When the Constituant Assembly decreed a patriotic contribution of 25 per cent of available income, certain Lyonnais declarations reached very large sums. Banker Etienne Delessert pledged 36,000 livres; the Provost Tolozan, 20,000; Régny, the treasurer, 15,000. The Finguerlins, Fulchirons, and Van Risamburgs enjoyed comparable wealth. On the other hand, famous designers like Pierre-Toussaint Dechazelles and Philipps de Lasalle were able to contribute only 1200 livres. This patriciate that controlled business, banking, and the silk industry, and held the principal city offices, naturally allied itself with the office-holding bourgeoisie and secured for itself ecclesiastical benefices. The pre-eminence of these consular families conferred its special character on Lyonnais society.

But at the same time, from 1778 on, the condition of the weavers, and of all workers in Lyons, was deteriorating. Orders were arriving irregularly. Foodstuffs were becoming more expensive. The debt-ridden Consulate was continually raising town tolls and taxes. Wages were not being adjusted to rising living costs, and the workers' purchasing power declined heavily throughout the century. According to a budget prepared in 1786, a household with minimal expenditures for food, clothing, and shelter could not avoid an annual deficit equal to one-third of the family's earnings. The abbé Bertholon gave dramatic emphasis to this state of affairs: "Someone has said that nowhere could factories be established like those of Lyons because one would have to find people who neither eat nor sleep like the workers of Lyons." They worked as many as eighteen hours a day, up before dawn, continuing their "work far into the night in order to compensate for the modest income they receive from their inadequate wages by the extended time spent at their trade." Such overwork produced physical deformities and hereditary degeneration. "We are told that no silk worker has been the grandson of a silk worker. They live on the lowest subsistence level and one may say that they eat not so much in order to live as in order not to die. The entire family is lodged in, or rather squeezed into, a small appartment where the air is inevitably filled with impurities."

Many documents confirm this picture which might appear to be inspired by the humanitarian sensibilities of the age. In their badly lighted rooms where oiled paper replaced window panes and windows were never opened for fear the humidity would break the silk threads, the workers lived sparingly on herring, dried codfish, and white cheese. On special occasions they treated themselves to fritters, bacon rind, pork cracklings, and coarse butter. In times of distress some had to sell their furniture and abandon their children. Recalling happier times, they cruelly resented their state of impoverishment, for people are always alert to changes in living standards, and even if they are resigned to poverty, they do not tolerate a further decrease in their economic resources.

To justify their parsimonious wages, merchants placed the blame on foreign competition. "Everyone knows," said one of them in 1786, "that it is mainly owing to cheap labor that our textiles are marketable in the rest of Europe." But Etienne Mayet, a Lyonnais who had become director of the factories of Frederick II, declared: "If necessity stops forcing a workman to accept from his employer whatever wages are offered him, if he succeeds in freeing himself from this kind of slavery, if his profits exceed his needs to the point where he can survive for a while without resorting to manual labor, he will use this time to form a union." The merchants thus considered that "the low cost of labor was not only advantageous in itself, it became even more so by making the worker more industrious, steadier in his living habits and morals, and more submissive to their will."

Certain contemporaries were astonished by the submissiveness of the Lyonnese weavers, a fact they attributed to overwork and the haunting fear of suffering. The skeptical Grimod de la Reynière, who was living at that time in Lyons, was outspoken: "The workman, sedentary by the nature of his work, tied down to this kind of occupation by the way he is paid, and forever breathing the same foul air, enjoys neither good health which accompanies physical exercise nor that satisfaction with one's work which reflects good health . . . . Chained from childhood to his joyless loom, he behaves mechanically like the machine he operates. His range of ideas is limited because their confines, circumscribed by routine, have never had the opportunity to expand. He is like the ox who plows each day his painful furrow and forever traverses the same terrain."

Such a judgment was valid perhaps for certain elements, but it did not apply to all the master craftsmen. Certainly their ideas appear rudimentary, especially their economic views. Relegated to technical jobs dependent on orders from the businessmen, those who did the manufacturing tended to become salaried employees of the merchants. But these master weavers were more advanced and more enlightened than a simple journeyman. Living together on the right bank of the Saône, on its slopes and hillsides, they had the advantages of residential contacts. They were all members of the guild. The truth is that their outlook and attitudes were complex. Working outside the merchant's surveillance, employing their own help, they took on the legal appearance of proprietors. Formally speaking, they were free men and heads of enterprises. They were in charge of a small workshop. They gave orders to journeymen. They trained apprentices. They enjoyed the pride and satisfaction of being "masters." They rubbed shoulders with the designers, genuine artists, whom the merchants sent to the various courts to study current fashion trends and who sometimes acquired the status of celebrities. These silk workers felt themselves an indispensable part of this brilliant production. Their long apprenticeship, their technical knowledge, and their interest in artistic problems set them apart from members of other industries. These 6000 master craftsmen were closer to the artisans of the *petite bourgeoisie* than to the proletariat. With simultaneous ties to the great merchants and to the other workers, they helped to mold public opinion.

Without letting themselves be blinded by questions of food supply, they were more concerned with discussing working conditions. they sought more long-range remedies than the routine distribution of charity. They envisaged the application of a "tariff" setting the price of piecework and regulating, within the jurisdiction of the community, the relationships between the two classes of masters: the merchants who distributed the silks and the workers who manufactured the cloth. They had scarcely any hope of becoming merchants themselves. Their professional specialization and their manufacturing equipment precluded any change-over to another profession. They were anxious therefore to clarify and fix the conditions of their career. They desired impartial professional justice, representation equal to that of the merchants in the *Bureau de la Fabrique,* and the right to name their *jurés gardes* [supervisors]. But above all they sought the abolition of the freedom that subjected them to the power of the merchant. "No regulation, it is true, obliges us to work for an inadequate wage. But the most imperious of all laws, the law of necessity, imposes this cruel requirement upon us . . . . Every day we must live and every day we must work." In times of unemployment unfortunate weavers accepted orders at a reduced price, voluntarily lowering their own remuneration. Only arbitration would prevent total devaluation. "Among men equal in means and in power who, for this reason, cannot be subjected to the arbitrary will of the one or the other, freedom can only be to their mutual advantage. But with respect to silk workers, deprived of all resources and whose daily subsistence depends entirely upon their daily work, this freedom leaves them completely at the mercy of the manufacturer who can, without harm to himself, suspend operations and thus reduce the worker to the wages he chooses to offer, well knowing that the worker, driven by the superior law of necessity, will soon be obliged to give in to his demands."

Their isolation was all the more apparent as the Consulate, partly made up of merchants, regarded the workers with suspicion and forbade them to form any association. In particular, they could not affiliate with the journeymen. They did, nevertheless, join secret societies which, with their ritual and mysterious ceremonies, were an echo of the past, but by their spirit also heralded the future. The authorities persecuted these organizations of defense and resistance. The merchants wanted to have them dissolved because they interfered with the recruitment of workers and because they maintained throughout their ranks, along with a concern for high professional standards, a determination to be independent and to express a certain degree of opposition. However, the intense rivalry among different groups of journeymen reveals to what extent the workers were as yet unaware of their collective interests. Rivalry prevented them from playing a wholly effective role and often degenerated into bloody brawls rendering them vulnerable to their adversaries. In 1778 the *Présidial* condemned thirty-six journeymen accused of having gathered at the Inn of the *Mouton Couronné* in Vaise and of having fought with members of different *Devoirs* [labor organizations of journeymen]. The judgment forbade "all workers, journeymen, and apprentices from forming any assembly under pretext of affiliating with the *Devoir*." The *Parlement de Paris* ratified the ban on associating with the "*Sans Gêne, Bons Enfants,* and *Dévorants*" [names of the several *Devoirs*] for the purpose "of securing a position or rendering mutual assistance."

Several times the workers proposed a better system for the allocation of jobs by creating a placement bureau. In a petition to the King in 1779 the masters and journeymen called attention to the fact that whenever there was an oversupply of orders, the merchants asked the brokers or their agents to canvass the number of vacant looms. An office established for that purpose would simplify this distribution. The master guards judged this proposal useless on the pretext that they were familiar with what was available inasmuch as silk workers, always sedentary, were not making a *Tour de France*. They also believed such an organization would be dangerous: it would reconstitute a kind of Journeymen's Association which would become "a rallying point for more than 6000 workers; disorders might result from it." In 1783 the project was rejected again by the guild which saw in it an opportunity "to form tumultuous assemblies contrary to public order."

In 1784 the Consulate again proscribed their calling themselves "by the name of journeymen of the *Devoir* or journeymen *Gavots* or by any other title . . . or to come together or assemble for any cause whatsoever or under any pretext whatsoever in any group greater than four in number." Nevertheless, the association of journeymen intervened in the strikes and riots of 1786. In September 1789 an impressive celebration took place and on October 25, 1789 there was a General Assembly of the bodies belonging to the *Devoir*: woodworkers, locksmiths, turners, glaziers, and harness-makers. An entire life of a somewhat secret nature which accustomed the employee to being part of a group greater than himself and which imbued him little by little with the notion of solidarity, was slowly developing and gaining strength within the heart of the working classes.

This movement was reflected in efforts undertaken to secure a fixed rate for wages. The request was first made in 1779. It was significant. In place of a loyalty that harkened back to feudal times, workers now wanted a contract which the middle class had demanded and which workers felt they were also entitled to. In order to obtain it, they appealed, out of strategic necessity rather than for ideological reasons, to the protective intervention of the Consulate, and they did so in strong language:

Manufacturing is a source of wealth for the State and a source of wealth for a large number of businessmen. It is like the mining industry which produces vast treasures by swallowing up thousands of slaves who never taste the comforts and pleasures they afford others. . . . The most persistent kind of work, nightime work in addition to daytime work, is far from giving us the basic necessities of life, and yet you are not unaware that we are subject to frequent unemployment whenever the luxury trade is forced to curtail its desires and demands. . . .

They secured a tariff improving their situation slightly.

The fluctuating cost of living demanded a periodic review of this wage scale. In 1783 the Treaty of Versailles, re-opening English markets to the Lyonnais industry, revived these dealings. The master guards proposed the development of a mobile "wage scale" tied to fluctuations in the market. The Consulate banned all discussion of the matter.

⊸§⊱⊷

Rigidity on the part of the patriciate caused the workers to take firmer stands. A prolonged exchange of notes lasted until 1786 and kept the dispute going. Everyone condemned the freedom that allowed a maximum reduction on the established wage scale in order to lower the cost of fabrics. Since businessmen were continually arguing the need to do so to meet foreign competition, the silk workers sought statistics on the manufacturing conditions in Venice, London, Vienna, and Berlin, and they declared that workers in Lyons were the most ill treated of all. In July 1785 a statement from the workers to the master guards asked that wages be adjusted to the cost of commodities and the cost of rents. Counting on "the tender sensibilities of the magistrates" the statement recalled that the petition of 1783, followed by a detailed budget estimate, had come to nought and that upon this tariff depended "the competitive spirit and zeal of the workers, the quality of their output, and even the preservation of the *Fabrique*."

Then the master guards addressed a memorandum to the Count of Vergennes, Secretary of State for Foreign Affairs, who had the department of Lyons under his jurisdiction. They stressed the deplorable situation among the workers despite the steps taken in 1779 and 1783 and emphasized the difficulties encountered in getting a hearing and the humiliating nature of the assistance granted. "There is nothing more burdensome and even more dangerous to society and to the state than a man who is reduced to charity." They advocated the adoption of two measures, first, the control of raw material. Merchants gladly furnish damp silk or silk dyed in English black which grows lighter in weight when handled. As the worker must return the same weight of fabric he receives, he is suspected of cheating and "his modest earnings evaporate with the water impregnating the silk." Second, a tariff must be imposed. Merchants will not increase payments of their own free will, "the majority of them having no other intention than to establish their fortunes on the debasement, impoverishment, and desperate needs of the workers." An equitable tariff will obviate the possibility "of making a worker leave the country or else die of hunger, a freedom one must not grant to industries whose chief advantage to the state is to provide a livelihood for hard-working men and women." The master guards resorted to an effective argument: the textile workers, finding only poverty and slavery in Lyons, "are leaving in droves and they are scarcely turning out any new apprentices to replace those who are leaving; the dearth of workers being felt there proves that the industry is perishing for lack of man power far more than from the jealousy and rivalry of foreign competition." And the results are justified: "Any industry which kills instead of giving life must be outlawed by the State which is being depopulated by that kind of industry. It is intolerable that businessmen, who have all kinds of ways and means open to them, should wish to preserve such an enterprise for the maintenance of their personal fortunes." To keep this wealth in Lyons and in the kingdom, "it is necessary to guarantee bread to the citizen worker." The argument carried weight. In transmitting the text to Devin de Gallande, Vergennes noted: "I do not doubt that this matter will seem worthy of your attention, particularly because of the migrating workers whose loss can only be most prejudicial to our economy."

In the name of a threatened economy, Tolozan was instructed to assist in effecting a reconciliation. He recognized the desperate plight of the weavers. "They are the principal recipients of public charity and our hospitals are overcrowded with members of this unfortunate class alone." He acknowledged the legitimacy of demands with respect to wastage, but he was opposed to subjecting the merchants to a system of (textile) conditioning. He advised an amicable agreement on a discount rate, "the gift," in order to compensate for the alleged moisture in the silk. As for the tariff, it seemed to him a dangerous measure. The workers "would soon be making new demands and charges perhaps less justifiable than the present ones without considering that they must compete equally with the merchant in the business fortunes of the industry. Insubordination and personal interest would become the sole basis for their actions." Besides, in order to be equitable a tariff would have to embrace too many variable factors and would dissuade the merchants from having materials made up in advance, at a reduced price, for fear of a business recession.

The master guards chosen from among the workers replied that it would suffice to fix the cost of manufacturing three representative cloths which would serve as a yardstick for the remainder. They added a new demand: modify the law of acquittal which imposes on wage earners an odious kind of servitude since it forbids them to leave a merchant who has employed them without a special permit certifying that they are free of debt. An exchange of letters on this subject continued throughout the winter between the Mayor of Lyons and the Intendant of Commerce. No precise measure was adopted.

In the Spring the workers became restless. About sixty of them arrived at the Town Hall in April "in a very tumultuous manner." They proclaimed once more that the lot of the workers superseded all else. "The Lyonnais silk industry would be an impermissible vice in the State, one that would have to be extirpated unless it could be maintained without subjecting its workers to the most frightful and unbearable living conditions." They invoked a kind of "iron law" which Turgot had already anticipated. "If silk workers were considered only as so many mechanical instruments needed to produce textiles or, disregarding the fact they are human beings and should, for that reason alone, be the concern of all society, if one were so inhuman as to treat them simply as domestic animals to be maintained and preserved merely for the profits accruing from their work, it would still be necessary to provide them with the subsistence accorded to animals unless one wished to risk being deprived of the fruits of their labors." And again they included the type of budget they wanted, carefully documented.

The government, the Consulate, the Mayor, and the syndics made evasive promises. The municipal magistrates began to perceive the existing contradiction between economic arguments and social considerations. If they allowed the price increase, the merchants would take it as "a justification for raising the price of textiles to the point where we would no longer be able to compete with foreign factories." A tariff would end any chance of price adjustments: the workers have their way when business is good; "the merchants in turn lay down the law when they are less pressed with orders." The Consulate feared above all that by ordering a wage rise in the *Fabrique* they would unleash a general movement among journeymen in other trades, notably the shoemakers and dyers who were ready to foment an insurrection. Therefore, they limited their action to naming a master hatmaker to arbitrate the difference. Tolozan was apprehensive. "No one knows better than I the sorry state of these workers. The price of labor is assuredly below their needs and," he wrote to Gallande, "I long to see them enjoy better conditions."

As Tolozan feared, there were three successive waves of strikes in early August. Perhaps they were triggered by a decision of the Archbishop. Malvin de Montazet demanded at that moment the arrears owing to him on his right to the wine tax (*le banvin*) which he deducted from the August sales. Yielding to a spirit of feudal reaction, his tax collectors carried out their mission with unusual harshness. The price of wine rose and tavern-keepers decided to close their shops, all of which increased popular discontent. The masons were the first to obtain the right to discuss contract conditions with the master masons. An order from the Consulate decreed a wage increase for those workers engaged in filling in the embankment along the peninsula. Other workers cited this precedent for their own demands.

For a long time hatmakers had wanted their wages to be paid "at the same rate as in Paris" and their work no longer to be paid for by the piece. The fullers voluntarily limited themselves to two hats a day. The masters declared that "this practice was the cause of debauchery and conspiracies. The skilled worker spends two and often three days of the week away from his shop, plunged in a state of inebriation." Then he rushes to finish his weekly task. Master craftsmen often hired day workers and unskilled labor at reduced wages, and they permitted *appropieurs* [cleaners] to work at home assisted by their children. They regarded it as an excellent means for assuring better and faster production, one that facilitated apprenticeship and which, "by dividing and separating the workers, reduced the likelihood of plots and conspiracies." The workers wished to abolish these practices.

To insure their control they established a sort of association which imposed fines and dictated regulations. They forbade one master craftsman to hire more than twenty fullers; they imposed on another higher wages than the tariff provided for in 1762; they demanded the presence of a domestic in another shop. Should the master refuse, the workers deserted him. "They can be heard in the cabarets, streets, and crossroads taking oaths not to work except at the wages they have set, and they mention aloud those masters whom they intend to confront with a conspiracy and an uprising." More often than not the employers capitulated and paid the fines.

As a matter of fact, the workers had chosen the opportune moment. They presented their demands while the Lyonnais hat trade was prospering. In 1782 it had had difficulties following a rise in the cost of raw materials. Its products had been prohibited, notably in Spain where its factories had enjoyed sizable markets. The masters continued nevertheless to manufacture hats at the risk of seeing fashion changes devaluate their stocks.

Our workers were aware of this. Therefore, we never knew them to be more

assiduous, more peaceful, better behaved, and more docile than at that time.
. . . Today when orders are substantial, today when the workers, although numerous, are not enough for our needs, today, in short, when we find ourselves
close to making up the losses we have sustained, there is no kind of insult,
unfairness, or irritation that we are not subjected to on the part of the workers.

~§§~

The Mayor was fearful of these hatmakers and attempted to forestall
collective action by the malcontents. It was futile. Those of the *Grande
Fabrique* left their jobs August 7 singing: "The shuttle won't work without
two sous." That was the amount of the bonus they demanded per yard of
English taffeta. The more determined persuaded those who were undecided,
and all of them assembled in the taverns of Les Charpennes to discuss ways
and means of obtaining satisfaction. The hat makers chose "the Perrache
works" as a rallying center. Was it to engage in earth work on the embank-
ments, as one of them was to allege at the tribunal? Was it to consider a
plan of action with the masons who had instigated a recent action? Without delay the Mayor, who had convoked the master guards, rebuked the
representatives of the merchants for their inhumanity and advised them to
accept the proposals offered. That night the silk workers returned, most of
them intoxicated. A large number addressed Tolozan "with respect and
decency." Reassured, the latter wrote to the Comptroller General: "What
gives me less cause for alarm at the moment is the confidence and loyalty
which the workers and common people have shown toward me."

The following evening, August 8, despite a consular decree banning any
gathering "in the streets, cabarets, and other public places," hat makers
and silk workers assembled in even greater numbers. They presented their
demands to Tolozan. In front of the splendid residence on the Quai Saint-
Clair the crowd grew larger. Soon rocks were hurled at the windows. People
began shouting. The bourgeois militia and a detachment of constables of
the watch were molested. The crowd massed on the Place des Terreaux. It
now included artisans, laborers, and Piedmontese who, with knife in hand,
"were conspicuous for their violence." The mounted police opened fire.
A comparable scene was taking place in Bellecour. The frightened Consulate gave in. Two decrees approved the increase agreed to by the master guards of the *Fabrique* and by the hat makers. But this concession
did not guarantee an immediate resumption of work. The hat makers
advised their colleagues "in the neighboring towns to come to Lyons to
reinforce their numbers," and they tried to persuade the fullers and dyers
to do the same. The Cathedral Chapter intervened on behalf of the wage
earners. Recruiting its members from among the nobility, it remained a
power to be reckoned with. The canons, counts of Lyons, had family ties
or relations with all the great families of the region. They employed a large
personnel—dignitaries, priests, and laymen—and they had at their disposal
a sizable clientele of poor people and workmen. They took pleasure in

playing the role of popular *grands seigneurs*. As a kind of survival of feudal times, they liked to oppose the Consulate and the bourgeoisie. The Counts of Pingon and La Madeleine distributed subsidies, promised relief measures, and begged the Consulate not to prosecute anyone.

The spreading of "the two cent strike" (*l'émeute des deux sous*) prompted the *Sénéchaussée* to take action. The King's attorney Barou du Soleil once again forbade "artisans, journeymen, workers, and tradesmen to come together, assemble, or make any agreements among themselves contrary to public order . . . or to carry canes, clubs, and other arms, and to call one another by such names as journeymen of Devoir, Gavots, or Draguins."

This decision suggests that meetings of journeymen were by no means unknown to the movement. Then the attorney interrogated those who had been injured—an apprentice pastry maker, a journeyman carpenter, an agricultural worker . . . . The Consulate, overwhelmed with work, abandoned its police powers to the civil and criminal courts (*le présidial*). The Mayor appealed to the Gévaudan company of riflemen stationed at Tournon. He did not like to do so. The people of Lyons did not approve the use of royal troops to safeguard their privileges. Lyons had no garrison. The mounted police (*la maréchaussée*), the riflemen of the city guard and the bourgeois militia took the responsibility for maintaining law and order. When riots threatened, the local authorities counted on force to "maintain calm" and resigned themselves to securing reinforcements from the neighboring districts at Vienne in the Dauphiné or in the suburb of Vaise "adjoining the district of Bourgneuf entirely populated by workers." The government sent a detachment of Royal Marines and a battalion from La Fère in which a Lieutenant Bonaparte was serving. The Mayor was reassured, for the harassed soldiers of Lyons were running short of ammunition. Repression began. Certain workers tried to leave the country, but they were arrested at Pont-de-Beauvoisin and Fort-L'Ecluse by orders of Tolozan who wanted "to prevent this migration from increasing and causing serious trouble for business." On August 11 the *présidial* condemned to death a hat maker and a taffeta weaver charged with being "among the principal instigators of sedition and revolt," and having "participated in the excesses, threats, and violence directed against the different troops of the city." They were executed the following day on the Place des Terreaux along with their "captain," arrested in Bourgoin when he was endeavoring to cross over into Savoy. Once again three canons of the Church, members of the Masonic lodge called *Le Patriotisme*, intervened to reduce the sentences. The Archbishop gave a pension to the widow of a condemned man. A canon is alleged to have fought a duel with the Provost of the mounted police. The execution was in progress when the official pardon arrived.

Faced with threats of reprisals, the workers returned to their shops little by little. As late as August 21, Tolozan was still suspicious of the hat makers. Those "wandering people split up into various associations" seemed to him the most turbulent. "The trouble makers who are numerous among them" were always ready to make common cause with other tradesmen. As for the majority of the master hat makers, they observed the decree but "only for a while . . . in order to calm down the excitability of their workers and to return them to their workshops." Several of them, declaring the increase abusive, were already lodging an appeal with the Parlement.

Tolozan was more lenient toward the silk workers and desired the establishment of a contract to be drawn up by the "arbitration commission" consisting of three merchants and three workers. The latter "insisted on their demand for a tariff because, without it, the announced wage increase would be no more than an illusory promise." It was fully justified, they argued, and if it were not applied, there was the risk of "seeing a repetition of scenes of horror" and the danger of a migration of weavers "from which foreign countries would derive all the benefit." The Mayor acknowledged that the resort to violence had hastened this act of justice. "It is even possible that without their mob action, unquestionably reprehensible, personal interest, disguised under the name of general business interests, would have forestalled these protests for a long time and prolonged the workers' misfortunes." The Consular ordinance thus ended negotiations initiated a year earlier. Tolozan was especially severe with the merchants. "It is unthinkable today that in spite of all that has just occurred, a number of manufacturers in this city persist in the injustice of not paying a slight wage increase to unfortunate workers who are responsible for their brilliant and rapidly acquired fortunes . . . ." After calling attention to the double peril of "creating a frightful carnage" among 20,000 rioters or seeing them leave the country, he deplored the greed of a large number of merchants. "They doubtless reject the wage increase because they feel that police authorities are vigilant and that any disorderly uprising would be harshly dealt with. Yet it is not right for the King's troops to act as perpetual guardians of the manufacturers' interests and serve as the agents of their vengeance upon citizens whom they need and whom they would like to oppress with impunity."

With order re-established, the Consulate at first refused to accept the tariff plan outlined by the master guards, and the king made two decisions: he granted a general amnesty and permitted freedom of assembly. His pardon resulted from a plea by the archbishop and was given in the hope that repentance on the part of the guilty ones would stifle any further expressions of insubordination "whose contagious example leads the multitude astray and often makes it the unfortunate victim of its ignorance and credulity."

An Order in Council of September 3 cancelled the concessions granted by the Consulate.

His Majesty, convinced that all these obstacles—the tariffs—are prejudicial to industrial progress, are also prejudicial to public tranquility, has deemed their abolition the best means of preventing further tumultuous demands in the city of Lyons. . . . The wages of journeymen, apprentices, and artisans of the city of Lyons will be regulated by mutual agreement arrived at between the merchant manufacturer and the worker.

It was of course forbidden to meet in large assemblies or to form any secret societies or conspiracies.

The Comptroller General commented on this measure. The tariff is un-workable: "It is impossible to establish just and precise laws in a matter so dependent on circumstances. A worker's wages must be based on his ability and on the greater or lesser degree of resources he finds for his sub-sistence in the place where he lives and works." Free discussion should, on the other hand, enable the worker to obtain better remuneration. "Lyons is the only city in which the merchant has imperiously laid down the law and has always . . . denied the artisan of his fortune a just and legitimate wage." Barracks were set up in the public granaries and the Intendant Antoine Jean Terray was sent to Lyons to supervise the execution of the decree.

Terray was even more severe. He was not afraid of a workers' migration. That would require "that the workers find elsewhere a happier state to attract them. But there is none." Only the undesirables can leave the coun-try. The silk workers falsely maintain that "as they are obliged to work because of their extreme poverty and no longer have in their favor a law requiring that they be paid at a certain wage rate, the merchants will take advantage of their plight to make them accept whatever they may wish to pay them. Freedom would be only an illusion for the worker and a reality for the manufacturer who would abuse his freedom." Terray, confident of the benefits of economic liberalism, advised as a guarantee of conciliation the payment for work in hand on September 3 according to the increased tariff rates and to allow a transitional period before reverting to the old rates.

Tolozan, more familiar with Lyonnais traditions, noted that the decree was ambiguous. It seemed to regulate relationships between masters and journeymen and to be unaware of the fact that in the *Fabrique* the struggle was essentially one between the merchants and those individuals who acted as *chefs d'atelier*, heads of shops. "Although in fact it was the journeymen who rioted to obtain a wage increase, it was not against the master crafts-men whose interests are the same as their own, but against the merchants who determine the wages." A mutual understanding prevailed between master craftsmen and journeymen. "One cannot overlook the fact that the masters themselves encouraged their journeymen in order to achieve their objective more easily." Tradition apportioned a certain percentage of the work cost to the journeyman: two thirds for unornamented cloth (*les étoffes unies*) and one-half for the figured materials (*les brochées*). However, there were wranglings from time to time. The announcement of a return to earlier wage rates caused dissatisfaction among the journeymen. Some fifteen of them criticized a master craftsman for having accepted the reduction and wanted "to spoil" the silk destined for piece work. "I note with regret," Tolozan wrote to Calonne, "that the merchants' refusal to reach any mutual agreement favoring their workers perpetuates the latter's discontent, keeps them from doing a steady job, and can only result in an upheaval that will be disastrous for our business."

The aftermath of the strike persisted. In disobedience to the law, master hat makers assembled to decide not to give out work except on a piece-work basis. On September 17, journeymen *approprieurs* [cleaners] numbering 250, who were demanding payment by the day, stayed away from their shops. As in August, the order to boycott had been transmitted by a society of journeymen. "They form a body among themselves," said Terray. "They have a leader whom they call grand master, a number of officers, a recording secretary, and a treasurer. They impose fines on their members, sometimes even prison sentences. The purpose of their association is to protect the weakest and to favor the most dissolute, to enable such workers to earn as much as the strongest and most dependable." That is why they insist on a uniform daily wage. But the Intendant found cause for reassurance. The masters had declared they could get along without these workers. Let them leave! "Their departure will be more useful than advantageous [to them] and is something to be desired."

On September 18 they went to the Patronal festival in Saint-Alban-en-Dauphiné. Others had crossed the bridges of the Rhône, the Saint-Clair Gate, or had withdrawn to the "Perrache works." According to informers sent into the taverns, everyone thought only of having a good time. On the 19th the strike was agreed upon by the decision of a "league." Many persons stopped work "intimidated by threats from fellow-workers . . . ." Otherwise, they would have returned to their jobs. The Mayor called upon them to go back to their shops assuring them "of all the protection of authority," and he blamed those "who sought to incite others to disobedience." On September 20 the Intendant, the Mayor, and the King's attorney attempted to hold conciliatory talks between masters and workers. The latter were intransigent. They were threatened with arrest "as vagrants and disturbers of the peace." Most of them were wandering aimlessly about . . . . The Mayor repeated that one-third of the workers "preferred piece work because they could get more out of it; but that they were held back by fear of their co-workers who threatened to mistreat those who might introduce any sort of novelty."

They again risked reviving the quarrels of the *Fabrique*. Merchants were now refusing to pay the increase for work undertaken between August 8 and September 3. A dozen of them gathered in the room of a Capuchin friar to decide their course of action. The Mayor reminded them "of all that was odious and reprehensible in their conduct." Terray then planned to employ the mutineers in work on the Perrache embankment. Tolozan persuaded them to leave the city and arrested the leaders who were preventing them from returning to work as well as the association's secretary and the tavernkeeper whose place had served as the association's head-quarters. Defections now began to occur. Seventy out of 250 had failed to return by September 25. Some of them left for Paris or Marseille. The strike had lasted for a week and Tolozan was rejoicing over its abatement. He had rejected Terray's suggestion because it threatened to embitter the workers and because it would have armed them "with pickaxes and shovels which they might use at the expense of public peace and tranquility." The return flow of workers was rising; the number of recalcitrants was decreasing; and the weavers were working.

Although the strike had failed, "popular emotion" had given evidence of a certain organization, at least some indication of a relative solidarity among workers. A feeling of collectivity, a sense of willingness to fight, an awareness of the fairness of their demands—all this was noticeable in their meeting places, in the measures they adopted, and in the lists of grievances they drew up. An appeal to workers in neighboring towns and other corporations betrayed a desire to break their isolation and to acquire new strength. Mediation by the clergy and the role of the journeymen's associations, although difficult to describe with precision, were also very significant. If French newspapers and periodicals kept a prudent silence, *La Gazette de Leyde* reported these events in a series of letters. Despite the presence of military forces, the silk workers' vigilance never faltered. The song [*la complainte*] which spread the story of the revolt expressed the desire "that the wives of manufacturers should stop arousing discontent among poor workmen by displaying their jewelry and adornment."

Bold words had been spoken. The wage earners had demonstrated that political economy must be imbued with morality. All forms of production and commerce involve a human effort on which the life and happiness of large numbers depend. Business considerations must be accompanied by social considerations. But the weavers and *approprieurs* [cleaners] carried on their battle as novices. They did not exploit the differences which set the merchants against the Intendant, the Mayor, and the Cathedral Chapter. In October, Terray evaluated the events that had occurred during the stormy period. The merchants criticized him for having permitted the provisional wage increase. He justified his position. This concession divided the workers since certain ones were still working on orders which included the bonus. No "collusion" existed between Tolozan and Terray, and the Intendant criticized the Mayor's lack of determination.

When the alarm subsided, the merchants wanted to take advantage of their new freedom. In November they addressed a report to the government directed against Terray: "Our intendant does not understand the situation at all. In matters concerning the *Fabrique* he lets himself be led by a certain abbé Jaquet who has always been a legal adviser to the workers and who has encouraged them in their insane hope for a new ruling." The merchants found fault with Terray's indulgence and especially his liberal interpretation of the decree. As for the Mayor, he behaved in his usual fainthearted manner when confronted by the populace. He was "not afraid of angering the solid citizenry in order to pacify the riffraff." Eighty velvet makers "conspired to get a pay increase on piecework, and small groups of four or five each went about stealing the tools of those who were working on this type of cloth." Tolozan looked the other way. The merchants demanded more firmness. "We depend on them because we cannot do anything without them. But they should feel dependent on us because we give them work and they should not attempt to subject us to tyrannical laws." To satisfy them, Tolozan redoubled his surveillance and intercepted notes urging workers to raise their prices "in a firm manner and in a spirit of genuine accord" in order "to secure a tariff." The author, a certain Denise Monnet, a master craftsman who had been a legal practitioner in his youth, was thought dangerous because of his knowledge and education. He wanted to intimidate the merchants by threatening them with a league. His endeavors were short lived.

From then on the master guards had to prevent merchants from speculating in human misery. They recalled that "the government's intention had been to allow each individual unrestrained freedom in bargaining for the amount of his wages." They tried to prevent employment of any weaver who "was forced by the need to provide for a destitute family to conform to the iniquitous law imposed upon him. The decree of 1786 had been enacted to maintain freedom and not to hand the unfortunate worker over to the oppression of a few unjust manufacturers." Indeed at that time an extremely high rate of unemployment prevailed in Lyons.

The unusual fervor of 1786 did not last. For the most part the workers regarded the heads of the *Fabrique* as their protectors. They trusted them and remained in their ideological camp. They felt this spirit of dependency especially in times of unemployment. It was then they realized that only the businessmen could affect policy changes at the court, find outlets for their luxury goods, and employ different techniques to revive business.

For their part, the bankers or merchants accepted this role. Their religious feelings inclined them always to show kindness toward the poor. And it was the part of wisdom to deal with them tactfully. Humanitarian sentiments encouraged philanthropy, and philosophy was introducing the idea of social responsibility. Unlike Anglo-Saxon puritans, they did not consider poverty as a sign of divine disapproval, as an opportune means for punishing idleness and vice. They were influenced by the sensitive feelings of the time which they found more acceptable than destructive criticism and cynical skepticism. The poet Thomas, who lived among them, spoke thus using strong language: "The Court is not the State, and the luxury of the few does not provide happiness for twenty million citizens." Many of them remembered the hardships they endured when they first started working in the big city. Did not the Mayor himself descend from a humble peasant in the Dauphiné? Market fluctuations had acquainted them with economic insecurity. An unspoken sense of solidarity united the different elements of the *Grande Fabrique*. To be sure, manufacturers envied the office-holding bourgeoisie. Certain ones dreamed of official posts for their sons. But in the final analysis they looked upon those who had become ennobled and even upon certain talented persons as parasites, for they were no longer producers and, far from living thriftily, often became impoverished. A hope for regeneration resided in the rising class: new workers, patient and courageous, were arriving from Auvergne. Ordinary shopkeepers were advancing socially. Skilled new designers were appearing . . . .

Everyone thought that the business slump would not last long and that to forestall any risk of social unrest it would suffice to relieve distressed workers by resorting to the usual methods. In the first place, in keeping with a typical eighteenth-century reaction, they wanted to prevent famine and to guarantee the community's food supply. Moreover, many of the wage earners, viewing their remuneration as something constant, sought to secure basic commodities, bread above all, at reasonable prices. They were concerned primarily with their interests as consumers. The city authorities took control of the *Chambre d'Abondance* (The Chamber of Abundance), an autonomous organization up to that time, established to facilitate the distribution of wheat.

The two hospitals fought against beggary. Their situation became worse in spite of the generosity of the rectors. Henry Decroix, a rich draper who was a syndic of his guild in 1776 and a magistrate in 1780, turned his entire fortune over to *La Charité* in successive contributions. It was found necessary to borrow funds from Genoa, to open shops and especially silk mills, in order to obtain resources. The overflow of impoverished workers inundated the *Hôtel-Dieu* and the *Journal de Lyon* launched a subscription drive to secure an additional 300 beds "so that all the patients in this hospital can sleep alone."

The royal *Bicêtre* [a home for the aged and mentally unsound], ordered in 1783 "to purge the city of these dangerous elements, people without status, occupation, or any kind of property, who subsist only on criminal activities," offered shelter to vagabonds, beggars, women of ill repute, the *insensés* [insane], and unemployed workers who had been housed until then at *La Charité*. Such promiscuity appeared dangerous for public morals. The unemployed "will return from these shelters given over to dissolute living, debauch, and indifference to crime," or so the rectors believed. They thought that many would allow themselves, "the workers and their children, to perish in the most extreme state of poverty" rather than accept such assistance.

Influenced by Rousseau's ideas, members of the bourgeoisie also took charge of the workers' children. Mothers who were busy at their looms entrusted their children to nurses in the villages. The infant mortality rate was high. To combat this very real social scourge, the Consulate sponsored the establishment of a bureau in 1779 under the direction of Dr. Pestalozzi, for the distribution of infant nurslings among healthy peasant women. This system, which lasted until 1783, was not altogether successful. Like Beaumarchais, who promoted in Paris a society to encourage breast feeding, the archbishop of Lyons founded in 1784 "a charitable institution (*Institut de Bienfaisance*) for the benefit of impoverished mothers with babies." Gifts flowed in. There was a benefit performance of *Le Mariage de Figaro*. Students in a boarding house in Ecully sent in their donation in 1786. Two Jews contributed alms to celebrate the issuance of their naturalization papers . . . . At the theatre in 1785 there were added to the comic opera *Blaise et Babet,* the hit of the day, verses written especially for the occasion, a practice common at that time. Actors praised the merits of the *Institut de Bienfaisance*. Lyons, said one of them, is "in the forefront when there is something good or beautiful to be done." To the tune of Figaro's *vaudeville* they sang the praises of Lyonnais philonthropy. Middle-class families supported the society that proposed to improve public morals, to protect the health of mothers, and to combat infant mortality. It distributed information on child welfare and practitioners provided free services in the home. This effort brought social groups closer together. The publicist Mathon de la Cour observed: "The result for some is good advice and assistance; for others the advantages are even more precious." The same kind of social concern prompted the abbé Lacroix to propose an insurance plan for the benefit of the hospitals. Using the mortality tables of Parcieux, he suggested depositing a sum of money on the occasion of each birth which would remain the property of the establishment in the event of the individual's death and would provide an annuity for the survivors. Whatever the motives, these institutions reflected a sort of paternalism which the latest crisis had accentuated.

The years 1787 to 1789 witnessed every possible misfortune: a shortage of raw materials, lowered output of textiles following the discontinuance of druggets and lampas [types of fabric], competition with textiles of foreign origin, and, for household use, competition from English wallpaper. The severe winters reduced food supplies by making the much-used water transportation impossible, and they interfered with or even halted operations of the mills established along the Rhône. In 1788 ice completely destroyed certain installations. To make matters worse, spring storms carried off part of the harvest in hail and wind. The Consulate, handicapped by the ban placed on exports by order of the Parlements of Dijon and Besançon, sent agents to Forez and Marseille. Expanding its prerogatives, it fixed the price of bread, granted compensatory allowances to the bakers, made financial advances to the workers, and exempted more than 10,000 heads of families from the capitation tax on account of their notorious poverty.

In the streets "30,000 livid, fleshless specters revealed their uselessness and destitution." When people of Lyons emerged from the theatre (a pleasure they were fond of), as they walked along the streets which were poorly lighted "by lanterns provided with tallow candles that the least bit of wind extinguished," they would encounter silk workers "at all the cross streets, each with a lantern in hand. In exchange for a few pennies they would guide the steps of those who accepted their services." A traveler reports that many of them would rush up to the theatre goers "to implore with heart-rending pleas an expression of pity that is latent in every heart. These unfortunate, intrusive individuals who present a picture of misery to these fortunate sybarites, who are they then? They are factory workers who, with their families, have been reduced to begging because of the shortage of silk. They are dying of hunger."

The bourgeoisie then undertook a vast program of public assistance. Beginning in 1785 the *Society of manufacturing merchants* assigned "all its (business) profits" to charitable works, and the *Société des personnes charitables* provided foodstuffs and an allowance to the unemployed. In 1787 the Mayor made an appeal to public generosity to help keep in Lyons a large enough labor force to meet industrial requirements. He authorized a public subscription under the auspices of the syndics of the corporation. "We do not doubt that the citizens of the second city in the kingdom will act in this moment of urgent need for charitable giving." An organization was set up with an office, a treasury, and distributors. Subscription notices were sent to all prominent people and alms collectors made house calls.

The response was generous. Malvin contributed 12,000 livres; Tolozan 4000; Terray 3000; the *Bureau des Collèges* 1200. The acting company of Monseigneur de Villeroi, under the direction of Collot d'Herbois, organized a performance "for the sole benefit of the unemployed workers of the *Fabrique*." The painter David turned over the proceeds from the sale of 200 engravings. The Freemasons were particularly active. Their philanthropic ideal was inspired by the principle of social utility so dear to eighteenth-century *philosophie*, and by the notion of brotherly love recommended by Christianity. They wished to establish "an active concern with feelings of brotherhood and assistance in all matters, to revive the social virtues and restore their practice." The Lyonnais affiliates took up a collection at every meeting to be given to the mutual assistance fund. In 1784 *La Régularité* lodge subsidized the *Institut des Pauvres Mères Nourrices* [The Institute for Poor Nursing Mothers]. When a subscription was launched for the Hôtel-Dieu, *La Sagesse* and *Le Patriotisme* lodges each contributed 600 *livres*. In 1787 the provincial Grand Lodge urged its members to organize fund drives on behalf of "the silk workers."

For allocating subsidies, one of the syndics of the *Fabrique* proposed three categories for assistance: master craftsmen with wife, children, and employees who were in charge of their own shops; then the journeymen, reelers, and all who worked for the master craftsmen; and finally, those who were sick or incapacitated. Knowing the psychology of the silk workers, he declared: "There are a vast number of master craftsmen, heads of families, who would consider it degrading to be assimilated in the assistance plan

with workers who are normally their own employees." He suggested forming in each parish a *Bureau de Charité* with the parish priest and members
of the leading families in order to effect a discreet and equitable distribution. And so it was that in December 18,000 workers were given public
assistance, chiefly in the districts of Saint-Nizier, Saint-Georges, and Saint-
Paul. As the crisis continued, the charitable organization functioned in
1788. The Provincial Assembly entrusted it with the distribution of food
cards for bread and meat, and the new archbishop, Yves de Marbeuf, recommended in his first diocesan letter the practice and duty of performing
works of social assistance. Villefranche then set the example of a permanent organization. The Duke of Orléans, thinking perhaps of creating for
his own advantage a political clientele in his patrimonial estate, founded in
March 1788 a *Société Philanthropique* modeled on the one in Orléans and
he provided it with its first funds. Property-owning Lyonnese in the Beaujolais became members, and in October 1789, the city of Lyons created a
similar office.

From then on, it was necessary to find regular sources of revenue. A pro-
jected *Caisse de Secours* [Assistance Fund], previously envisaged in 1779,
was again rejected since this kind of *Mont-de-Piété* [pawn shop] would
have encouraged the theft of gold threads and the *piquage d'once* and
would have induced the poor to convert their valuables to cash, "the husbands for purposes of debauchery and the wives to satisfy their love of luxury
and vanity." Rast de Maupas proposed in 1787 "a public and royal assessment on bales" of silk. Each merchant would contribute one sou per
pound entering the city. He also suggested setting up a mutual assistance
fund to be maintained by a withholding tax on wages.

There was a preference for seeking royal favors. The Intendant of Commerce, Jean François Tolozan, brother of the Mayor, agreed to advance
credits on condition they were used to re-activate the *Fabrique* or to open
charity workshops. The Provincial Assembly also deemed the work stoppage dangerous for industry, morals, and public security. Donations and
collections were no longer adequate. "For every day the numbers of beggars
increases; the habit of begging gradually lessens the sense of shame in so
doing, and the example it sets is contagious . . . . Songs, more likely to cause
a public uprising than appeal to people's sense of charity, are repeated
aloud at all hours and in all places, and more than one unfortunate person
will perhaps end up guilty of some misdeed." The *Fabrique* noted the same
thing: "All writers, publicists, and economists agree with the view that it
would be better to take losses on manufactured products and textiles in
order to keep the worker occupied than to turn him loose to live a life of
idleness and sloth which often leads to dire consequences."

The Assembly studied the possible alternatives. To ask the government
to advance money for the purchase of silk and to pay the cost of manufacturing the materials would cause a rise in the price of textiles and a stock-
piling of unsold merchandise. To give jobs to the unemployed in the manu-

facture of printed cloths or cotton, in the spinning factories or the cotton print industry, was scarcely feasible. There would have been a need "to find sufficient work at once for 22,000 persons." Now these factories, located in the suburbs or surrounding countryside, already had their complement of workers. They attempted to organize shops for knitting stockings or weaving hemp and cotton. But the silk workers were not a versatile labor force. Having learned "from the cradle only the art of handling silk . . . , they have no skill or aptitude for any other profession."

The *Fabrique* did not insist on this "conversion." It readily concurred in the impossibility of using silk weavers for any other task. "His sedentary way of life affects both his psychological and physical nature, and he knows no other trade. He is utterly lost if he is deprived of it." He has no resistance "to the damp workshops required by the cotton industry." As a general rule, it is dangerous to let a worker remain idle: "It accustoms him to idleness and tempts him to disturb public order . . . but we are dealing with a class of workers that has no strength or energy for any other occupation." And indeed the merchants themselves did not want to have mixed cloths woven with filoselle (floss-silk) or wool just to avoid purchasing silk at an exorbitant price. To obtain fibers to occupy "more than 30,000 people" would inevitably force a price rise. So the wisest thing to do in the spring of 1788 was to await the new harvest. To prevent workers from migrating, which "would have the most serious consequences on business in the second city of the kingdom," it would be sufficient to provide temporary relief for the unemployed. The King finally authorized the floating of a loan. But his opinion was unchanged: Lyons should follow the example of the city of Tours where it was decided to buy the raw materials and to weave and sell the merchandise even at a loss if necessary.

When the preparatory campaign for the meeting of the States General began, Lyonnais opinion pondered the possible solutions to the crisis: a social reorganization or a resumption of economic activity. The authorities were becoming alarmed.

When a committee composed of businessmen, doctors, and lawyers . . . called on Tolozan to summon the principal citizens, without regard to social rank, to meet at the Town Hall "to deliberate on all of the most important questions ever to be discussed" and to draw up a list of their recommendations "on the great plans for regenerating the kingdom," the Mayor was fearful of agitators that might get out of hand. He wrote to Necker: "Under present circumstances when the rigors of winter force us to devote all our attention and all our vigilance to furnishing this city with supplies of every sort, it would cause anxiety and alarm should large numbers of citizens be seen holding a meeting. Those unaware of the true motives would attribute it to fear of a total shortage of basic commodities and foodstuffs." On January 12, the Third Estate called attention to the workers' plight. "The severe winter and widespread unemployment having reduced the poor workers of this city to a state of extreme poverty and destitution, the citizens here present, wishing to enable the workers to share in the results of this patriotic assembly, will make a contribution for their relief."

United in their struggle against the privileges of the nobility, two groups were soon in opposition to one another within the ranks of the Third Estate: the merchants and the master craftsmen, supported by their journeymen. In a brochure they issued, the latter rebuked the Consulate "for tolerating the unscrupulous greed of certain manufacturers who are so inhuman as to make the weavers work at a loss exceeding half the price of their finished products in normal times." When the notables discussed electoral requirements in January, with certain demagogues outbidding each other for attention, some bold pronouncements were made: "Wealth does not produce intelligence, and patriotism is found in all ranks of society"; money is not "the infallible criterion of virtue and esteem." Noting this fervor and excitement, Terray notified the government and reminded it that no regiment was stationed in the *Généralité* of Lyons. He begged Tolozan to take precautionary measures. But the Mayor refused "to impede the freedom of convoked assemblies by the appearance or use of troops. Such a measure might incite excesses on the part of the many municipal guilds of Lyons all of whom will be active at one time or another."

In February the corporations named the electors who would be responsible for choosing the deputies to the States General. No incident arose among the tailors, hat makers, shoemakers, or stocking makers . . . but the fabric trimmers (*passementiers*) elected three members whom the Consulate had removed from the function of master guards and who were considered factious individuals. On February 26, twenty printers chose Périsse-Duluc and Rosset "universally esteemed for their integrity and intelligence." The workers, who had not been convoked, protested and nominated two of their number who, despite recriminations from the Chamber of Booksellers, were permitted by the ministry to sit with the Assembly of the Third Estate alongside two masters.

On the same day 2651 members of the *Fabrique* met in the Cathedral of Saint John. There was stormy debate. Several master craftsmen proposed that no merchants, syndics, or sworn guards should be admitted. According to some of the townsmen, "whenever a few voices were raised in favor of the latter, they were immediately drowned out by shouts of the master craftsmen who forced the dissenters to retract." Thus they imposed the election of thirty-four silk workers most of whom were in disfavor with the Consulate, especially the militant Denis Monnet who had been imprisoned as an author "of libelous and seditious writings." Merchants protested with a notarized statement and advised Necker that those "who initiate industrial activity not only for the benefit of the corps of the *Fabrique* but for all business enterprises in the second city of the kingdom—400 citizens controlling in real estate and personal property more than 60 million livres—were without representation." They demanded in turn the right to be seated separately, to have their own elected representatives, and to draw up their own recommendations. The Consulate recognized that this class, "by creative invention of our beautiful textiles and through correspondence with the outside world, has made wealth flow back into our city." But it did not intervene in favor of the merchants for fear of causing "murmurings of discontent among the working class."

The Assembly of the Third Estate, which counted 183 delegates on March 14 in the Church of Saint-Bonaventure, was "very tumultuous." The workers, especially those of the *Grande Fabrique* who were the most numerous, wanted to control the deliberations. The truth is that these delegates who had demonstrated their pugnacity, were incapable of expressing an original thought in the reports they submitted. They clung to their autonomy and their property. They did not want any social changes. Their grievances were limited to a series of complaints which never took the form of constructive proposals. They were unable to produce coherent notions about corporate government, tariffs, or forms of assistance. The nobility, on the other hand, who had risen from the upper middle class and achieved nobility by acceding to municipal offices, outlined and advocated a substantial economic program touching on free trade, rural activities, and coal mining. As for the parish *cahiers*, they reflected the views of the commercial bourgeoisie. Saint-Bonnet-le-Troncy, for instance, explained that it "had undertaken the spinning of cotton and the manufacture of linen. These measures would have prevented poverty had business conditions held firm. But since the trade agreement with England, business was so unprofitable that workers could no longer earn a livelihood and manufacturers could no longer make a profit and often sold their merchandise below production costs."

⋙§⋘

Lamartine claimed that the city of Lyons was "more inattentive than any other city in France to the movement of ideas and social philosophy announcing the Revolution." He was not the only one to fail to recognize the specific nature of local problems. The central government also neglected them during the revolutionary crisis, and that accounted for the attitude of the bourgeoisie. It felt gravely threatened by the economic decline during the reign of Louis XVI, more than any other group perhaps in view of the instability of its luxury trade and the fragility of its business forever at the mercy of international events. The solid wealth of the *haute bourgeoisie*, the upper middle class, was able to withstand the crises, but the working class suffered from chronic unemployment which was greatly aggravated by the slightest recession.

However, the presence of an intermediate group—the master craftsmen —exercised its own influence on popular reactions. Sufficiently well educated and of independent judgment, they were in charge of the guild. The journeymen, who regrouped into secret professional associations, accepted their directives. All of them fought strenuously against the privileges of the Old Regime and even against the merchants who exploited them. Rather than a regular distribution of subsistence wages, they demanded the formulation of a "collective contract," including a discussion of working conditions, manufacturing costs, and sales abroad. They rejected freedom of bargaining and in order to get a tariff, they resorted to rioting in 1786, hoping to unite the entire Lyonnais proletariat. They dared to oppose the merchants once again when preparations were in progress for the States General. In such circumstances these artisans became the vanguard of the working communities of every guild. They became its living conscience.

However, these rebels did not have in mind a new kind of social organization. The master craftsmen did not want a revolutionary upheaval to reach down to the journeymen and apprentices. Their task in no way resembled that of a worker in a huge industrial complex. Their goals were to be accomplished within the framework of a family arrangement. They did not want to be assimilated to their assistants who were growing panicky in the face of scarcity and were begging for some help. Master craftsmen felt a sense of solidarity with the *Grande Fabrique*. Like the merchants, they hoped for an economic recovery and did not envisage "a conversion" in their production. They all applauded the philanthropic efforts of the bourgeoisie who responded to every appeal for funds, made strenuous efforts to set up charitable institutions, and succeeded in rediscovering markets for their goods. In this manner contact was maintained between the wealthy bourgeois and the humble apprentice through the intermediary of the master craftsman.

There were two opposite poles of attraction. On the one hand, there was solidarity in the quest for economic remedies, paternalism on the part of manufacturers, and pride on the part of the master craftsmen in belonging to the *Grande Fabrique*. On the other hand, there was antagonism between merchants and producers, the wealth of the former and the poverty of the journeymen. There was pressure from the workers in other corporations, demands for a fixed wage scale even to the point of violence, and the election of militants in the spring of 1789 . . . . From the days of this pre-Revolutionary crisis those sentiments emerged and developed which were to plunge the working world, on the heels of certain bourgeois elements, into the Rolandine secession of 1793. And there were intimations of the zeal that would one day animate the militant groups of 1831 and 1834.

PART *II*

The Beginnings of the Revolution

THE MOVEMENT OF PRICES
AND THE ORIGINS OF
THE FRENCH REVOLUTION

◄§ By Georges Lefebvre

For some years, undoubtedly as a result of the economic crisis which has
overtaken the entire world,[1] the movement of prices has been of special
interest to economists, sociologists, and historians. An International Committee, in which France is represented by Mr. Hauser, was formed to
organize a systematic study of the problem. It was only in the second half
of the nineteenth century that, in the nations with highly developed civi-
lizations, the State decided to make frequent inquiries and to publish
statistical documents periodically. For the preceding periods, research necessarily presupposes the exploration of local sources: grain-market prices,
notarial minutes, archives of religious orders and of hospices, and the all-
too-rare papers of banks and of commercial or industrial establishments.
Nevertheless, these preoccupations are not new. Restricting ourselves
to France, and not referring to the collections of prices published during
the nineteenth century—the best known of which is that of d'Avenel—it was
only in 1912 that François Simiand, in his doctoral thesis,[2] opened the way

[1] This article was originally written in 1937.
[2] François Simiand, *Le salaire des ouvriers des mines de charbon en France* (Paris, 1907).

to research and to the scientific presentation of facts. Not long ago in a series of voluminous works [3] he summarized, in part at least, the results of investigations that he had been carrying on for thirty years. Also, C.-E. Labrousse has recently published an important work on price movements in France during the eighteenth century.

SIMIAND'S WORK

Simiand's method goes far beyond a simple study of the movement of prices, to which, however, he, and Labrousse after him, applied this method. His method aims at nothing less than a regeneration in the study of social and economic data.

We are all familiar with the classic methodology of political economy. It uses as a point of departure a *homo oeconomicus*, identical to himself in time and space, and constructed with the aid of information procured by introspection about human nature. It is true that this methodology has recourse to observation, but in a fragmentary way and without being able to reduce the results to numerical formulas which alone are capable of eliminating individual variations by application of the law of great numbers. Similarly, sociology until now has usually proceeded by description and by comparison. Economic and social history, even when it is a question of the eighteenth and nineteenth centuries, also shows a marked penchant for description. Let us admit, if you wish, that the a priori and subjective notions of introspective psychology play no role in the use of these procedures. They still never lead to anything but establishing purely *qualitative* causal relationships between facts. To the contrary, the natural sciences proceed by enumeration, measurements, and weights, and what they strive to discover are *quantitative* causal relationships. Simiand's plan was to transplant into political economy, sociology, and economic and social history, the search for these *quantitative* relationships, without which there is no *science*.

We can immediately observe that he encountered great difficulties. The natural sciences work directly with facts. For Simiand, research is applied to statistical data which come between the sciences and reality, like the document between the historian and the past. Now, what are statistical data worth? This is the chief problem, one which is identical to that encountered by historians whose solution to a large degree depends upon the application of the rules of criticism which the historians have developed. Besides, statistics, even today, almost never proposes to inform the scholar, and consequently does not always make a direct reply to his questionnaire. He must know how to ask questions of it. For example, Simiand saw the need for calculating the volume of *exchanged* merchandise. He made the ingenious decision to estimate it on the basis of the volume of *transported*

---

[3] François Simiand, *Le salaire, l'évolution sociale et la monnaie* (Paris, 1932, three volumes).

merchandise. He wished to know the total amount of *profits*. He estimated it by deducting, from the total value created by production, the values of the raw materials, of the machines, and of the salaries.

But these were only the first steps. The essential procedure of the natural sciences is the experiment or, to be more precise, the experimentation by means of which the fact under study is elicited under the most favorable conditions for observation, isolated from such and such a factor, or combined with them. This is impossible here. An attempt at adaptation is therefore necessary which will permit us roughly to place the economist, the sociologist, and the historian in the same situation in regard to the facts as the physicist, the chemist, or the physiologist. Simiand devoted an extensive part of his great work on salaries to laying down the principles of this new *methodology*.

First of all, he observed that laboratory experimentation analyzes not *states* but *changes* and that, on the other hand, the study of social events through successive states permits no explanatory conclusion. Thus a person examining trees in June, and then in December, without studying what has happened in the interval, might conclude that the cold resulted in growth. Likewise, a person describing the French economy in 1720, then in 1860, would concede that it was Napoleon III who launched the industrial revolution. If, at such a moment, one observes that salaries on the one hand and wealth on the other are superior in England to those in France, one would conclude that salaries increase along with general wealth. However, it could be that wealth was decreasing and salaries increasing in the two countries; or that such was the case in England, while in France wealth was increasing and salaries decreasing; or inversely. It is therefore the movement or, if you prefer, the evolution that must be discovered. Speaking like Simiand, it is *the fact producing itself*, which, for historians at least, in my opinion means not that the study of *states* is useless, but that it constitutes merely a point of departure for that *coherent and complete* study of phenomena which alone can provide an explanation.

To the scholar who undertakes such research, let us now comment that the laboratory permits the organization of experiments so as to eliminate, or introduce, or combine the factors considered. This method is forbidden to us. Let us suppose that the salaries in an industry increase as a result of a strike, and that they also increase in the others in which work was not stopped. We cannot materially separate the first from the rest, in order to achieve what Simiand calls an *independent integrality*. Consequently, we are not in a position to decide whether all salaries increased as a result of this strike, or whether the general increase in reality depends upon another factor. But being unable to materially attain *independent integrality*, Simiand judged that he could come sufficiently close to it by means of intellectual operations. This is the essential point.

In what conditions? The first is to eliminate the individual variations with the aid of averages, by isolating the bodies of facts which correspond to a collective reality. This is the precept of *homogenous segregation*. We shall see below how salaries have apparently met this requirement.

The second precept is that of the *basic identity* which excludes the comparative method that for some time has been so widely used. The comparative method compares, for example, the evolution of salaries in England and in France, consequently acknowledging that from one country to the other, this category of facts is independent of other factors. But, the influence of these other factors cannot be excluded *a priori*; for they differ from one country to the other, so that the comparison which, in principle, would imply that we can apply to it the formula, "all other things being equal," is obliged to the contrary, to make this reservation: "all things being unequal in other respects," which makes it all the less conclusive. The situation changes if we study the evolution of salaries, for example, in France, because, at least for such a carefully chosen period, the factors in question can be considered as constant or only moderately variable.

Third, we must review all the possible factors of action upon the phenomenon under study, that is to say, in the question under study, salary movements. This is the *selective review*. This review must be complete for, in the laboratory, if one factor has been neglected, the experiment does not work or gives unexpected results. The scholar is thus warned. But here we have nothing which ought to put off the researcher. The value of his conclusions depends solely upon the rigorous application of selective review.

Finally, the method leads to the construction of curves which sometimes express the progress of the principal phenomenon which it is a question of explaining, sometimes that of the phenomena which are capable of modifying it. It is by the detailed comparison of these curves that causal antecedents will be discerned. In order for the operation to be productive, the curves must naturally make the least variations evident. Success therefore depends to a great degree upon the processes employed in drawing up the graphs. This is why the study of the technical methods which statisticians have created for this purpose is of great importance in the training of the economist, the sociologist, and the historian. Ideally, it should be included as soon as possible among the "auxiliary sciences" of their respective disciplines. Let us limit ourselves to observing that Simiand's curves never take absolute measures into account—for example the nominal sum total of salaries—but only the *growth* of these measures, which is related to these measures as acceleration is to speed. These curves, to use the technical terms, are on a logarithmic scale. This presupposes that, to simplify calculations, indices calculated in terms of a basic year whose index equals 100 have been substituted for these absolute measures. In his study of salaries, Simiand chose the year 1892 for this purpose. Therefore, the salary of miners in 1858, for example, was represented by sixty, and all absolute measures disappeared from the work.

Never before had anyone undertaken in such a deliberate manner and with such disdain for the constantly invoked pretext of the complexity of human phenomena, to elevate the science of man and his society to the level of the natural sciences. But it goes without saying that this effort would have been less impressive if, at the same time that he presented his method, Simiand had not presented the results of its application during thirty years of labor. It is in his study of salary movements that we shall see him at work, for economic matters were his special field of study. Nevertheless, sociologists include him as one of their own, for his principle of *homogenous segregation* led him to look upon salaries as the remuneration of a working class and, consequently, to make dependent upon them not the expression of individual caprice, but the reactions of a group endowed with a social reality. Moreover, it is in short his method which Mr. Halbwachs applied in his book on *Les Causes du suicide*, so full of original insights. There is even more. For example, the causal relationship which Simiand established between prices and salaries is not in the least automatic. It functions in the group consciousness of the salaried workers by the intermediary of collective images, so that research, based upon statistics, ends up enriching the collective psychology. Economic and social history has much to learn from these innovations. As we shall see, Labrousse—without trying to discover like Simiand the origins of changes in prices and incomes, and to the contrary focusing his attention upon their social and truly historical consequences—has shown brilliantly how we can profit from Simiand's work.

"The salary," according to Simiand's definition, "is the sum of money in exchange for which one rents the pure or relatively pure labor of a worker." Thus the study is limited to the *nominal* salary and does not take into account the *real* salary, that is to say the quantity of merchandise which the nominal salary allows the worker to procure and which varies according to the cost of living. This is an important restriction, especially for the historian, and one to which we must return. Let us for the moment observe that this definition is related to an economy based upon exchange or, still more precisely, to a monetary economy, as contrasted with a closed economy in which the producer would live upon his own products, or with an economy in which exchange would be limited to bartering. Moreover, it makes a clear distinction between the salary and the retribution granted "for the action of direction and sales characteristic of the employer's function, and also the retribution which is granted to the employee whose activity does not include, at least as an essential element, a manual function." The study of salaries is therefore in accordance with the precept of *homogenous segregation:* "The pure furnishing of labor appears to constitute a framework of distinct economic reality." It is a basic form of income for a very extensive category of society. The mass of French workers and even better the different types of trades form *independent integralities.*

The framework of his inquiry is contemporary France, during the period from 1789 to 1928, the only conceivable one owing to the documents available to Simiand, so that the precept of *basic identity* is respected as much as reality permits. The sources are examined in great detail according to historical methods. As they are more or less fragmentary, this use involves ingenious *adjustments* that we cannot discuss here. We shall give a concrete example of them during our discussion of Labrousse's book. The results are summarized in the form of curves relative to the salaries of men and to those of women, for Paris on the one hand, and for France excluding Paris on the other. It is therefore clearly the *phenomenon occurring* which is observed. Actually, this is not true for each curve, from one end of the period to the other; the curves are not continuous. But for four industrial groups (coal mines, sugar factories, textiles, and metals), they are much more extensive and continuous. Between the first and the last, reproduced on a sheet of transparent paper which can be placed over the general diagram, the agreement is striking. Since these curves thus confirm one another, one finds himself therefore authorized to use one group for the years which the other does not cover. In this way the author strove to establish a single curve for all of France.

The following conclusion can be drawn from an examination of the graphs. On the eve of the Revolution, salaries were on the increase and this increase continued into the second decade of the nineteenth century. A new period of increases began about 1850 and continued until 1880. A third began about 1900 and ended in 1928. Simiand calls them A *Phases*. They are separated by periods of low salaries or rather of stagnation, B *Phases*; one from 1820 to 1850, the other from 1880 to 1900. In Simiand's opinion, a third began in 1928. Salaries are thus subject to *fluctuations over long periods*, each lasting twenty to thirty years, without, as Labrousse has shown, its being excluded that during the other periods these fluctuations would be more extensive. This observation is very new, for in the studies made by economists since the eighteenth century, salaries always appeared to increase in a continuous and regular manner or to be affected merely by accidental variations which had no relation to prices.

It now remains to determine the causes of these fluctuations. Here one must make that *selective review* of the possible factors which, without being infinite in number (especially since upon examination a part of them are seen to have no appreciable effect), are nevertheless very numerous. Each of them necessitates a new inquiry and operation of the same sort: discovery and critical examination of the sources, drawing up of tables, construction of curves. In doing this, Simiand had to overcome multiple difficulties and in a very original manner he expanded our economic and social knowledge, for example in regard to the numerical expansion of the working class, of its *durability*, that is to say the greater or lesser degree of change which circumstances provide for escaping from it, in regard to variations in prices, money and the means of credit, production, the amount of agricultural and industrial enterprises and their extent calculated according to the amount of surface under cultivation, the quantity of workers hired, the number and power of the motors.

All the curves are not parallel, and some vary inversely. Those that show the closest agreement with salaries concern the movement of prices and that of profits. Now, these price curves change direction before the others. From this Simiand concluded that it is the price movement that determines the variations in salaries and profits. Nevertheless, their curves are not exactly parallel. In Phase A salaries follow the price increase, but without equaling it. As a result profits increase in relative as well as in absolute value. In Phase B, when prices collapse, salaries decrease much less or remain constant. The unit profit (by unit of production) decreases, but as the number of employers also decreases, the individual income of the employer decreases only slightly or remains stable. The relationship is never an automatic one. In order to provoke the increase in his salary or to halt its reduction, the worker must act through strikes and labor unions. In order to take advantage of the price increase, the employer must create or develop his business and, in order to maintain his income during periods of price reduction, he must perfect his tools or his methods. Moreover, there are no grounds for saying, as it has often been said, that it is to the detriment of salaries that profits increase, since their movements are concomitant. But it remains true that the capitalist's profits take the lion's share, for in Phase A they increase more than salaries, while in Phase B they decrease only slightly or remain constant.

❧§§❧

These conclusions are already striking. However, we have not taken into account the most original one. It is the price movement which marks the passage from Phase A to Phase B, and reciprocally. But what is the factor that provokes the price variations themselves? One of our curves provides the clue through its variations in the same direction. It is the abundance of money, real and paper, and of auxiliary means of payment: transfers and clearing houses, credit balances in current accounts.

Does this mean that Simiand is only confirming the *quantitative* theory of money, according to which the speed of monetary circulation and the quantity of merchandise exchanged being assumed constant, the prices vary in *direct proportion* to the abundance of money? Not in the least. First of all this theory obviously rests upon a postulate that is in fact a tautology. Without recourse to observation, we do not know whether the speed of monetary circulation and the quantity of merchandise exchanged remain constant. In fact, Simiand's curves indicate that the latter at least is a variable. In Phase A it increases like monetary abundance and prices; in Phase B, when the increase in money slows down and prices drop, its rate of growth progresses. On the other hand, there is no immediate and proportionate link between monetary abundance and prices; the extent of monetary fluctuations is much greater; price variations are much slower.

Finally, while in Phase A prices increase with monetary abundance, in Phase B they decrease, while monetary abundance only slows its growth coefficient. But the fact remains that in an economy based on exchange, monetary abundance is the principal driving force of activity.

Why? Because money is an *anticipation*, and this remark of Simiand's, precious to political economists, is even more so to collective psychology. The economist looks upon money as an instrument for measuring, representing, and preserving values. We must add further that it is also, for its possessor, a means of immediately realizing a *future* value. Indeed, the economy based upon exchanges is characterized by the fact that, from the beginning of production until consumption, a series of transmissions takes place which each time involves a monetary settling of accounts, while a more or less long period of time must pass before the resultant income, upon which the final value of the quantity produced depends, can be realized or even discovered. Money thus permits its holder at any moment to realize, for his personal advantage, a part of the future value. In other words, it is the ideal instrument for credit. On the other hand, at a given moment the sum total of values and income, while awaiting the final realization, is as a result normally superior to the sum total of the goods immediately connected with production and distribution. If this difference is only covered through personal promises, it is not actually realizable and, consequently, the movement of economic expansion risks remaining limited. On the other hand, as a growing rush of monetary means offers the expanding economy a display of general and immediately realizable value, it no longer has inconveniences for individuals, and it will lend itself all the better to the economy's extension as, through monetary abundance, the realization will be easier. It seems to me that the accuracy of this analysis is implicitly agreed to when they say that business is favored if money is abundant and credit is consequently easy and cheap. But it is apparent that a psychological element is involved. This abundance, this easiness, and this cheapness create *confidence*, the conviction that the final value will live up to expectations and will be rapidly realized without obstacles. Confidence stimulates the spirit of enterprise and, as a result, triggers an increase. It is noteworthy in this regard that the increase appears first in the price of mass-produced merchandise—for example in steel—which serve as raw material for the conversion industries and are as a result the farthest from the terminal realization and which thus require the most confidence on the part of the producer, since there is greater risk involved here. It is then that the increase reaches raw materials and finished products, the retail price being the last to rise.

It is this characteristic of anticipation which, for Simiand, also explains the relationships between prices, production, profit, and salaries, that is to say the psychological reactions that determine them. Salary movements, for example, appear to have as an immediate antecedent, a series of inclinations among the workers and employers which Simiand classifies as follows according to decreasing strength: (1) the inclination to maintain the monetary income already achieved; (2) the inclination not to increase one's own efforts; (3) the inclination to increase the monetary rate of income; (4) the inclination to diminish one's efforts. Why does the attachment to monetary income occupy first place? And why do the workers defend it during Phase B, when by making concessions about the rate of salaries they would perhaps be able to decrease unemployment? The explanation is that monetary income involves an undetermined possibility of realization, an anticipation which is all the more precious when, during Phase B, prices decrease. It is also that, in a monetary economy, the social situation, the *social standing*, is expressed by the total monetary income. In contrast, the increase in this income does not involve a decrease in attraction when the known needs are satisfied, because it opens a perspective toward new, diverse, and unlimited satisfactions, and results in an elevation in social *standing* and the prestige that this involves. The nature and sum of the effort thus present a certain value in this last respect. One therefore does not increase his effort in order to increase his gains. What is above all appreciated is the increase in gain without new effort, that is to say, a windfall. On the contrary, the increase in gain is in certain cases accompanied by a decrease in effort. But the decrease in gain results in a greater effort, because it is the most obvious index of a step down in the social ladder. Thus statistics, translated into appropriate curves, have permitted us to shed a light on the psychological reactions provoked by a certain external stimulation—in this case, the increase or decrease in prices—and, as a result, of the permanent traits of human nature, integrated in a specific social environment, the economy based upon exchange or money.

☙§§☙

Having reached this point, we become aware that in searching for the conditions and the causal antecedent of salary fluctuations, Simiand finally succeeded in formulating a general theory (an experimental theory, not an *a priori* and conceptual one, for no amount of reflection could have forseen the directions that so many variations would take) for economic activity in contemporary society. It is dominated by a double movement of ebb and flow, and the alternation of Phases A and B, first discovered in salary variations, is of general significance.

In Phase A, monetary abundance—inflation—causes a price increase, which, once established, is then accelerated by the multiplication of purchases stimulated by the prospect of a greater increase. The movement is profitable not only to large businesses but to enterprises of all sorts and sizes. The number of small employers, of more or less independent artisans, of retailers, and of agricultural exploiters keeps increasing. The same is true for the quantities produced, at least in absolute value, for the return does not increase or even decreases in relation to the capital invested and to the number of workers. The prospect of gain as a result of the increase weakens the search for technical progress and even the efforts of the salaried workers. The increase in the number of businesses means that a certain number of them are those of artisans or small businessmen. Likewise, agricultural day laborers rise to the position of small landholders, tenant farmers, or sharecroppers. The number of salaried workers can increase in absolute value; in relative value, as compared with the whole group of producers, it decreases. Unemployment is also reduced, so that the worker's individual income increases perhaps even more than the rate of salaries. This is a period of great ease, of frequent climbs up the social ladder. Competition becomes less bitter between classes and between nations as well. Circumstances are favorable for economic liberalism at home and for free exchange abroad. The race to discover new markets becomes less heated. All other things being equal, one might say that Phase A presents less probabilities for social troubles and war. But these advantages are counterbalanced by the slowness of economic transformation, by the slowing in the progress of the differentiation of businesses, and, consequently, of the division of labor, of technology, and of mechanization.

In Phase B, monetary means can continue to grow, but the rapidity of their increase diminishes. This is deflation. Credit is tightened and becomes more expensive. As a result businesses are in jeopardy and lower their prices. Once established, the deflation accelerates as a result of the rarefaction of purchases in the face of a still greater decrease. Anxiety and discouragement ruin the business spirit. In addition, indebtedness, deliberately contracted during Phase A, crushes a growing number of entrepreneurs. Thus a crowd of artisans, of shopkeepers, and of small land-owning peasants or tenant farmers are cast down into the proletariat. On the one hand, the number of workers thus increases, and their condition becomes more *durable*. Society is in the process of becoming proletarian. On the other hand, businesses merge and the number of employers decreases. In addition, the situation of salaried workers worsens because of the spreading unemployment, so that, even if salaries remain stable, the income per head decreases considerably, while those employers who escape disaster frequently defend their income successfully. Thus class antagonisms become clear and worsen. The State itself is affected by the decreased receipts, and the fiscal problem becomes insoluble. Each nation withdraws into its shell in order to protect its domestic market. This is a period favorable to *mercantilism*, to protectionism, and governmental controls. At the same time, the conquest of foreign outlets becomes all the more necessary, and rivalries between nations risk worsening. All other things being equal social troubles and international conflicts become more probable. But it is during this period of economic crisis and great individual suffering that humanity makes the technical progress which, in the new Phase A to follow, will raise it to a greater degree of prosperity. The head of a business, in order to keep up his income despite the decrease in unit profits, improves output by perfecting his equipment and his methods; the worker himself frequently increases his efforts or takes willingly to innovations.

The link between one phase and the other is indisputable. They are joined together and the final result is the product of each of them. It is in Phase B that technical progress occurs, but this is only possible because the businesses which manage to survive were able to save the indispensable capital during Phase A. If during Phase A men were able to slacken their efforts and to improve their general standard of living, it was because Phase B created technical conditions which are more advantageous for production. Therefore, an antagonism exists between the pleasant life and economic progress. The latter can be achieved at the price of individual suffering, but the capitalist who stood fast suffers lease, just as in Phase A he made sure that he would make the greatest profits.

Unquestionably, the more the economic structure has evolved, and the more the natural economy has been eliminated by the economy based upon exchange, the more marked are the effects of these joint phases. Since these characteristics are not very old and since, it being a question of long-term fluctuations, it took a certain amount of time to observe these fluctuations, it is not surprising that the phases which we have just briefly described were not brought to light until our time. If the economic movement continues in the same direction, their dissonance will become increasingly striking and the B Phases will become increasingly painful and threatening, unless we succeed in shortening them by the directed inflation which Simiand apparently proposes, as we shall see below. This is a major problem for the economist and the statesman. For the historian, it is no less interesting to go back into the past as far as the origins of the monetary economy and to see whether Phases A and B can be found, what effects they produced, and how long they lasted. This is the type of inquiry which Simiand sketched in his *Recherches anciennes et nouvelles sur le mouvement général des prix du XVIᵉ au XIXᵉ siècle*. We are a long way from knowing with certainty the beginning and the end of the phases, but from the end of the fifteenth century a general pattern appears. Phase B dominated at that time and at the beginning of the sixteenth century. The arrival, after 1530, of galleons loaded with silver from Mexico, and later from Peru, opened an A Phase.

Since then, the phases have continued to alternate according to the following approximate dates, which take into account the new precise information contributed by Labrousse: about 1650 to 1732: Phase B; 1733 to 1817: Phase A; 1817 to 1850: Phase B; 1850 to 1880: Phase A; 1880 to 1900: Phase B; 1900 to 1928: Phase A; 1928 to ?: Phase B.

❧

In the light of these observations, we should re-examine all of economic and social history since the end of the Middle Ages. For example, Colbert's work takes on a new light when we observe that he took over finances in the midst of a Phase B, which was restricting receipts at a time when the Great King was demanding that expenses be increased. Therefore, his mercantilism does not appear as the application of a doctrine or of "the offer to France" of which Lavisse spoke, but as a real necessity which forced him to increase the monetary stores in order to enter Phase A. Likewise Napoleon, after the deflationary period during the Directory, which incidentally Simiand did not mention, was forced to follow the same policies, and to continue them under the Empire in even greater proportions thanks to the conquest which provided him with new markets and which permitted him to increase the monetary wealth by requiring war indemnities and tributes. But before the sixteenth century? Marc Bloch correctly observed that a vast field of research was opening up for medievalists. Though the weakening of real money and of money of account is a well-known fact, the economic and social effects have not yet been studied. The devaluation of feudal dues and the evolution of the seigneury undoubtedly depend upon it. Unfortunately, when we go back into the past, Simiand's specific method becomes increasingly difficult to apply. The documents will probably not permit us to reconstitute continuous series of numerical estimates any farther back than the seventeenth century.

Since money is the motivating force of economic activity, we seem obliged to admit that in the end the explanation is irrational or contingent. Since money is provided by precious metals, the explanation lies in the discovery of new mines, which is apparently a matter of chance. In the case of inconvertible paper money, the explanation is to be sought in the historical *events* about which the least we can say is that the intervention of certain individuals introduces a share of irreducible irresolution. We can doubtlessly ask whether it is not the scarcity of monetary resources so cruelly felt in Phase *B* and their constantly increasing value which spark the search for new mines or the more extensive working of the old ones. In this respect, the needs of the State could also be taken into consideration, at least in our day and in those nations with controlled economies, so that it might happen, for example, that the search for gold mines by the Soviet State, by flooding the world with unexpected quantities of the precious metal, would in the end reopen an A Phase and consequently save the capitalist economy. But up to the present, Phase *B*'s role in stimulating the discovery of new mines is not clear.

Nevertheless, we are not irrevocably abandoned to the contingent and the irrational. In fact, Simiand observed that paper money, the inconvertible bank note, at least at the beginning of inflation, which he calls *Phase A'*, leads to the same results as the inflation of the metallic currency. It is only when the multiplication of paper money becomes excessive and uncontrollable, during *Phase A'*, that because of an increasing lack of foresight, these beneficial effects are destroyed, then replaced by a contrary tendency. This reversal can be all the better understood because history shows that inconvertible money has frequently been issued solely to serve the purposes of the State and, in time of war, for nonproductive or even destructive ends, and in order to distribute allocations without [demanding] the corresponding work. It is even more easily understood if we reflect that inconvertible money has no intrinsic value and therefore does not assure the individual that come what may he will keep at least a part of what he hopes will have been reserved for him in the final value of production. In this case, paper money, having fallen to zero, must be withdrawn from circulation, so that Phase B is characterized not by a slowing down in the growth of monetary resources, but by the abrupt decrease in their absolute size, and therefore by an enormous deflation which makes the crisis catastrophic. But it can still happen that inflation undertaken in cold blood, for exclusively economic ends, and methodically calculated so that it will not go beyond Phase A', can maintain money at a low price, spare the economy the horrors of deflation, and make it move from Phase B into Phase A.

Moreover, history offers numerous examples in which the state, overwhelmed by the weight of its debt, or threatened, in our day, by the troubles which arise from indebtedness on the part of individuals, has obtained analogous results by weakening the real money standard or by devaluating the money of account. The Middle Ages and the Old Regime resorted to these two methods, and we have in our own day seen the second one employed frequently. Without even officially devaluating the money of account, a state whose life depends upon exportation obtains the desired effect by suspending the gold standard and by temporarily making paper money inconvertible, which brings about a lowering in the exchange rate. England has done this on two memorable occasions, the first time from 1797 to 1817, the second in 1932. Roosevelt's experiments have the same basis.

Since one of the basic results of these expedients is to annul all or a part of credit, we could therefore say that bankruptcy is one of the rational means of putting economic activity back into action. Owing to a lack of new mines for precious metals, the *rentier* would be offered as a sacrifice so that society, threatened with collapse by the suffering of Phase B, can move on to Phase A. It is acquired and consolidated wealth which, in the end, would pay the costs of the technical progress of production.

THE HISTORIAN'S REACTION

As short as this sketch is, I hope it will inspire the respect which Simiand's work deserves. This, however, does not mean that his work arouses no objections.

In regard to economics, I wonder if the extension of the market should not be considered more fully, at least during a period of capitalist economy, one of whose fundamental characteristics is precisely such a constant search for new outlets. Capitalism is essentially *conquering*, that is to say that it progresses, within the state, by ejecting the artisan and small businessman, and that, on the other hand, it can only realize total profits by annexing foreign markets into which it pours the products which salaried workers, *rentiers*, and civil servants cannot buy since their incomes represent only a part of the final value of production. Let us agree, with Simiand, that the conquest of new outlets or the restriction of the market cannot be the cause of long-term fluctuations in economic activity. They could, however, be a *permissive* condition: in Phase A production would be able to increase, owing to the extension of the market; in Phase B, the stringency would contribute to aggravating the decrease while a new extension would favor a revival. If, therefore, one day the earth came to be completely exploited according to the capitalist system, the problem arises of knowing if money would still be capable of playing the role which Simiand assigns it. In truth, we would undoubtedly reply that in such a period capitalism would no longer exist and would have been replaced by an economy of another sort, since one of the conditions necessary for its existence—the constant conquest of new outlets—would have become unrealizable. Yet the field of application of the economic rhythm which Simiand elucidated would still be limited in the future, just as it has been in the past, to a period of monetary economy, without being able to be expanded to that of the natural economy.

It seems to me that the influence of demographic matters would also justify some reservations. According to the curves constructed by Simiand for the nineteenth century, demographic conditions undoubtedly cannot be considered as the cause of Phases A and B since, during that period, the population continued to increase, while the price curve changed direction several times. Yet we must still verify whether demographic variations have any influence upon prices. As far as the last decades of the Old Regime are concerned, I have considered the rather rapid increase in population as one of the causes of price increases. From now on let us agree with Simiand that this population increase is not the principal cause; yet I am nevertheless inclined to think that it helped reinforce the price increase. Or in the opposite direction, such an increase in the number of inhabitants could halt a decrease in prices, at least as far as the most essential foodstuffs are concerned. As for the decrease in the population as a result of the ravages of war or of a great epidemic, both so common from the fourteenth to seventeenth centuries, it seems an undeniable fact that this decreased population acted at least to raise salaries and to decrease farm rents. The price of food supplies may have been lowered because of decreased demand, but we should examine whether the accompanying reduction in production did not produce the opposite results. In short, the question arises as to whether demographic conditions intervene to attenuate or to accentuate the characteristics of Phases A and B.

Now we come to the objections made by historians, several of whom have not been very receptive to Simiand's work. First of all it must be admitted that he had left his flank exposed to their criticisms by being too complacent about some of his sources. Some historians are still outraged by one of his remarks, *one can weigh accurately with inaccurate scales.* It is, however, irreproachable in the sense Simiand intended it to be. If a certain series of prices shows that it is spoiled because of an error, the *absolute values* which it provides cannot be trusted. The scales are inaccurate. However, if the cause of the error has been employed consistently, the appearance of the curve constructed with these values will nevertheless faithfully express the price *variations*. The weighing will be accurate. This will be true, for example, if the author has made a mistake about the contents of a measure or a monetary unit, or if we can show that, in establishing the grain market quotations, they regularly took only the highest or lowest price into account. In reality, historians' reservations are still justified because the cause of the error is generally not constant. Such is the case with d'Avenel's collection, the principal object of the debate, which Simiand believed he was entitled to use in his *Recherches anciennes et nouvelles sur le mouvement des prix*. D'Avenel does not indicate from which documents he drew his information. He publishes only a part of the prices which he had copied without explaining the reasons for his choice. He does not seem to realize that, from one region to another, and sometimes from one period to another in the same region, a measure may vary. Since his work embraces an extensive period, the value of the monetary unit undergoes numerous variations which it is not easy to estimate. The work therefore cannot be used as it is if we are looking for *absolute values*, and it would lead astray the historian who wanted to establish a curve of the variations for a short-term period. Simiand has therefore been justly reproached for not having verified d'Avenel's work by archival research. But Labrousse has done this verification as far as the eighteenth century is concerned, and he concluded that, although d'Avenel's collection does not in fact permit a study of the cyclical and seasonal variations, we can still make a sufficiently approximate observation of long-term fluctuations. Since Simiand was not looking for anything more, we can therefore avoid condemning him, though we cannot of course recommend that anyone else run such a risk.

If this question of sources had not arisen, Simiand's work would still have disturbed historians because of its abstract nature. His principal book —the one concerning salaries—is really difficult to read. The sentences follow step by step the workings of the mind. When stating a proposition, he tries hard also to mention all the variables upon which the proposition depends. Complicated though it is by incidentals, suspended by parentheses, often very long, it must be read, if I may say, very slowly, yet without losing the overall view; it requires a simultaneous effort at analysis and at synthesis which does not permit the attention to wander for even a moment. As absolute values never appear, any more than do events, the historian, deprived of his customary landmarks, is completely lost.

When at last he becomes accustomed to this new "climate," the principal objection soon becomes evident: man, living and suffering, does not appear in Simiand's work. Marc Bloch remarked that he forbade himself to refer to documents which express man's reactions in the presence of economic events, his feelings of insecurity or of confidence, of anger or of satisfaction. It is not, as we have seen, that he makes abstractions of psychological matters, since, to the contrary, it is through them that he establishes causal relationships. But he eliminates the documents which Bloch mentioned because they are tainted with subjectivity, and also because the collective representations which he retains refer strictly to the social significance of money and of effort. However, there are other representations of this sort whose influence is undeniable, for example, about the workers' activities which provoke the increase in salaries or halt their decrease, without taking into account that, for the periods in which statistical data are very rare, it is upon these subjective documents that we must rely.

◆◆◆

This absence of man or, if one prefers, of the individual, is made even more noticeable by two grave gaps which can undoubtedly be justified by Simiand's plan—the study of the *nominal* salary and of long-term fluctuations—but which his turn of mind must have prevented him from being tormented about, as an historian would have been.

Having defined the salary as a *sum of money*, he said nothing about the *real* salary, that is to say about the quantity of merchandise which this sum of money is capable of procuring or, if one prefers, of the relationships between the nominal salary and the cost of living. He is applauded for having objectively shown that man attaches a particular value to his nominal income because his social dignity depends upon it, and because of the possibilities of future and undetermined purchases which are implied in it. But we cannot agree that the real income is immaterial and must be even less so the lower down the social scale we go. When the worker defends his nominal salary, he is also thinking of past possibilities, of the level of material life which he has attained and without which he judges that life would now be intolerable. This observation does not contradict Simiand's conception, but it completes and enriches it. In addition, the importance of the real salary had not escaped him, and he had promised to study it separately. He died in 1935 at only sixty-two years of age, and his work, as too often happens, remained unfinished. This is all the more regrettable because for the historian the importance of the problem goes beyond the explanation of the movement of the nominal salary. As the latter increases and decreases less than prices, we might wonder if, from the point of view of the real salary, Phases A and B are adequately named. It could happen that the real salary would decrease in Phase A and increase in Phase B, the advantage in the latter case being naturally counterbalanced by the ravages of unemployment. Besides, prices increase unequally. Thus, during the course of Phase A, it could happen that a worker might be obliged to modify the composition of his budget. Food supplies hold first place in it, and their share was formerly much larger than today. Now, until the middle of the nineteenth century, the prices of these very food supplies varied to a very great degree. The social and historical consequences of long-term fluctuations were not elucidated by Simiand's analysis.

That is not all. Prices are affected by other fluctuations which were not included in his plan of study, but which are nonetheless important to the historian. They are studied for a longer time because they are shorter and therefore more easily perceptible and observable. There are, first of all, the *seasonal* fluctuations whose reality, at least, is common knowledge. Next there are the *cyclical* fluctuations which bring an alternating maximum and minimum in prices during a period whose duration keeps becoming shorter since our civilization has reached the industrial and capitalist stage, but which, in the eighteenth century, still essentially agricultural, was commonly estimated at eleven years. The cyclical minimum corresponds to one of those economic crises whose historical importance can be seen on all too many occasions. These seasonal and cyclical fluctuations exaggerate to a considerable degree the extent of the long-term movements. Into Phases A and B they introduce temporary variations of increase and decrease which make the curve look like the teeth of a saw; it is through them that the long-term movement is perceived by the vast majority of human beings. It is these fluctuations which provoke the reactions which form the course of history. Therefore, the nature of Phase A is once again questioned: in principle, it seems that class antagonisms should in such a case be weakened; however, the cataclysm of 1789, which was chiefly the result of a class conflict, occurred during Phase A. The analysis therefore had to be reworked by historians. Such was the work of Labrousse.

LABROUSSE'S INQUIRY

There is more than one similarity between the way his mind and Simiand's react in the presence of facts. Moreover, though Labrousse was unable to use the *Recherches anciennes et nouvelles sur le mouvement des prix*, he is familiar with the great work on salaries. He too seeks to reduce economic and social realities to statistical data and curves, and he consequently tries implicitly to elevate the study to the dignity of a science, by introducing the methodology of the natural sciences. Without making a dogmatic statement, he in fact applies Simiand's precepts, notably those of basic identity and homogeneous segregation. By comparing curves, he draws conclusions that shed light upon the collective psychology and upon the causal relationships to which the curves provide the key.

Yet the differences are equally noticeable. Though Labrousse is an economist and a sociologist due to the nature of the problems which especially interest him, he is also an historian; and in my opinion, at least after having read the first great work which he published, he is above all an historian. Simiand starts with the facts which he gleans from statistics, established by others, in order to find their causes and to develop a theory, with an ill-concealed disdain for the *historical events* which were, in part, their consequences. Labrousse, on the contrary, at least for the moment, makes no claims to be searching for the cause of long-term or cyclical fluctuations, or even to be observing whether the movements of prices and salaries and other income, which he observed during the chosen period, are also to be found in those which precede or follow. He declares that he is purely and simply concerned with presenting a *description* of them. Actually, he does not stop there. He also establishes causal relationships; but they are aimed at the *historical consequences* of these movements, not at their *rational antecedents*. We are undoubtedly not misrepresenting the workings of his mind in supposing that his research was inspired by the attraction he felt for a great historical event, the French Revolution, several characteristics of which were begging to be explained, without his deciding in advance whether the explanation would be contingent or rational. In short, he worked as an historian who is well aware that the facts which he is establishing will form the tested materials for the economist and the sociologist. Consequently he works along with them, but whose own function is, first and foremost, in part at least, to construct history, that is to say to determine subsequent events, some of which are both economic and social and which statistics, in its turn, will reduce to numerical data and to curves. The others are purely *evenemential*, as Simiand called them, and are outside the statistician's discipline.

Between these two scholars, as between the economic and social discipline on the one hand, and the historical one on the other, the difference, at least to a certain degree, is reduced to two inclinations of the intellect: one more abstract, and perhaps more philosophic, which incidentally is confirmed by the mathematical discipline of statistics; and the other more concrete. Of course this distinction is not an absolute one, for I am convinced that nothing will prevent Labrousse, after having studied other periods, from in his turn constructing a theory of economic movement which will undoubtedly confirm Simiand's, but which also will show slight differences and make it more complete.

But as far as method is concerned, his attitude gives rise to a capital difference. While Simiand begins with facts that are provided for him, assuredly not without testing them, Labrousse has searched for new facts from new sources; while thus enriching our knowledge, he was able to examine the old sources experimentally. What this process loses in generalizing power, it gains in analytic strength. It restricts the extensiveness of the research in order to investigate it to the fullest. This is the method which wins the historian's approval. In my opinion history shows that one of the conditions for progress in political economics and sociology is that the historian must ply his own trade in all sureness of conscience.

Labrousse proposed studying the movements of prices, income on land holdings, and salaries in France, with their long-term, cyclical, and seasonal fluctuations, during the period from 1726 to 1789 and which thus covers the major part of Phase A—which on the basis of grain prices he established as beginning in 1734 and ending in 1817. However, he permitted himself to go back to the years before 1734 in order to establish a more solid base for his comparisons. Sometimes, on the other hand, he went as far ahead as 1817; but in general he stopped at 1789. It is certain that the Revolution upset the conditions for these movements, especially in the case of money, and that it merits special research; but here we cannot help recognizing the author's original preoccupations, and his "historicism" is, as a result, emphasized.

Having thus defined the period under study, the principle of basic identity appears to have been respected. Beginning in 1726, money remains stable. There are few legislative, technical, or social changes. The Kingdom is scarcely affected by war. But one reservation must really be made: in 1764, in 1774, and in 1787 the freedom of the grain trade was proclaimed. But, replies Labrousse, it did not equalize prices in the various regions. Because of the lack of communication, the market did not properly speaking become national. The conditions of his observation therefore remained basically unchanged. And exportation, permitted in 1764 and in 1787, had always been insignificant: between 1 and 2 per cent of total production. Although free exportation probably exerted a certain influence in a few frontier regions, it could not have modified the general price curve of grains, and even less so the cyclical and seasonal movements. I consider this reply to be on the whole pertinent. It is, however, one of the points that will ultimately be verified by local studies. The regions through which the great lines of communication ran could have been more affected than Labrousse thinks. Mr. Dion has drawn up a price curve for wheat at Beaugency which shows, after 1764, a sudden increase which could be explained by the exportation possibilities provided by the Loire.

Until now we have had at our disposition two general tables for wheat— and for wheat alone—showing the average price for the Kingdom. One accompanied the Creuzé-Latouche report of December 8, 1792; the other was published in 1837 in the *Archives statistiques* of the *Ministère des Travaux publics, Agriculture et Commerce*. Both of them begin in 1756 and stop in 1790; both come from a manuscript table, kept in the *Archives Nationales* (F [20] 108), apparently drawn up with the help of the papers of the *Bureau des subsistances* of the *Contrôle général des finances*. Indeed, after 1756 the subdelegates were ordered to submit every fortnight, and beginning in 1771 every week, a summary of the prices of the principal commodities on the basis of the grain-market quotations in their administrative area. The intendant used them to draw up a recapitulatory table every fortnight. He sent it, with the summaries of the subdelegates, to the *Bureau des subsistances*, which then calculated the average for each *généralité* and the national average. The documents cited above have preserved for us the results of the Bureau's work, but as its archives have disappeared, it is impossible to verify them without referring to the departmental archives or to the summaries of the subdelegates and of the intendants, for which a part of the original duplicate copies has survived. Labrousse's research has permitted him to make new calculations of the prices in the *généralités* corresponding to seven-tenths of the general table that has been handed down to us. The examination indicates that there is agreement within a variation of between 1 and 2 per cent on the average. The difference can probably be explained on the whole by the different procedures used to convert measures or calculate weights. And we must realize that the intendant and the Bureau did not automatically register the information received, but verified it as best they could and tried to improve its preparation. Of course we could not fail to make allowances for bureaucratic routine. But we also have a means of verification, which is to refer to the market quotations themselves. We should not deny the value of the principle of agreement as a test of the summaries of the subdelegates. If the subdelegates, working separately, provide us with prices whose curves present concomitant variations, we would be abandoning ourselves to hypercriticism if we questioned the reality of these variations. Last, Labrousse concludes that the general table, which has until now been used without verification, is trustworthy.

It remains to be seen whether the market quotation which he uses as a base can be trusted. Their agreement should again be taken into consideration here. But we can also examine what factors were likely to alter the operator's sincerity. On this point I must refer to the work itself. Yet there is a good argument to invoke when justifying the confidence which Labrousse definitely places in the market quotations: it is that they were referred to in the tribunals and between individuals when converting dues and farm rents in kind into currency. If they had been systematically erroneous, it is unlikely that people would have put up with them.

We must nevertheless note that the prices which they indicate are inferior to those marked down by the subdelegates and the intendants, because the higher authority only recorded the highest market prices. The average difference is 4.47 per cent. Now, we have only the market quotations for the years preceding 1756. The indications can only be fitted into the general table by increasing them. Since, in fact, the difference varies, this adjustment, carried out on the basis of the average difference, involves something of the arbitrary. Although it is too slight to change the direction of the movements, we must still remember that the curves, from 1734 to 1756, represent only *qualitative* values. A local historian should refer to the market quotations themselves in order to find the *quantitative* values.

For the other cereals, everything remained to be done, for we had no general table, since the *Bureau du contrôle général* was only concerned with wheat prices among all the commodities quoted by the subdelegates and intendants. Labrousse therefore returned to the summaries of these local civil servants to draw up tables for the *généralités* and the nation as a whole. Since there were gaps in these series, he had to make adjustments by taking as a base the relationship between one cereal and another observed in the years when the series are complete. For example, the price of rye averages 68 per cent that of wheat; when the price of rye is missing, it can be hypothetically re-established in terms of that of wheat.

The difficulty increases for the other commodities: dry vegetables, wine, fodder, meat and suet, textiles, iron, and firewood. The gaps are much more frequent and the adjustment is often impossible. Let us add that certain products, like candles, are not represented and, finally, that Labrousse had to give up making a distinction between wholesale and retail prices.

For income on land holdings, the situation becomes even worse. There is no public inquiry, nothing but private sources, that is to say the leases preserved in the ecclesiastical and seigneurial archives or among notarial records. Actually, research here is simplified by the fact that, especially in the case of the large estates, the leases were generally for nine years. Labrousse chiefly used the information collected by Zolla; [4] the calculations are based principally upon the data relative to seventy-four domains belonging chiefly to the clergy or to hospital establishments.

We are the most poorly informed concerning salaries and are reduced to local sources which do not permit us to construct any continuous tables. Nothing remains of the government inquiry begun in 1729; the first usable one dates from 1777 when the salary increase had already begun; then came the information concerning the salaries of 1790 collected for the price controls of 1793. In all, Labrousse was able to establish sixty-one series, divided among eleven *généralités*, and each concerning a profession, mainly construction, textiles, and the agricultural day laborer, in one locality and during one season. This is not very much. But these indications have a great representative value because in the eighteenth century observers were agreed in their statements concerning the stability of salaries which they contrast with the variations in prices, so that the figures for one year have a representative value for a whole period.

Studying, among others, the cyclical variations, Labrousse used the process of *mobile averages*, which consists of calculating the average price not for a year, but for a group of years including those which precede and those which follow, plus the year under study, the whole forming a cycle. The difficulty lies in evaluating its duration. Labrousse thinks that it can be extended to thirteen years, six before the year under study and six after. But having no delusions about the fact that the duration of the cycle can vary, he preferred to substitute the real cycles for this theoretical rhythm, and he took, as points of comparison, the cycle 1726 to 1741 on the one hand, and the cycle 1771 to 1789 on the other, while adding a subsidiary comparison with a cycle 1785 to 1789 as the most likely to shed light upon the situation at the beginning of the Revolution.

The effort of research, criticism, and elaboration is praiseworthy, and we

[4] "Les variations du revenu et du prix des terres en France au XVII et au XVIIIᵉ siècles," *Annales de l'Ecole des sciences politiques*, 1893.

can agree with Labrousse that future investigations will not change the meaning of his conclusions. But it does not seem that such investigations will be useless and that anyone willing to undertake one should be discouraged. First of all, it will not be presumptuous to confirm the inquiry and to perhaps arrive at a more precise estimate of the percentages. Also, certain commodities are represented by discontinuous or scanty series which can profitably be augmented; other commodities are missing. Labrousse did not take the price of bread into consideration, and it would be very useful —we shall soon see why—to compare it with the grain prices. As far as salaries and yearly incomes from investments are concerned, the data are really much too scarce. We should also like to see the venal value of the soil taken into consideration. And last, the history of monetary matters still remains to be done. Local scholars should therefore become convinced that they will not be wasting their time in establishing new series with the help of the archives at their disposal, especially the notarial records. In addition, Labrousse aspired to establish national prices. A certain region of the Kingdom could profitably be taken as the basic unity. France under the Old Regime was extremely diverse, and it is one of the tasks before us to clarify this complexity by the same statistical procedures that have brought so many innovations, as we shall soon see, in the history of the national community. If we have dwelt at length upon Labrousse's method, it is because it will be of precious aid to researchers; for them his work will be a guide and a tool from now on.

THE MOVEMENT OF PRICES AT THE END OF THE OLD REGIME AND ITS SOCIAL REPERCUSSIONS

The phase of price increases, which began in about 1734, not to end until 1817, is by far the longest we have known up to the present. The upsurge, slow until 1758, became very strong between 1758 and 1770; then the increase took root and again became accentuated on the eve of the Revolution. Labrousse's calculations concerned twenty-four commodities or items of merchandise. If the cycle 1726–1741 is taken as a base and is given the index 100, the long-term increase for the period 1771–1789 averages 45 per cent; it climbs to 65 per cent for the period between 1785–1789.

But one of the great merits of our author is that he so forcefully showed that the increase is very unequal depending upon the product. For all the cereals together, the corresponding percentages are 56 and 65. The price of wheat increases by 56 and 66 per cent; rye by 60 and 71 per cent; buckwheat follows a similar pattern; for barley the change is a little less extensive; and for oats it is superior to all the others. The price of fodder, which dominates that of the products of livestock raising—especially meat—is equal to or superior to that of oats. From 1726–1741 to 1771–1789, meat increases by 55 per cent and in 1785–1789 by 67 per cent; suet by 47 and 58 per cent. Wine is a very special case: from 1726–1741 to 1771–1789, the increase is only 41 per cent; after 1781 it even decreases considerably and is not more than 13 to 14 per cent during the years 1785–1789. Firewood breaks all records; its percentages are 63 and 91 per cent. On the contrary, textiles and iron remain below the average; the coefficients are 41 for spun wool between 1726–1741 and 1771–1789, 44 for raw wool, and only 22 for woolen fabrics. Linen and hemp follow the cereals rather closely, but linen cloth only increases by 36 per cent and cloth made of hemp by 38 per cent. In addition, beginning in 1786, the prices of all fabrics drop considerably. Iron only increases by 30 per cent.

These observations characterize an economy that has remained essentially agricultural, is backward and still poor. If cereals increase more than the other foodstuffs, it is because at that time they occupied an enormous place in the budget of the common people, because production was growing only slightly while the population was increasing rather rapidly, and finally because foreign competition was not able to intervene. The cereal curves are interdependent because, if one cereal was lacking, they relied upon the others. Rye wins out over wheat because it constitutes the basic food in the rural areas, and often even of the [urban] lower bourgeoisie. If wine, on the contrary, did not follow the pattern of cereals, it is because the conditions of its production are different, because its abundance is more variable, and because here substitution does not apply.

The relative stagnation of manufactured products indicates that industrial activity was still weak. Iron holds last place, while the price of steel is today one of the most sensitive indications of a *conjuncture*. Wood, it is true, increases by enormous proportions, but the weak position of industry is reflected clearly in this. It lacked a cheap fuel, for it had ruined the forests but did not yet make use of coal.

The social consequences are of no less importance. The crisis in the vineyards, in the last years of the Old Regime, has until now never received the attention that is deserves. Many vines had been planted in the eighteenth century. Wine was sold at a loss from 1770 to 1775, and especially from 1780 to 1785; on the eve of the Revolution prices had recovered, though the increase, in comparison with the years 1726–1741, did not go beyond 13 per cent, while it was at least 66 per cent for meat. Winegrowers, who were very numerous and many of whom were small producers, were taken unawares and left totally unprovided for by the scarcity of 1788–1789.

But cereals must also claim our attention. Their prices increased the most. The prices of the other foods and manufactured products, used by those in comfortable circumstances much more than by the poor, increased the least. Thus the long-term increase affects the Frenchman in inverse proportion to his wealth. In addition, we must note that, with the exception of barley, which is not very desirable for use in bread, the poorer the type of cereal, the more the price increases. Rye, buckwheat, and corn increase more than wheat, oats more than all the others; so that the lower the standard of living, the heavier the burden.

A reservation of some importance still seems necessary in regard to the nourishment of workers and artisans in the cities. There the price of bread was controlled, and I have shown that, in the future district of Bergues, especially at Bourbourg, in times of high prices the municipal administration increased the price of bread for the rich considerably more than for the poor. The study of the price of bread should therefore come to complete the information supplied by Labrousse. But the corrective which it could bring would concern only the urban population and would make no modifications in his conclusions concerning the enormous proletariat of the rural areas.

Now let us bring in the cyclical variations. From cycle to cycle (1726 to 1741, 1742 to 1757, 1758 to 1770, 1771 to 1789), their extent grows and the maximums go increasingly beyond the index of the long-term increase. In 1789, the cyclical maximum brought the increase of wheat to 127 per cent (the long-term index stood at 66 per cent) in comparison with the basic price of the cycle 1726–1741, that of rye to 136 per cent, and that of barley even higher. The sharpness of the cyclical increases is especially intensified in regard to buckwheat, whose production is very irregular and which is very sought-after during periods of scarcity because it provides almost as much flour as rye. Corn, even more economical, also varies much more than wheat and rye. However, the abruptness of the cyclical movement only reaches its peak with wine, because of disconcerting failures in the vineyard. The index of 1781–1789 being 100, that of 1780 is 150; that of 1785 is 55; that of 1789 is 100. Fodder, in this respect, closely follows the pattern of wine. In contrast, there is only a moderate variation for suet and wood, a slight one for meat, and an even smaller one for textiles and fabrics; again, iron is in last place.

We must still superimpose the seasonal variations upon the long-term and cyclical fluctuations. For cereals, they are almost imperceptible in time of abundance, but become enormous during bad years. The price of a commodity can then increase from 50 to 100 per cent, and even more, between autumn and the following summer. In 1789, the seasonal maximum (which coincides with the first two weeks of July) brought the increase for wheat to 150 per cent as compared with the basic price of 1726 and 1741, and that of rye to 165 per cent. Buckwheat and corn, in the same situation, were once again the most affected; fodder, meat, and wine were only slightly so; manufactured products were not affected at all.

The cyclical and seasonal upsurges therefore act in the same direction as the long-term increase. Quantitatively, they increase excessively the extent of the long-term movement, especially the maxima. Qualitatively, they affect cereals, aggravating the instability of their prices in a frightening manner and increasing in the same proportion the margin of insecurity for the popular classes. Although today the *conjuncture* is seen chiefly in the prices of the major manufactured products, while the cost of living changes only slightly, at least when the currency is stable, owing to the always possible expedient of importation, the eighteenth century was subject to the inverse situation.

As we have previously mentioned, the inequalities in the increase affected the various classes of the population in different ways, according to the organization of their budget. With cereals increasing more than all the rest, it is evident that in the eighteenth century the common people were the most hard-hit. But can we study the question even more closely and construct an index of the cost of living for the common people? For that, we realize, the proportion of the various categories of expenditures in the worker's budget must be determined approximately. Labrousse has tried to do this: he allocates half the income for bread (this is a minimum); 16 per cent for vegetables, bacon, and wine; 15 per cent for clothing; 5 per cent for heating; 1 per cent for light. In applying his long-term indices to the price of each of these different articles, he concludes that, when compared with the basic period of 1726–1741, the cost of living during the cycle 1771–1789 had increased by 45 per cent and, during the years 1785–1789, by 62 per cent. Now, here again the seasonal variations introduce the disastrous effect of their maxima. On the eve of 1789, the share of bread in a worker's budget was already at 58 per cent as a result of the general increase; in 1789, it climbed to 88 per cent, which left only 12 per cent of the income for the other expenditures.

In this rapid survey we can see to what degree Simiand's analysis has been enriched and completed. But, since the price increase thus treats those in easy circumstances kindly and overburdens the poor, it is time for the historian to investigate whether the movement of incomes righted the imbalance or whether, to the contrary, it aggravated it even more.

❧§§❧

The governmental inquiry of 1777 and the data supplied by the price controls of 1793 concerning the situation in 1790 show an increase in salaries of 16 per cent during these last years of the Ancien Régime. The local series drawn up by Labrousse gives 17 per cent between the basic period of 1726–1741 and that of 1771–1789. In more than half the cases, it does not reach 11 per cent. As compared with the years 1785–1789, the increase is 22 per cent but in all except three généralités it does not go beyond 26 per cent. The respective figures for construction are 18 and 24; for agricultural day labor, 12 and 16; textiles seem to have remained in the middle. The long-term increase was thus very slight; for prices, the percentages are 48 and 65. Simiand's analysis is proven: salaries followed prices but without catching up, but the margin is greater than in the nineteenth century. But the cyclical and seasonal variations in salaries aggravate the discrepancy since they are in the inverse direction of prices. In fact it was universally recognized in the eighteenth century that excessively high prices provoke unemployment: an insufficient harvest reduces the need for manpower; the general rise in prices also forces the agricultural exploiter to reduce the number of his personnel. On the other hand, it forces the peasant family which works its land without employing salaried workers to seek extra money for itself by working for others. The agricultural crisis unleashes an industrial crisis, because when prices rise the excessive share of bread in the worker's budget reduces the number of other purchases made by the common people. We may ask, however, if in a normal year the stagnation or the minimal increase in salaries does not, to the contrary, result in a decrease in the number of working hours or in unemployment, so that the hourly salary or the annual income would have increased more noticeably than the daily wage. But nothing indicates that the length of the working day had been cut; nor does anything show that unemployment wreaked less havoc. The wool and linen industries scarcely developed at all and even declined during the last years of the Old Regime; cotton made progress, but this involved the introduction of machines; construction prospered and land was cleared but, as I have indicated for the future department of the Nord, the population appears to increase much more quickly than job openings. If cultivators often complained of a lack of manpower, it is because industry was contending with them for workers and was already preferred by day laborers. These workers' change of residence does not necessarily result in an absolute decrease in unemployment.

Comparing the increase in the nominal salary with that of the cost of living, we therefore see that the real salary decreases rather than increases. Labrousse estimates that, from 1726–1741 to 1785–1789, the difference is less than one fourth. If we take into account the cyclical and seasonal price maximums, it rises to more than half. The eventuality which has been envisaged thus is found to have taken place for the A Phase of the eighteenth century: the increase in the nominal salary which characterizes this phase, as Simiand's analysis asserted, nevertheless corresponds to a decrease in the real salary; and since the standard of living in this period required that the reduction be chiefly on food supplies, Phase A brings about an augmentation of poverty for the working classes. To the historians, who are chiefly interested in economic fluctuations in terms of their social and political consequences, Simiand's theory is therefore only acceptable if it is completed by observations of the movements of the real salary. As we move on into the nineteenth century, the equilibrium in the worker's budget changes and the fluctuations in the prices of food supplies lessen. It is therefore possible that the real salary modifies its curve to come closer to the nominal salary, even to the point of varying in the same direction as it does. But this remains to be seen and, in any case, when we go beyond the eighteenth century, everything leads us to believe that, to the contrary, it is Labrousse's observations which will be confirmed.

We know how economists define ground rent: the surplus income, the windfall, which the price increase procures for the property holder and the cultivator of the soil, without his having increased either his investment or his efforts. We must therefore make a distinction between the augmentation in income that can result from an increase in productivity—that is to say of the yield of an agrarian unit, as a result of the introduction of supplementary fertilizers, of new cultivation, of perfected equipment, or of drainage or irrigation work—or in the population, through the drying-up and clearing of land, because, in both these cases, the improvement is the return for capital invested or for exceptional work done. When we succeed in estimating the income on land, we do not therefore arrive at the same time at an evaluation of the *rente*. In the eighteenth century, there does not appear to have been much growth in productivity and in production, and the leases, especially for the great estates, do not mention an increase in the amount of land under cultivation. However, there is some uncertainty about this. It is true, as Labrousse rightly observes, that since the rich farmer was capable of bargaining about the rate of rent to be paid for a farm, we can agree that in the case of the leases under consideration, the increase upon which the *rente* depends must have been curbed, which would compensate for the error attached to the possible development of productivity and production. But we must again add that sales for exportation and the decrease in the real salary could have acted in a contrary manner, and we must take into account the attractiveness of land in a basically agricultural society where the population was increasing, while the working of even a small plot, no matter how mediocre, seemed the only means by which the peasant could acquire relative security. In short, it seems to me problematic that Labrousse has in fact arrived at the *rente* in its theoretical form. We would thus have to deduct a few points from his estimates. But the increase is such that his conclusions would not change their meaning. The study naturally requires that we make a distinction between farm rents in money and income on land collected in kind.

As far as the first of these is concerned, the leases used by Labrousse indicate an increase of 82 per cent between the period 1730 and 1739 and the period 1770 to 1790; of 98 per cent if we compare them with the years 1786 to 1790. After a certain delay, the increase in the *rente* follows the price increase, but its extent is much greater, since cereals over a long period only show corresponding increases of 56 and 63 per cent. In Phase A, according to Simiand, profits increase more than the nominal salary. This assertion is thus confirmed, but only, it is true, as far as land profits are concerned. We see to what point, since the nominal salary only increases by 17 per cent.

Farm rents paid in kind are still more profitable for the landowner. To the long-term increase is added, since he can sell at the most favorable moment, the advantage of cyclical and seasonal maximums. For example, Labrousse calculates that from 1763 to 1770, with a difference of 128 per cent for rye between the lowest annual price and the maximum of the cycle, the corresponding increase for the *rente* was 195 per cent, from the lowest price of 1763 to the average price of the last quarter of 1770. Markedly different, however, is the case of the landowners who turn over their land to sharecroppers. Their income varies with the harvest (it is most often a half) and, in addition, the seed for sowing—an amount which does not vary—and also the *dîme* and the *champart* [field rent in kind to the lord] are set aside before the crop is divided up. In this way, in the event of high prices, that is to say of a poor harvest, the price increase is to a large degree or entirely compensated for by the decrease in the quantity. Now, sharecropping was prevalent in two-thirds or three-fourths of France. Labrousse's observations on the *rente* paid in kind would therefore be much less forceful if we did not know that to his share of the produce the landowner frequently added a payment in money, *corvées*, and small fees of all sorts, which have not been taken into account here. The problem of the *rente* in the case of sharecropping would merit being re-examined and studied more closely.

To summarize, the *rente* on land would decrease at one rate or another depending on whether it was paid—in descending order—in kind, in money, or was determined by sharecropping. As a result regional inquiries which would inform us about the respective percentage for each of these types of tenure would be most valuable. In addition, all research on the division of property and of the exploitation of land will greatly contribute to clarifying the social influence of the increase in the *rente* on land. From now on we know, however, that the greater share of the land rented out, and especially rented farms, belonged to the privileged classes, priests, nobles, and bourgeois exempt from the *taille*.

The Old Regime knew another form of land profits, which was solely to the advantage of these same privileged classes. It was that which resulted from the previous deduction of the *dîme* and of the feudal or land dues paid in kind. As in the case of sharecropping, this deduction varied with the harvest; but much less so because it was calculated on the total harvest, without deduction of the seed for sowing. Labrousse has made a detailed study of the value of this income in correlation with the inverse variation of productivity and prices, using the physiocrats' estimates as a base. In estimating the *dîme* as one-thirteenth, he concludes, for example, that in an abundant year it would bring in 6 livres 67 per *arpent* and would increase as the harvest decreased until it reached 7 livres, 10 sols in a bad year. Consequently, the feudal dues in kind—like the farm rent paid in kind, and also like farm rents paid in money since the latter, being fixed, became more oppressive as the abundance of the harvest decreased—increased as production decreased. For the *rentier*, a year of scarcity was one of abundance. Between the privileged classes, especially the feudal lords, who were almost the only ones to profit, on the one hand, and the agriculturalists on the other, the conflict was thus obvious and brutal.

We must, however, ask if this conflict was not mitigated by the profit which the agriculturalist could also make by selling his food products. But his case was not the same because the costs of cultivation were paid by him. Now at least a part of these costs was fixed: seed and food for the personnel. In bad years, it reduced the amount at one's disposal to almost nothing, so that the price increases did not bring profits to the agriculturalist or left him with a deficit. The conflict therefore remains and the less fertile the soil, the more marked it becomes, since the land then requires more seed. Only the rich farmer, paying his day laborers in money, is relatively on a level with the feudal lord. Here we can see one of the issues that puts him into opposition to the mass of peasants. Yet the rich farmer would still profit considerably from the disappearance of the *dîme* and the *champart*; this is why he would one day side with the peasantry against the feudal lords.

The question can obviously be approached from still another angle. The *rentier* and the agriculturalist only profit from the price increase if they have something to sell. If they consume their income paid in kind, the increase makes little difference to them. If they do not collect enough to be self-sufficient and must buy, the increase affects them as it does the nonharvester. We can see immediately that the *décimateur* and the feudal *rentier*, as well as the noncultivating landowner who in the majority of cases is in one of these two categories, fit into the first category. On this point, the big farmer has the same interests as they, and that is why he demands along with them the freedom of the grain trade, including the right to export. On the contrary, the vast majority of the peasants are buyers. At best the most fortunate among them manage to be self-sufficient. Here we see how right I have been in insisting upon the necessity, when studying the distribution of property and of its exploitation, of determining approximately what amount of land, in the region under consideration, the cultivator needed in order to live independently. The conflict between the feudal lord and the rest of the nation, the consumer in the cities being in a worse situation than the peasant who must buy, is seen here even more clearly.

There is not the least contradiction between the feudal institutions and the long-term movement of prices, of salaries, and of the *rente*. For the monarchy, it was of more immediate interest. All other things being equal, public expenditures should increase along with prices, while the yield from taxes upon consumption—which should have increased along with the increase of prices and the growth of the population—was to the contrary checked by the inadequacy of the nominal salary and by the decrease in the real salary. Therefore, indirect taxes were increased as the buying power of the popular masses continued to decline. It was a vicious circle, and we can imagine how it eventually appeared impossible to fill the deficit through indirect taxes. Therefore, we can much better understand the fierce hatred toward them evidenced in the *cahiers*, their suppression in practice at the time of the municipal revolution and of the agrarian revolts of 1789, and the Convention's realization that it would be absolutely impossible to re-establish their collection. The royal budget should have been buoyed up financially by direct taxes since the price increases augmented incomes and gave those living upon the income from their land enormous profits. But these *rentiers* were chiefly of the privileged classes, did not pay the *taille*, and were only scarcely affected, or not affected at all, by the *capitation* and the *vingtièmes*. The fiscal problem was therefore insoluble, and the State could no longer govern if the aristocracy was not made subject to the common law. We understand why it put up a resistance, for it would not only have had to pay its share, but probably to increase it in order to liquidate the arrears. We also understand, even better than before, how its resistance unleashed the Revolution.

THE REVOLUTION AND THE PRICE MOVEMENT

The origins of the Revolution involve several problems. It was the bourgeoisie who took control of it and who gave it juridical form, inspired by its own ideology, which agreed with its own interests. The problem—which Jaurès stated precisely and for which he had sketched a solution—is to know how the bourgeoisie finally came to understand, thanks to the progress of the capitalist economy, that the feudal institutions constituted an obstacle to capitalism's progress which it was absolutely necessary to eliminate; and how it simultaneously acquired the strength, the knowledge, the talent, and the means to grab power and keep it. The study, in Phase A, of *profit*, the equivalent of the *rente* for a merchant, industrialist, or financier, would obviously cast a new light upon these questions. Labrousse has not touched upon this problem, and though we must point out this omission, we surely have no right to reproach him for it.

Second, the revolt of the aristocracy gave the signal for the Revolution. Chérest, and later Sagnac, had already shown this. Mathiez then very penetratingly elaborated upon this important idea. Labrousse, in his analysis of the movements of prices, salaries, and *rentes*, proved that the fiscal problem facing the royalty was insoluble unless the aristocracy was made subject to the common law, and that the aristocrats, in refusing to do so, ruined the State of the Old Regime.

But the bourgeoisie only triumphed through the help of the popular masses. Why did they begin to move? The counter-revolutionaries, from the very first, denied that the masses had a reason to complain seriously and blamed their uprisings upon the criminal instincts of the populace (this is the thesis whose success was assured by Taine) and to the seditious schemings of the bourgeoisie (this is the plot thesis, so dear to Barruel, which was revived by Cochin). Historians favoring the Revolution have usually agreed that the popular classes had the same interests as the bourgeoisie; at the most they add that scarcity and unemployment helped to mobilize them. I have tried, for my part, to show that hunger played a more important role than had been thought, and I am pleased to observe that Labrousse stresses, in concluding, that the insurrection of July 14 coincides, as I once observed, with the culminating point of price increases during the eighteenth century. But his fine work, along with Simiand's, has singularly expanded the scientific basis for this observation. It has ceased to be purely contingent and appears now as the result of the general characteristics of Phase A, elucidated by Simiand but given nuances and deepened by the examination of the real salary, related to the cyclical and seasonal movement, and explained by the historical traits of the economy of the time. As far as the peasants are concerned, I have tried to show that the feudal institution and the fiscal regime were in contradiction with the extension of agricultural progress and with the vital necessities that the population increase was imposing upon the rural areas. Labrousse has also provided his explanation with a scientific base, with which Simiand would have agreed, through the analysis of the movements of the *rente* and salaries. But I have added that the majority of peasants, though associated with the bourgeoisie against the feudal nobility, nonetheless had their own interests which were in conflict with the progress of capitalism, that they were hostile to commercial liberty, to the enclosure and division of communal lands, and even to the freedom of culture. Labrousse, without stressing this theme, has provided new arguments for it. In as much as he was a land-owner, the bourgeois was in this respect a supporter of feudalism, and revolutionary legislation confirmed and brought to term the efforts which the monarchy in the eighteenth century, under the pressure of economists and of the feudal nobility, had developed to promote the application of capitalism to agriculture. Even more, the bourgeoisie acted in this way, when it was put into possession of a great portion of the national lands. Through his study of the movements in the *rente*, Labrousse has rationally explained the antagonism which was subsequently to be seen, during the Revolution, between the crowds of peasants and the bourgeoisie, and the disappointment that did its share to extinguish revolutionary enthusiasm.

He has also clarified in a very original manner the fiscal difficulties of the Revolution. We hope that grievances will no longer be held against the Constituent Assembly for having sacrificed the taxes upon consumption. But Labrousse has also clearly shown how the direct tax, or, more exactly, the tax upon land—which was the Treasury's principal resource since the bourgeoisie refused to establish a suitable global tax upon personal income—was difficult to establish and collect. Called upon to provide the greatest part of the receipts, such a tax had to be heavy and relatively stable. Yet economic conditions affected the cyclical and seasonal variations to an enormous degree, so that, in bad years, the burden of the land-tax became unbearable. This difficulty was not to be eliminated until under the Empire, through the dimunition of the land-tax; but if it was possible to grant this abatement, it was only upon condition of re-establishing taxes upon consumption. And why did they once again become tolerable? Because the rate undoubtedly remained moderate, but also because after 1790 salaries, accelerating their increase, became—on the whole and, taking into account periods of unlimited inflation—kept in step with the increase in prices or even went beyond it, so that the real salary improved and the tax upon consumption once again became productive without being excessive. This is one of Labrousse's most penetrating and far-reaching observations. Since Simiand established the link between prices and salaries by means of psychological relationships, he would undoubtedly not contradict this explanation. However, we must certainly note that if salaries were able to catch up with and pass prices, it is thanks to an *event*, to the Revolution which, by momentarily liberating the popular classes from the control of the State and even, during the period of the Revolutionary Government, by putting this government on their side, permitted them to raise their *social standing*. In any case, the improvement in the living standards of the common people, which was observed by the prefects of the Consulate, is thus explained, and I admit that the pessimistic conclusions which I had made concerning the influence of the Revolution in this respect are now much less so. Nevertheless, we still know so few things about the movements of prices, the *rente*, and salaries during the Revolution, that we can easily see that an inquiry, continued along with the lines of Simiand's and Labrousse's, remains indispensable and offers a vast field of work to local researchers.

❧❀❧

Thus the origins of the Revolution having been attributed, in part, to these movements, it still remains necessary, as in Simiand's study, to explain them. In the case of the cyclical and seasonal fluctuations and, consequently, of the crises, the causes must be laid to the general conditions of production and to the state of communications. An agricultural economy that was still backward and the impossibility of transporting heavy and cumbersome merchandise such as grain explain why each region still lived off itself and why the size of the harvest consequently decided the cost of living. Industry, made up almost entirely of artisans and exporting only very little, was subordinated to internal consumption and was therefore closely dependent upon agricultural fluctuations. Thus the industrial crises were sparked by poor harvests. The one which followed the trade agreement of 1786 should be re-examined. It is usually blamed upon English competition, and undoubtedly the effects of this competition were not negligible. But if such competition had been lacking, the crisis would have broken out anyway after the disastrous harvest of 1788.

But the cyclical variations would not have been enough. It was the long-term increase—and its unusual duration—which in the last analysis provides the key for the entire economic movement, to which the Revolution, in part, owes its origins. And what caused it? Here Simiand once more becomes our guide. According to him, it comes from the multiplication of monetary resources. According to Soetbeer, between 1661 and 1680 the world had produced 337,000 kg of silver and 9260 of gold; from 1681 to

1700, the results had not been much higher: 341,900 kg of silver and 10,765 kg of gold. At the beginning of the eighteenth century, the increase becomes clear: 335,000 and 12,820 kg from 1701 to 1720. Between 1721 and 1740 it becomes really noticeable: 431,200 and 19,080 kg. The acceleration does not continue beyond this date for gold, but for silver, which formed the principal medium of exchange, it continues. From 1741 to 1760, there were 533,145 kg; from 1761 to 1780, there were 652,740 kg; from 1781 to 1800, there were 879,060. From period to period, the increase is therefore 3700 kg (1701–1720), 75,600 kg (1721–1740), 101,945 kg (1741–1760), 119,130 kg (1761–1780), 226,320 kg (1781–1800). The coefficients are: 1.08 per cent, 21.26 per cent, 23.64 per cent, 22.34 per cent, and 34.67 per cent.

The relative slowing down, between 1761 and 1780, would explain why the long-term increase abated after 1758 only to resume its growth after 1780. The increase in mining production is due chiefly to Mexico, where new veins were opened: 2,204,000 kg of silver between 1680 and 1700, the production reached 4,615,000 kg between 1721 and 1740, and 11,249,000 between 1771 and 1800. Alexander von Humboldt, in his *Voyage to the Equinoctial Regions of the New Continent* provided abundant information on this point.

But Simiand was only referring to precious metals, and the problem is to learn to what degree the appearance of paper currency and the multiplication of the means of payment through banks contributed to the inflation. This is a study that remains to be done in its entirety. The banknote dates from 1694. The end of the reign of Louis XIV was marked by an extensive use of paper money that was crowned by Law's experiment. After that, France used no more banknotes until the establishment of the *Caisse d'Escompte* in 1776, but the monarchy continued to resort to the same expedients as Louis XIV. Outside France, during the second half of the century, Austria, Russia, Sweden, and Spain issued paper money. In England, commercial paper came into common use; the clearing house was established. The continent was much less advanced, but commercial paper slowly made progress there.

Finally, we might wonder, along with Simiand, whether this growth of monetary resources had the contingent and irrational nature which disturbed him, and whether the taking of the Bastille, having to a certain degree been prepared deep in the mines of Mexico, does not owe even more to chance than we would be inclined to believe. Upon reflection, we conclude that the prosperity of the mines of the New World must come from the needs of the Spanish State and from the growing value of precious metals at the end of the seventeenth century, while the development of paper currency and of commercial means of payment is the result of the policies of the monarchies and of the progress of the European economy. Thus this monetary inflation will ultimately find its explanation in the evolution of the society of the Old World which, through the circuitous road of prices, contributed to unleashing the Revolution.

THE ORIGINS
OF THE REVOLUTION
IN BRITTANY (1788-1789)

৶ৄ By Jean Egret

Augustin Cochin credits the philosophy of the Enlightenment with the desperate resistance with which the Breton aristocracy opposed the revolutionary edicts conceived by Loménie de Brienne and Lamoignon, and which the Parlement of Rennes, like the other parliaments of France, registered under military duress on May 10, 1788.

In reality, the Breton nobles were not visibly the dupes of any subversive idea. They were simply obeying a reflex of self-preservation. Against precise threats, they defended with all their strength their seignorial courts, their parliament, and the liberties of their province, which were above all their liberties.

Without suppressing seignorial tribunals, the new *ordonnance* concerning the administration of justice dealt them a blow which might become mortal, by authorizing, in civil suits, "each of the parties to immediately accuse the other before the tribunals of royal justice." On the eve of the Revolution there were, in Brittany, 2500 seignorial jurisdictions which sometimes interposed between the plaintiffs and the first royal tribunal two, three, and sometimes as many as five degrees of seignorial jurisdiction. A

136

great number of jurists desired the suppression of these parasitic organs. Intendant Bertrand de Moleville had previously prepared a plan for a decisive simplification. But he knew how attached the Breton seigneurs were to an institution which was the principal guarantee of the income from their seignorial rights, and he was certain that they "would see in these reforms a debasement of their seignories and a serious blow dealt to their property."

The same *règlement* which attacked seignorial justice almost annihilated the judiciary activity of the Parlement of Rennes. It created, in Brittany —at Rennes, Nantes, and Quimper—under the name of *grands bailliages*, three rival courts of appeal which would leave the Parlement, in addition to the rare cases concerning the domain, the duchy-peerages, and the admiralties, only those civil suits whose value exceeded 20,000 livres, and those criminal cases concerning the privileged classes. The decrease in activity naturally resulted in a reduction in the number of offices, provided for in a special edict. Now, this fallen parliament—the best *constituted* one in France—recruited its members solely among the nobility. If we believe an unindulgent but well-informed observer, the Breton nobility could only congratulate itself about this sovereign court's partiality for noblemen and seigneurs. "What!" another ministerial propagandist had a nobleman say, "they would destroy the authority of the Parlement and we, who are attached to that company, will let them do it! Thirty-odd parliamentary families would be deprived of their positions and we would sit by and watch that attack upon property without opposing it with all our might?"

No less hateful for the aristocracy was one of the edicts of May which established a plenary court, located in the French capital, and qualified to register all general laws, in the place of the provincial parliaments. It was the expression of a visible desire for national unification. The judiciary organization of Brittany was already being overthrown without consulting the Estates. Now, every blow to the authority of the Estates first injured the nobility, which enjoyed an "absolute preponderance" in the assembly. All noblemen over twenty-five years of age had the right to sit in the Estates of Brittany, and the number present rarely went below 500. Active and noisy, they had no trouble intimidating and winning over the Order of the clergy—recruited solely among the bishops, the canons, and the abbots— and the Third Estate, represented uniquely by the mayors of forty-two privileged cities. And last, the *procureurs-généraux syndics* of the Estates, guardians of the liberties of the province, were obligatorily noblemen.

Nothing was more real than the bitterness with which the Breton nobility gave the signal for the struggle against the May edicts and supported its main efforts. The essentially noble character of the revolt was cleverly pointed out by a defender of the edicts: "Is Brittany inhabited only by noblemen? Who would not ask this question, seeing that it is a matter of the so-called violation of the privileges of an entire province, and since only noblemen are protesting?"

⋙⋘

The aristocratic Parlement of Brittany was undoubtedly the one which put up the most stubborn resistance to the laws which were dealing such a hard blow to the magistracy. It multiplied its decrees: Before May 10, to denounce the coup it anticipated; after May 10, to declare nul the registration of the new laws and to forbid their application. Finally, *lettres de cachet* exiling the magistrates to their own estates having been distributed during the night of June 1 and 2, forty-eight members of the Parlement met again on June 3, and nineteen on June 6, to renew their anathemas. They did not, however, go so far as to issue decrees of arrest against the Commandant and the Intendant, as a more resolute minority had demanded.

This resistance was naturally supported by the protests of the aides of the judiciary—lawyers, *procureurs, huissiers*—living in the shadow of the court and by those of the municipality of Rennes, spokesmen for all the inhabitants, especially the artisans and merchants, "whose life [depended] upon the activity of the law courts and upon the comfortable existence of all the citizens."

The law clerks, the law students, and the lackeys and sedan-chair porters of noblemen and magistrates formed tumultuous and more or less spontaneous assemblies: on May 10, in front of the *palais de justice* which was laid siege to by the band; on June 2, in front of the Hotel de Cuillé, where the members of *Parlement* had entrenched themselves as a result of the *lettres de cachet*. These disorganized scuffles, mildly repressed by the Comte de Thiard, Commandant of the Province, who had to reckon with the defection of a part of his officers, supporters of the noble revolt, provoked the inglorious flight of Intendant Bertrand de Moleville. The riots only stopped when a camp of 8000 men under the command of Maréchal de Stainville was established at Rennes on July 30.

⋙⋘

The noble Order, closely linked to the Parlement, was on its own preparing a solemn petition to be presented to the Sovereign. Two assemblies bringing together hundreds of noblemen, one held at Saint-Brieuc on June 13–14, the other at Vannes on June 19–20 each named six deputies. The "twelve" carried the protestations of the aristocracy to Versailles. The King refused to receive the representatives of these illegal assemblies. At a loss, during the afternoon of July 12 they summoned all the Breton gentlemen or landowners residing in Paris, for consultations at the Hôtel d'Espagne, on the rue de Richelieu. But during the night of July 14–15, the "twelve" were arrested and taken to the Bastille, while the court nobles who had gone to their meeting—the Duc de Praslin, the Duc de Chabat, the Marquis de La Fayette, the Marquis de Sérent, and the Comte de Boisgelin—were deprived of royal favors.

The arrest of the twelve gentlemen resulted in a clandestine meeting of the *Parlement* of Rennes at the Château du Pargo, near Vannes, on July 24, and the dispatching to Versailles of a deputation of twelve members bearing remonstrances. But the magistrates were arrested at Houdan, fifteen leagues from Paris, by express order of the King; and despite the efforts of the Marquis de Caradeuc, the *procureur-général*, son of the illustrious Lachalotais, the Breton parliamentarians prudently beat a retreat.

It was not until July 30 that Louis XVI consented to receive eighteen members of the three Orders of Brittany belonging to the Commissions sitting at Rennes. He promised them a meeting of their Estates in the near future. "It is through them that the wishes of the province should reach me, I will listen to their remonstrances, I will be regardful of them to the degree they merit it. . . ."

❧⟨§⟩☙

However, from the middle of July, the Breton nobility, obviously inspired by the example of the Dauphiné, endeavored to win over the clergy and the Third Estate to the revolt of the nobility. To this end it organized active propaganda in all the Breton dioceses.

In Brittany, as in Languedoc, the diocese had remained an administrative unit. In the capital of the diocese of Rennes sat a *Commission intermédiare des États* or *Grand Bureau*. Under its direction in each of the eight other dioceses, were commissions of nine members (three from each order) called *bureaux diocésains*. The *Commission intermédiaire* and the *bureaux diocésains* took over the major provincial services (collection of the *impôts abonnés* and public works). During July, within the shadow of each *bureau diocésain*, a *Comité de correspondance de la noblesse* was installed, which received its instructions from the Committee in Rennes and worked within its jurisdiction to promote the insurrection of all the orders.

The aim was to have two deputies from each of the three orders selected in each diocese. The King would consider their combined membership an imposing and, at last, an authentic delegation from the province of Brittany, voicing its opposition to the edicts of May.

It was not difficult to form a new deputation from the nobility, all of whose members, on their guard since the beginning of the crisis, were strong supporters of the twelve prisoners of the Bastille. As for the clergy, although the bishops balked, the chapters of the nine Breton cathedrals docilely chose the requested delegates. But it was much more difficult to select a deputation for the Third Estate.

Forty-two cities were entitled to represent the Third Estate in the Estates of the province. These cities were naturally invited—within the framework of each diocese—to take part in the full deputation. They were not always in a great hurry to do so. Although the edicts of May unanimously horrified the nobility, bourgeois opinion was more nuanced. The creation in Brittany of three large *bailliages* and of fifteen presidials promised considerable promotions to all the subordinate judges of the province and rather considerable profits to the cities which would serve as seats for these tribunals. Through his subdelegates, Intendant Bertrand de Moleville, after having fled Rennes on July 9, attempted to maintain within the Third Estate a frame of mind favorable to ministerial undertakings. A more or less bitter struggle pitted the *parlementarians* against the *royalists* in each city. All the details are not known, but the results are significant.

In only two dioceses—Saint-Brieuc and Saint Malo—every city adhered to the movement, naming deputies. In five dioceses, Rennes, Vannes, Nantes, Dol, and Saint-Pol-de-Léon, the municipalities were content to grant, usually without much enthusiasm, a more or less vague power-of-attorney to the delegates selected uniquely by the capital city of the diocese. Last, in two dioceses, Quimper and Tréguier, the capital itself chose no one.

We must give up the conventional image of an entire province aroused during the summer of 1788 by a "storm of anger." In fact, the full deputation of fifty-three members from the three Orders was formed rather laboriously at Rennes during the first days of August. Reaching Paris on August 11, it was not permitted until August 31 to present to the King a memorandum whose tone and contents no longer suited the circumstances—it was five days after the disgrace of the Archbishop of Sens, fourteen days after that of the Keeper of the Seals Lamoignon.

On October 11, the Parlement of Rennes, its functions re-established, registered the Royal Declaration of September 23. By its abandonment of the judicial reform, it sanctioned the victory of aristocratic resistance. But by announcing the coming meeting of the Estates General without giving a specific program, it opened the way—in Brittany and in all of France—to the bourgeois Revolution.

II

Augustin Cochin shows that the Breton nobility from October on was eliminated from the leadership of that "machine," the work of the *sociétés de pensée*, which was destroying the Ancien Régime. The bourgeoisie, after having docilely followed the aristocracy's lead, turned against it. After having helped it undermine the King's authority, they attacked the privileges of the nobility. This was a requirement of the "progress of the enlightenment." The split of October is only the first of the *purifications*: "and the same fate awaited the victors and, after them, all the social teams and all the philosophical programs from Épremesnil to Danton."

We have seen how the revolt of the nobility was really not very "philosophical." A careful observation of facts forces us to realize the equally down-to-earth nature of the bourgeois uprising.

The Third Estate was very imperfectly represented in the Estates of Brittany by a deputation "presided over by a nobleman and made up of nobles and ennobled persons or officers, or agents of the nobility." After 1782, Lanjuinais, a young professor in the Faculty of Law in Rennes and *avocat-conseil* of the Estates, had proposed a plan for reform. While waiting—bound spokesmen for the forty-two cities they represented—the deputies of the Third Estate protested against the unjust distribution of the *capitation* and against allowing the common debt paid under the name of *fouages extraordinaires* to fall solely upon land owned by commoners. In August 1788 the lawyers of the Parlement had had, it is true, an indictment printed against the laws of Brienne and Lamoignon. But in it they had stressed above all the particular grievances of the Third Estate, which was not represented in the *Cour plénière* and which was subject, in criminal matters, to the *grands bailliages*, and not to the parliaments, which were reserved for the privileged classes. The lawyers even dared to approve the suppression of seignorial justice, a measure greatly feared by the aristocracy. Apparently, the Breton bourgeoisie did not wait for the split of October to become aware of its own interests and of the serious discord already troubling this unexpected alliance formed against the May edicts. Outside Rennes proper, this alliance was only an illusion.

We can imagine the impression made upon this expectant bourgeoisie by the appeal of the inhabitants of the Dauphiné, on July 21 at Vizille, demanding a new constitution for their Estates and obtaining from the King on August 2 the calling of a deliberative assembly of the three Orders charged with drawing up this constitution, which would grant the Third Estate its legitimate place. Such compliance by the government with bourgeois demands was enough to reassure the most timid. Had they not been encouraged to rise up against the aristocracy by the Intendant and his subdelegates, who a short time before had been mistreated by the revolt of the nobility, and who desired revenge? Above all, how could they measure the unpredictable repercussions of anti-aristocratic broadsides, published with the aid of the provincial government? An oral tradition claims that the Angevin Volney, a civil servant on leave whose establishment at Rennes in 1788 remains a mystery, was a government agent. His periodical pamphlet *La sentinelle du peuple* incensed the Breton bourgeoisie, without doubt going far beyond the hopes of the ministers.

Two texts, which were disseminated in large numbers upon the announcement of the coming meeting of the provincial Estates, provided this bourgeoisie with the theme for its insurrection: the decision made on October 20 by the general assembly of Rennes, and the petition addressed on November 4 by some of the notables of Nantes to the municipal officers of that city.

Those deliberating at Rennes authorized their deputies to the Estates to demand a more equitable distribution of the *capitation* and the *fouages extraordinaires*, and the replacement of the *corvée en nature* by a tax on the three Orders. There should, in addition, be a reform of the provincial Estates introducing deputies from the rural areas into the representation of the Third Estate, excluding from this representation the nobles and seignorial agents, and making room within the Order of the clergy for the parish priests. More radical, and closer to the new constitution for the

Dauphiné, the petition of the notables of Nantes—in addition to the reforms demanded by the city of Rennes—insisted upon a representation of the Third Estate equal to those of the clergy and the nobility combined, and consequently the vote by head and the abandonment by the nobility of its traditional right to sit as a body in the Estates. Finally, the men from Nantes called upon the Third Estate to refuse all participation in the coming provincial deliberations, organized according to traditional patterns, if the demands of the Third Order were not accepted beforehand by the two others.

The instructions given by the city of Rennes to its deputies foresaw a moderate reform respecting the basic organization of the Breton constitution: the separation of the Orders. But the committee at Nantes intended to overthrow the existing institutions, to bring together the three Orders, and to permanently destroy the preponderance of the nobility in the Estates. The former text provided a basis for discussion; the latter one was an ultimatum announcing a test of strength. The conciliatory program came from a parliamentary city where, willingly or unwillingly, the aristocracy and the lawyers had struggled side by side in the recent crisis, and where the bitterness of the grievances was tempered by habitual deference and by a traditional dependence. The revolutionary program was the work of a clique dominated by the business-oriented bourgeoisie of a great merchant port, independent and audacious, and led by a rich new nobleman, Jacques Cottin.

At the beginning of November 1788, nothing was less sure than the victory of the revolutionaries in the forty-two municipalities whose mayors were the legal representatives of the Third Order in the Estates of Brittany. These municipal governments—observed the new Intendant, Defaure de Rochefort—"are composed of a *bureau ordinaire d'administration* which, on important occasions, meets with a fixed number of citizen from the three Orders, and it is this body which is called the *communauté de ville* or municipality. This body presumably represents all the inhabitants of the city, but, in all the cities of Brittany, with the exception of three or four, it forms but a poor shadow of a truly representative system. . . ." Indeed, the holders of municipal offices, bourgeois of the robe, seignorial judges, property owners, *rentiers*, were too committed to the aristocracy to break with it abruptly. Richard de la Pervenchère, Mayor of Nantes, a newly created nobleman who had married the daughter of a gentleman, was anxious to be received into the circles of the old nobility, which had nothing to fear from him in the way of too audacious an initiative. Le Normant de Kergré, Mayor of Guingamp, *procureur fiscal* of the Duc de Penthièvre, also had every reason to wish, as he did, the preservation of "the so very desirable union between the Orders."

The master stroke of the Committee of Nantes, directed by Jacques

Cottin, was to give the Breton cities the signal and the model for a municipal revolution which would shake the protectorship of the reigning oligarchies. On November 4, at Nantes, a crowd of 300 persons forced the
registration of the famous petition of the patriots of Nantes upon the
hesitant *bureau* of the city. On November 6 a new irregular assembly,
meeting at the *hôtel de ville*, selected twelve deputies to the government.
They asked the ministers to grant the Third Estate of Nantes the right
"to assemble for the purpose of being able to name and choose their
representatives themselves, either to the Estates General or to the Estates
of the province." They got nothing because of the timidity of the men in
power. But the deputies of several other Breton cities joined them, the
Parisian patriots welcomed them, and advised them. Emboldened, they
sent instructions to the forty-two cities represented in the Estates.

The dazzling insurrection in the city of Nantes, [wrote a contemporary] came
along to precipitate the Revolution. A newly created nobleman renouncing his
privileges, a crowd of distinguished citizens signing a petition and bearing it
in pomp to the *hôtel de ville*, opulent merchants contributing funds to send
twelve deputies to Versailles: all these extraordinary happenings produced a
sort of explosion.

The researches of Augustin Cochin permit us to measure the repercussions of the appeal made by the citizens of Nantes. Eighteen *hôtels de ville*
in the province, between November 6 and December 15, opened their
doors, sometimes upon the initiative of some member of the municipal
government, to assemblies of the inhabitants, more or less numerous, who
gave a new accent to the demands of the city. Pressured by these commoners, at least seventeen cities (out of forty-two) charged their deputies
to the forthcoming provincial Estates to require the vote by head, that is
to say the overthrow of the Breton Constitution.

In Brittany, as in the other provinces, there were noblemen ready to
attempt, in order to avoid the worst, a reconciliation with the moderate
elite of the Third Estate, by offering it a henceforth equitable share of
public offices, which was contrary to the preservation of the basic principles
of the Constitution. The Bishop of Rennes, François Bareau de Girac,
President of the Estates, tried to rally to his cause this liberal nobility,
which came primarily from the dioceses of Rennes and Nantes. But the
needy and narrow-minded country squires who, at the end of December,
flocked in droves to the capital of Brittany did not expect to cede any of
their prerogatives. The Chevalier de Guer, in his *Lettre au Peuple de
Rennes*, expressed their intransigeance and the hatred which they bore the
opulent bourgeoisie. "Common people of Brittany, an odious injustice is
being committed—do not doubt it—is being committed in the distribution
of taxes in France, but it is not between the Third Estate and the nobility
. . . it is between the poor and the rich that this inequality exists. . . ."
The intractable mood of the *épées de fer* (iron swords) served the cause

of the partisans of violence in the special assemblies which the representatives of the Third Order held in the *hôtel de ville* of the city of Rennes between December 22 and December 27, before the opening of the provincial Estates. In addition to the ordinary deputies, twenty-nine cities had sent deputy commissioners. They supervised and led the mayors, who were always suspected of weakness, in the direction indicated by the fourteen extraordinary deputies of Nantes, led by Jacques Cottin. They broke the resistance inspired by Le Normant de Kergré, Mayor of Guingamp; they established, despite the moderates, the doctrine and the conduct of the deputies of the Third Order to the provincial Estates, by a motion voted on December 27. These deputies not only would insist upon an equal share of public offices, but upon a basic reform of the provincial Estates, anticipating the double representation of the Third Estate and the vote by head. They were to refuse to deliberate "all requests by the King, on any matter whatsoever, before having obtained justice concerning the more perfect representation of the Third Order in the Estates and concerning the equal and proportionate distribution, among the three Orders, of all taxes both real and personal."

The instructions were carried out, willingly or unwillingly, by the mayors, who opposed the entreaties of the first two Orders calling upon them to deliberate with passive resistance. Possibly dissident individuals were intimidated by the resolute attitude of the young patriots from Rennes, who occupied the galleries. "A member of the Third Estate who dared give in ran the risk of a cold bath or a stoning," observed the editor of *Héraut de la Nation*. They became convinced once and for all by the "Results of the Council meeting of December 27," which, by granting the Third Estate double representation for the Estates General, clearly indicated the government's preferences, and by the Council order of January 3 which, rejecting the stern measures against the insurgent communes demanded by Intendant Defaure de Rochefort, merely suspended for a month all deliberations of the provincial Estates.

The aristocracy, abandoned, denounced the treason of the ministers. On January 8, in the assembly room of the Estates, every gentleman took an oath to "remain inseparably bound and united for the defense of the Constitution." They refused to accept the suspension of the Estates. They declared the "Results of the Council of December 27" to have been an abuse of the King's good faith, inspired by a minister "who dares to put his opinion into opposition with the forms adopted and consecrated by the French nation in its previous assemblies, and with the opinion of princes and notables."

Putting aside its prudent reserve, the *Parlement* issued an order aimed at paralyzing the municipal revolution, so feared by the aristocracy. It forbade the citizens to hold any illicit meetings, for the purpose of influencing the municipal assemblies "established by the laws of the kingdom, to express the wishes of the commoners." It promised prosecution of the administrators of the parishes of Rennes, guilty of having stirred up such assemblies. It urged energetic intervention by the Sovereign against the fomenters of troubles. But this parliamentary thunder no longer intimidated anyone. "The *Parlement* does not dare to act," observed the Comte de Thiard. "It is afraid of revolts, does not wish to compromise itself, and does not have the strength to have the offenders arrested and punished."

Such unexpected and utter impotence exasperated the nobility and led it to undertake hazardous schemes. A few gentlemen, Guer, Trémargat, Coataudon, setting off a maneuver prepared since the beginning of the crisis, stirred up the sedan-chair bearers and domestic servants, common people devoted to them, against the insolent bourgeoisie. Such is the origin of the strange demonstration before the Parlement of Rennes on January 26, which demanded both the preservation of the Breton Constitution and the lowering of the price of bread. It degenerated almost immediately into a confused scuffle between the liveried servants and the young patriots, on the alert since the assembly of the Estates. The next evening, after several bloody encounters, the nobility, entrenched in the hall of the Cordeliers and anticipating an imminent attack, addressed a desperate and imperious appeal to the Commandant: "The nobility of Brittany expects you, Monsieur le Comte, to join with it to either repress these people, or to fight them at our head." Indeed, the Comte de Thiard succeeded in obtaining a general disarmament on January 28. But the *journées* of Rennes stirred all of France. They made the break between the aristocracy and the bourgeoisie irreparable, and made the insurrection of the Third Estate for the redress of its grievances irresistible.

❅

Paralyzed by the dissention among the Orders, the Estates of Brittany, assembled at the end of December and almost immediately suspended, had not carried out their usual functions. They had granted the King, for two years, the traditional free gift. But they had not voted the *impôts abonnés* (*vingtièmes* and *capitation*); they had not confirmed the powers of the *commissions intermédiares*; they had not authorized—except temporarily and for two months—the collection by the tax-farmers of the tax on beverages known as the *devoirs*. "And if the farm of the *devoirs*, upon which the payment of the province's debts basically depends, is once destroyed," wrote the Comte de Thiard to the Minister, "it will perhaps be as difficult to re-establish it in Brittany as it would be to establish the *gabelle* there."

The administration's disarray obliged the government to prudently prepare the new session of the Estates fixed for the beginning of February. To give some satisfaction to the Third Order and to calm its intransigeance, the *arrêt du Conseil* of January 20 authorized the privileged cities to add to their ordinary deputies double the number of representatives, freely chosen by the "community." What did they mean by that word? For Intendant Dufaure de Rochefort, declared enemy of the popular assemblies, *"communauté de ville* [did not] mean generality of inhabitants, but municipal body." But convinced by the renewed activities of the deputies of the Third Estate at Court that it was necessary to destroy the privileges of the oligarchies in power, Necker, justifying the municipal revolution, agreed in the interpretive *arrêt* of January 30, that the new deputies would be "named and elected by the generality of inhabitants in the said cities, in one or several assemblies either general or partial."

Also, the Breton patriots, heedless of the Intendant's instructions, had not waited for the Minister's tardy interpretation, which was not even brought to their attention. In nineteen out of forty-two cities, the new deputies were elected, with the aid of or through pressure exerted by persons foreign to the traditional community. At Nantes especially, on February 1, on their own authority an assembly of 700 persons added Jacques Cottin and three of the most energetic leaders of the commune of Nantes as associates of the Mayor, Richard de la Pervenchère, and of the *échevin*, Chardot, the ex-officio deputies, known for their sympathy toward aristocratic resistance.

On January 18, a group of 164 students and "young citizens," assembled at the Law School of Rennes, had declared their adhesion to the demands of the Third Estate. The *journées* of January, during which the young patriots of Rennes fought with noblemen and their domestic servants, aroused the youths of the principal Breton cities. Several hundred inhabitants of Nantes entered Rennes on January 31, followed two days later by a detachment from Saint-Malo. News of support from other cities in the province and the neighboring university cities, Angers and Poitiers, reached the leaders of the movement. On February 4, the Bishop of Rennes was able to notify Necker of the conclusion of an agreement: "There was an assembly at the Law School attended by the deputies of the detachments from Nantes, from Saint-Malo, and individuals from the various neighboring provinces. It was agreed that eight of those from Nantes and four of those from Saint-Malo would remain, to notify the others, who would come at the first warning."

From the beginning of January on, the patriots had made an appeal from Rennes, calling upon all the communes of Brittany to support the efforts of the deputies of the Third Estate. This appeal was immediately answered by a declaration by the Order of the nobility, affirming its solicitude for the people of the rural areas scorned by the urban bourgeoisie. These two manifestos, of which several thousand copies were printed, were translated into the Breton language for the benefit of the rural population of Basse-Bretagne. Thus began a struggle which, after the beginning of February, attracted the anxious attention of the King's commissioners and which continued until the elections for the Estates General.

The initiative seems to have belonged mainly to the urban bourgeoisie, which sent its resolutions to the neighboring parishes and added to them writings reflecting current problems which were likely to excite the peasants. "It is in Quimper and its vicinity," wrote the Intendant to Necker, "that there is the most ferment. The Sieur Le Goazre, *l'avocat du roi* in the Presidial and my subdelegate, is accused of adding coals to the fire by a text in bas-Breton which has been quietly spread abroad, and of exciting the common people and the peasants to a revolt against the nobility and the clergy." The aristocracy protected itself by putting to use the means of influence at its command. The *procureurs fiscaux* received from their seigneurs, and the parish priests from the vicars-general of their diocese, the order to paralyze the deliberations of the rural communities. Sometimes the nobles intervened personally: "I know a gentleman," wrote a correspondent to the Minister, "who threatened to dismiss all his farmers if they took the least part in the deliberations of their parishes. . . . He therefore delayed in renewing the leases, which are on the verge of expiration."

The documents published by Henri Sée and André Lesort, about the communities belonging to the *sénéchaussée* of Rennes, give a few indications concerning the insurrection in the rural areas of the dioceses of Dol, Saint-Malo, Saint-Brieuc, and Tréguier, which had been neglected in A. Cochin's research. They provide some new details about the diocese of Rennes proper. Out of 161 parishes in the *sénéchaussée* of Rennes which belonged to this diocese, seventy supported the deliberations of the Third Estate, most of them purely and simply, some by adding original detailed descriptions about the particular burdens of rural areas and especially about seignorial rights. Twenty-six parish priests, eleven *sénéchals* or *procureurs fiscaux*, dared to participate in these seditious assemblies, which were expressly forbidden by order of the Parlement of Brittany. But the deliberations of the seventeen notables, who normally constituted the *général* of a parish, should create no illusions about the sentiments of all the inhabitants of a community. As the Bishop of Rennes remarked, "We must not confuse what they call the *général* of the parishes with the inhabitants of the parishes. The former is mainly composed of men of the legal profession. . . ." In fact, out of the seventy parishes belonging to both the diocese and the *sénéchaussée* of Rennes, who participated in the campaign of the Third Estate, there were only twenty-five in which a part, and a modest one at that, of the inhabitants of the community became associated with the deliberations of the *général*. The movement of the Breton Third Estate during the first months of 1789 remained a bourgeois insurrection.

❧

The organized violence of this insurrection surprised and disturbed Necker. Malouet, who was then one of his close associates, retraces the hesitations which tormented the Minister of the people, who was "uncertain about certain basic points" beneath the mask of firmness he wore. In a personal letter to Mgr. Bareau de Girac, Bishop of Rennes, who was vainly trying to effect a reconciliation in the Estates of Brittany, in the midst of violent hatreds, Necker reveals his confusion. "I would have to write a great deal . . . in order to tell all about it, and unfortunately I have only a few spare moments in the midst of this torrent in which we find ourselves. Make up for all the deficiencies with your wit. You have here, Monseigneur, a fine opportunity to do a brilliant job, but we agree that the situation is extraordinarily difficult."

Necker undoubtedly recognized the need to reform the Estates of Brittany as the Third Order requested. But an immediate reform seemed to him inopportune and, amenable to the suggestions of the Comte de Boisgelin, President of the nobility, and concerned with at least retarding the unavoidable day of reckoning, he consented to refer the problem to the Estates General. For the moment, avoiding making a decision about the future, he limited his ambitions to handling current problems. After the insurrections of January, a plenary meeting of the Estates, as then composed, had become impossible; an attempt would be made to obtain agreement on ordinary taxes from each of the three Orders, meeting successively. Then some way would be found to assure the representation of Brittany in the Estates General, without having to resort, for the Third Order, to the Estates of the Province.

On February 1, the Breton nobility and clergy, wishing to leave Rennes as quickly as possible and to escape the terrible hatred which they had unwisely aroused, granted the votes necessary to the administration of the province. That very evening the Bishop of Rennes, President of the Estates, told Necker about it: "There were only sixty-eight opponents. All of the King's requests were granted as they had been in 1786. They prolonged the power of the *Commission intermédiaire* for tax collection and administration, and all the projects entrusted to them. The collection of the *devoirs* (taxes upon beverages) was agreed to and the administration of it entrusted to the present tax-farmers, the whole until January 1, 1790, in conformity with the King's desires. The treasurer of the Estates was authorized to deposit in the royal treasury the same sums and on the same terms as during the years 1787 and 1788, to make all the necessary expenditures . . . in the same manner as in the above-mentioned years, with the express reservation that the Third Order agree to it. . . ."

The most difficult thing to obtain was the consent of the 140 representatives of the privileged cities forming a new deputation of the Third Estate, by virtue of the *arrêt du Conseil* of January 20. Indeed, this implied the abandonment of the still essential requirement that the grievances of the Third Estate first be satisfied, a demand which the Minister turned over to the Estates General for consideration. While Malouet was busy questioning the deputies of the Third Estate at Court, in Necker's name, Mgr. Bareau de Girac, the Comte du Thiard, and Defaure de Rochefort multiplied their entreaties to the representatives of the cities, assembled at

Rennes. Their influence was opposed by that of a crowd of unofficial deputies from the guilds and the market towns, which filled the *hôtel de ville*, preaching intransigeance. "There are, among these guilds," observed the Bishop, "wool-carders and people of the lowest sort."

On February 14, having finally isolated the 140 regular deputies, the Comte de Thiard attempted the decisive move. The man, unjustly scorned by Bertrand de Moleville, had been courageous and adroit during the fever-ish *journées* of January. His witty, relaxed manner and his elegance im-pressed the bourgeoisie. The editor of the *Héraut de la Nation*, a patriotic newspaper, describes his triumph as follows: "Monsieur Chaillon, Deputy from the guilds of Nantes, rose and cried out, 'Gentlemen, long live the King and Monsieur de Thiard! The King's requests by acclamation!' . . . Then all the deputies and a considerable amount of the visiting public covered the voice of the eloquent man from Nantes by cries of: 'Long live the King! Long live Monsieur de Thiard! Long live Necker! . . .'"

The provincial Estates, in their traditional form, had obviously lived out their life. There could be no question of calling them to a plenary session, as the Church and the Breton nobility demanded, to undertake the selec-tion of deputies for the province to the Estates General. The *règlement* of March 16 stipulated that the privileged orders alone would meet at Saint-Brieuc, to draw up their *cahiers* and to elect their deputies. The deputation of the upper clergy would then be completed by ecclesiastics of the Second Order, chosen in diocesan assemblies. As for the deputies of the Third Estate, they would be elected, according to the law in force in the rest of France, in assemblies of the *sénéchaussées*.

Greeted with satisfaction and applied by the Third Estate and the lower clergy, the *réglement* was rejected by the privileged orders, assembled at Saint-Brieuc from April 16 to 20, who refused to name representatives to the Estates General. Once again, they followed the lead of the ringleaders of the nobility. "They did not vote, they did not even ask for opinions, they did not allow the president any time. The decision was made by accla-mation: a way to cover up the opinions of those who did not cry the loudest." As for the upper clergy: "Nothing could have persuaded them. They were restrained and intimidated by the Order of the nobility. . . ."

By proclaiming the exclusive right of the Estates of Brittany to send deputies from the three Orders of the province to the Estates General and by loudly disobeying the King's order, the Breton aristocracy remained faithful to the policies they had adopted a year earlier. However, the aristo-crats decided to carry out two measures which had long been refused. They accepted among their members the newly created noblemen who had acquired transmissible nobility. They declared their "express desire, in the coming constitutionally assembled Estates of Brittany, to consent to an equal distribution of the taxes which would be voted by the aforesaid Estates."

Six months earlier, the first concession might have robbed the Third

Estate of two of its most energetic leaders, Cottin and Le Chapelier, newly created noblemen who were exasperated by the scorn of gentlemen from older families. The second would undoubtedly not have disarmed the most resolute patriots, but it would have given the conciliatory members, rather numerous at the beginning in the Third Estate, an impetus which might have been irresistible. In April 1789, both were ridiculous in the face of the unlimited prospects being offered to the victorious bourgeoisie.

III

By making the revolt of the nobles in the summer of 1788 and the bourgeois insurrection of the following winter proceed from a common mystique, and by making the second movement emerge from the first by the so-called normal means of a purge, Augustin Cochin constructed a fascinating thesis which does not stand up to the careful study of the facts.

The revolt of the nobility—in Brittany as in the rest of France—is the natural resistance of the aristocracy to the concrete threats included in the laws published by the men who directed the French government after the assembly of the notables in 1787. It is a defensive reaction; it is not a revolution. To this resistance were associated, willingly or unwillingly, the bourgeois of the robe who were still bound by ties of dependence and solidarity with the parliamentary aristocracy, which was particularly threatened by the May edicts. However, the vast majority of the Third Order maintained, in regard to the movement, an indifference and even a hostile reserve, which is not difficult to discover beneath the illusions spread by well-prepared propaganda. Once the May laws had been retracted, the bourgeoisie had no trouble rallying together for the common defense of demands which were already old—born of daily experience and of the critical observation of social reality—and which the approaching meeting of the Estates General and the arrival of a presumably liberal minister were making especially pertinent. In a *Mémoire pour le tiers état de Bretagne* published in February 1787, Gohier, a lawyer, was to sum up the essential point, in terms which require a great deal of good will to find in them the expression of a "dream ideology": "No exemption, no derogation, no exclusion. No taxes not paid by all; no profession that all cannot honorably exercise; no positions of prestige which all cannot attain. . . ."

The revolutionary activity of the Third Estate was the work of a minority of new men who, by municipal revolutions and the mobilization of a resolute group of young people, were able to intimidate, neutralize, or sweep away the hesitations or resistance of the traditional representatives of the Third Order, too involved with the system to combat it energetically. We could even agree that this active minority was principally recruited from among the membership of the "reading rooms," really very well informed about public affairs and naturally disposed to participate in them.

But it is impossible to accept the affirmation that these revolutionaries received their instructions from the thirty-nine Masonic lodges of Brittany, themselves affiliated with the Grand Orient of France. It is certain that there was an appreciable number of Freemasons among the ringleaders of the Breton revolution, and Augustin Cochin has identified some of them. Nevertheless, if Mangourit, editor of the *Hérault de la Nation*, an important patriotic newspaper which began publication on December 10, 1788, is an authentic Mason, the Masonic membership of the famous Volney, whose *Sentinelle du Peuple* gave the real signal for the bourgeois Revolution, remains very doubtful. Above all, nothing permits us to vouch for the unity of doctrine and of action among the members of Breton Freemasonry, and certain pieces of information betray strange divergencies. In the hypothesis accepted by Augustin Cochin, what must we think of the two-sided game played by Le Normant de Kergré, Mayor of Guingamp, obstinate orator of the moderates in the assembly of the Third Estate of December and members of the *Vertu triumphante* lodge of Saint-Brieuc? How could we reconcile the declared hostility of Intendant Dufaure de Rochefort in regard to the popular party, and his membership in the *Parfaite union* lodge of Rennes?

By playing down the role of the Grand Orient of France in the conduct of the French Revolution, we must not disregard the links established by means of the deputations sent to Court between the Bretons and the patriotic circles of Paris. Precise references to this point remain extremely rare. However, Augustin Cochin published an important text proving the existence of an agreement aimed at making the demands of the French Third Estate "as uniform as they are general."

The vigorous nature of the bourgeois Revolution in Brittany, which developed to the point of violence, comes from the absolute intransigeance of a nobility closely associated with a parliamentary aristocracy, whose leaders were able to neutralize all dissenting parties and to prevent all compromises, all reconciliations of the type which occurred in the Dauphiné, between the notables of the three Orders. It was by struggling against the obstinacy of the *"epées de fer"* that the ringleaders of the Breton movement, who had become the deputies of the Third Estate, acquired that rigidity which was to make them famous after the first sessions of the Estates General.

But another striking aspect of the Breton insurrection of 1789—along with its notorious energy in the struggle against the aristocracy—is the sincere desire for an alliance with the royal government, supposedly faithful to the political program inaugurated after the Assembly of Notables and which the popular Minister seems to have confirmed in the "Results of the Council of December 27." "The Revolution will certainly take place in Brittany," wrote Blin, a lawyer from Nantes, to Malouet, on February 12, "without trouble and without civil dissension if we are helped by the government, with stress and trouble if we lack the necessary support." And the Breton deputies at Versailles, in a letter of March 10 addressed to the Ministers, wrote:

All France has its eyes on the Breton nation. The latter is glorying in having been one of the first to have dealt a blow to the aristocratic system, concocted long ago by the enemies of the prosperity of the State and of the glory of the King. Determined to preserve legitimate authority with all its might, it will maintain this firmness until the destruction of this odious system . . . .

The confidence, the hope expressed by these texts rested on the reasonable belief in a firmness in the thoughts and a constancy in the plans of a government whose ministerial correspondence reveals—in reality—disarray and hesitation. The later events of the French Revolution are already to be seen in this tragic misunderstanding.

THE PRE-REVOLUTION
IN PROVENCE (1787-1789)

 By Jean Egret

In Provence the agitation began on the day after the first Assembly of
Notables, when the news spread that the Estates of Provence, suspended
since 1639, might be re-established in the near future.

In the important speech which Loménie de Brienne had made when
dismissing the Notables, on May 25, 1787, one sentence had attracted
attention. In announcing the coming establishment of the provincial assemblies, he had clearly asserted that the traditions of certain provinces would
be respected, "uniformity of principles not always entailing a uniformity
of means." Such condescension offered the people of Provence the opportunity to renew, with a greater chance of success, their request for a restoration of their Estates, which the *Parlement* and the *Corps de la noblesse*
had presented several times.

The Estates of Provence, at the time of their suspension, were—like the
other provincial Estates—a fortress of the aristocracy. The clergy was represented in it by the Archbishop of Aix, who presided over the group, the
Archbishop of Arles, the twelve bishops of the province, a few abbots, and
a few commanders of the Order of the Knights of Malta. All gentlemen
owning fiefs had the right to sit in the Estates, with no limit upon their
total number. An imposing mass, which overwhelmed the small delegation
of the Third Estate, formed by the mayors of the thirty-six cities or privi-

leged towns and by the Consul of a community selected by rotation in each of the twenty *vigueries,* or administrative circumscriptions.

The re-establishment of these aristocratic Estates was in keeping with the compelling desire for action which at that time animated the French nobility. In addition, those nobles of Provence who owned fiefs saw in it a more efficient means of defending their fiscal immunities, which the statements of successive ministers, Calonne and Brienne, had recently threatened before the Assembly of Notables. The properties of the nobility were exempt from the free gift and the majority of local charges. Their attachment to these immunities was all the stronger among the owners of these properties, because they had already been forced to share in the *vingtièmes* and in various accessory contributions.

The gentlemen possessing fiefs were not very numerous: 205 provided the proof necessary to entitle them to sit in the re-established Estates. But they were organized, quick to work together for their own interests in the general and private assemblies, directed by the *syndics* of the sword and of the robe. They were supported by the Parlement of Aix, thirty-four of whose sixty-two members were also fief holders, and they had won over Gallois de La Tour, its *premier président*—who was also the Intendant of Provence. The establishment of the provincial Estates, which they unanimously demanded, was ably solicited by Monseigneur de Boisgelin, Archbishop of Aix, and by Le Blanc de Castillon, *Procureur général* of the *Parlement.* Both of them had earned Brienne's gratitude in the recent Assembly of Notables by taking part in the intrigue of which former *Controleur général* Calonne had been the victim. They joined their prestige to that of the Comte de Vintimille, *Syndic* of the nobility of Provence, nobleman at Court, gentleman Councillor of State, and personal friend of Keeper of the Seals Lamoignon.

Another faction rose against the re-establishment: that of the principal members of the administration in office. This administration—a curious survival of the suspended Estates—was presided over by the Archbishop of Aix, and was under the control of the municipality of Aix and of the representatives of the thirty-five other privileged communities. The "General Assembly of the Communities," meeting yearly at Lambesc, voted the free gift, divided it and the other taxes among the *vigueries* of Provence, and carried out those projects within its authority relative to public works and relief. The intermediate administration was formed by the eleven *procureurs du pays,* who were a part of the Assembly. The guiding force of this entire administration was a member of the municipality of Aix, always selected from among the important lawyers of the capital, who bore the title "Assessor." In 1787, for two years, this was the lawyer Pascalis, fifty-five years of age, whom an impartial contemporary portrayed as follows: "An upright man, who has wisdom, insight, and experience, but who is too eager, too hot-headed, sometimes impassioned, always believing he is so only to support the good cause, but then easily humbled to the point of pusillanimity."

Pascalis, in close collaboration with several of his colleagues, former assessors themselves, Pazery, Barlet, Portalis, Dubreuil, Siméon . . . , organized as early as the month of June 1787 a stubborn resistance to the attempts of the fief-holding nobles. Losing all hope of being able to prevent the re-establishment of the Estates and of maintaining what Le Blanc de Castillon called "assessoral domination," he strove to have two preliminary conditions to this re-establishment accepted by the government. The first was the abandonment of their fiscal immunities by all property-owning fiefs. "We say to the nobility: either pay your share or else do not meddle in an administration which can be of no interest to you since you do not pay its expenses . . . ." The second condition anticipated a new composition of the Estates, which would grant fourteen representatives to the clergy, twenty-two to the nobility, and fifty-two to the Third Estate, the only proportion—according to Pascalis—which would enable the Third Order to cope with the allied aristocracy. "It is useless to conceal the fact that the nobility will always dominate in the Estates owing to its rank, its wealth, its birth, its influence, its relations, and even more its union with the clergy, even if the voices of the common people were of a number equal to those of the two other Orders . . . ."

Were these demands—which seemed excessive at the moment they were made—sincere or merely, as *Procureur général* Le Blanc de Castillon maintained, a lawyer's method of obtaining the retraction of the demand formulated by the nobility and the preservation of the administration in its functions? Whatever might have been his thoughts on this, Loménie de Brienne took shelter in arbitration. He referred the examination of the problems stated by Pascalis to the Estates themselves, which would be convoked in the old manner. The Parlement of Aix publicly expressed the aristocracy's gratitude to the Minister of October 6, 1787. A few days later, the committee of former assessors brought the debate before the public opinion of Provence. Upon the committee's advice, Pascalis published a "*Mémoire sur la Contribution des trois Ordres aux charges publiques et communes de la Province*," which he addressed to the principal communities and to the chief towns of the *vigueries*. In it he developed, for the information of the Third Estate, the argument that he had vainly supported before the ministers, in favor of the necessary equality of all inhabitants of Provence in respect to taxes.

The Estates General of the *Pays* and *Comté* of Provence, whose sessions lasted from December 30, 1787 to February 1, 1788, showed clearly the desire of the fief holders to profit from the government's complacency in order to organize a provincial administration which would be faithful to them. With 128 members of the enfeoffed nobility present, docilely joined by the nineteen representatives of the upper clergy—as compared to the sixty deputies from the communities and *vigueries*—they were assured of an absolute majority.

Men of experience and authority led them: *Syndic* Vintimille; Arbaud de Joques, and Arlatan de Lauris, *Présidents à mortier* of the Parlement;

Mazenod, President of the *Chambre des Comptes*; Cymon de Beauval, Councillor in the Parlement; Gallifet, Prince de Martigues . . . The modest and wisely calculated concessions which they were resigned to grant in response to the demands of the Third Estate, had been planned with the ministers and were stipulated in the instructions to the Commissioners of the King: the Comte de Caraman, Commander of the Province and Gallois de La Tour, Intendant and *Premier Président* in the Parlement. Assured of their support, they could count upon the total devotion of Monseigneur de Boisgelin, President of the Estates, who desired to please the men in power. This prelate hoped to obtain the *cordon bleu* [1] from Brienne, after the death of Cardinal de Luynes. Throughout the entire session, he would place his seductive eloquence in the service of the fief holders.

In the hopeless struggle forced upon them, Réguis, Mayor of Sisteron; Mougins de Roquefort, Mayor of Grasse; and de Baux, Mayor of Saint-Maximin saved the honor of the Third Estate, the first two with polite firmness, the third with less civility and more impetuosity. The threats and jeers with which he was assailed overwhelmed Assessor Pascalis. "The Assessor plays the saint," Le Blanc de Castillon noted cruelly. "He shows that, after having been lacking in prudence, he is lacking in character and is only an insolent coward like so many others."

Dismissing the Assessor's claims to grant the Third Estate sixteen votes more than the first two Orders combined, the nobility had merely promised the ministers to accept equality between the privileged classes and the others in accordance with the principle accepted for the provincial assemblies. The promise was kept. But this equality was a mere shadow for, among the mayors of the cities represented in the Estates, several were noblemen or owned fiefs and voted with the privileged classes. This could be seen during the course of the debates in which Demandols de La Palu, Mayor of Aix and Gineste, Mayor of Toulon, joined their voices to those of the first two Orders.

In addition, the ringleaders of the nobility took every necessary precaution to avoid surprises. They were careful to eliminate from the clergy's future representation the ecclesiastics of the Second Order, even the cathedral provosts whom the bishops would have been willing to admit. "The provosts," observed President Fauris de Saint-Vincent, "are not to the liking of the dominant groups. It is to be feared that since most of them are related to bourgeois families by marriage, they might side with the Third Estate on some occasions." The nobles insisted that the deputy from each *viguerie* not be freely chosen by their constituency, but selected in rotation from among the consuls of all the communities of the *viguerie*, even the smallest ones. This method of selection was very reassuring to

[1] The *cordon bleu* was the insignia of the *Chevaliers de l'Ordre du Saint-Esprit* (Knights of the Order of the Holy Ghost) founded by Henry III at the end of the sixteenth century. It was second only to the *Ordre de Saint Louis* as a distinction, a sign of honor accorded only to members of the top layers of the nobility.

the interests of the privileged classes for it introduced into the Estates a few deputies "absolutely worthless or totally enslaved to the wishes and power of their seigneurs." The nobility obstinately refused to grant this deputation—which would always remain partially under its control—that "*Syndic des Communautés*" which the Third Estate was demanding to direct its defense. "This help," we read in a letter from the municipality of Pertuis, "is all the more necessary to it because its deputies usually change each year, because the majority are poorly informed about the affairs of Provence, and because they know little about its administration, are not used to speaking in public, and are far too timid to make the necessary demands and protests."

The *Commission intermédiare* was organized on January 26 in the same spirit. Out of seventeen *procureurs* of the region, ten would of necessity belong to the clergy of the First Order and to the fief-owning nobility.

Therefore, while affirming the fundamental immunity of its noble possessions and while confirming its refusal to pay the free gift, sure of the future, the aristocracy decided to make a conciliatory gesture before the cloture of the Estates. It offered to share, in the future, in the construction of roads in the province and in the upkeep of foundlings, in addition to the local charges it already paid.

❦

On February 1, 1788, at the moment when the Estates were breaking up, twenty-one of the sixty deputies from the Third Estate, who would not accept defeat, signed a protest addressed to the King to complain about the injustice of which they were the victims and to solicit the calling of a "General Assembly of the Communities" in which "they could choose their own defenders and provide everything necessary to the preservation of their rights."

This manifesto, carried back by the mayors to the privileged communities which they had represented in the Estates, provided the theme for municipal deliberations. On its guard ever since Pascalis' memorandum on the contribution of the Three Orders, the bourgeoisie became aware of its own interests and of consequent opposition which would cause it to rise up against the enfeoffed nobility.

At Aix the municipal government was closely watched by the aristocratic Parlement; and the Mayor, Demandols de La Palu, was himself a fief-holding gentleman. It was only on February 26 that the majority of the municipal council, overcoming the Mayor's opposition, joined in the protests of the deputies of the Third Estate. It resisted the Parlement which, the next day, tried to silence it. Exasperated, Le Blanc de Castillon demanded sanctions from the Minister against that "cabal of furious cowards whom we must render incapable of troubling the Estates." But the critical letters which Breuteuil, Secretary of State for Provence, sent to the municipalities on March 13 and April 16 did not in the least intimidate the Third Estate.

In fact, it was encouraged by the progress of the movement of protest which gradually spread to other cities. Between February 17 and March 24, eighteeen municipal deliberations in privileged cities and towns supported the demand of the Third Estate and the request for a General Assembly of the Communities. The eighteen mayors, acting as ringleaders, who suggested this motion were mainly bourgeois, either through assuming this title without other qualification or by belonging to bourgeois professions (five lawyers, three doctors of medicine, one royal notary). Three, however—Barrème of Tarascon, Sauteiron of Manosque, Désidery of Rians, all former soldiers—were nobles without fiefs, and had been relegated to the Third Estate by the intransigeance of fief-owning noblemen. In view of the authority which their birth and past conferred upon them, they naturally came to lead the Third Estate. This was the first symptom of an alliance which was to prove formidable for the aristocracy.

The spirit of revolt against fief holders made its way into the most distant rural areas. This is evidenced in the assemblies of the *viguerie*, which brought together the first consuls of all the communities in the chief town of these administrative districts. The most important assembly, that of the *viguerie* of Aix, which included ninety-one cities and communities, met from March 31 to April 3. Its turbulence tormented Le Blanc de Castillon, who could not keep those deliberating from agreeing to every request of the Third Estate of Provence, and who had to be satisfied with forbidding the printing of their *cahier de doléances*.

Intendant Gallois de La Tour thought the insurrection of the Third Order could be appeased by giving it a semblance of satisfaction. On his advice, the government accepted a meeting of the "General Assembly of the Communities." It was understood that this assembly would not be entitled to deliberate on a new proportion of the Orders in the Estates or on the manner of selecting representatives of the clergy or the nobility. It would be limited to the matters concerning only the Third Estate, and would make no decisions about these questions, merely addressing its complaints to the Sovereign.

The Assembly of the Communities, comprising fifty-eight deputies, met at Lambesc from May 5 to 9, 1788. Caught in the web of ministerial regulations, it settled for repeating already familiar grievances in order to obtain a *Syndic général des Communautés*, free elections for the Third Order within the *vigueries*, an intermediary administration not so completely enfeoffed to the aristocracy, and an equitable distribution of the fiscal burden.

The Sieur Pascalis [observed Gallois de La Tour] came daily to tell me what he was to propose in the committees which preceded the daily assemblies. He did not hesitate to withdraw those propositions I showed him were contrary to instructions and even those about which I expressed some doubt. He continually directed the discussions concerning the interests of the Third Estate in such a way as to eliminate all bitterness, to prevent uncalled-for difficulties, and to prepare the way for a general reconciliation, and all the deputies complied with these principles.

However, during this same month of May, Charles-François Bouche, another less timid advocate, was reviving and developing Pascalis' demonstration of the necessary equality of all in regard to taxes, by publishing his *"Droit public du Comté État de la Provence sur la contribution aux impositions."*

ᦥᦥ

The final session of the Assembly of the Communities meeting at Lambesc, had been troubled by the news of a great storm which had just broken over the French magistrature, in revolt against the government for some months. Satisfied with the re-establishment of the Estates, the Parlement of Aix had not taken part in this revolt. It nevertheless suffered the consequences set down in the six *ordonnances*, edicts, and declarations which it had to register on May 8, 1788. The sovereign court of Provence, like the other Parlements of France, saw its right of remonstrance transferred to a plenary court common to the entire Kingdom, and its judicial activity singularly reduced by the creation of two *grands bailliages* at Aix and at Digne.

This coup did not stir up a riot at Aix, as it had in other capitals of the judicial system. However, except for certain desertions in a few subordinate tribunals, aroused by hopes of promotion, or in a few municipalities dazzled by the luster and profit which the establishment of a *grand bailliage* would bring, the opposition was general among those connected to the Parlement by ties of dependence and solidarity. The opposition brought together the *Chambre des Comptes*, almost all the *sénéchaussées*, the lawyers of Aix and Toulon, the mass of the nobility of Provence, the *commission intermédiaire* of the Estates, and especially the city of Aix, a parliamentary city whose prosperity was threatened by the destruction of the Parlement.

The truce in the struggle between the Orders lasted until October 22, 1788, the day when the Parlement of Provence registered the royal declaration of September 23, which made official the victory of the magistracy over the disgraced ministers and announced the coming meeting of the Estates General. From that time on the problem of the deputations to these Estates held the public attention and reawakened the quarrel between the aristocracy and the Third Estate.

ᦥᦥ

In Provence there was no uncontested tradition fixing the manner in which deputies to the national assemblies were to be selected. It was generally felt that they should be selected in the provincial Estates. Abbé de Coriolis, an expert in the field of the administration of Provence, agreed that each Order meeting individually should name its deputies, the election then to be approved in a plenary assembly of the Estates.

Each Order [he said] knows its members best, and can place its confidence in a manner more in agreement with its views; but the private proceedings of each Order are only preparatory; in order to have the force of a real deliberation, the work of their commissioners must be reinforced by the wishes of the Nation assembled, since it is the Nation which must be represented by the deputies of the Orders of which it is composed.

The plenary assembly of the Estates of Provence therefore was considered to possess the precious right of controlling the selection of every deputy. In the coming sessions of the Estates, the principal concern of the fief-holding nobility was to maintain the superiority which it had gained through the traditional right of all its members to sit. It asked Necker, the new Minister, once again to exempt it from the anticipated and promised reduction in the number of its representatives. The Minister, without doubt poorly informed and not suspecting the gravity of his decision, found the request "very reasonable," and the authorization was granted on November 3.

This oversight by the popular Minister surprised and astounded the leaders of the Third Estate. Pascalis, who was serving as Assessor until the end of the year, demanded in compensation a considerable increase in the representation of the Third Estate in the coming provincial Estates. For example, the number of deputies from each *viguerie* would be increased to three, and new privileged communities would be created to send delegates directly to the Estates. "If the Estates are to be plenary for the nobility, they should be so for the Third Estate as well. In fact it is the only way the Estates can be a real spokesman of the Nation and can send to the Estates General persons who will express the wishes of the Nation."

While Pascalis was sending the Minister this prudent proposition which saved what could be saved of the traditional organization, a much more energetic manifestation of a really revolutionary nature was being prepared, without the knowledge of the municipal council. On December 21, 1788, a petition signed by more than 200 persons was delivered to the Consuls of Aix. It denied the traditional Estates the right to name deputies to the Estates General. "How can the Nation entrust this precious right to them, since it is itself so illegally represented in the Estates of Provence?"

The example of the neighboring province of the Dauphiné clearly inspired the authors of this petition. The inhabitants of the Dauphiné had obtained from the government the right to hold at Romans a real provincial constituent assembly of the three Orders, which worked out a new Constitution for the Estates, suspended like those of Provence since the reign of Louis XIII. From January 2 to 6, 1789, these regenerated Estates would elect the Dauphiné's representatives to the Estates General.

The "petition" of the citizens of the city of Aix demanded an assembly of the three Orders of the provincial capital. It personally would ask the King for the calling of this general assembly of the three Orders of the region, which the people of the Dauphiné had been granted, to carry out both the necessary reforms of the provincial Estates and the selection of the deputies to the Estates General. Consequently, the Consuls of Aix were required to

convoke on the earliest possible day, an assembly . . . in which every ecclesiastic in the holy orders or owning ecclesiastical property and residing in the city will be able to vote with the Order of the clergy; every gentleman likewise residing in the city will vote with the Order of the nobility; and every non-ecclesiastical or non-noble head of a family will vote with the Order of the Third Estate.

It is important to observe that the initiative for this step came from those members of the nobility not possessing fiefs, who were especially numerous and active in the capital of Provence. Fauris de Saint-Vincent indicated that the leader of the movement was Monsieur de Levesque, about sixty years of age, former President in the *Chambre des Comptes*, and former Consul. And the author of the petition submitted to the Consuls was d'André, a young twenty-nine year-old Councillor in the Parlement. "I am a nobleman," he wrote Necker on December 22 to justify himself, "but I do not possess fiefs and I share this fate with 500 other gentlemen of Provence. We are not represented in the Estates; those possessing fiefs do not allow us to join their group; the Third Estate excludes us from its Order. The King certainly does not want us to be creatures absolutely incapable of cooperating with His Majesty in the great work of national regeneration . . . ."

Levesque and d'André could count upon the declared support of several magistrates from the *Chambre des Comptes*, of whom merely eight out of twenty-four owned fiefs. Within the Parlement itself, that citadel of feudal aristocracy, *Avocat général* d'Eymar de Montmeyan, an important member of the *Amitié* Masonic lodge at Aix, and a fief holder besides, supported d'André. Some other owners of fiefs, *Avocat général* Cymon de Beauval and Councillor Arnauld de Vitrolles, did not disapprove of the assembly of the three Orders, and President Fauris de Saint-Vincent, who criticized it, was not very sure of the legitimacy of his colleagues' claims: "The nobility of Provence," he recorded in his journal, "is arrogant. It is as attached to its rights and privileges as it ever could have been in the fifteenth century. Of course philosophy has changed this way of thinking in several provinces . . . ."

This divided Parlement, overtaken by the feeling that it had been abandoned, did not dare forbid the planned convocation of the three Orders of the city. The twelve members of the Parlement, who deliberated on December 28, simply asked d'André and Montmeyan not to participate in this revolutionary assembly.

◆◇◆

The assembly of the three Orders of the city of Aix met at nine o'clock in the morning on Monday, December 29, in the College Church. According to Fauris de Saint-Vincent it was composed of "about thirty lawyers, as many *procureurs*, several bourgeois, a very small number of gentlemen who owned fiefs, and a great number of artisans, merchants, farmers, and householders. In all about 1000 or 1200 men." The new Consuls of Aix declared that as they were "the *Procureurs* of the three Estates they should not take sides but restrict themselves to reconciling all the Orders." And they withdrew. Pascalis, the former Assessor, led the debates and read a remarkable petition intended for the King and drawn up by Councillor d'André. After having pointed out the faults of the Estates of Provence in which neither the lower clergy, noblemen without fiefs, nor communities without privileges were represented, d'André demanded the calling of an assembly which would be really representative of the three Orders, to remedy the situation. "The assembly for which we are asking Your Majesty will not delay the Estates General of the Realm. It can be held during the month of January, it will give its consent to the ordinary taxes, and it will send representatives as promptly and more lawfully than the so-called Estates of Provence could have done."

The text of the petition was received enthusiastically, and they went on to elect the deputies who would carry it to the Sovereign. "It was then," wrote Fauris de Saint-Vincent, "that the plans of the Assembly's leaders were spoiled. They wanted to have Messieurs Portalis and Siméon selected as representatives and proposed their names. Someone shouted: 'Monsieur Bouche, Monsieur Barlet' . . . The latter said he could not undertake the mission, but Monsieur Bouche was selected by acclamation . . . ." The following day a strengthened municipal council selected former President Levesque, the lawyer Pochet, and the bourgeois Mollet de Barbedelle to accompany Bouche.

A new spirit moved the insurrection in Provence, giving the really popular classes the chance to express themselves for the first time. The "*Caté-chisme du Tiers-Etats*," a lampoon published at Aix during this period, showed a profound distrust of the upper bourgeoisie of the robe, and of the clique of ex-assessors suspected of timidity, sympathy for the traditional Constitution, and doubtful discretion. "I only know one of them," declared the author, "who has dared to defend us: that is Bouche. This must be said in acknowledgment of his patriotism and courage."

The famous lawyer Pascalis, former Assessor, was one of these now disowned ringleaders. While the deputation, from which the voice of the people had excluded him, was setting out to carry the demands of the three Orders to Versailles, he wrote Necker a strange letter which was almost a defection. "Monseigneur, I am speaking to you and to you alone. If you think that from now until the Estates General it will be impossible to tend to the demands of the region, a single word from you will sustain all hopes and calm all fears. We realize we must know how to adapt ourselves to circumstances and not multiply embarrassing situations. . . ."

Perhaps Portalis was not completely unaware of the warnings his colleague, the lawyer Gassier, *Syndic de robe* of the nobility, had just addressed to the upper bourgeoisie in a speech for the defense of those owning fiefs, published during the month of December.

You attack the fiefs and you want to provide the disastrous example of an attack upon the right to own property. But can you not foresee that that part of your Order which has only its two arms and little or no land may ask for such a partition? Therefore, if you want to preserve your own property, respect that of others. Do not be led astray by those so-called reformers whom you call publicists and who are merely dangerous innovators. Be just, at least through self-interest, and remember that the fire you should like to kindle against the fiefs would only spread and then devour your own patrimony.

Whatever Portalis' regrets, the impetus had been given, and the movement spread rapidly through Provence.

On January 30, 1789, without running the risk of being contradicted, Mirabeau could declare before the Estates meeting at Aix: "No one is unaware that a great part of the Nation is asking for a general assembly of the three Orders. The capital was first to express the desire; many entire *vigueries* have adopted it . . . ." The assemblies, held during the month of January for the selection of deputies to the Estates, had indeed provided an opportunity for the councils of the communities, meeting in the chief town of the *viguerie*, to give massive support to the watchword issued at Aix-en-Provence.

Also of great significance is the interest in public affairs which all classes of the population began to show. At Aups, a town never distinguished by a demonstration, the new municipal government, bowing to public opinion, had to support the general wishes. To add more weight to their demands, the municipal councils—at Antibes and at Cuers—strengthened themselves with notables. Finally, real popular assemblies in which all categories within the Third Order were represented, were formed as they had been at Aix: on January 7, at Rians around the Mayor, Doctor Casimir Messié— the ninth at Cucuron, around Mayor Clémentis—the fourteenth at Tarascon, around Guigue, Second Consul. Though noblemen were not very numerous in the meetings, called "of the three Orders," the lower clergy was never absent.

The spirit of revolt against the current Constitution of Provence was again seen in the scorn for the traditional rules on the occasion of the election of deputies of the Third Estate to the provincial Estates of January 1789. Several deputies—representing *vigueries*—were not selected by rotation from among the community consuls, but were selected freely from among the inhabitants of the entire circumscription. The majority of the privileged cities were not represented by the current Mayor but by the one of the previous year. The *viguerie* of Saint-Maximin and several cities had two deputies instead of one. "Most of the credentials," observed the Intendant, "were in a position to be rejected as contrary to the regulations . . . ." This is why the members of the Third Estate obstinately refused during the first two days of the Estates (January 27 to 28) to have their credentials verified by a commission accountable to the plenary assembly in which the nobility, sitting as a body, was assured of the majority. "They wanted to keep those persons of fervent spirits who would have been excluded by an exact and official examination," observed Gallois de La Tour.

The King's commissioners and the President of the Estates were from the beginning appalled by the growth of the spirit of independence among the deputies of the Third Estate who the preceding year had been discontented, of course, but docile. These deputies henceforth showed an irritated distrust of the heavy eloquence of Monseigneur de Boisgelin. The representatives of the Sovereign (Caraman and Gallois de La Tour), men of maturity and experience, vainly tried formerly effective methods of neutralizing the opposition. The communication of the government's instructions justifying the plenary convocation of the nobility for this session only, and "the announcement of an *arrêt de Conseil* nullifying the decisions made by the three Orders at Aix on December 29, "neither appeased nor intimidated anyone." "Authority," wrote the Intendant, "is neither recognized nor respected. It is the greatest of misfortunes. We are performing our duties with decency and firmness. But they are painful to carry out."

The principal concern of the King's commissioners was to have the traditional free gift voted by these Estates which they could not succeed in organizing. On January 29 they learned with stupefaction that on the preceding night the deputies of the Third Estate had signed before a notary an act which, confirming their protestation against the present composition of the assembly, nevertheless expressed their faithfulness to the Sovereign by granting "in the name of their communities and of their *vigueries*, the free gift, taxes, and royal subsidies as they were determined in the last Estates. . . ." Caraman and Gallois de La Tour rescinded the unprecedented act and succeeded in negotiating a compromise between the nobility and the Third Estate. The nobility agreed not to dispute the irregular credentials of some of the representatives to the Third Estate; all credentials would be declared legal. In exchange, the deputies from the communes would agree to vote the free gift in the Estates in conjunction with the other two Orders. This was done, and on January 31 the free gift was granted in the established manner.

In the meanwhile, the quarrel which had died down for a moment burst forth more bitterly than before. On December 30 the Comte de Mirabeau, a member of the nobility and son a fief holder but linked with those nobles not owning fiefs whom he had defended in the past, repeated before the Estates the demands for an assembly of the three Orders of the region.

The critique of the existing Constitution of the Estates of Provence had already been excellently done by Councillor d'André, and Mirabeau added nothing. What is new about his memorable intervention is the still more daring appeal to natural law, the irreverence in respect to the Sovereign.

I wish someone would tell me if it is really true that the King alone has the right to form the Constitution of the nation of Provence; if it is not up to the Nation . . . to correct its laws since it originally created them itself . . . ? Let no one any longer refer to that testament which bequeathed men like an inheritance. I only see the grounds for our union with the Crown of France in free elections, by a people exercizing their rights.

But what especially irritated the nobility, called upon to demand the general convocation of the three Orders, was the "insulting tone" of the gallery toward it. The turncoat gentleman was robbing the aristocratic faction of the privilege of being insolent.

The population of Aix excitedly followed the tumultuous debates of the Estates. As early as December 27, the Archbishop was insulted by the common people when leaving the *hôtel de ville* where the assembly was being held. On December 29, the tumult increased. "The Bishop of Toulon, passing before the cafés at the beginning of the *Cours* (public promenade), was pursued by unrelenting hooting and was obliged to hide in the first open house." In vain the Parlement issued an *arrêt* to forbid the tumultuous gatherings. On January 31, thirty grenadiers were obliged to escort the Archbishop; Mirabeau and his deputies of the Third Estate were cheered. On the same day the King's commissioners suspended the work of the Estates after they had voted the free gift.

But the entire province had been won over by the agitation in the capital. While the numerous deliberations of the municipal councils approved the action of the deputies of the Third Estate and sometimes paid hommage to the Comte de Mirabeau, we see new popular assemblies being formed. They grouped together 400 to 500 persons of all professions at Draguignan and at Sisteron, more than 300 at Lorgues, more than 200 at Solliès.

A few documents permit us to observe the rural population's rather fervent participation in the movement. Between February 2 and 18, the councils of nineteen towns and communities of the *viguerie* of Apt met to express their satisfaction to Clementis, the deputy of that *viguerie*. And these councils sometimes assumed the aspect of real assemblies of the heads of families, as at Lourmarin on February 15, when more than seventy persons grouped about Mayor Gorgier. On February 8 the twelve communities forming the distant and mountainous *viguerie* of Seyne, simultaneously held general assemblies, which numbered about 100 persons at Seyne, chief town of the *viguerie,* and at least twenty in the smallest parishes which were not even counted as having one household.

To the powerful activity of the Third Estate were added the steps taken by those nobles not owning fiefs, who despite Mirabeau had been permanently eliminated from the Estates by the assembly of the fief-holding nobility of January 23. They urgently demanded that the government assure their representation in the Estates General. The clergy of the Second Order, more timid and less well organized, nevertheless continued to show its desire to be henceforth included in the Provincial Estates and above all to participate in the approaching national convocation.

The echo of this unanimous demand reached Necker. At dinner he had received the deputies of the three Orders of the city of Aix—Levesque, Bouche, Pochet, and Mollet de Barbedelle—who had seemed to be "good folk." He had read with interest the entreaty drawn up by Councillor d'André, then had asked for new clarifications on the traditional manner of selecting deputies from Provence to the Estates General. The man was hesitant by nature; he was not aware of French provincial traditions; but he was moved by the sincere desire to be informed and to be fair. The demonstrations of public opinion reassured his timidity and strengthened his decisions. Besides, he did not have the same reasons as Brienne for treating with respect the fief holders of Provence, who on January 21 had dared to condemn the "unconstitutional propositions" contained in his famous report to the Council of December 27, which sanctioned the doubling of the Third Estate.

Necker, however, did not agree to the calling of a general assembly of the three Orders, an audacious measure which the King's representatives in the province expressly advised against and whose dangers to sovereign authority were to be seen in the Dauphiné.

The best solution appeared to be to submit Provence to the common law of the nonprivileged provinces of the kingdom, that is to say to have the deputies to the Estates General elected not by the assembly of the Estates of the region but by the electoral assemblies of the *sénéchaussées.* In the first two Orders, access to these assemblies was very freely granted to nobles without fiefs who were in possession of acquired and transmissible nobility, and to parish priests.

The *règlement* of March 2 which put forth the Sovereign's wishes, was accepted by all except the fief-holding nobility, which could see in it only the overthrow of the Constitution of Provence and the destruction of its own privileges. It deliberately disobeyed by proceeding to elect a dissident deputation on March 12 and 13. President Fauris de Saint-Vincent had few illusions about the efficacy of this step. "The prelates and the Third Estate," he noted in his journal, "have decided to go to the *sénéchaussées.* The nobles without fiefs will also go and make an appearance. These groups will name deputies for the Order of the nobility and it seems very likely that these deputies and not those owning fiefs will be accepted . . . ."

❧§§❧

The delegates of the Third Estate to the assemblies of the *sénéchaussées* were selected in the cities and rural communities during the last ten days of March. In Basse-Provence these first electoral meetings were accompanied from March 23 to 27 by popular insurrections which seriously troubled the large cities (Marseilles, Toulon, and Aix) and several communities of the *viguerie* of Aix and adjacent *vigueries*. These riots were directed against members of the upper clergy, seigneurs, municipal officers, and fiscal agents. The demonstrators pillaged public granaries and called for the establishing of price controls upon foods, the abandonment of credit, and the renunciation of seignorial rights. At Aups a seigneur who tried to defend himself was killed. The violence and the disconcerting instability of the common people of Provence astonished the Archbishop of Aix, a Breton. "The fury of the riots is terrible," he wrote on April 7. "The common people, in their hatred, threaten nothing but death, speak of nothing but tearing out hearts and eating them. And these same common people return repentant the next day, bring back what they have taken, and love as they hate . . . ."

In explaining this brutal burst of excitement, contemporaries naturally gave credit to exasperation with poverty, to the end of a winter which had destroyed orange, almond, and even olive trees, and during which the grain monopolized by speculators "was more expensive than rare." They also did not fail to see in it the final results of that revolutionary agitation which since the end of 1787 had gradually spread to every community of the province and which exploded into violence here and there on the occasion of the popular assemblies preliminary to the elections of the deputies in accordance with the *règlement* of March 2. But, going infinitely far beyond the original demands of the Third Estate's first leaders, the common people declared "that it wanted to pay nothing: neither taxes, nor dues, nor debts."

What attracted the attention of every observer is that the popular revolution did not spare the bourgeoisie, especially those in municipal governments, who in order to pay the community's taxes, were quick to create taxes on alcoholic beverages so odious to the common people. In some places, observed Fauris de Saint-Vincent, the insurrection became "an open war of the poor against the rich, not only against holders of fiefs, but against the bourgeois, against the parish priests . . . ." And the Comte de Caraman wrote in a letter to Necker: "As the attack by the peasants was directed against everything which seemed to dominate them, the upper Third Estate, closer to them, was also the worst treated. This pushed that class, which was greatly opposed to the nobility, toward the nobility, into an alliance against the common enemy. . . ."

The principal craftsman of the reconciliation was Monseigneur de Boisgelin, who finally succeeded in the mediation he had vainly pursued for more than two years, and whose disappointments still wrenched this resentful cry from him on April 11: "It is true that there has been nothing more unjust than the Third Estate, nothing more stupid than the nobility, and nothing more worthless than the clergy." He was seconded by the Parlement of Provence, which had members in both camps.

The Archbishop set the example by sending on March 25 a circular letter to the ecclesiastics of his diocese, in which he formally expressed his desire for the proportional taxation of the clergy. On the morning of March 27, while a militia made up of nobles and bourgeois succeeded in re-establishing calm, which had been troubled for two days by the popular insurrection, the Parlement invited "the three Orders to be reconciled, to unite their feelings, their desires, their interests . . . ." That evening, about sixty fief-holding noblemen, gathered at the home of their *syndic*, Monsieur de Pourrières, unanimously supported a declaration by President de Jouques "by which he swore that he desired proportional taxation on all his noble and commoner possessions and invited all those possessing fiefs to do likewise."

On the same day the committee of ex-assessors, which had given the signal for the insurrection of the Third Estate in the autumn of 1787 by publishing the *Mémoire sur la Contribution des trois Ordres*, announced the end of the struggle to Necker.

The nobility, the burgeoisie, and the artisans have united, mingled, and armed themselves together, in order to control the multitude or rather those vagabonds, thirsting for pillage, who had stirred up this multitude. These movements are merely the war of the ill-intentioned poor against the rich. It has already ended and the example made of one or two wrong-doers will strengthen public calm. These events have nothing at all to do with the questions raised among the various Orders and perhaps the fact that they saw they were all threatened and that they have the same interests to defend presents an opportunity for reconciliation.

Denying all solidarity with the popular revolt, the upper bourgeoisie of the robe thought it could establish limits for the revolution which was beginning—a common illusion among the notables of this period.

The way has been prepared for the regeneration which is going to take place in the National Assembly. The pre-eminence of the first two Orders will be recognized, the special protection of their property will be assured. They will themselves offer the motherland the sacrifice of their exemptions, which cannot be included among their legitimate property and which must finally end along with the motives which had established them. The common people will realize that they must be succored but submissive, that they are the strength of the State, but that they would be only a blind force if they were not directed.

❦

On March 27, 1789, the former assessors of Provence, who for years had led the deliberations of the assembly of the communities, had still not understood that their reign had ended and that control over the Third Estate had escaped them.

They stirred up the Third Estate on the day following the Assembly of Notables, against the attempt by fief holders to assure themselves of control of the provincial administration. But, paralyzed by the cleverness of their adversaries, the hostility of Brienne's government, and their own timidity, they did not lead it on to any victory.

A few months later, the announcement of the Estates General created great hopes and brought forth new leaders not impeded by any superstitious or selfish attachment to traditional institutions, some of whom, like Councillor d'André, had that independence and authority which—sometimes—is characteristic of a gentleman. They proposed the recasting of the Estates of Provence, carried out in a general assembly of the three Orders which would be formed like that of the Dauphineé. They demanded legitimate representation for the social groups which had until then been neglected: nobles without fiefs and the clergy of the Second Order. They welcomed the popular classes into the assemblies of the Third Estate, which became impressive before becoming tumultuous. Mirabeau, who had reached Provence during January 1789, put his oratorical genius into the service of a cause which his political intelligence showed him to be already won. And Necker, impressed by the strength of the movement, abandoned the fief holders and the last defenders of the Constitution of Provence. While the former assessors, willingly or unwillingly, had to step aside, the principal ringleaders of that victorious campaign, Bouche, Mirabeau, and d'André, became deputies from Provence to the Estates General.

PART III

The Popular Movement in the French Revolution

REVOLUTIONARY CROWDS

*§ By Georges Lefebvre

The specific notion of *crowd* was introduced into the history of the French Revolution by Dr. Lebon. It implied the existence of problems which before him had scarcely aroused concern. But if this author's contribution is, in this respect, undisputed, it goes no further. Prolific and hasty, he remains confused and superficial. He did not state the problems; he did not elucidate the notion of the crowd itself. Sometimes he means by crowd a heterogeneous aggregate of individuals; elsewhere he contrasts the crowd with the elite and then it becomes nothing more than the diffuse mass of the lower classes. He passes from one notion to the other and arbitrarily confuses them; this is probably because he thinks that man is generally guided by what he calls *"mental contagion,"* a contagion which, however, he has neither studied nor even defined. These weaknesses are only half surprising. Indeed, Lebon had no direct knowledge of either the social or the political history of the Revolution and found his documentation in Taine. We can draw two conclusions from his books. The first is that, in speaking of the *crowd*, he was not at all concerned with studying it, but concealed behind this term a certain conception of mental phenomena so that the specificity of the crowd in reality disappears to make room for a problem of individual psychology. The second is that revolutions in general and the French Revolution in particular are the work of unconscious gatherings, prompted by more or less sincere leaders, and they therefore have no causes other than the works of the *"philosophes,"* who inspired the leaders themselves. It is rather curious to see a man who claimed to be a realist thus joining the partisans of the purely ideological conception of revolutionary movements.

Dr. Lebon's assertions have haphazardly made their way into so-called historical works which are really polemical works, but serious historians have gleaned nothing from them and have not touched upon the problem of the crowd. This is regrettable, for they alone can provide sociologists with the indispensable source materials. We must also add that the sociologists themselves have scarcely been interested in the problem because the crowd constitutes a collective rather than a social phenomenon, a "degraded" phenomenon whose fluctuating characteristics are not easily grasped.

Historians of the Revolution implicitly seem to consider the Revolutionary crowds as voluntary meetings of individuals animated by a common emotion or an identical way of reasoning, for the purpose of a more or less concerted action or a holiday celebration. These are not crowds in the specific sense of the word, but *assemblies*. Historians are evidently thinking of manifestations such as those of June 20, 1792 and June 2, 1793; of insurrectionary marches, of those of August 10, 1792, for example; of the celebrations of August 10, 1793, and 20 Prairial of Year II. These assemblies differ from the crowd in that they indisputably show a certain organization: the National Guard and the *sections* provided the framework.

But we might reply that the crowds of 1789 did not assume the same characteristics. First of all, the combatants of July 14 and the marching column made up principally of women, directed by Maillard, on the morning of October 5, show no trace of organization. The same is true for the agrarian riots. But above all we can see that before assuming the characteristics of assemblies oriented toward action, the gatherings of 1789 were at first formed, if not always by chance, as a pure crowd, at any rate for reasons foreign to revolutionary activity. On Sunday, July 12 a part of the Parisian common people had collected around the Palais Royal to stroll about and enjoy the fine weather, when the news of Necker's dismissal suddenly modified its state of mind, created a *"state of crowd,"* and prepared the abrupt change of the aggregate into a revolutionary assembly. The women who met on Monday, October 5 probably wanted, or at least most of them did, to demonstrate against the scarcity and high prices of bread, and it is only later that the aggregate was abruptly transformed into a marching column headed for Versailles. At Igé, in the Mâconnais, on Sunday, July 26, the peasants had attended the mass as usual and had very naturally begun to collect outside the church. This assembly turned into a revolutionary assembly directed against the château, which was the point of departure for the agrarian revolt in the province. During the Great Fear, the gatherings at first formed at the news of brigands' approach. If a person conquers panic, he proceeds to organize his defense. It is only later that sometimes—this is not most frequently the case, far from it—the

assembly assumes a revolutionary character, that is to say, hostile to privileged persons and to the king's agents. Throughout the entire Revolution,
we encounter similar abrupt mutations of a crowd into an offensive assembly, notably in market places or at the doors of bakeries, during periods
of scarcity. They are much more interesting for our study than the preparation of a methodically organized insurrection.

Second, when faced with an assembly, we cannot consider it as a simple
meeting of men whose ideas or passions have been aroused, independently,
in the consciences of each of them; if they form a group to act, it is first
of all because an intermental action and a formation of a collective frame
of mind had already taken place. The sudden mutations which we have
just described make us look for a similar preliminary operation. The con-
vulsive movements of the Great Fear can be explained in no other way.
Doubtless, historians implicitly admit it, and they sometimes even describe
the aims which the gatherings pursued or analyze their feelings. But we
must agree that they have not done very extensive research on this question.
They prefer to study the conditions of economic, social, and political life
which, in their opinion, lie at the heart of the revolutionary movement—
and to also study the events which marked it and the results it achieved.
Now, wedged between these causes and effects is the formation of the
collective frame of mind. It establishes the true causal link, and we can
surely state that it alone permits us to understand the *effect*, for it sometimes seems disproportionate compared with the *cause*, as the historian
too often defines it. Social history can therefore not be limited to describing the external aspects of antagonistic classes. It must also come to understand the mental outlook of each class; in this way it can contribute to
explaining political history and especially the revolutionary assembly's
actions.

Last, though a gathering is a concerted action, the men included in it
do not as a result think and act from that moment on in the same manner
as if they had remained isolated. In the formation of the collective mentality we also take into account the more or less involuntary aggregates
which can bring individuals together in their daily life. If we define the
revolutionary gathering as an *assembly*, we must then study its relationship to the *crowd* itself.

These are the three questions which we propose to examine briefly.

THE CROWD IN ITS PURE OR "AGGREGATE" STATE
SEMI-VOLUNTARY AGGREGATES
THE ABRUPT MUTATION INTO AN ASSEMBLY

In its pure state, the crowd is an involuntary and ephemeral aggregate
of individuals like those who collect around a railroad station when a train
is due, or in a street or public square at the moment when schools, offices,
and factories pour out their population which mingles with shoppers and
passers-by. Urban topography imposes a certain itinerary upon them; the

density of the crowd depends upon it as well as upon the time of day and the weather.

In its "social" aspect, this crowd is characterized by a provisory disintegration of its various groups. Halbwachs clearly demonstrated that between the workshop he is leaving and the family to which he is returning, the worker, in the crowds of the street, momentarily escapes the institutions which socialize his activities.

This undoubtedly explains the feeling of joy experienced by certain individuals upon losing themselves in the crowd; it also explains the anxiety felt by others. The former feel liberated, the latter are terrified by the idea of being abandoned to themselves.

Composed as it is of disintegrated social elements, the pure crowd seems devoid of a collective mentality. This is simple on the surface, and we shall see what we should really think about this.

It is principally to this pure crowd that the hypothesis of "mental contagion," upon which Lebon relied so heavily, applies. But we must remember that Durkheim has peremptorily demonstrated that it includes under one name a number of essentially different operations: (1) the leveling of ideas by intermental exchange; (2) the adoption of an idea by reasoning, by considering its utility, by sympathy or concern over conformity, by fear of material or moral constraint; (3) last, the contagion itself, which is a contagion of movement, as manifested in animal aggregates. The first two types of operations include intellectual components and could not be considered mental contagion. With this reservation in mind, the contagion of movement can be effectively seen in the crowd, but this possibility can not be considered the essential characteristic of the crowd.

Having thus defined the *aggregate* or pure crowd, we must first of all notice that between it and the voluntary *assembly* are a number of meetings of an intermediate character which might be called *semi-voluntary* aggregates. We will discuss those which we believe played a role at the beginning of the Revolution in forming the collective mentality and in preparing *assemblies*. This role is particularly important in the rural areas where conversations in the workshop, the street, and the café are not as important as in the city.

Agricultural life under the Ancien Régime brought the peasants together much more often than today, at least in many regions. The French plains were generally areas with open fields. The village land was divided into parcels where crop rotation was compulsory, either because there was indeed *contrainte de soles* (compulsory rotation) or because free grazing and division of the land into small portions made this practice absolutely indispensable. During the periods of plowing, sowing, haying, and reaping, to say nothing of the vintage, the peasants thus all went together to the same piece of land. It is not impossible that, from the point of view which concerns us, there was a principle of differentiation between these regions and the *pays d'enclos* (enclosed countryside)—especially the West and the

Limousin—or the mountainous regions. We must add that during reaping and the vintage, migrant workers and the practice of gleaning in bands also played their part.

More apparent is the influence of the Sunday Mass which was invariably followed by a meeting in the church or the public square, after which groups would form in the cabarets. It is also known that Sunday played an important role in the agrarian troubles; we have already cited the example of Igé in the Mâconnais. For the same reason Monday was equally feared; on that day the plans made on Sunday were carried out.

The market place also is of prime importance. We know that the peasant could not sell his goods at home, especially his grain. He was obliged to transport it to town and to display it before the customers' eyes at a specified time and place. Afterwards he would make the most of his journey and go shopping. Thus the rural population came into contact with that of the towns; this is how it learned the latest news. But circumstances permitting, it was also touched by the ideas fermenting among the city-dwellers. If there were commotions at the market, the peasants told the village about it, and the village became frightened. If there was scarcity, the peasants came to the market to buy, and the townspeople were frightened in their turn to see these starving men come in such great numbers.

During such periods of crisis, the circulation of grains, which in that era could only be done by boat or, more commonly, by wagon, constantly stirred up gatherings which stopped or pillaged the vehicles. Mendicity developed and soon bands began to circulate. But nothing was more feared than the line which constantly formed at bakery doors in large cities; no gathering is more apt to be suddenly transformed into an assembly of rioters.

In all the cases we have just enumerated, the meeting is not voluntary. Men go to work, to Mass, to market, to the bakery in order to tend to their affairs, not to form groups. Still they know perfectly well that their fellowmen will do much and that they will find themselves caught up in the crowd—and they consent to it. Even better: they are happy and most of the time would be very vexed to be alone. Others look upon the meeting as a distraction and a pleasure which are not the essential objects which they pursue, but whose loss they would sharply feel. They are also the reasons why they continued to go to market after having been authorized to sell at home in 1774 and in 1781. This habit continued well into the nineteenth century for grains and has persisted for minor produce.

Arthur Young would still be able to make fun, as he did in 1788, of the peasant who wastes his time going to sell vegetables or eggs for a price which is not worth the time he spends. But he did not take into account the distraction which the peasant finds in doing so.

We are thus led to mention purely recreational meetings. In towns they are daily, or occur at least every Sunday, in fixed locations which serve as tacit meeting-places. The role of the Palais Royal in Paris is well known.

An assembly of this sort was, as we have recalled, the origin of the revolutionary assembly of July 12, 1789. In the rural areas, "votive" festivals or *"baladoires"* fulfill the same function in a way which is naturally more intermittent. They had always been feared. In July 1789 the agrarian movements in the Beaujolais were hastened, we are assured, by the votive festival of the Holy Manger. With these assemblies we obviously advance one step further. One undoubtedly takes a walk and goes to a festival to enjoy the fine weather, to look at the shop displays, and to listen to the buffoons, not, strictly speaking, to talk or to gather together. But the pleasant prospect of seeing people also counts, and all the other prospects would be spoiled or perhaps would even vanish if one were afraid of being alone.

Last, once the Estates General had been called, then assembled, one last type of meeting deserves to be pointed out. First of all it is a question of the electoral assemblies held in the parishes to elect delegates and draw up the *cahiers de doléances*. It is also a question of the spontaneous gatherings which formed in towns to await the mail and to listen to the reading-aloud of letters sent by deputies or friendly correspondents. These meetings had great influence upon the evolution of the collective mentality. In the electoral assemblies, the members of the Third Estate recapitulated all the grievances which they had once expressed individually. Nothing was more suited to encouraging the leveling which we shall discuss and at the same time to reviving bitterness and anger. The gatherings which formed to hear the latest news more than once, at Rennes in July 1789, for example, changed into groupings for revolutionary activity. Here we almost have the voluntary assembly. The local inhabitants were convoked by the King into electoral assemblies, but it is evident that they did not come against their will and that they expected to act collectively. One came to hear the news for his own purposes, but at that moment the collective revolutionary mentality had already been born and, if a person was impatient to be informed, it was in view of possible action.

However, we move even a little closer to the revolutionary assembly with the assemblies convoked in a great number of towns at the end of June and in July 1789 to draw up and sign addresses to the King and to the National Assembly concerning the events in Paris and at Versailles. This step doubtlessly remains legal and even respectful in theory, although the words employed are not always so. But these addresses, usually planned with the deputies, already constituted public acts.

If the preceding explanations offer, as we believe they do, a glimpse into how several of these aggregates were able to be abruptly transformed into *assemblies*, it is no less true that considerations of another sort, which we will now discuss, make the phenomenon still more intelligible.

In describing above the simple *aggregate* or *pure* crowd, we made one reservation about the absence of a collective mentality in which we might be tempted to recognize one of the characteristics of the aggregate. Indeed, we believe that this absence has never been anything but apparent. Every human aggregate forms within society. It is true that, to become a part of it, the individual must provisionally break away from the social group to which he normally belongs; but he cannot for all that completely throw off the collective mentality of the group. The ideas and feelings which it involves are only pushed into the back of his consciousness. The degree to which this repression occurs depends upon the degree of heterogeneity in the aggregate. In the aggregate formed at the exit of a factory, the workers escape from the ascendancy of the economic institution of the employer, but they escape from the collective mentality of their class much less easily. In the rural aggregate we have described, there is no reason why the peasants should completely lose sight of the interests and emotions of the village community. Besides, these men share in the collective mentality of groups which do not find expression through institutions, for example the consumers' group *vis-à-vis* producers and speculators. It can happen that the aggregate, far from weakening this collective mentality, on the contrary strengthens it. This is the case of the market-place aggregate, for example, and of the line outside the bakery. We might even affirm that within the aggregate, the individual escaping from the pressures of the small social groups which form the limits of his daily life, becomes much more sensitive to the ideas and feeling which belong to the more extensive collectivities of which he is also a part. Finally, no matter how involuntary and heterogeneous the aggregate may be, its members are to no lesser degree a part of society, in the broadest sense of the word, and it is impossible to erase from their consciousness the elementary collective idea without which a society cannot be conceived, that is to say that its members have the right to see their life and their goods respected. Lynching has been looked upon as the symbol of the crowd phenomenon. In our opinion, it proves that within the aggregate is the collective idea that whoever attacks the safety or property of one of the members of the social body should be punished. When the aggregate turns against the *gendarme*, or policeman, a collective idea of a more complex nature can be observed, that is to say that the guardians of public order can very well attack individual liberty, either by error or voluntarily, and that it is the collectivity's duty to control their actions. In this sense, the typical phenomenon of the aggregate or of the pure crowd would be panic. When its members become convinced that they are no longer able to protect themselves collectively against the peril which threatens their existence, the social tie is definitely broken, and the individual has no other recourse but to seek his salvation in flight.

From these observations we can draw two conclusions:

1. We can say, without paradox, that for the human species the simple aggregate or crowd in its pure state does not exist. For we have defined it as heterogeneous, and it is never completely so, its members always participating to some degree in a collective mentality. This of course does not mean that certain characteristics of the pure aggregate, which is animal, are not encountered in the human aggregate.

2. The components of the antecedent collective mentality being simply

repressed into the depths of consciousness among the members of an aggregate, it suffices that an external event recall them to the surface for these men to abruptly regain the very vivid feeling of their solidarity. The sudden awakening of the group consciousness, provoked by a violent emotion, gives the aggregate a new character which could be called the "*state of crowd.*" In highly cultivated contemporary nations in which civic feeling is highly developed, the phenomenon is especially impressive when, within an aggregate, the news spreads that the existence of the nation, its leader, or its basic interests are in peril. Instantly the aggregate once again becomes aware that it belongs to the nation.

Is it not therefore easy to understand how an aggregate can be abruptly transformed into a revolutionary assembly? It suffices that a collective revolutionary mentality be first developed in the population and that an event occur which recalls it to the surface level of the consciousness from which it had momentarily been dismissed by the causes which had determined the aggregate's formation. The mutation will be all the easier if the aggregate provokes a psychological over-stimulation as would a votive festival, or if by nature it permits a collective mentality of opposition, as in the market place or the line outside the bakery in periods of scarcity.

Consequently we conclude that there is no revolutionary assembly or, if one prefers to use the word *crowd* in the imprecise sense commonly given it, that there is no revolutionary crowd unless an appropriate collective mentality has been previously formed.

THE COLLECTIVE REVOLUTIONARY MENTALITY

Its formation clearly implies economic, social, and political conditions which vary according to the situation and which it would be impossible to examine here. In 1789 these conditions led to the insurrection of all who belonged to what it is agreed to call the Third Estate against privileged persons and against the King's agents who had been entrusted with maintaining an oppressive legality and a good share of whom, moreover, were members of the aristocracy. But the Third Estate's mentality was far from being uniform. The peasants suffered much more under the Ancien Régime than did the city-dwellers, and they were grappling directly with the seigneurs. Food shortages, which accentuated the irritation against privileged persons and against the King's agents, also tended to break up the Third Estate by putting into opposition the poor and the rich, the consumer and the producer, the city-dweller and the peasant. In other periods, the problem is stated in a completely different manner. In 1830, national sentiment played a predominant role; the July Days undoubtedly had a political and social character. The former Third Estate wanted to defend the Charter and put an end to the government of the nobles and clergy, but above all they reproached the King and his allies for having come to power with the help of national disasters. The tricolored flag took its revenge upon the white flag. In February 1848, the political ideal—universal suffrage and the Republic—was combined with class conflicts exasperated by the economic crisis. In June 1848 these class conflicts alone were involved. The commune movement of 1871 was even more complex.

It is very clear that the revolutionary mentality is first formed in individual consciences, more hastily, to be sure, in some of them. But its collective features result from intermental action. How is this intermental action expressed?

Above all by conversation. Until a period very close to our own, the inadequacy of public instruction, communication difficulties, and material and political conditions allowed only a limited scope to the propaganda methods with which we are familiar: the brochure, the newspaper, and the public meeting. Today conversation is still the major instrument of propaganda; it alone can reach indifferent persons. But it is not as such that it played the greatest role in the formation of the collective mentality, at least in the past. In the course of daily conversation men unconsciously and without premeditation exerted upon each other the mental activity which unified their thoughts. Thus we must not believe that the collective revolutionary mentality was suddenly formed on the eve of the Revolution. Its germination goes far back. In 1789, it was based upon the common people's memories, upon a very old popular tradition in whose formation and transmission evening chats surely played an essential role. This oral tradition already included leveling and processes of abstraction. The antagonism between the peasant and his seigneur was as old as the feudal system and had been expressed throughout history by countless jacqueries which popular traditions kept alive if not as a precise and detailed account, at least as a sentimental impression.

Once revolutionary agitation begins, one of the peculiar traits of conversation, which is to deform the news, exerts a powerful influence upon the evolution of the collective mentality. The news is transformed so it will harmonize with the collective mentality, and thus comes to confirm its constituent notions and to excite its emotive elements. In 1789, and for a long time afterward, the news was in most cases spread orally; the state of communications and of the press permitted no control over it. The Great Fear can not be explained any other way. But it is evident that, since then, the distortion of the news through conversation has not ceased to occur, especially in time of crisis and, of course, this need not necessarily be a revolutionary crisis. The war of 1914 provided striking examples of this distortion.

Next to conversation, propaganda can also contribute to forming the collective mentality through the printed word, songs, and speeches. In 1789, the printed word played an important role in the ranks of the urban and rural bourgeoisie, but it did not directly reach the popular masses. Until the meeting of the Estates General, speeches were unable to gain acceptance except in urban electoral assemblies. But once the Revolution had begun, this form of propaganda developed greatly, and clubs were created partly for the purpose of organizing it. After 1815, it became permanently established, and repression was never completely able to suppress it. Indeed, we must observe that propaganda can very well assume an almost unconscious form, the printer, the peddler, the wandering minstrel spontaneously flattering the collective mentality in hope of profit. The almanac, the prints from Epinal, and the popular song must be taken very much into account when one studies, for example, the formation and spread of the Napoleonic legend.

Finally, the collective mentality also develops under the influence of the coercion which the collectivity exerts upon the individual. It is above all a moral coercion, and the feeling of calm and irresponsibility gained through conformity comes powerfully to its aid. But the fear of losing customers or of no longer finding work is far from negligible, and as passions break loose the fear of corporal ill-treatment or of crimes perpetrated against property becomes increasingly important. The study of these different factors would make an especially profitable study for historians. Naturally it is not easy to discern the traces of these factors at work and above all to collect an adequate amount of documentation. There are no files on them in the archives. But the component parts are not lacking. Every study of "the public spirit" or "opinion" should include a description of the economic, social, and political conditions and a re-creation of the collective mentality which reflects it, with the most precise indication possible of the processes by which it was formed. Unfortunately, not many of the numerous books whose titles arouse such hopes, actually fulfill them.

The intellectual operations for which intermental action serves as the point of departure of necessity only reveal themselves to the historian by induction and are not, strictly speaking, within his purview. It seems that first of all there is a leveling. Also, the wrongs which each peasant may have suffered as an individual are blamed entirely upon his seigneur, then upon all the seigneurs, each one of them being jointly and severally deemed responsible for all the complaints. Even today the various categories of feudal rights, in their infinite variety, are sometimes described as if every peasant had invariably borne all of them. The natural consequence of this leveling is that through abstraction it forms a seigneur-symbol, so that the individual characteristics of a particular seigneur are observed with increasing difficulty, or so that, in any case, one is less and less disposed to take into account any moderate or beneficent characteristics they might have. It also happens that in the course of the agrarian revolts, peasants excused themselves from doing violence to "such a good seigneur"; they nevertheless burned his archives. At Lisle-sur-le-Doubs, Arthur Young, called upon to say whether he was on the side of the aristocracy, defended himself vigorously, but he added, "Suppose I were a seigneur, what would happen then, my friends?' . . . 'What would happen?' they replied in a harsh manner. 'You would be hanged, for you probably would deserve it.' "

We must, however, realize that this process never attained perfection. All through the Revolution we see seigneurs escaping banishment and remaining tranquilly in their châteaux during the peak of the Terror, because their former vassals did not personally wish them any ill.

The collective image of the seigneur attributes to him a perverse, egoistic will which leads him to oppose and to frustrate by all possible means any reforms which would threaten his supremacy. We can certainly admit that the peasants generously attributed this desire to him because, being closely attached to their lands, they knew perfectly well that in the seigneur's place they would not have acted otherwise. As soon as the peasants learned that the King had called the Estates General, they interpreted this news as proof that Louis XVI wanted to relieve their misery; and since, to their minds, he could only succeed by suppressing at least a part of the taxes, all the feudal rights, and the *dîme* as well, they concluded that the privileged classes would strive to prevent at any cost the reforms for which they would be bearing the financial burden. From this arose the suspicion of an "aristocratic plot" which was only too fully vindicated by the privileged class's opposition to the vote by head and then the attempted military coup against the National Assembly. This is a fundamental trait of the collective revolutionary mentality of 1789. It was reinforced during the succeeding years by foreign intervention, but from 1789 the collusion of the privileged classes with the European aristocracy had been predicted and played an important role in the Great Fear.

Once the adversary symbol has been created, the inability of a common man to analyze the causes of an economic crisis—which "experts" themselves do not always identify with certainty—does not fail to blacken the picture if material circumstances become unfavorable. No distinction is made between permanent abuses and the temporary hardships resulting from unemployment and scarcity. The dominant class is held responsible for both of them, and not always unjustly. This is what happened in the course of the years 1788 and 1789, and the economic crisis also contributed greatly to unleashing the revolutionary movement. The same was true in 1848, and that time it was the bourgeoisie which was taken to task. In 1789 the seigneur, the *décimateur*, and the King's agent were accused of gouging. Even better: the food shortages were linked to an "aristocratic plot," organized by the adversaries of the Third Estate to punish it for its rebellion. This explains the murder of Foulon and Bertier.

If the portrayal of the adversary is pessimistic, that of the long-suffering classes is to the contrary optimistic. During the revolutionary years the poor were endowed with every virtue. In addition, it is true that literature since Jean-Jacques Rousseau had exploited this theme, and that it—rather than the collective mentality of the *sans-culottes*—is responsible for the clichés to be found in parliamentary speeches and newspapers of the period. But it is certain that the *sans-culottes* spontaneously created the image of an ideal *sans-culotte* whose basic attribute was poverty. Even today, a militant labor-unionist or socialist more or less consciously imagines the proletarian to be like him and confers upon him the idealism and disinterestedness with which he is himself personally, very truly, endowed.

It follows that, to achieve the social good and to assure the happiness of mankind, one has only to suppress the hostile class. And since the individual happiness of each depends upon this suppression, all the members of the oppressed class become animated with an ardor often completely lacking in the dominant class. But this is what the revolutionaries do not know or do not wish to believe. They attribute their own emotions to their adversary. And since the adversary is rich, since he benefits from the support of the State, and since in 1789 the revolutionaries saw his weapons, numerous servants, and more or less fortified chateaux, they overestimated his strength and greatly feared him. We know today that in 1789 the French aristocracy only realized the danger very belatedly, that it did nothing to organize the "crushing" of the Third Estate, which it was accused of premeditating, and that when the Court tried its coup it proved to be lamentably incompetent. This is doubtless why no importance has been attached to the idea of the "aristocratic plot" which exerted so great an influence upon the popular masses. Yet it holds the key to many events, and in it we have a conclusive proof that it is not enough to tell how things really happened at Court and in the château. We must also, and above all, reveal in what manner the revolutionaries thought things would happen or had happened—and this is a study of the collective mentality.

We still must say a few words about the affective and moral characteristics which are associated with the revolutionary mentality. To us the most striking seem to be anxiety and hope.

After what we have said above, anxiety is self-explanatory. One has everything to fear from an adversary as one imagines him to be. In 1789 they thought that the seigneur was going to make an appeal to the King's troops, to foreign powers, and to "brigands," that is to say to the vagabonds and beggars who had multiplied because of food shortages and unemployment. On July 14, nothing seemed more legitimate than to credit a concerted plot with the senseless acts of the governor of the Bastille, who suddenly ordered his men to open fire upon the crowd, which had not fired a shot, and then upon a delegation bearing a white flag, sent by the Hôtel de Ville. This anxiety turned to fear at the end of July. We find it again throughout the entire Revolution in the form of suspicion, and it explains the *loi des suspects*. It turned into an illness, the illness of suspicion. We shall not discuss whether or not it is normal for revolutionaries to be suspicious of their adversaries and to organize themselves to resist them. But we must point out that, even agreeing that suspicion was unreasonable until June 1789, it became legitimate after the attempted *coup d'etat* by the Court, and that all the information we possess today concerning the plots of subsequent years and the appeal to foreigners, shows that suspicion became increasingly well founded.

This anxiety is not cowardliness. It would be childish to deny that it caused many persons to act with reserve and that during the Great Fear it frequently degenerated into panic, but the "Great Fear" is basically very improperly named. In reality the event is much more accurately characterized by the very rapid reaction which led the revolutionaries to arm themselves for defense and for the counterattack. And, in the cities, the announcement of the military *coup d'etat* which began on July 11 with the dismissal of Necker did not arouse any fear at all but, to the contrary, a very sudden burst of indignation and very precise measures of defense against royal power. The bravery, audacity, and offensive spirit were certainly very unequally distributed among the partisans of the Revolution, but these are qualities which the revolutionary mentality in its final form unquestionably includes. Class solidarity in the presence of peril is more widespread. Beginning in the spring of 1789, we find uncertain persons addressed with the threatening question: "Are you part of the Third Estate?" Even more widespread, naturally, for it involves less risks, is the punitive will to which were joined hatred and a thirst for vengeance. Hence we have the murders and the destruction or burning of chateaux. But to attribute these excesses to the "collective madness" of a "criminal crowd" is to present only an incomplete picture. In such a case, the revolutionary assembly is not unconscious and does not feel it is guilty; to the contrary, it is convinced that it is punishing justly and in good earnest. Even the September massacres sometimes took the trouble to organize a tribunal. Throughout the entire Revolution here and there we encounter the idea of a "popular justice," summarily organized and at times even more summarily applied, but which would merit being studied closely, for it would surely throw a great deal of light upon the collective revolutionary mentality and even upon the collective mentality of the popular masses in general. Likewise, when peasants systematically demolished or burned a chateau when they could have contented themselves with destroying the archives if they had been thinking only of feudal rights, it was not madness. It was the desire to punish the seigneur through the goods which were so precious to him and which were the symbol and the basis of his power.

But hope, which we earlier placed at the top of the list along with anxiety, seems to us more important than these last traits. Once the perverse will of the dominant class has been broken, universal happiness will immediately arise. The optimistic picture that the revolutionary class forms of itself excludes all difficulties. It will suffice if the dominant class disappears. In this respect the collective revolutionary mentality obviously is akin to the millenarianism of certain religious groups: the revolution is also a "gospel." The French Revolution has very likely been portrayed as a religious crisis because it was a great hope. Objections to this are self-evident. Yet it still seems true that the sentiment we are discussing was in part the origin of the revolutionary cults. The new society which is born or will be born worships itself, conscious of its perfection. Mathiez was not wrong in trying to apply Durkheim's ideas when undertaking a study of the beginnings of the revolutionary "religion." Hope also explains, at least in part, the disinterestedness and spirit of sacrifice—in short, the idealism—shown by the insurgents, the soldiers, and the obscure "militants" during every revolution.

The affective characteristics of the revolutionary mentality take into account this tendency to action which distinguishes the revolutionary assembly from the aggregate. During such periods, when men meet to celebrate a holiday, the *state of crowd*, which we have defined above, is established from the very beginning, and without the intervention of an external event—and this *state* is already a deed because it invincibly implies the resolve to attain the new society. When men intentionally meet to give battle, the revolutionary assembly occurs in its most characteristic and pure form. The aggregate's abrupt transformation into a revolutionary assembly requires, on the contrary, the intervention of an external event which awakens affective feelings. In the market place, this would be the quarrel between a buyer and a merchant; in the line outside the bakery, the invectives of an audacious individual; in the village, the arrival of the tithe collector; during the Fear, the announcement that brigands are coming. But there will always be a will to act, either defensively or offensively.

Finally, these characteristics shed some light upon the relationships between the revolutionary assembly and social conditions, and upon the manner in which the collective mentality tends to spontaneously create institutions. It is generally held that the revolutionary mentality and assembly are essentially destructive. And indeed, the assembly, whether its planned action is defensive or offensive, always attacks lawfulness. The collective revolutionary mentality is even more pernicious because, from the moment of its birth it tends to break down the traditional collective framework by contesting its legitimacy and by ruining the authority of the traditional leaders.

Now, every institution rests on the conviction that it is just and beneficial, and it only endures if the men who represent it inspire respect and confidence. But we forget to add that, if the assembly born of an aggregate through an abrupt mutation is naturally lacking in organization, the pure and concerted voluntary assembly on the contrary procures a staff and leaders. The day after July 14, the revolutionary masses in Paris organized themselves into national guards and into districts which later became the *sections*. It is these batallions of the National Guard and these sections which serve as a nucleus for the insurrectional movements of 1792 and 1793. During the troubles of July 1789, the revolutionaries replaced the former royal authorities with committees of their own choosing. Yet we must turn to the collective mentality, especially if we want to understand the constructive power of the revolutionary movement. Indeed, it grants the new leaders their indispensable authority; it recognizes that they are necessary and trusts in them. These leaders can be elected. The Constituent

Assembly owed its unparalleled prestige and authority to the collective revolutionary mentality. But these leaders can also suddenly reveal themselves and impose themselves during the course of events. Moreover, the elected ones often were nominated because their activities and speeches had attracted attention. In short, we are here touching upon the question of the "*meneurs*" or "ringleaders," which deserves a detailed study in its own right. We have succeeded in giving the word "ringleaders" a pejorative sense, and it cannot be denied that, if certain leaders were disinterested idealists who sacrificed their personal interests and even their lives to the cause which they had embraced, there were others on the contrary who were *agents provacateurs* and who made money on the influence they had managed to acquire. More numerous are those who are consumed by the desire to play a role, either through vanity or ambition, or who are predestined to command because of their authoritarian temperament. But we should admit that we have no proof that the majority of the ringleaders were corrupt, and the character of the others is most often complex. The vain, the ambitious, the authoritarian are not necessarily lacking in sincere convictions, and we cannot even be certain *a priori* that the man who profits from his personal influence does not to some degree share the ideas and emotions of those whom he leads. Ringleaders are like other men, and those who defended the established order were similarly moved by complex motives among which disinterdness and love of the public good did not necessarily hold first place. Far from it! In any case, whatever their secret motives, the ringleaders were only heeded if their speeches and orders fitted the needs of the collective mentality. It had given them their authority, and they only received because they gave. This is why their position was difficult and their prestige often ephemeral. For since hope is one of the essential elements of the collective revolutionary mentality, confidence in these leaders vanishes if an event belies hopes.

Moreover, the creative efficacity of the revolutionary movements varies with the extent and intensity of the collective images. One becomes especially convinced of this in studying those born of food shortages. If rioters can find no other causes for their misfortune than the greed of a certain merchant whom they have before their very eyes, they will limit themselves if successful to imposing some rules upon the market or some relief measure. If, on the contrary, they blame the municipal government and the royal agents for conniving with the monopolists, it can happen that they take authority away from the government to confer it upon groups of their own choosing. Finally, if they accuse the central power itself and realize that to put an end to scarcity and high prices, legislative measure, price fixing, requisition, and national controls over basic commodities are indispensable, their rebellion can provoke, as in 1793, a complete reorganization of the national economy. We can add that the effectiveness of the movement also depends upon its territorial extent. If it is the act of a small portion of the nation, the reaction or inertia of the majority will promptly result in its

downfall. The great Revolutions cover all or almost all of the State's territory. This is why revolutionary parties are unitarian; and counter-revolutionary parties are either conservative, particularist, or federalist. Here we
can catch a glimpse of a special case of the question remaining to be examined, that is to say the influence exerted upon the mentality of the
individual and also upon the collective mentality by the very existence of
the aggregate or assembly, an influence which is related to their density and
their extension.

THE SPECIFIC ACTION OF THE AGGREGATE AND THE ASSEMBLY

In attempting to define the revolutionary assembly and to explain the
formation of the collective mentality which serves as its support, we have
until now only relied upon individual psychology and intermental action.
This does not mean that from the historical point of view the aggregates'
role, which we discussed at the beginning of this study, can be considered
as inconsequential. To the contrary! Since the collective revolutionary mentality is formed by conversation and propaganda, everything which puts
men into direct contact is favorable to its development, and at a time when
propaganda by means of the printed word and the public meeting was not
in use or did not directly reach the masses, it is evident that aggregates
exerted a capital influence. It is none the less true that, after what we have
said up to now, there is no distinction between the mental operations which
took place in them and those which were to be seen in daily collective life
where men exert an intermental action upon one another by occasional
contact. They are alike; the aggregate merely speeds up the rhythm.

The moment has come to examine whether this outlook explains everything and whether the aggregate and the assembly, by their mere existence,
do not exert a specific pressure upon the individual. An affirmative reply is
certain. First of all, the aggregate creates the impression of a force which it
would be folly for the individual to attempt to resist. If constraint con-
tributes to forming the collective mentality, the aggregate, by its very size,
confers a special effectiveness upon it. But we must say more: it exerts a
constraint for which the intermittent relationships between men could find
no equivalent. At heart the individual is not only attracted by the feeling of
quietude which conformity confers; or uniquely by fear of cruelty that one
or another of his fellow men can inflict upon him. The aggregate, by its
very size, destroys the will to resist, somewhat like the tempest and the
unleashed ocean.

But the aggregate's activity becomes particularly effective as soon as the
collective revolutionary mentality is pushed into the foreground of the
conscience, by inciting it to action. This feeling of collective force, which
imposes the collective mentality upon hesitant persons, at the same time
encourages all those present to take up the offensive against the political
or social authority which is resisting them. The aggregate and the assembly

are inventories and, into the balance of power, they throw the force of pure number, by making it visible and tangible. Their influence is particularly strong upon the most emotional persons. It takes into account the audacity which is abruptly aroused in some of them during the riot, and thus we see how in the course of a popular movement, ringleaders appear who had taken no notable part in the propaganda and whose role ends with the violence. On the other hand, the feeling of individual responsibility is weakened or disappears within the aggregate. The phenomenon is in part an unconscious one. As the individual more closely assimilates the collective mentality, he becomes its instrument, and his activities cease to be autonomous. But the phenomenon can also be conscious in one respect. The individual calculates that, in the crowd, he will not be recognized, or that no one will want to testify against him, or that it will be impossible to punish everyone who has participated in the uprisings. Last, we must pay great heed to the anguish resulting from the attack. In the aggregate which forms upon the announcement of a danger, as for example during the Great Fear, and even more so in the insurrectional assembly, organized for the purpose of activities involving a risk, individuals exert an intermental influence upon one another which is also undoubtedly physiological and which stimulates their nerves and increases anxiety to its peak. In this case they plunge into action to free themselves from it: they flee forward.

We have now only to indicate one last aspect of this research. We have tried to create a distinction between the aggregate and the voluntary assembly. But we must now say that, in some manner, the latter always has something of the former. When an assembly is formed, it cannot prevent indifferent persons, unhealthy elements which want to fish in troubled waters, and *agents provocateurs* from incorporating themselves into its mass. As a result, it loses a part of its homogeneity. It once more becomes heterogenous like the aggregate, although to a lesser degree. Second, the topographical configuration also exerts a certain influence upon the assembly. It is undoubtedly less powerful than on the aggregate. All the same, the ravages of a band of urban rioters or of peasants in revolt are not solely determined by the hatred they have vowed for one individual or another, one public authority or another. It happens that they strike at one point and spare the other because the street plan or the layout of roads led a band to one particular house or château. Last, the contagion of movement which enables us to recognize the animal aggregate within the human aggregate cannot be excluded, although there is no need at all to attribute to it the importance Lebon attached to it. In the demolition of châteaux, in physical cruelty and murders, one gets the impression that certain individuals began to strike because they saw others doing so. They would undoubtedly not have done it if they had not been a part of the collective mentality, but it is not sure either that all of them went into action consciously and this is what establishes the particular responsibility of those who serve as examples. It is not even forbidden to wonder whether, in the course of the phenomena we have tried to classify and describe, a sort of physiological magnetism does not intervene, which may play its part in the formation of the collective mentality, in the going-into-action and in the contagion of movement. Nothing would be more likely to encourage its action than the aggregate and the assembly.

We do not deny having adopted a middle position between Lebon who, in his idea of a crowd, postulates an identification between the animal and the vast majority of men, and those who, to the contrary, see in the crowd only a juxtaposition of autonomous individuals. To us the great gap in both of these theses comes in treating the collective mentality as an abstraction. We will willingly concede to Lebon that it tends to stifle in the individual the critical spirit which is the characteristic of man. But we will not agree that this mentality is in some way formed by a purely mechanical process, without the intervention of the operations which occur in the formation of every individual mentality. The collective mentality and, consequently, the mentality of the revolutionary "crowds" does not constitute a return to animalism.

THE BREAD RIOTS
OF MAY 1775 IN PARIS
AND THE PARIS REGION

ᴇᔆ **By George Rudé**

The popular movement of May 1775—the famous "flour war"—although often commented on by historians has never been the subject of a serious study. Contemporaries, however, never ceased to be much impressed by the extent and importance of a movement which, in the space of two weeks, took hold in Paris and Versailles as well as in the provinces bordering on the Capital—Normandy, Picardy, the Orléanais, the Ile de France, Champagne and the Brie; the bookseller Hardy speaks of it in his *Journal* as "an event which (some people) think of as epochmaking in the history of the monarchy."

We have wanted to study this movement "from below" and to follow its course and range in the areas where it was most extensive: in Paris itself, in the Ile de France and in the Brie; to this end, we have consulted above all the Archives of the Commissaires of the Châtelet of Paris and the minutes, reports (procès-verbaux), and sentences of the *Prévôté* of the Ile de France (Series Y in the Archives Nationales); we have also consulted Series B in the Archives Départementales of the Seine-et-Marne and of the Seine-et-Oise. This documentation, although partial, has permitted us to

191

"situate" the riots of May 1775 more exactly, call attention to their extent, and to correct the tendency of many historians to present them, following the example of Turgot and his disciples, as the expression of a plot of the great and the rich, rather than as popular unrest concerning the grain supply. Our work has also perhaps a certain value for the study of the French Revolution in so far as it allows us to look more closely at the participants in a movement that arose at the end of the Old Regime and to call attention to the rather remarkable similarities that exist between this movement and certain of the social movements of the Revolution.

Having taken over the *Contrôle général* in August 1774, Turgot was not long in applying the idea of the freedom of the grain trade so dear to the Physiocrats. The *Arrêt du Conseil* of September 13 re-established the freedom of the grain and flour trade within the realm; despite the resistance of the Parlement, it was registered on December 19. Although the new minister did not have much difficulty in convincing public opinion that all of the work of his predecessor, the abbé Terray, the protector of monopolies and partisan of state intervention, had to be swept away, the moment was badly chosen. "The harvests of the years before 1774 had not been very abundant," an official report of the time declared; the harvest of 1774 was not very abundant either. When the stocks were exhausted at the beginning of the year, the scarcity became evident, and the prices of grains went up rapidly. In the Paris markets, the price of the four pound loaf, which had been selling since the summer at 11 sous, went up to 11 sous and a half on March 8 and, on May 15, to 12 sous; and, according to Hardy, people were saying out loud in the markets: "What a fu . . . reign!" On April 12, bread was sold at 12 sous and a half, on the 15 at 13 sous and, on April 26, at 13 sous and a half. Reporting the price rise of April 12, Hardy observed: "People were all the more affected by this rise as a still greater one was already being spoken of, which fact did not cease to arouse the tempers of the *menu peuple* against the government." Still more indicative of the state of mind is the following incident reported by Hardy on April 26: "A *maître d'hôtel* having just bought a liter of green peas that he had paid 72 *livres* for, it was thrown in his face with the following comment: 'If your goddamn boss has the means to pay three *louis d'or* for a stinking liter of peas, let him give us bread'; and the *maître d'hôtel* withdrew prudently without daring to complain."

It was in this atmosphere of popular excitation that the movement of May 1775 was being prepared in Paris and the Paris region. Even before, there had been, in the course of the month of April, popular riots in the provinces, caused by shortage and the dearness of grains: at Dijon, Tours, Metz, Reims, and at Montauban; and an official report of the Parisian events of May 3 would note: "Finally we learned that in almost all the provinces and cities there had been a lot of ferment and uprising among the people."

The movement that historians have called the "flour war" was begun at Beaumont-sur-Oise on April 27. It will be seen later that what characterizes it above all is the ardor and unanimity with which the little people of the cities and villages around the Capital fixed the prices of bread, wheat, and flour at the "just" or traditional price—most often at 2 sous the pound of bread, at 12 francs the *setier* of wheat, and at 20 sous the bushel of flour. Moreover, it is a movement which, most often, took its point of departure at the local market from which it spread to the villages, the farms and the bakers' shops of the surrounding area. In general, one can summarize its course and chronology as follows: starting at Beaumont on April 28, it descended the Valley of the Oise, got to Pontoise on April 29, crossed the Seine at the bridge of Poissy and arrived at Saint-Germain on May 1. While a secondary movement spread out toward the east and was felt the same day in the markets of Saint-Denis and Gonesse, the principal current passed to Versailles on May 2, from whence it reached the Parisian suburbs and broke out in Paris on May 3. To the south of the Capital, a movement started on May 4, at Choisy-le-Roi and at Limours; at Arpajon and at Montlhéry on May 5; and at La Ferté-Alais on May 6. Meanwhile, the movement from Gonesse on May 1 was spreading to the districts situated to the east and northeast of Paris; but it was to the southeast of the Capital, and in the Brie especially, that the movement was to become most extensive: having left Choisy and the environs of Lagny on May 4, it got to the markets of Lagny, Brie-Comte-Robert, and Fontainebleau on May 5 and to those of Meaux, Coubert, Melun, and Nemours on May 6; May 7 it reached Corbeil and, on May 9, Beaumont-en-Gâtinais. On May 10, movements were reported in the environs of Rabais and Milly; but by that time the movement had already lost its main drive.

In order to understand better the nature of the movement, it is necessary to follow its course more closely. At Beaumont-sur-Oise, according to the testimony of Nicolas Bailly, dean of the notaries and *procureur* of the city, it was the indiscreet remarks made by a grain merchant which, as early as April 22, had provoked popular anger. On April 27, about noon, some street-porters of the town had come to the *procureur* to complain of the conduct of bakers who were refusing to sell bread. An hour later, the "populace" came back holding by the collar a grain merchant who was said to have offered his wheat at 32 livres the *setier*. The *procureur* was asked to set grain prices. He did not want to have anything to do with this proposition, "because he could not set a price on wheat." Upon hearing this refusal, the people occupied the market and fixed the price of wheat themselves at 12 livres the *setier*. The next day, upon the insistance of the merchants, Bailly made a search in several houses of the city. He was mistreated by the people who said to him: "Louse, you don't want to enforce the regulations nor lower the price of wheat; O.K., louse, I'll do it myself"; he refused, however, to make any arrests "because he had no armed force and no help from anyone at all."

At Pontoise, where the popular movement broke out on April 29, it was the public authorities who themselves fixed the prices of wheat and flour. According to the report of Saffrais de Boislabbé, counselor and *avocat du roi* at Pontoise, "the populace having come down to the port to pillage the boats," it was agreed "that the gates of the city would be closed and the bourgeois militia put under arms"; the lieutenant general himself fixed the price of wheat verbally at 12 francs 10 sous the *setier*, and it was at that price that "a number of individuals" bought the wheat at the port. The next morning, de Boislabbé, warned "that all the peasants of the environs were assembling to continue the pillage of the previous day," orally authorized the merchants to sell their wheat at 20 francs and their flour at 40 francs the sack, on condition of a promise to sell them at current prices as soon as military help arrived. Despite his complaisance, which caused him to spend seven weeks in the Bastille, de Boislabbé could declare to his interrogator at the Châtelet "that on that day there was no outbreak, not a single *setier* was sold in the fauxbourgs at less than the current price."

The next day, May 1, the riots started at Saint-Germain-en-Laye. Among those who came to the market to pillage and fix prices of grains and flour, there were many from the neighboring villages. They crossed the Seine at the bridge of Poissy, where the millers Leclerc and Sauvage reported to the commander of the *maréchaussée* of Triel that, about 10:30 A.M., "there had passed several peasants about whom they knew nothing except that they were from Triel and the surrounding villages and who had spoken to them threateningly, saying that they were going to Saint-Germain to look for flour." At eleven o'clock, the lieutenant general of police of Saint-Germain "having learned that the populace was rioting in the grain market" went to the market where he learned "that the people of both sexes, both from the city and the surrounding countryside, were doing violence to the merchants; that one part was forcing these same merchants to furnish them flour at 20 sols the bushel and wheat at 12 and 20 livres the *setier*; and another and principal part was throwing down piles of merchandise, cutting open the sacks with knives, taking and carrying away the merchandise without paying . . . which lasted until seven o'clock in the evening."

The same day the riot, before passing the next day to Versailles, spread out toward the east and, to the west and north of the Capital, reached Nanterre, Gonesse, and Saint-Denis. At Nanterre, a woman named Jarry, a baker, saw herself forced to sell at a loss sixty-one sacks of flour, a part of which was paid for at the rate of 40 sous the bushel "although it had cost her fifty-five." A weaver, arrested for having taken part in the affair, tried to excuse himself by declaring that it had been said that bread and flour had had their prices fixed. It was for having another baker woman of Nanterre to sell her grain below the current price that Marie-Geneviève Le Noble, wife of a vine grower, was condemned to be exhibited publicly in an iron collar and locked up for three years in the Salpêtrière. We have little information about the events that took place at Gonesse on May 1; but, according to a *procès-verbal* of the Châtelet, it was Pierre Cadet, called

Porcher, a thresher, who had taken over the leadership of the riot by provoking the people to pillage and inciting them to fix the price of grain at 12 francs the *setier* at the market; and it was Jacques Hazard, a laborer from Goussainville near Gonesse, who is supposed to have incited the rioting people against the *maréchausée*, crying out: "Hit the damn s.o.b.s; they're made out of flesh and blood like you."

Up to this point, the riots do not seem to have made a great impression upon contemporaries, but, having reached Versailles, the very threshold of the Court, on May 2, the movement created a great scandal. Hardy reports that "a kind of popular uprising supposedly caused by the dearness of bread" had begun at Versailles, that the King had been forced to give up going to the hunt and that "the Queen had shed tears over this event." According to Métra, whose testimony is often suspect, the riot was the work "of women especially who, as is well known, are more dangerous in this sort of crisis than men. He added that when the King came out on the balcony to harangue the 8000 demonstrators, "they scarcely listened to him, so excited were they." From a *procès-verbal* drawn up by the *Prévôté* we learn that the riot started as a result of the arrival in the city of people from about twenty surrounding villages, who, having joined with the Versaillais, pillaged the flour stocks or fixed its price from 20 to 24 sous the bushel and afterward invaded the bakers' shops. According to an official report of the day's activities:

Between eight and nine o'clock in the morning several audacious persons tumultuously entered the *Poids le Roy*, a warehouse for the flour sold in this city, where they are supposed to have cut open and pierced several sacks of flour which they then seized by violent means and without paying for them. . . . Some then went to the bakers' shops and pillaged bread; others having encountered in the streets wagons loaded with flour for the supply of Versailles made them turn back and then stole their merchandise.

Overwhelmed by popular action, the young Prince de Poix, the governor of the city, ordered the bakers to sell their bread at the price fixed by the people—at 2 sous the pound—a decision which, although annulled the same day by the intervention of Turgot, was to have important consequences, as we shall see.

The same morning, the riot broke out at Poissy. Peasants from the environs had entered the city and, re-enforced by those from Poissy, had gone to miller Souard's and the shop of Dame Blancharde, a grain merchant, to pillage and fix the price of flour and wheat. Among those who were arrested for participating in this affair was Robert, a day laborer from Poissy, "who seems to have been the one who led the troop of peasants . . . and who cried out 'Let's go, peasants, let's break into the house, because that's where the grain is.' " In the afternoon the price of flour was fixed at miller Robinet de Rennemoulin's, about 10 kilometers from Versailles, by about sixty persons who had come from Noisy and Bailly. "They said . . . that they wanted to pay only 20 sols the bushel, and in fact they bought or took about twelve sacks at that price."

Under the impetus of the events of Versailles, the movement reached the suburbs of Paris. At Colombes, an apprentice gardener was arrested on May 2 for having uttered seditious words on the subject of bread. At Boulogne, a vinegrower ("former baker") having been arrested for seditious activity admitted having gone with several other persons that same evening to two bakeries, where they had caused to be delivered, "without either threat or violence," bread at 2 sous the pound. At Epinay, on the main road between Pointoise and Saint-Denis, a carter who was transporting twelve sacks of flour to the Paris market was stopped by a wheelwright and a joiner "who were followed by a prodigious quantity of people"; his flour was taken from him and its price fixed at the rate of 25 livres, 5 sols the pack. In Paris itself, at the *Petite Pologne*, a certain Guérangé, having heard tell "that bread was being sold at 2 sous the pound in the *Pologne*," caused two butchers to sell him and its price fixed at the rate of 25 livres, 5 sols the sack. In Paris itself, next morning, Rémy Girier, a ragpicker from Bougival, having got bread from several bakers of Rueil at 2 sous the pound, explained his conduct in the following way: "Having seen bread being sold at Versaille at 2 sous the pound, he had thought that it was not worth more than that price . . . ; that he was ready to make restitution if it was worth more." The same day, at Vaugirard, when prices of baker's bread were fixed, it was reported that a woman linen worker had several times entered a shop "to ask for white bread at 2 sols the pound, saying that it was the wish and order of the King that it be sold only at that price."

On that day, Wednesday, May 3, "toward eight o'clock in the morning," the price of the four pound loaf was raised from 13 sous and a half to 14 sous in the Paris markets. It was almost at the same instant that the riot, passing through the barriers, reached the Parisian markets and then spread out to the bakers' shops of the city and *faubourgs*. Hardy, an eyewitness to part of these events, noted in his *Journal*:

The populace, stirred up by troops of bandits and brigands and which was said to have entered Paris principally through the St. Martin, Conference and Vaugirard gates, got rather excited in the *Halles* and pillaged the bakers' bread there. The rising soon became almost general within the city and the *faubourgs*; most of the shops were closed, such was the fright caused by the people running around the streets inviting the citizens to take this precaution. This populace undertook to pillage the *Halle aux grains* and to open all the sacks of flour found there; but, happily, they could not carry out their plan; but they compensated for this by going into all the markets and forcing the bakers to sell them their bread. They also forced private individuals who had [stocked up on bread?] to give it up, sometimes going so far as to break down the doors which the householders did not think it wise to open with good grace. The bread of the markets having been pillaged, the same populace became occupied with forcing the bakers' shops in the various quarters to open. To this end, they struck with poles, sticks, and even iron tongs the door of those who seemed to want to put up some resistance.

The *procès-verbaux* of the commissioners of the Châtelet, the declarations of the bakers and the interrogations of persons arrested allow us to make more precise the report of the day made by Hardy and even to correct him in those places where he allowed himself to be too much influenced —which happens rather rarely, by the way—by rumor. Unfortunately, as the police did not venture into the market until three o'clock in the afternoon, we are very poorly informed about what happened during the morning. The few indications we have come from the interrogation of about ten vinegrowers and others who, having come from Montesson, Rueil, Nanterre, and Argenteuil to buy wheat and flour, were arrested by the troops in the course of the afternoon, accused of having stolen grain and of having been "found with an empty sack in hand." According to their declaration, some of them had arrived at the market at eight o'clock "to buy flour at the rate of 20 to 24 sols the bushel" and, as early as ten o'clock, the gates had been closed; one of them claimed that he had succeeded in obtaining some flour—at the rate of 30 sous the bushel.

It does not seem, as Hardy among others suggests, that the rioters waited for the pillage of flour, wheat, and bread to be finished in the markets before going off to the bakers' shops in the city and *faubourgs*; the *procès-verbaux* of the commissioners of the Châtelet indicate rather that these movements took place simultaneously and that it is certainly not a question, for one or the other phenomena, of small bands of pillagers following a preconceived plan. A laborer arrested for having stolen a cheese worth 6 livres in a grocery store declared to Commissioner Serreau that he had seen the riot break out about eight o'clock at the *Barrière des Sergents* and that he had followed the rioters into the rue des Petits Champs, passing by the Porcherons and the Chaussée d'Antin. It was in this same quarter that a certain Rosier, a master baker of the rue Saint-Denis, saw come into his shop "about eight-thirty or nine o'clock in the morning a crowd of people, made up of men as well as of women and children . . . , who seized all the bread that was there, the product of six sacks of flour, to the value of 408 livres purchase cost and 21 *livres* for cooking." A certain La Roche, master baker of the rue de l'Arbre Sec, was to declare to Commissioner Chénon *fils* that, in the morning about nine o'clock "the populace entered tumultuously into his shop and forcibly seized and took away all the bread of all sorts without paying for it. He had used one and one half sacks of flour in its manufacture at 66 livres the sack, which came to 99 livres, plus 12 livres for the cooking." The baker Chappe of the rue Beauregard was obliged "at ten o'clock in the morning" to throw his bread out a first floor window to a group of individuals gathered in the street "in order to avoid having the door of his shop beaten down." And it was in the same quarter that, between ten o'clock in the morning and one o'clock in the afternoon, the crowd came to pillage and fix bread prices in the bakeries of the rues Neuve des Petits Champs, Tirechappe, Babille, and du Champfleuri.

Profiting from the absence of the guards, who showed themselves only in the afternoon, the movement quickly passed from the center to the left bank and the *faubourgs*. A water carrier of the rue Mazarine was accused of having entered a bakery in his quarter, where he was supposed to have refused to pay more than 8 sous for a 4-pound loaf, saying that it was by "order of the king." The laborers and water carriers of the place Saint-Michel were supposed to have fixed the prices or bread in the bakeries of the rue de la Harpe and neighboring streets at 2 sous per pound, and the widow Suire, baker of the rue des Boucheries, St. Sulpice parish, making a complaint to Commissioner Chenu "said that . . . her shop was assailed at about eleven o'clock in the morning by a bunch of riffraff, among whom were to be found many laborers and street cleaners, several of whom usually hang around the Luxembourg gate" and that they had taken 200 four-pound loaves "very few of which were paid for at the rate of 8 sous for 4 pounds."

On the place Maubert, according to Hardy, Commissioner Des Ormeaux "was constrained to allow the riffraff to enter his house and to give them the bread that a baker of the marketplace had deposited with him; his gates were forced open to make sure that there was no bread in his lodgings or his basement. A little boy of 10 to 12 years of age had the effrontery to enter the reception room, his study and to go to the back of his garden in order to carry out a more exact investigation."

Once again according to Hardy, it was a part of the rioters of the place Maubert who "went to the Abbaye Saint-Victor, marched right in and took three ovenfuls of bread from the nuns saying that their intention was not to steal the bread, that they were willing to pay for it at the rate of 2 sous the pound, but, nonetheless, the nuns got only 12 livres for the entire supply from those who were in good faith."

In the rue Mouffetard, *faubourg* Saint-Marcel, the crowds entered en masse into the bakeries; a wigmaker is supposed to have threatened a certin Jardin, a baker, saying to him: "You are not going to close your shop, you are going to be pillaged. How much bread have you?" Meanwhile, at the other end of the city, the workers and artisans of the Saint-Laurent and Saint Martin *faubourgs* were fixing prices in the bakeries as early as eight or nine o'clock in the morning. Workers employed in paving the Rue Faubourg Saint-Martin were arrested; one of them, whom the police asked how he knew that bread was selling at only 2 sous the pound, answered: "that his comrades had spoken to him of the revolt that had taken place the day before at Versailles and told him that bread had been fixed at 2 sous the pound." In the *faubourg* Saint-Laurent, "men had been seen to defy the watch company of the Paris Guard, showing them pieces of paving stones while they were loading their rifles." In the *faubourg* Saint-Antoine, several persons had been arrested for pillaging or for buying bread at less than the current price in the bakeries of the rues du Faubourg Saint-Antoine, Charenton, and Saint-Marguerite. About seven o'clock in the evening, the mounted musketeers were still seeking to disperse "a very numerous populace," and the crowd succeeded in liberating from the guardhouse "a poor woman who was creating a disturbance at the door of a baker's shop, where she was demanding bread."

But we are best informed about the events of the *faubourg* Saint-Victor and part of the *faubourg* Saint-Marcel. Commissioner Roland, whose jurisdiction covered the Saint-Benoît Quarter, was the only one of the twenty-eight police commissioners to have drawn up a comprehensive report on what happened in his quarter. This document, which is most important for the study of popular price fixing in Paris, contains the testimony for the study of popular price fixing in Paris, contains the testimony of twenty-eight bakers who often indicated the professions of the rioters, the hour of their arrival, and the amount of bread taken away. In his preamble, Commissioner Roland reports "that a gang of brigands who were gathering and entering into the baker's shops of the rues du Petit Pont, Gallande, Saint-Jacques, des Noyers, du Mont-Saint-Hilaire, des Bourguignons, des Lyonnais, Saint-Etienne des Grès, Faubourg Saint-Jacques, enclos Saint-Jean de Latran . . . took bread and threw it into the street to people of their own kind who were following them . . . . That the said bakers fearful of being exposed to a repeat performance of the same scene did not furnish their shops; we immediately ordered the bakers to knead and bake bread as usual, to supply their shops, telling them that they could be certain that the king, ministers, and magistrates would provide for their security and tranquillity."

It results from the declarations of two bakers of the enclos Saint-Jean de Latran that the riot began there at nine o'clock in the morning; the shop of one of them was invaded by a "quantity of boys and small boys whom his wife recognized as being apprentice shoemakers . . . he cooked three ovenfuls and gave them to all who came for them at 8 sous the 4-pound loaf." In the other bakery, "a troop of brigands carrying aprons, hachets and sticks, who resembled workers . . . among them the shoemakers of the street" entered and asked for bread at 2 sous the pound, but took away everything without paying for it. At ten o'clock, "a great quantity of vagabonds" entered a bakery of the rue du Petit Pont "saying that they wanted bread at 8 sous the 4-pound loaf. . . . They took away or threw to people following them everything in the shop." At 10:30, "a great quantity of brigands, who had small aprons, sticks, and sacks" took everything in a bakery on the rue Saint Jacques. Sibert, a baker of the rue des Lyonnais, testified that at eleven o'clock "brigands resembling apprentice hatmakers and repairers of procelain pottery" entered his shop and took 1200 pounds of bread. At 11:30, according to the declaration of a baker of the rue des Bourguignons, "some small boys wearing aprons made of hide entered and some men who seemed to be porters followed them" and carried away all his bread. At the same hour a little man "with a stick in his hand" went into a bakery of the rue Galande. "The people following him seemed to be Savoyards (that is, messengers and street workers)." At noon, "a large number of brigands who seemed to be merchants of rabbit skins" took all the bread from a bakery of the rue Saint Jacques. The declaration of a baker of the rue du Faubourg Saint Jacques is rather significant: he declared that "although there was a post of the Gardes Françaises almost directly opposite his door" the thieves, having already visited him once at 12:30, came back twice more in the afternoon. The losses suffered by these bakers were considerable; according to their declarations, they came to a total of 19,667 pounds of bread, an average of 700 pounds per head.

Despite the numerous arrests carried out in Paris in the course of the following days, nothing indicates that the riots went on there after May 3. Once the guards were mobilized and the patrols posted in the markets and at the bakers' doors, which began in the afternoon of May 3, the popular movement in Paris calmed down; but it continued or started again in the suburbs and especially in the countryside to the east and south of the Capital. On May 3, in the morning, an individual entered a bakery in Neuilly-sur-Seine and took away a 12-pound loaf "throwing a coin of 24 sous on the counter and saying that was what it was being sold for in Paris." In the afternoon, "several individuals dressed as peasants and armed with sticks" entered the same shop and took all the remaining bread "paying for it at the rate of 2 sous the pound." The same day, millers' warehouses were pillaged in Montmartre and the faubourg du Gloire in Paris. Laforge, miller at the mill of Couronnes, behind the enclos Saint Lazare, was invaded by 600 persons who took away twenty-six sacks of flour, while a gang of 1500 to 1600 "who had already pillaged the surrounding mills" came to the miller Egret in the same area and took away "forty sacks of flour, ten sacks of groats, and 17 *setiers* of wheat." At four in the afternoon, a woman named Glezy saw several individuals bring home some flour stolen from Pierre Devaux and Dame Coupe, millers at Montmartre. The next day and the day after, the police helped by the *maréchaussée*, searched Saint Denis, la Chapelle, and the *faubourg* du Gloire and were able to return to the millers part of the flour taken from them in the Paris market and the environs of Montmartre. Still on May 3, a riot broke out in la Villette, where the *little people* went to all the bakeries of the village and stole or fixed the prices of flour and grain in the market. The sieur Garmont, a baker, testified to the courtesy of the rioters, whose chief, a certain Charrois, a horseskinner, is supposed to have said to him upon entering his shop: "I'm very sorry about this, Monsieur Garmont, but we have to do it." His confrère, Jean Leduc, master baker of the chaussée de la Villette, got an altogether different impression of Charrois and his companions; he declared indeed, that "those wretches" having stolen all his bread, flour, and groats, "which he estimated at about 600 livres . . . were not content with having broken and pillaged all his merchandise; they threatened to kill him, which makes him fear much for his life." "On the same day there were riots at Dammartin and Louvres, to the northeast of the Capital. At Dammartin "a troop of bandits" were said to have pillaged a grain storehouse, and, at Louvres, gangs of peasants went to the farmers and forced them to sell wheat at 12 livres the *setier*."

Meanwhile, the movement that had reached Gonesse market on May 1 had spread, starting on May 2, to the countryside located to the east and northeast of Paris. According to a declaration made to Commissioner Chenon *fils* by Lorinet, schoolmaster and recordkeeper of the *bailliage* and *seigneurie* of Gagny, as early as May 2 it had been said in his village that "wheat was being distributed cheaply" at the great Charlemagne farm at Bobigny. On the morning of May 3, therefore, Lorinet and his companions went by coach to Bobigny where they found, however, only one *setier* of "*briblanc*" (a poor quality grain) for which they paid 6 livres, 6 sous. The next day they had better luck and got wheat at 12 livres the *setier* from Charlemagne and from the farmers of Groslay and Drancy. Meanwhile, the villagers of Sevran and Aulnay went to the local farmers and "had wheat given them at 12 francs the *setier*." The same day at Sevran, a farmer complained that the laborers "came to his place . . . asked him for wheat . . . . They paid what they wished, that is, 12 francs for the *setier*." They returned the next day and took "a total of 16 to 18 *setiers* for which he got a sum of 120 livres." Again on May 3, the people of Bondy, neighbors to those of Gagny, went to Charlemagne at Bobigny. Finding no more wheat there, they went as far as Petit Drancy to the Royemont farm, "belonging to the brothers of the Saint Lazare Order" and to a farm in Clichy. Everywhere they had wheat given to them at 12 francs the *setier*.

[The movement continued in the same region on May 4.] On that day, Nicolas Chartier, a *laboureur* of Blanc Mesnil, was obliged to deliver wheat at the rate of 12 francs the *setier* to villagers of Groslay and Sanat. His declaration seems to prove that often, despite the popular price fixing, relations between farmers and villagers remained good: "Seeing himself obliged to give them grain at this price, he wanted the people of his own area to profit from the cheapness; consequently, with all possible orderliness and without violence, he had 69 *setiers* measured out for all these people. From that moment on, inhabitants of villages other than his own, having been told that they had behaved badly, came back and brought with them what they had taken or paid for it at the current price; following their example, several persons of his area had also brought back grain, so that in a few days he hopes to be completely [indemnified] for his loss."

The movement that started in Versailles on May 2 and reached Paris on May 3 spread toward the east in the following days—into the countryside and villages south of the Capital. [The same pattern of pillage and price fixing was repeated in this area. The movement to the south and southeast of Paris was the strongest of all. Each new episode seemed to breed another one in the immediate vicinity. At Meaux, not only was the market pillaged but also the flour mills and the houses in the city popularly supposed to be stocked with grains. The bakeries were, of course, not spared. The movement spread to the countryside where *laboureurs*—and sometimes priests and seigneurs—were forced to sell their wheat at 12 francs the *setier*. The movement that had started in Choisy and north of the Marne spread into the center of the Brie, where it went on for three or four days, reaching its peak on May 6, in places like the region around Villeneuve. On the seventh, the movement picked up once again in the west on the banks of the Seine. The price of wheat was fixed at 12 francs the *setier* in the market at Corbeil.]

But by May 8, the movement, although still spreading, had lost its momentum. At Tournan, wheat was being sold in the market at 22 francs the *setier*. Near Brie-Comte-Robert, the *maréchausée* dispersed with blows of their swords a crowd of 2000 people who were preparing to advance on the market . . . . Before dying out, the movement crossed the Seine south of Melun and would reach as far as the Gâtinais. Already on May 5, a riot had broken out at Fontainebleau and, on the sixth, at Nemours. On May 9, at Beaumont-en-Gâtinais, Françoise Martin, the wife of a vinegrower, is supposed to have "incited the people to revolt and to pillage by boldly fixing the price of wheat at a figure well below its value." On the tenth, women were supposed to have set grain prices at Dammarie, near Melun, but the reports become rarer and less precise. The popular price-fixing movement, having raged for about two weeks, had exhausted itself or had succumbed to government repressions.

Indeed, to put an end to these riots, the government had, from the very beginning, refused to lower the price of bread and had chosen to use repressive means. On May 2, the day of the riot of Versailles, the "stupid manoeuver" of the Prince de Poix, who had fixed the price of bread at 2 sous the pound, was already being vociferously criticized. The next morning in Paris, although warned of the imminence of a riot, the government gave a new pretext to the rioters as the price of bread was allowed to rise by another half sou. At 11 A.M., after three hours of pillage and price fixing among the grain merchants and of flour in the bakeries, a police ordinance was published forbidding anyone to force bakers to sell bread at less than the current price. Lenoir, the lieutenant general of police, who, it was said, was opposed to the repressive measures suggested by Turgot, was obliged on the next morning to send his resignation to the King. He was replaced by Albert, an ex-*intendant de commerce* and a faithful partisan of the Controller General. A resolution of the Parlement, in which the King was asked "to be so good as to order more and more steps to be taken, steps inspired by his prudence and his love of his subjects, to bring down the price of grains and bread to a rate proportionate to the needs of the people," was annulled. On May 9, the Minister had the bishops send an "instruction" to priests ordering them to proclaim from the pulpit the pure doctrine of free trade. "The pastors do not need to be told to make their parishioners see that any usurpation of [this] foodstuff, even if paid for at a price inferior to its value, is a true theft, censured by human and divine laws and which no excuse can change in the slightest."

Meanwhile, the government had recourse to more rigorous measures. Gatherings were forbidden under penalty of death. Turgot mobilized two armies, one of which, under the command of the Duc de Biron, was to watch over Paris, while the other, commanded by the Marquis de Payanne, was to act in the Ile de France. Two rioters were hanged in the Place de Grève; numerous arrests were made in Paris as well as in the markets and the surrounding countryside. Strong patrols guarded markets and the doors of bakeries until October. As a result of these measures it was possible to suppress the riots and to impose upon the people respect for the principles of free trade. The prices of bread and wheat remained high for a long time: it was only on October 14 that the price of the 4-pound loaf, which had remained at 13½ sous since May 6 in the Paris market, went down by half a sou, and the price of the *setier* of wheat, which was worth 32 livres, 10 sous at Rozay-en-Brie at the beginning of April, went to 32 livres at the beginning of July, and went down to 26 livres, 5 sous only at the beginning of October. Popular intervention, despite its extent and the fear it had aroused in the governing classes, had thus been of little value against the tenacity of Turgot and military repression.

How is one to explain this "flour war"? Is it really a question of a popular movement provoked by famine and the rise in the price of wheat and bread, as our presentation of the events would lead one to suppose. Or was it rather, as contemporaries and most historians have it, an aristocratic or clerical plot, whose aim was to starve out the Capital and to bring about the fall of the Turgot ministry. This last point of view certainly does not lack supporters. To be convinced of this, we have only to cite the following judgments. Among contemporaries let us cite:

Métra: "All of this did not come at all directly from the people, but from a strong and wicked cabal which wishes to destroy the Controller General . . . . The abbé Terray is strongly suspected of being at the heart of the Cabal."

Hardy: "The party of financiers, and that of the Jesuits and the clergy were suspected of having had some part in the present troubles."

The author of the "Instruction . . . to All Parish Priests": "It seems that the goal of the plot was to produce a true famine in the provinces surrounding Paris and in Paris itself, in order to incite the people, through need and despair, to the worst excesses."

And Miromesnil, the *garde des sceaux:* "It would seem that there was a plan formed to lay waste the country . . . to starve out the big cities and especially the city of Paris."

And to put this "plot" into execution, to arouse the villagers and the little people of Versailles and Paris, there is supposed to have been an avant-garde made up of carriers of watchwords and "orders of the king" and of "foreigners" and "unknown persons," professional press gangs. "Brigand-age," one reads, "was incited by men foreign to the parishes they have just devastated." In the Parisian region, "troops of unknown persons with sav-age faces swelled the ranks of the people and directed their movements." Near Chartres, "there are unknown persons running around the villages, inciting the people, saying that it was an order of the king to sell wheat at 12 francs the *setier*." The day of the riot at Saint-Germain-en-Laye "it was said with confidence that emissaries were spreading out in the cities and villages persuading the *menu peuple* that they were going to die of hunger." And Métra added that "in the pockets of most of the seditious commoners arrested there were many half louis d'or."

It is evident that the commissioners of the Châtelet did not think of the origins of these riots in any other way; that is what results, at least, from their way of interrogating their prisoners. Let us cite, as an example among many others, the following excerpts from the interrogation of a woman named Tanton, arrested for having put herself "at the head of a gang of pillagers of wheat" in the market at Brie.

Asked to declare who had incited her to commit this sedition;
She answered that no one had incited her;
Asked if it were true that a few days before some ill-intentioned persons had not passed through the village of Hierre, saying that they were bearers of orders to set the price of wheat at 12 francs and showing papers which they said con-tained the said orders;
Answered that she knew nothing about it, that she had not seen the persons and had not heard it said that they had been seen at Hierre or in the environs;
Asked if these same persons had not incited her and others to go to the next market at Brie and to those in the environs to riot, promising them a reward for such action;
Answered, no;
Asked if it were not true that she had received money to incite her to riot;
Answered no and that she had only the 50 sous she had spoken of to us.

To uphold the thesis of a supposed conspiracy, we find, it is true, a cer-tain number of "proofs" in the documents we have consulted. Did not the first riot begin at Beaumont-sur-Oise, not far from the Château of Ile-Adam the home of the Prince de Conti, the zealous defender of the Parlement and bitter enemy of Turgot? Among the thirty persons locked up in the Bastille as a result of this affair, were there not ten priests and country vicars, a grain merchant, an ex-consul of the King at Tripoli, a police coun-cilor, an ex-president of the Conseil Superieur of Rouen, and—a convincing proof—the sieurs Sorin and Doumerc, who had been the administrators of the grain supply under the abbé Terray? Had not an officer of the house-hold of the Comte d'Artois distinguished himself among the most muti-nous of the rebels at Versailles? It is incontestable, moreover, that in the

Brie, it was two gamekeepers of nobles, Louis Chevalier and Simon Bodart, who were most often noticed as leaders of the gangs of villagers that had gone to the farmers' and the vicars' homes to fix the price of grain. At Roissy, in the Brie once again, the farmers were supposed to have incited persons to "pillage" by giving money to their domestics and others to go buy grain cheaply; and three of the vicars locked up in the Bastille admitted having lent money to their parishioners to do as much. Had not the administrator of a bakery at Vaugirard, where bread prices were fixed at 2 sous the pound on May 3, declared to the police that one of the individuals who had entered his shop "had taken a handful of money from his pocket, in which the deponent noticed several louis (d'or), that he had thrown a 2-sous coin onto the counter and had gone away, crying out in the village . . . that the price of bread had been fixed at 2 sous by order of the King?" And, on May 20, Commissioner Chenon had in fact received from Albert, the lieutenant general of police, the order to go to Écouen to arrest and bring to the Bastille "a man named Petrer, a glazier, and a man named Badran, a groom . . . . They are the creators of the disorder and pillage that took place at Villers-le-Bel and other places. They have declared that it was some rich people who had sent them to pillage and had given them money."

Here are rather more striking proofs than those invoked by Métra and certain historians to support the thesis of a noble or clerical plot. Nonetheless, the minute study of the facts will suggest that this explanation is ill-founded. That the Prince de Conti, like many other privileged persons, desired the fall of Turgot and that he may even have sought to profit from his troubles, would not be astonishing; but nothing permits us to conclude that he organized and provoked the riots in order to achieve his ends—not even the proximity of Beaumont-sur-Oise, the point of departure for the riots, to his château at Ile-Adam. Indeed, more than one riot would begin in this region without our being able to indict, for this reason, the Prince or his heirs. The revolt against "the overly large quantity of game" for example, which on the very eve of the Revolution would break out at Gergy, Pontoise, Ile-Adam, Beaumont and so on, "whose hunting rights are the property of His Highness the Prince de Conty," and some months later, as Georges Lefebvre has pointed out, one of the currents of the Great Fear —the Fear in the Clermontois—would follow exactly the same Valley of the Oise, passing through Beaumont, Ile-Adam, and Pontoise. The arrest of Sorin and Doumerc does not indicate the existence of a plot on the part of the monopolists and the financiers. These gentlemen, who had acquired a very bad reputation as administrators of the grain supply, were not arrested as suspected of having participated in the riots, but rather for having wasted public funds during the administration of the abbé Terray. Nothing suspect having been found in their papers, they were released on June 20. It is very probable that, as Hardy claimed, they were arrested at this time "to give a kind of satisfaction to the people."

The arrest of a dozen priests or country vicars ought not to permit us to rally to the thesis of a Jesuit or clerical conspiracy. There is nothing in the interrogations of the vicars that allows us to suppose that any one of them had consciously incited his parishioners to riot against the farmers of the royal authority. All that can be ascribed to them is that they showed themselves a bit too indulgent toward their parishioners who were attracted by the opportunity to buy grain cheaply and even that they caused grain to be bought for their own account. One of them had even presided over the distribution of their grain by farmers of the environs of Meaux, but it was at the suggestion of the farmers themselves, who were afraid of a general pillage of their goods; moreover, the difference between the current price and the price that had been fixed was restored to them several days later. In any case, no one of the priests was judged by the Courts that took jurisdiction over the affair; none remained more than two months in the Bastille. As to the other "great persons"—and there were many—whom the popular imagination or the agents of the Ministry thought to be involved in this affair, it was never established exactly what role they supposedly played: the King destroyed the dossier of reports he had received.

Even if the so-called conspirators-in-chief escape us, do we find in the documents incontestable proof of the existence of carriers of orders, of "unknown persons," of "foreigners," or of hired gangs so dear to certain historians? In general, not at all. At most, it can be claimed in this respect that, in a few places, it is possible that some local leaders had shown farmers and bakers false Orders in Council and false orders announcing the fixing of prices of bread and grain. The case is rare enough, and we have found no example of such documents in the archives of the Châtelet or elsewhere. This accusation was made, however, against more than one of the prisoners by the police. A woman named Tanton, for example, arrested as a rebel in the market of Brie and of whom we have already spoken, was accused of having given herself out as "a titled person who had certain orders"; and it was in regard to her, no doubt, that Chevalier, the gamekeeper, declared in his deposition "that he had heard it said that a woman disguised as a man had caused grain to be sold at Brie at 12 francs the *setier* and had said she had orders to this effect." Tanton defended herself against this accusation energetically, claiming that it had been the rioters who had called her "our princess" and that "it was this qualification repeated as a joke that had given rise to the remarks brought up in the trial." [An investigation of the police reports reveals that these carriers of orders, "unknown persons" and "foreigners" were figments of the imaginations.] Among the hundreds of prisoners arrested in Paris and the Paris region, we do not find a single one who can be called a foreigner to the place of his arrest; and the declarations of the farmers are especially remarkable for the long lists they give of persons who were perfectly familiar to them among those who had come to set prices on their grain.

[Those persons accused of distributing funds to the rioters and who were found in possession of some money had perfectly good reasons to have had it with them. In short, there is no reliable evidence of such a distribution, and none of the bakers or farmers whose grain was taken at fixed prices made reference to having been paid in the large coins that had supposedly been given out. As to the allegation that the riots were part of a plot to starve out Paris, once again there is no evidence. Grain was taken wherever it could be got, not only from convoys destined for the Capital.] The accusation of a plot against Paris was commonly made in the eighteenth century against those who got in the way or seemed to get in the way of the free circulation of grain toward the Capital. It was, indeed, easy to cry out against a plot when it was a question of social and economic movements that people did not understand.

If the study of these documents does not allow us to rally to the thesis of a plot supported by hired gangs, how are these riots to be explained? Who were these rioters who were so freely called "brigands"? It is incontestable that, in general, they were not persons without means of making a living (*gens sans aveu*) or vagabonds, but rather the rural and urban little people stirred up by hunger and by the opportunity that presented itself to buy bread, grain, or flour cheaply. In the cities there was, among the local rioters, a predominance of workers; in the countryside and among those who, coming from neighboring villages, went to the markets, we find especially vinegrowers (but fewer in the Brie, obviously), agricultural day laborers, and small artisans. We have already noted the role played by the streetporters in the riot at Beaumont-sur-Oise, by worker masons at Versailles, by the sackcarriers at Meaux, and in Paris by the laborers, watercarriers, pavers, worker hatmakers and shoemakers, and others. Among the 145 persons arrested in Paris on May 3 and the following days, we can count about one hundred salaried workers, a dozen small merchants and heads of workshops, and fifteen rural persons. A great proportion of these workers and artisans were illiterate: two thirds of them did not know how to write their name. There were many "non-domiciled" persons—about forty lived in furnished rooms and ten in their employers' homes—but very few persons without means of making a living; there were only four who claimed not to have a fixed domicile. Thus, the proportion of workers among the rioters was very marked. In the Parisian region, on the other hand, especially in the villages, the rioters were drawn from wider strata of the population. In the Brie, among the villagers, there have been noted gamekeepers, schoolmasters, wealthy peasants, and even a surgeon; and we have already noted the equivocal role of certain farmers and vicars. Altogether, the village population seems rather well represented in the gangs that went to the farms: of the 260 persons arrested in the Brie and the Ile de France about whom we are best informed, there were about forty vinegrowers, forty small merchants, tavernkeepers, and shopkeepers, forty agricultural day laborers, and about sixty journeymen and heads of workshops of various trades. Of 170 other persons whose names are mentioned in the farmers' declarations, there are a dozen vinegrowers, twenty small merchants, twenty agricultural day laborers, and sixty artisans. And of all of them there are scarcely two or three without fixed domicile, whom we can call vagabonds. Moreover, among all these "brigands," whether from Paris or the surrounding countryside, there were very few criminals: of 252 persons on whom we have details as to this question, there was only one habitual offender, and about fifteen others who had served earlier prison terms, usually of very short duration.

Why did this *menu peuple* of the cities and rural areas engage in a movement of revolt of so great a magnitude? It is without doubt that the shortage and the rise in prices were at the origin of this movement. We have seen that, following on the bad harvest of 1774, hunger riots had broken out as early as March and April 1775 in various regions of the country and that, as early as April 12, Hardy noted the ferment provoked in Paris by the rise in the price of bread. The reports of the commissioners of the Châtelet indicate the excessive poverty and lack of grain as the motives of popular intervention. But the form of popular intervention—price fixing of bread and grain—and the range of the movement cannot be explained by poverty and shortage alone. We must also take into consideration the popular mentality, resolutely opposed to the new ideas of freedom of trade and partisan of the notion of the "just price," a notion which, moreover, was not limited to the people: the Parlement, a part of the clergy and of the royal officers held to it is well, as we have seen. It was as a result of the persistence of this notion, no doubt, that popular action, provoked by shortage, took the form of price fixing of grains.

Once the movement had begun, it was not necessary that there be organized gangs of carriers of orders or distributors of money in order for it to spread. In certain markets, no doubt, the popular explosions were provoked by special causes—at Paris, for example, where the price of bread was raised on the very morning of the riot—but, in a general way, it was the rumor of the price fixing which, carried from market to market and market to village, served as the principal motor for spreading the movement. . . . We must not believe that this contagion emanated from the example of popular action only: in Pontoise, Brie-Comte-Robert, and especially in Versailles, the magistrates themselves set prices of grain and bread; and the people believed firmly that the prices of foodstuffs had been set "by order of the king." That is why many respectable, even responsible, persons allowed themselves to be persuaded that they were committing no crime by summoning bakers and farmers to sell their bread or grain at the set price; and many paid the rest of the price, in money or kind, once they had understood that they had bought their goods below the current price. Moreover, we must not lose sight of that "electricity" or "nervous excitation" of the revolutionary crowd, of which Georges Lefebvre speaks. The Tanton woman, for instance, asked to explain her seditious conduct, "answered that she had been carried along as she had just said and agreed that she had got excited and no longer knew what she was saying or doing." Others excused their conduct by claiming to have "acted like the others," having been "carried along by the multitude," by a "bad example." How many, indeed, did no more than follow the example of their neighbors, profiting from the opportunity presented to pillage bread, grain, or flour or, most often, to buy them cheaply?

In sum, it is essentially a matter of a spontaneous movement provoked, first of all, by the shortage of grains and the rise in prices; a movement in which the people intervened with violence to lower the price of grain and bread to their "just" value—in the present case to 2 sous the pound or 12 livres the *setier* of wheat. In this, the "flour war" was clearly related to the tradition of great popular hunger revolts of the Old Regime.

Then again, we find in this movement elements which are forerunners of the social movements of the French Revolution. This popular mentality, resolutely opposed to the freedom of trade desired by the mercantile bourgeoisie—was it not a forerunner of the demands of the "fourth order" or of the *sans-culottes* on the eve and in the course of the Revolution? Does not this extended movement of popular price fixing seem to foreshadow the Parisian *journées* of October 5 and 6, 1789, of February 1792, and of February and September 1793? There are very special resemblances between it and the October days: the gathering in front of the château of Versailles; this cry of a master locksmith arrested in the *faubourg* Saint-Antoine: "Long live the king, and may bread reappear!"; the hatred for bakers: "bakers are thieves" and "all the bakers ought to be hanged." One would think one were already in July 1791 on the eve of the "massacre" of the Champ de Mars, if one listened to the answer given by a journeyman bath attendant to an officer of the musketeers, who asked him about the price of bread: "Answered that the gentleman had asked him if he found bread too expensive. He had answered that for an officer who had means it was not too dear: but for people who did not have them, it was." And then there is the expression attributed by the widow of a Parisian shoemaker to the women of the *Halle*: "that if bread were not given at 2 sous, the workers of the manufacture of the faubourg Saint-Antoine would revolt." There are still more striking, and even hallucinatory, resemblances to the Great Fear and the rural movements that preceded it in the spring of 1789; the bourgeois militia that took up arms—at Pontoise, Melun, Meaux, and Rebais; rumors of price fixing carried from market to market and village to village; the fear of "brigands" or of "enemies" given out as being hirelings of an "aristocratic plot."

However, despite their importance for the study of the Revolution, we must be careful not to push these resemblances too far. That there were in the "flour war" elements which tie it to the social movements of the Revolution ought not to surprise us, given the continuity of social and economic conditions and the vital interest the people had, in 1789 and 1793 as well as in 1775, in assuring themselves a sufficient quantity of cheap bread. But, in the end, the differences are, perhaps, just as marked. In 1775, the ideas of the Philosophes, which had already been current for a long time among the privileged orders and the bourgeoisie, had not yet reached the people. We do not find perforce, in the course of these riots, any trace of a popular conception of the Nation, of the Sovereignty of the People, of Equality. The hatred for the privileged classes, which was to rally the people to the revolutionary ideas and watchwords of the bourgeoisie in 1789, could only be glimpsed and rather feebly at that in 1775: in the "flour war" we do not see, as later on, the hatred of the people burst forth against the landed proprietor as owner of the feudal dues and hoarder of food-stuffs; and if a part of the clergy felt threatened by popular action, they were for the most part small village vicars whose storehouses were within reach of the excited villagers. The popular revolt, on this occasion, was aimed mostly against the commercial bourgeoisie both urban and rural— notably against the farmers, bakers, and merchants of grain and flour. Therefore, there is no trace of any solidarity within the Third Estate, which is not at all astonishing; and despite the few signs of a fighting mentality on the part of the *menu peuple* which we have reported, there was also very little of that popular social consciousness that was to reach so great a magnitude in the *sans-culotte* movement of 1793 and the Year II.

The popular movement of May 1775 suffered, as we have seen, a total and crushing defeat. In order for the people to win a victory, however small, on a social matter, it had to ally with the revolutionary bourgeoisie against the privileged classes and all the apparatus of the Old Regime. In 1775, this alliance was lacking; in order for it to be realized, it was necessary to await the experiences of the years 1788 and 1789.

PROBLEMS OF WORK
IN YEAR II

By Albert Soboul

The Revolution of 1789 was not, like that of 1848 or the others which
followed it, chiefly preoccupied with labor problems. A bourgeois revolution, it was much more concerned with ownership of property, which the
Declaration of 1793, like that of 1789, included among the inalienable
rights of man, after the total abolition of feudalism had made it a universal,
absolute right.

The eighteenth-century bourgeoisie had rehabilitated the "arts and
trades," it had given an incomparable vigor to invention. But as it was
above all sensitive to the problems of technology and production, it had
no conception of work as a social function. From 1789 to 1794, the bourgeoise never considered labor problems in themselves or in terms of the
worker, but rather as they were related to its own bourgeois class interests.
This is proved by Le Chapelier's law of June 14, 1791, which by forbidding
coalitions and strikes, in the name of liberty, left the workers helpless
before their employers. And though on September 29, 1793, the Convention granted the general price controls demanded by the sans-culottery,
the Montagnard bourgeoisie never looked upon it as anything but a tac-
tical concession. Again price controls were essentially related to food supplies, and salaries were by no means viewed as proportionate to labor.

Divided between the dominant economy of artisans and the nascent

211

large-scale industries, and lacking any class consciousness, how could the working world have opposed its conceptions to those of the bourgeoisie? In its all-out fight against the aristocracy, to a great degree it entrusted the bourgeoisie with the presentation and the defense of its interests. Its stand on labor problems could only be one influenced by the dominant social and political structures. The development of commerce and of industry had clearly brought the bourgeoisie into the forefront. The traditional forms of production still were predominant; large-scale industry was just beginning to make itself known. Economic evolution remained insufficient to give workers an awareness of the rank which they held in society as a group, and of the place of labor as a function in society. All the more reason not to comprehend the role of work in the development of the individual.

Although the bourgeoisie placed ownership of property at the heart of the social problem, the san-culottery itself, under the former's influence, never conceived of labor in terms of anything but property.

❦

The vocabulary of the period bears witness to these limitations.

Workers were not distinguished by their social function, but simply by their clothing. Workers adopted trousers buttoned to a short jacket, a costume which became characteristic of the common people: the *sans-culottes*. Who imagined making a social distinction as well as a political one of this fashion of dress? The answer is unimportant. It suffices to note here that the bourgeoisie correctly understood the social meaning of this term: ". . . In speaking of the *sans-culottes*," declared Pétion before the Convention, on April 10, 1793, "we do not mean all the citizens, nobles and aristocrats excepted, but we mean men who have not, in order to distinguish them from those who have." Property, and not work, formed the line of demarcation.

At the end of the eighteenth century, property-owners, whether aristocratic or bourgeois, called the mass of those who worked with their hands by the somewhat disdainful term *peuple* (common people). In reality, between the lower bourgeoisie and the proletariat, the nuances, as well as the antagonisms, were numerous. Jean-Jacques Rousseau had already written in his *Confessions* that he had been born "into a family whose means distinguished it from the common people." His father was a watchmaker. This situation is echoed by Duplay the carpenter, landlord of Robespierre. The remark of his daughter, the wife of Lebas, member of the Convention, has often been cited, according to which her father, in his concern for bourgeois dignity, had never allowed one of his "servants," that is to say one of his workers, at his table. Jaurès reminds us that the "carpenter" Duplay received between 10 and 12,000 livres rent from houses he owned, to say nothing of the profits from his business. The vocabulary takes into account the imprecision of social limits and of the indelible mark which being an artisan left upon the members of this group. It was the trade or the guild which earned them the title, not the notion of work. But had the "carpenter" Duplay, actually a rather important master of a carpentry workshop, manipulated a plane in his youth? Or had his father? Or his grandfather? Perhaps we do not have to go into details, but this matter should be clarified in the interests of an accurate social history of labor. The head of a business maintained his professional title, still being called "joiner" or "carpenter," even when he employed several dozen workers. This was also the case for the "fanmaker" Mauvage, a good *sans-culotte* of the *faubourg-du-Nord* section. His history must be carefully investigated in order to observe that he owned a fan manufacture employing more than sixty workers.

Thus it is almost always impossible, in the documents of the period, to make a distinction among the journeyman, the small artisan, and the entrepreneur. Many nuances distinguished them from one another, and the transitions were made slowly. A disorganized, poorly defined notion of labor can be found in these words. This linguistic situation corresponded to the social reality.

❧

In 1789 Paris was a city of 5 to 600,000 inhabitants, of whom almost half depended upon manual labor for its existence. In the beginning of 1791, the exchange by employers of large bills for assignats worth 5 livres to be used for workers' salaries, enables us to see how the workers were distributed in forty-one of the forty-eight Parisian sections. Their total number can be estimated at 75,000, or with their families at about 300,000 persons.

The workers were much more widespread in the various quarters of the capital than they are in our day. With the exception of certain sections of the West, workers could be found in every section. But the most famous sections in the history of the Revolution were not those with the most workers. The *faubourg* Saint-Antoine grouped 4519 workers, for an average of fourteen per employer; the *faubourg* Saint-Marceau 5577 or twenty per employer. The great popular masses were in the heart of the Capital. The sections between the Seine and the boulevards and beyond, as far out as the exterior boulevards, counted 21,884 workers. There were textile and hosiery factories there which employed between 200 and 300 workers; the average, however, was nineteen workers per enterprise. The sections of the center (*Louvre, Oratoire, Halles*) included 5897 workers, or about twenty per employer. Finally, on the south bank of the Seine, from the Pont-Neuf to the Pont Saint-Michel, the *Quatre-Nations, Théâtre-Français*, and *Thermes-de-Julien* grouped another 5656 workers, with an average of sixteen per business.

Thus a wide dispersion and multiple nuances characterized the working population of Paris at the end of the eighteenth century. It is noteworthy that the *faubourgs* Saint-Antoine and Saint-Marceau had neither a dense working population nor large businesses. The average number of workers per employer in Saint-Antoine was even inferior to the average for all of Paris, which was between sixteen and seventeen. Among the urban popular classes, the most revolutionary element was not made up of a factory proletariat, but of small master artisans and their journeymen. This milieu of artisans formed the marching wing of sans-culottery. It was the nerve center of the social group of workers.

❦

These conditions gave rise to a certain behavior, just as the ambiguous situation resulted in certain contradictions. Working and living beside his journeymen, very often a former journeyman himself, the small master artisan exercised a decisive ideological influence over them. Through him, the bourgeois influences made their way into the world of the worker. Even though they were in conflict with their masters, the journeymen in the minor trades shared opinions about the major problems of the day with these men who had trained them, under whose roof they often lived, and at whose table they often ate. The lower bourgeoisie of artisans formed the workers' mentality. We should undoubtedly introduce a few nuances here. In particular, beside the independent artisans were the perennial dependent artisans. The classic example remains the silkweaver of Lyons. The artisan worked at home, under the control of the *négociant* (wholesale merchant) who supplied the raw materials and commercialized the manufactured product. The artisan owned his stock of tools, he could even engage journeymen. Legally, he was free and the head of a business, he appeared as an employer. Economically, he was only a salaried worker closely dependent upon the *négociant*. The interests of the dependent artisan and of the journeymen were the same. In the face of merchant capitalism, they demanded the *tarif*, that is to say a minimum living wage. But they did not go so far as to establish a relationship between the rate of the work and the rate of the salary. The salary was determined in terms of the price of food supplies, not in terms of the value of the work. This provides further proof that the social function of work was not clearly understood. The dependent artisan thus occupied an intermediary position between the journeyman and the independent artisan who was on the fringes of the lower bourgeoisie.

In the case of the already silent and anonymous salaried factory worker, when the situation arose they would act in a more independent manner which in some ways anticipated that of the proletarian of a large contemporary industry. Note, for example, the strike in the Réveillon wallpaper factory, which developed into the riot of April 27, 1789. But frequently the salaried workers of the large companies began in small workshops. They remained imbued with the spirit of the artisan, which was further strengthened by the milieu in which they lived, among the journeymen in comparison to whom they formed only a feeble minority. The working world on the whole clearly bore the traces of the mentality of the lower bourgeoisie and, like it, shared the ideology of the bourgeoisie. Neither by their thoughts nor by their actions were workers under the Revolution to form an independent element.

This position was not without serious contradictions which lay heavily upon the image which the *sans-culottes* had of work, and upon their political activity. Tied to their journeymen by living conditions and often by poverty, the artisans nevertheless owned their shops and their tools, and were considered independent producers. Having journeymen and apprentices beneath them and under their discipline accentuated their bourgeois mentality. But the system of small production and direct sales put them into irremediable opposition to the new bourgeoisie. As a result, a social ideal which ran contrary to economic evolution developed between these artisans and shopkeepers who were to form the main body of the *sans-culotte*. movement. They were to rise up against the concentration of the means of production; but they were themselves property-owners. In year II when the most advanced demanded the maximum of property, the inconsistencies between their social position and this demand escaped them. The demands of these artisans were to become sublimated into emotional pleadings, into bursts of revolt, without ever forming a precise, coherent program about the rights of labor or the right to work. This was also the case for the political groups which shared their mentality; the *Enragés*, then the Hébertists, and finally the Robespierrists themselves.

It is worth observing that workers were then chiefly concerned with their interests as consumers much more than with the general problems concerning their social position. The sans-culottery did not revolt because of strikes and salary demands but over the question of food supplies. The increase or the decrease of the prices of the chief articles of popular consumption, of grain, and especially of bread which represented at least half of family expenditures, was the decisive factor which favorably or unfavorably affected the salaried worker's budget. The *sans-culottes* would ask for price controls on foods, but the demand for the *tarif* would remain exceptional. This point of view is indicative of the economic and social conditions as well as of the ideology of the period.

In the combined characteristics by which the *sans-culottes* can be distinguished as a social group, work does not necessarily appear in an explicit manner, the *sans-culotte* being distinguished rather by his opposition.

The social antagonism which can be most clearly seen in the popular consciousness is that which brought into opposition the aristocracy and the sans-culottery. Privileges, wealth from real estate, seigneurial rights, in short everything which characterizes a society which is still feudal—it was against all this, in the person of the aristocrat, that the *sans-culotte* rose, whether he was a worker or a peasant. The noble was also, but only secondarily, one who took part in no productive activities, who did not work with his hands under penalty of forfeiting his nobility. Thus the opposition was strengthened. The address by the *Société des Sans-Culottes* of Beaucaire before the Convention on September 8, 1793, is in this respect significant. The members called themselves "artists" (by this they meant artisans) and peasants. "We are *sans-culottes* . . .; poor and virtuous, we have formed a society of artists and of peasants . . .; we know who our friends are, those who have freed us from the clergy and from the nobility, from feudalism, from the *dîme*, from royalty, and from all the scourges which make up its retinue."

After 1789 the economic crisis contributed to making social antagonisms more clear. To the fundamental antagonism between the *sans-culottes* and the aristocracy was added, as the crisis worsened and as the Patriot Party of 1789 broke apart, the antagonism between the *sans-culottes* and the upper levels of the former Third Estate. A note intended for the *Comité de Sûreté Générale* in Pluviôse of year II (January and February 1794) points out the existence of two parties in the *Brutus* section: that of the common people, "of sans-culottism," the other composed "of bankers, of stockbrokers, of the rich." The notion of manual work still does not appear here, except implicitly. Such is also the case for that speech before the Convention on 27 Ventôse of year II (March 17, 1794) in which "the worthy *sans-culottes*" are contrasted not only with the clergy and the nobility, but with the *procureurs*, the lawyers and notaries, and "*ces gros fermiés ces égoystte et tous ces gros riche marchand*" [those fat farmers, those egotists, and all those fat, rich merchants]. Was this an opposition between the haves and the have-nots? We cannot be sure, for among the *sans-culottes* were artisans and shopkeepers who were property-owners. It was rather an opposition between the more or less perceptive partisans of a certain conception of limited and controlled property, and the partisans of the universal right to property, which had been proclaimed in 1789. Even more, it was an opposition between the partisans of strict regulations and of price controls, and the proponents of economic liberty. Last, and from a secondary point of view, it was an opposition between those who work with their hands and those whose activity is not based upon manual work.

Besides these elementary reactions, texts permit us to discern the nuances and to clarify at the same time the position of the *sans-culottes* as a social group.

They denounced *les honnêtes gens* (honest folk), meaning by this those who, if not wealthy, at least lived a life of ease and were cultivated. The expression appears after June 2, 1793 and the elimination of the Girondins, when moderates and *sans-culottes* came into opposition on political and social policies. It meant essentially those bourgeois opposed to equality. Though the *sans-culottes* ironically called their adversaries "honest folk," the latter did not fail to treat them as *la canaille* [riffraff]. Thus social antagonisms were precised by the use of two expressions. A text of year III provides us with the key to the expression *honnêtes gens*. On 16 Pluviôse (February 4, 1795), the committee of surveillance of the sixth *arrondissement* called attention to the stormy scenes in the general assembly of the *Lombards* section between the *hommes aux quarante sols* [men with 40 sous] and the *honnêtes citoyens* [honest citizens]. The *hommes aux quarante sols*, or the *quarante sols* for short, were the workers to whom the law of September 9, 1793, had granted a bonus of 40 sous to enable them to attend without financial loss the assemblies of the section. The *honnêtes gens* did not receive these forty sous.

Equally significant was the animosity of the *sans-culottes* toward persons with independent incomes, which was particularly marked during the autumn of 1793, when the economic crisis and the difficulties of existence exacerbated antagonisms. From then on, having an independent income was a reason for being suspect, and therefore for being arrested. On September 18, 1793, the revolutionary committee of the *Mutius-Scaevola* section ordered the arrest of Duval, First Secretary for the police of Paris, as suspect for two reasons: for having shown contempt for the assemblies of the section and for being in possession of 2000 livres in income from investments. Jean-François Rivoire, former colonist at Saint-Domingo, was arrested on 2 Germinal of year II (March 22, 1794), by the revolutionary committee of the *Mont-Blanc* section. In addition to his political conduct, he was reproached for receiving 16,000 livres income from investments. An extreme case was that of a certain Pierre Becquerel, who was arrested on 19 Ventôse of year II (March 9, 1794), during a police operation in the gardens of the Palais-Egalité (today called the Palais-Royal) simply "for having said that he lived on an income." Here again, the *sans-culotte* who worked with his hands was distinguished from those who did not work with them.

The hostility of the sans-culottery toward persons of independent income was only one of the more emphasized aspects of its instinctive opposition to the rich. The most perceptive *sans-culottes* were not far from considering, as did Babeuf in year IV, the Revolution to be an open war "between the rich and the poor." But usually they had only an abstract notion of what a rich man was. Their attitude toward the rich was most often a purely affective one. In the *Amis-de-la-Patrie* section, Pierre Fotier was arrested on 10 Prairial of year III (May 29, 1795) during the anti-terrorist repression. He had in year II made a show of "jealous feelings toward the rich." The texts permitting us to glimpse a more developed analysis on the part of the *sans-culottes* are not very numerous. Vary rare indeed are those showing a clear perception that at the base of this wealth which they both scorned and envied lay the exploitation of another's labor. There are, however, a few examples. On 26 Ventôse of year II (March 16, 1794), Godefroy, a merchant *mercier*, was arrested by the revolutionary committee of the *Lombards* section. In addition to his political conduct, he was reproached for possessing a cotton-spinning mill at Vernon, in the department of Eure, where "120 women, old men, and children" worked. In *faubourg-du-Nord* section, Santerre, a former gauze merchant, was arrested on 24 Germinal of year II (April 13, 1794). He lived on his profits, he "had grown fat since time immemorial by the sweat of day-laborers." Thus it can be dimly seen that the antagonism between the *sans-culottes* and the rich rested upon the relationships of production, function, and activity. Thus the place of the various social classes in relationship to work was becoming clear.

A few *sans-culottes*, who were, however, really on the fringes of the middle bourgeoisie, attempted to go beyond the negative positions of the sans-culottery and to define it explicitly by means of its social function, labor. In this difficult *prise de conscience* they were aided by the representatives of the Montagnard bourgeoisie which saw that the salvation of the Revolution lay in an alliance with the common people. Such was also the case with the Robespierrists. And, on another level, with Hébert, who by conviction, but not without a touch of demagogy, exalted in his *Père Duchesne* "the most precious class" of the nation, the sans-culottery. "Nothing is worth the *sans-culottes*," he wrote in September 1793, ". . . It is they who are watering with their sweat the earth which nourishes us, it is they who work the metals and who manufacture the weapons which serve to defend the Republic." And he contrasted the bankers, the financiers, the merchants, and the men of law, "in a word, all the leeches of the sans-culottery," with "these hard-working artisans who become exhausted from toiling so hard."

In the same tone as the *Père Duchesne*, the *Poissonnière* section, in its address before the Convention of September 24, 1793, contrasted "the rich egoists" and "that laboring portion of the common people that lives by its labor alone." Sometimes the eminent dignity of work and of the workers comes through. Thus on 16 Messidor of year II (July 4, 1794), the revolutionary committee of the *Bon-Conseil* section suspended three commissioners in the manufacture of saltpeter. "They were enjoying finanical comfort and ostentation which was not in keeping with that of their workers." Arrested on 17 Germinal of year III (April 6, 1795) and questioned about his section, the *sans-culotte* Vingternier replied that he had no section other "than that of the common people and of the workers." Though this militant repeated the usual vague characteristics in defining the *sans-culotte*, he nevertheless incorporated a new idea. Answering in May 1793 to "the impertinent question: but what is a *sans-culotte*?" he declared "He is a being who always goes on foot . . . and who lodges very simply with his wife and his children, if he has any, on the fifth or sixth floor." Jacques Roux also was to refer to the attics inhabited by the *sans-culottes*, and "Père Duchesne" was to write: ". . . if you wish to become acquainted with the fine flower of the sans-culottery, just go and visit the garrets of the workers." For Vingternier, the material conditions of existence were not sufficient; in his definition he introduced a new notion of social utility. The *sans-culotte* knew how "to plow a field, forge, saw, file, do roofing, and make shoes." Here work was defined in terms of social utility.

During the repression of year III, the former terrorists were often re-proached for having exploited for political ends the popular presentiment that work introduces a differentiation into society. According to a note of 17 Nivôse of year III (January 6, 1795), the chief aim of the aforesaid commissioners of the *Bonne-Nouvelle* section was "to lead astray the vast numbers of the working class lodged in furnished rooms."

Denouncing the former terrorists on 20 Germinal (April 9, 1795), the *honnêtes gens* of the *Bon-Conseil* section essentially reproached them for having aligned the citizens into two antagonistic classes. "In the first class, as if there should be two among republicans, these evil-minded persons placed the wholesale merchants, the shopkeepers, the merchants, the men of the law, persons of independent income, clerks, and artists. In the second . . . they allowed only those estimable citizens accustomed to working with their hands."

Not very successful in defining their place in society as workers, the *sans-culottes* did not have a clear and distinct notion about work itself and its social role. They did not think that work could have a social function by itself; they only looked upon it in relation to property.

Work, and by this we mean manual labor, forms the foundation for property, which must remain in proportion to it. Artisans and journeymen or peasants working small parcels of land, the *sans-culottes* were small, independent producers. Personal labor legitimized the peasant's possession of his field, the artisan's possession of his shop and of his tools. And so the *sans-culottes* were closely bound to their small possessions, a right which would never be questioned. What they feared above all was being reduced to the level of dependent workers, of proletarians, as a consequence of the concentration of property. When it asked the Subsistence Administration on 27 Nivôse of year II (January 16, 1794), to indemnify a baker of the section, the popular society of *Poissonnière* section declared that "the small fortunes acquired by labor which is useful to society cannot be too highly respected and preserved from all harm." This demand was affirmed by the sans-culottery in a more or less vague way throughout every period of crisis. Let appropriate legislation render the concentration of property and of the means of production impossible, and let it maintain as a result the inde-pendence of work.

From this point of view, the clearest demand was formulated on Sep-tember 2, 1793, at the peak of the popular movement, in an address to the Convention by the *Sans-Culottes* section, formerly called *Jardin-des-Plantes*. After having affirmed the right to existence for workers and having defined property by "the extent of physical needs," it demanded that the Assembly "establish a fixed level for the price of the most essential foods, workers' salaries, the profits of industry, and the gains of commerce." A vast program of control over economic life, which finally was to be resolved by the establishment of a maximum on property. "That the same individual cannot possess more than a maximum; that none can hold more land to rent than is needed for a determined number of plows, that the same citizen can have only one workshop, one shop." These radical measures, concluded the *Sans-Culottes* section, "would gradually make the excessive inequality of fortunes disappear and would make the number of property-owners increase," that is to say, of independent workers.

At no other moment in the Revolution do we find as concise and clear a formulation of the ideal of the *sans-culottes* concerning the regulation of property and the organization of labor. It is an ideal in keeping with the artisans and shopkeepers who formed the greater part of the Parisians sans-culottery and who exercised a decisive ideological influence upon their journeymen and clerks. This ideal was also suited to that mass of consumers and small urban producers, hostile both to the direct or indirect sellers of food supplies and to the entrepreneurs whose capitalist undertakings threatened to reduce them to the position of dependent workers.

What were the theoretical or political sources of this social ideal of ownership based implicitly upon labor and remaining within its confines? Many leaders of the Mountain or of the Jacobins drew up similar proposals. In his *Eléménts de républicanisme*, Billaud-Varenne stated that "the accumulation of great masses of money in the hands of a small number of individuals progressively leads to all the social calamities." On the other hand, "the comfort of the greatest number, resulting from labor, and from industry and commercial speculations, brings a nation to the highest level of prosperity and imparts a real grandeur to its government." Saint-Just in his *"Institutions"* fixed the Republic's aim as "giving to all Frenchmen the means to obtain the chief necessities of life, without depending upon anything but the laws and without mutual dependence within the civil state." In other words, all Frenchmen should be small property-owners, independent producers, or free workers, and ownership should be based upon labor. As for Robespierre, who on April 24, 1793, has defined ownership not as a natural law, but as a social institution, his ideal was a society of small producers: the peasant owning his field, the artisan his workshop, both of them able to provide adequately for the needs of a family.

Georges Lefebvre correctly discerned in this ideal a double moral and social concern. "Man living by his labor, without owing money to anyone, it is he whom Robespierre calls the poor man; individualistic production and a very small bit of property guarantee him his independence; but in order to be acquired and preserved, this property requires a certain initiative, and personal virtues of work, frugality, and thrift." Although rarely explicit, this moral concern was no longer foreign to the sans-culottery. Hence there were certain harangues against laziness and luxury.

On one point, however, the Parisian *sans-culottes* outdid the Montagnard leaders. The latter were chiefly interested in agricultural production and in land-holdings. They desired to maintain a complete freedom of enterprise within the sphere of commerce and industry. In his Declaration of Rights of September 1792, Momoro, if he set a certain legal limit to "territorial property," nonetheless declared "industrial property" to be inviolable. At about the same time, an essay on popular government established a maximum for land-holdings, but set no limits "for the increase of fortunes made up of any property which is purely personal, such as money, public notes, merchandise, ships, etc." Consumers of agricultural products but also small urban producers, concerned with the independence of their shop or of their workshop, the *sans-culottes* went much farther. They were hostile to the concentration of commercial or industrial property as well as to large land-holdings. This explains the demands of the *Sans-Culottes* section.

❧

The ideological ambiguity, based on a contradiction between function and representation, was expressed by a social and political contradiction. One example will prove that this popular demand for independent work which legitimizes small possessions was not in harmony with the historical necessities of the period. The politics of national defense in year II required having recourse to large private businesses for clothing and equipment supplies, nationalization having only been adopted for the manufacture of weapons. Concerned with efficiency, the committees of the government were inclined to concentrate orders in the hands of capitalist entrepreneurs instead of dispersing them among the multiple small workshops. During the course of year II this was a source of conflict between the revolutionary government and the Parisian *sans-culottes*.

The crisis at the beginning of 1793 and the enlistments which it inspired having multiplied needs, the sections taxed their ingenuity to equip the volunteers. To this end, certain sections, such as that of the *Tuileries*, opened workshops. The considerations motivating the decisions of this section are illustrative of the hostility of the *sans-culottes* toward concentrated big business and toward commercial capital, and of their attachment to independent work. "First, the rapacious, ill-intentioned, or inept purveyors will no longer be able to impede the movements of the armies, to hinder our successes. The fate of liberty will no longer be at the mercy of the speculations of a monopoly. Second, a small number of rich entrepreneurs will no longer appropriate for themselves all the profits from the prodigious number of items supplied. The profits will be divided among all our merchants, among all our workers, among all of us. Third, cooperative enterprises being always directed with intelligence and economy, we will provide more while spending less, and supplies will be better." No better praise could be given in favor of small, independent production. But could such production be reconciled with the great needs of national defense?

The clothing administration was naturally led to organize large workshops in which production was established upon rational bases. The administration encountered constant opposition from the workers, who were accustomed to working freely and who constantly demanded the organization of small workshops in the sections. Thus opposition arose between two conceptions of organizing labor, and also between governmental policies and popular demands. On July 30, 1793, the commissioners of the forty-eight Parisian sections explained to the *Conseil général de la Commune* "how many inconveniences are caused by the assembling of a great number of citizenesses within a single workshop." They considered it "as much more advantageous" to have work divided among workshops in the sections. Though the work was finally divided among the sections, the difficulties and complaints did not stop. Although the section workshops corresponded to the popular ideal in regard to the organization of work, they had one weakness. Lacking operating capital, they were forced to have recourse to private capital. This meant sinking back under the control of the entrepreneurs and contractors from whom the *sans-culottes* had been striving to free themselves. Their demands began to be heard again.

On October 1, 1793, a deputation of cobblers asked the Convention that they alone be allowed to provide shoes for the troops. On 4 Pluviôse of year II (January 23, 1794), the popular society *l'Unité* proposed a law which would annihilate and suppress all the contractors of the Republic who, by cunning maneuvers, had worked their way into supplying equipment for the troops. Who suffered from this? "It is the Republic, it is the indigent artist, it is the workers without money who, in order to eat bread, are forced by the needs of life, to go to these egoists and ask for work to do for a paltry sum." The workers of *Invalides* section made a new attempt of 30 Pluviôse (February 18, 1794) and asked "that clothing to be made for the soldiers of the Republic be divided among the workshops of the section and not given to rapacious tendering parties." The general assembly agreed to support them, feeling "that it was just that the profits to be made on public works be for the benefit of the greatest number and of the poorest." It did not say: for the benefit of the workers. On 1 Floréal of year II (April 20, 1794), *Bonnet-Rouge* section again denounced the aristocracy of entrepreneurs. "A single one, always the richest, is sure to accumulate from all sides all the lucrative business, a fair division of which would offer to a multitude of good citizens the means of livelihood for their families and lawful profits." A few entrepreneurs must not grab all the work. Thus the Convention must decree that no one will be able to become a contractor unless he has a certificate of civicism. The large entrepreneur had very little chance of obtaining one from a popular assembly. As for the *sans-culotte*, there was no difficulty, and he would take "only that portion of the work which belongs to him, without standing in the way of his brother *sans-culotte*." The militants of the *Bonnet-Rouge* section intended to turn the Terror against commercial capital and big business. The refusal to grant a certificate of civism generally resulted in being arrested as suspect. But times had changed. In the spring of 1794, popular influence declined, and the Committees of the government defended the economic Terror on behalf of the property-holding classes.

The clothing workshops in the sections were not immediately carried away by the Thermidorian reaction; but they did not survive the crushing of the Parisian sans-culottery during the insurrections of Prairial of year III. On 25 Prairial (June 13, 1795), the Committee of Public Safety authorized the *Commission des approvisionnements* to liquidate the workshops and the distribution bureaus of the Commune of Paris, and to have clothing for the troops made by private entrepreneurs. History was retracing its steps. It could not be a question of favoring the work of artisans and small, independent production when there had been a return to economic liberty and when manufacturing war supplies appeared to the businessmen of the bourgeoisie as a field reserved for their capitalist ventures. At any rate the concentration of work, characteristic of developing industry, was nonetheless in its technical and social aspects opposed to the ideology of artisanal work.

◆⑤❦◆

The *sans-culottes'* inability to define their place as workers in terms of a social group, and that of labor as a function, is a characteristic which was in keeping with the conditions of the period, as was the conception of limited ownership based upon personal labor.

Peasants or artisans, in order to freely make decisions about their person and their labor, the *sans-culottes* had to first cease being enfeoffed to another, to cease being bound to the land or being prisoners within the framework of a guild. Hence their hatred for the feudal aristocracy, all the more detested because it was unproductive and scorned manual work. Hence their bitterness toward the Old Regime and its corporate organization. Direct producers themselves, they believed that personal labor alone could justify ownership. They dreamed of a society of small property-owners, each possessing his field, his workshop, his shop. In order to maintain a relative equality, the State should intervene. By inheritance laws, progressive taxes, and public relief measures, it should protect labor and reconstitute small property holdings to the degree that economic evolution tends to destroy them. It was above all a question of preventing the formation of a monopoly of wealth and of a dependent proletariat. The *sans-culottes* did not imagine that having reached a certain level of evolution, this regime would give birth to the agents of its own destruction. The individual and subdivided means of production would of necessity be transformed into socially concentrated means of production, and the small property of a mass of direct producers would be supplanted by large capitalist property.

During that spring of 1794, in which the supreme crisis of the Revolution developed, despite the efforts of the revolutionary government, and of the Robespierrists in particular, their failure became obvious to the common people. Had the confiscation of the clergy's and later of the emigrés' possessions, and the sequestering of the possessions of suspect persons resulted in the distribution of even a small plot of ground to landless peasants? Had the abolition of the corporations been sufficient to permit journeymen to establish themselves independently? Had the Revolution made independent workers of the *sans-culottes?*

However, the more perspicacious bourgeoisie asserted in opposition to the artisans' ideology of labor, that it was impossible to desire to maintain production based upon personal labor, when capitalist production was being developed. The *cahier* of Augny parish, in the *bailliage* of Metz, undoubtedly drawn up by some large property-holder, protested in 1789 against the division of the communal possessions which had already taken place in Lorraine and in the Bishoprics. "These breakings-up of land are ruinous for the public since individuals, personally concerned with their own shares, can be of no help to our cultivators, or to our manufacturers, or to our entrepreneurs." On 30 Nivôse of year II (January 19, 1794), Representative Delacroix wrote, "We think that, in such a large population, the indigent should be able to find resources not in agriculture but in industry, commerce, and the arts." Especially worthy of being cited are the observations made by Lozeau, deputy from the department of Charente-Inférieure, before the Convention of 22 Fructidor of year II (September 8, 1794). ". . . a great society only forms a respectable whole because all its members are bound to one another by the mutual services they perform . . .; it is impossible for the majority of a nation to be landholders, since in this hypothesis, each one being obliged to cultivate his field or his vineyard in order to earn his livelihood, commerce, the arts, and industry would soon be annihilated." It was impossible to suppress salaried manpower; it was even indispensable to preserve it. If all the peasants and all the artisans had lived by the fruits of their labor, upon their small plot of ground, or in their workshop, where would the big farmers, the manufacturers, the pioneers of large-scale industry have found the manpower so indispensable to their enterprises? The bourgeoisie of the Mountain itself considered the transformation of independent workers into salaried workers unavoidable. It was a necessary condition for the economic order as they conceived of it. As for those who, like the Robespierrists, considered state intervention in favor of free work and of small property-holders indispensable, they could not free themselves of their contradictions. They perished as victims of 9 Thermidor.

Sans-culottery struggled with itself over equally insoluble contradictions. Hostile to the capitalism which threatened to reduce it to a proletariat, it was, however, bound to the bourgeois order because it already owned its field or workshop, or hoped one day to do so. It demanded price controls, and the limitation of property, a property based upon personal work; but at the same time it demanded the independence of the shop, or the artisan, and of rural property, and was in this way partisan of the economic liberalism so dear to the capitalist bourgeoisie. These contradictions reflect the social composition of the sans-culottery which, not forming a class, could neither imagine its exact place in society nor establish a coherent economic and social program. Attached to the traditional system of production and of ownership based upon personal labor, it was doomed to decline as the capitalist organization of production founded upon salaried labor developed.

These are a few aspects of the labor problem of year II; they are basically social aspects. Many others could have been considered here: technical and economic aspects, aspects more strictly psychological . . . . Let us stress the difficulty of doing research, to say nothing of the absence, for the period which interests us, of documents enabling us to make a precise social analysis of the working world. We must comment that the popular classes left few documents, and that as a result it will always be difficult to write their history. Many aspects thus escape us, about which it would, in our opinion, be sometimes difficult to draw conclusions by analogy. We might make conjectures with some accuracy about the oppositions to be found among the workers, for example between the common laborer or the day-laborer and the worker at a craft, such as the jeweler, the engraver, or the carver, aware of the value of the object he is producing. Or else one can reveal that opposition, at least that differentiation, in the cleavage of the political personnel of the sections. Specialized workers, more perceptive and more educated, were to be found among civil and revolutionary commissioners, while laborers rarely rose above the position of simple militants. But owing to a lack of documents, research cannot be carried further. Whole sections of social reality thus remain in obscurity.

They were to become clear with the development of the new economic organization. Still poorly delineated at the end of the eighteenth century, established by retrogressive traditional structures, the notion of labor would gradually extricate itself under the influence of economic evolution, to the point that laborers would finally become aware of their place and of their role in society. Work would then appear as an essential social function.

THE SANS-CULOTTES AND THE FRENCH REVOLUTION

₰ By F. Furet, C. Mazauric, and L. Bergeron

When discussing the French Revolution, we can still begin with Clemenceau's statement: "The Revolution is a whole." For the word not only provides a key to a political sensitivity in which a reference to 1789 marks the watershed, defines before and after, separates the antagonists. It also indicates, in the face of a continuing royalist intellectual tradition, the unity of a republican historiography which brings together very diverse generations, from Michelet to Aulard, from Mathiez to Georges Lefebvre.

But this revolutionary "block" only appears as such in the face of the enemy, and in a negative way. That is to say that above all it has had a political vocation. In the scholarly world, many elements have disunited it. The enemy front has never been a very formidable one, consisting more often of ideologists than of historians, of emotional men rather than researchers. And a divine malediction was on the whole a less foolish explanation than a Masonic plot. In addition, everything forced revolutionary historiography toward analysis, nuances, progress. Everything—that is to say the very object of the research, the Revolution itself, both a profound necessity and a jolting adventure made up of brutal gaps, bloody ruptures. The political drama of these years, 1789 to 1794, is too diverse, too discontinuous, to be told with an impartial heart.

For it is indeed a matter of the heart. Nineteenth-century historians and

226

even some twentieth-century ones have given their sympathies to one certain aspect, one certain period, one certain person of the Revolution to the extent that this aspect, this period, this person provide precedents or ancestors for their own history, and make the interpretation of their own time easier. If there is still something mysterious in Michelet's fondness for Madame Roland, there is none in the relationships which tie Lamartine to the Girondins, Aulard to Danton, Mathiez to Robespierre, for these relationships are political. The French Revolution provided great ancestors or great examples for all the families of the French left. The history of this fascination on the whole has still to be written.

For fifty years socialist thought with its Marxist line, in the broad sense of the word, has made the French Revolution the principal domain of its historical research. For the moment let us not be concerned with nuances: from Jaurès to E. Labrousse, from Mathiez to Georges Lefebvre, it has not only delved into the study of those popular masses which then played, for a short time, an important political role. It also wanted to measure, in the strict sense of the word, the economic movements and the social disequilibriums which toppled the Old Regime. And it is thus that socialist thought discovered that not only are there several successive revolutions within the French Revolution, the Monarchists, the Feuillants, the Girondins, the Montagnards, and so on . . . , but that there are also several revolutions occurring simultaneously, whose convergence makes the Revolution.

Georges Lefebvre had already shown some time ago the lasting originality of the peasant movement in the bourgeois Revolution. He had also observed, in continuing along a path marked by Mathiez and his "high-cost-of-living," the specificity of another political current: that of the urban common people, animators of price fixing and terrorist campaigns, fanatics about the maximum and the guillotine. But we do not know them very well. This great gap is bridged by the thesis of A. Soboul.

What is meant by a political current? And where can we find it? First of all, it is very naturally an object of political history, which enables us to measure the limits of a camp, its real weight in the struggle. The so-called evenemential insights of history are thus indispensable, but it is history which has already been redone, because it has been seen through an original prism. For this *sans-culotte* movement—this is the least pejorative word—is not only autonomous; until the spring of 1794, it is constantly at odds with the groups directing the Revolution, the masters of the Convention and of the Committees. Its history was waiting to be written. Here it is.

But Soboul states a second problem, which is of general value: what is the relationship between the leaders of a political current and their supporters? In modern terms, what is the "base" upon which Jacques Roux or Varlet rely? This question, too long neglected by the historians of the Revolution, leads the author to a sociology of Parisian "sans-culottism."

His analysis consequently takes on the dimensions of a global history, which nevertheless remains based more upon politics and ideology than upon economics. This is not only due to a lack of statistical documentation. It is also because there is no economic definition of the *sans-culottes*, on the production level, and according to Marxist standards. Among these *petits* who mingle with salaried workers, artisans, and all their intermediate forms, among these fierce enemies of monarchical despotism who are at the same time nostalgic about economic Colbertism, it is not a fraternity of producers which unites. It is an egalitarianism of consumers.

Soboul consequently put his political documentation into full use, beyond evenemential history, toward the study of a social group which is distinguished by a particular sensitivity. For this exacerbated hatred of the aristocracy and of wealth in general, this obsession with a plot, this constant appeal to the guillotine to settle political problems, this cult of revolutionary martyrs and this deification of the Revolution finally appear to be more essential to defining the *sans-culottes* than membership in one particular level of society whose limits cannot possibly be clearly defined. Must Soboul's study be seen merely as the fruit of an irremediable poverty in statistical documents, or to the contrary, on another level, of the inevitable inflexibility of a Marxist scheme, when it is a question of pre-capitalist social groups? Soboul's important thesis still asks the historian of pre-industrial urban societies a fundamental question concerning method. The following articles by Claude Mazauric and Louis Bergeron will permit us to size it up.

I

In the study of the Revolution of 1789, Albert Mathiez had to appear before French historians could calmly investigate the attitudes and social conditions of the popular masses. But in Mathiez himself, the point of view still remains too narrowly political. Whether it was analyzed sympathetically or, to the contrary, with hostility, popular participation in the revolutionary *journées*, or insurrections, and, more generally, popular intervention in the cycle of history, from 1788 to 1795, was only appraised from a purely qualitative point of view. The history of those who after 1791 are called the *sans-culottes* remained to be written.

A group of historians inspired by A. Soboul, and encouraged by Georges Lefebvre until his death, came to bridge this obvious gap and, shedding a new light upon the entire history of the French Revolution, contributed to stating new problems. It may even be that the works of Rudé Soboul, and Tönnesson, whose research—they do not conceal it—is based strictly upon the methods of historical materialism, will have repercussions upon a great deal of research concerning the social strata of the different cities during pre-industrial revolutionary periods.

It is our intention to evaluate here only their contribution to the historiography of the Revolution.

An anonymous text of April and May 1793, answering the unwonted question, "But what is a *sans-culotte?*" defined it essentially by what it was not. "It is a Being who always goes on foot, who has no millions, as you would all like to have, no châteaux, no Valets to Serve him, and who is lodged very Simply with his wife and his children, If he has any, on the fifth or sixth floor—he is useful, for he knows how to till the soil, forge, saw, file, put on a roof, make shoes, and pour out His Blood to the last drop for the Salvation of the Republic . . . ." Such definitions, picturesque though they be, remain too vague. The first question asked was therefore one of method. How can "sans-culottery" be defined, counted, and localized, in time and place?

Before any definition, Soboul and Rudé decided to study the *sans-culottes* through their revolutionary development, and not to isolate them from the events in which they are known to have participated, for fear of laying colorless diagrams upon the moving reality of such a period. By beginning with political history, we can discuss types of *sans-culotte* activity and, to the degree that it is possible, can establish their links with the whole of Parisian society, still very poorly understood despite recent research. Everything considered, this was the only method possible, since the original fiscal registers and a great many other documents of a quantitative nature dating from the revolutionary period were destroyed when the Hôtel de Ville of Paris burned in 1871. The greater part of Soboul's and Rudé's documentation, like that of Tönnesson, was collected by the more or less systematic, according to the authors, scrutiny of *sous-série F7 (fonds du Comité de Sûreté générale)*, of the registers of official proceedings of the sections of Paris, of the jailbooks, and of reports and inquiries of public services or of the police, some of which have been published; to which are added the great mass of printed publications such as newspapers, decrees, petitions, in all a documentary mass which is appropriately enormous and which explains in particular the abundance of references and citations in Soboul's thesis.

Under the circumstances, starting with the political aspects was not in the least a backward method. For, in as lively a period as that of the French Revolution, in which political history is a daily thing, in which the material life of men and their mental outlook are, at least in Paris, constantly being threatened by tumbling monetary values, the situation at the frontiers, the recurring fear of an "aristocratic plot" or of a "famine pact," observing political reality is the best way to penetrate the life and attitude of social groups. Let us also observe that in selecting the *sans-culottes*, the authors did not select a socially defined group as a subject for their analyses. In fact, one of the characteristics of "sans-culottery" is that, aside from certain social aspirations, it is distinguished by political action in common. This is a point to which we shall have to return.

◈

The Parisian *sans-culottes* formed nothing less than a social class, if by this term we mean men bound together by a certain common position in the economic process and subject to the same ideological tendencies. The *sans-culotte* is one who lives by his work, whether he is a salaried journeyman, an occasional day-laborer, a self-employed artisan, or a keeper of his own shop. There is no "class consciousness" in the modern sense of the word. But there is a great awareness of social inequalities: for example, of what puts into opposition the *culottes dorées* (gilded breeches) and the *ventres creux* (hollow bellies) as they came to be called during the great social crisis of year III studied by Tönnesson. Among the master artisans themselves, we find a diversity of social positions. We also find the independent artisan in easy circumstances, such as Duplay, the joiner, who collected 10,000 livres income from his houses, or "Mauvage, the fanmaker, a militant *sans-culotte* of the *faubourg* du Nord, whose records had to be carefully investigated in order to discover that he owned a fan factory employing more than sixty workers." More numerous, without doubt, are the legally independent artisans subject to the ascendancy of commercial capitalism, of whom the silkworker of Lyons is the classic example. Salaried workers in factories, who are rather numerous in the center of Paris, between the Seine and the customs gates, will show an independent attitude if the favorable moment arrives. Take, for example, the occasion of the riot in front of the Réveillon factory, on April 28, 1789, which George Rudé has masterfully re-examined, or during the demands for increases in salaries in the autumn of 1793 and in Messidor of year II. On the whole, however, the salaried workers, who often began in small workshops, remain imbued with the artisan's spirit of the journeyman and small master craftsman which they dream of becoming. Finally, to these productive workers is added the mass of indigents so numerous in Paris although their number is undetermined. This floating population played a decisive role in the popular uprisings triggered by famine, in year II and especially in year III. Tönnesson has pointed out that the insurrections of Germinal and Prairial of year III "for bread and the Constitution of 1793" in actual fact only attracted participants from the two most wretched *faubourgs*. And when they (the authorities) wanted to liquidate the insurrectional menace, it was the *faubourg* Saint-Antoine which was disarmed (Tönnesson, page 309).

An evaluation still had to be made of the quantitative importance of this *sans-culotte* milieu, of that "crowd," as Rudé says, and, if possible, what proportion of the total Parisian population it constituted. There were an estimated 524,186 inhabitants in the capital city when the Estates General were convoked. The *tableau sommaire* of the Parisian population of 11 Fructidor of year II, which was prepared from resumés of the bread-ration cards listed in the registers of the sections, indicates 640,504 inhabitants. The figure is certainly exaggerated, but we must be satisfied with it since the census of year II was never completed. The inventory of the population in relation to supplies in year III gives an almost equivalent figure. Two heavily populated zones appear on each bank of the Seine (the section *Panthéon-français* is the most densely populated with 24,977 inhabitants, and on the right bank are 180,000 inhabitants in the twelve central sections). The *faubourgs*, where courtyards and gardens covered vast pieces of ground, are less populated and are occupied either by indigents or by artisans and journeymen working side by side. This will be the special domain of the sans-culottery. The great mass of salaried workers is located in the most densely populated sections, that is to say the center. The average number of workers per employer for Paris is 16.61, but it rarely goes above 10 outside the central quarters. Yet the most restless sections were not the most populated ones, but those characterized by a certain social norm, "that class of artisans which, at the end of the eighteenth century, left its mark upon the Parisian working world." An important observation, for it permits up to grasp the ambiguity of the social program of the *sans-culottes*, to realize that the political personnel of the sections, recruited mainly from those elements closest to the bourgeoisie, only partially represented the *sans-culottes*. Perhaps Rudé, whose book is primarily concerned with a study of the *journées*, was wrong to combine in a single revolutionary crowd the "militants," the only ones on whom we have abundant documentation, and the mass of the anonymous participants in revolutionary movements. More justifiably, Soboul, who relies upon several lists of participation in section meetings calculates that if, "in a period of crisis the Parisian sans-culottery in its vast majority pushed the revolutionary movement to a paroxysm"—as Rudé amply demonstrated in his study of the *journées* of 1789, of the manifestation of the Champs de Mars of July 17, 1791, of August 10 and June 2 when the crowd was armed, and as Tönnesson has shown in the insurrections of year III—"in a period of calm, less anxious about being fed, it only paid sporadic attention to political life."

Nevertheless, to isolate the politically engaged *sans-culotte* group, Soboul strives to define the "personnel of the sections," which leads him by analogy to discover the nuances and to make more precise the social contours of the entire sans-culottery. Despite its gaps, the abundant alphabetical *sous-série du fonds du Comité de sûreté générale*, enabled him to successfully complete this enterprise for the year II.

The political personnel of the sections can thus be divided into three groups: the participants in the *Comités civiles*, the "oldest, most stable, most affluent" nucleus of the sans-culottery, of whom 20 per cent represent the liberal professions and among whom there are no proletarians; the revolutionary committees recruited more democratically: 63.8 per cent of the revolutionary commissioners in the autumn of 1793 are artisans and shopkeepers (cobblers, joiners, wigmakers, artisans in artistic trades), and 9.9 per cent are salaried; last, the simple militants, participants in the assemblies and in the societies of the sections, where the salaried element is best represented: 20.1 per cent are journeymen, workers, day laborers, or clerks, compared with 0.8 per cent in the *Comités civiles* and only one man of independent means, an owner of houses; the shop and the studio are present in lesser proportions although in the majority, and besides their representatives come from the trades requiring a modest amount of skill.

Thus we see that the political personnel which surrounds the mass of *sans-culottes* has scarcely any social homogeneity and does not constitute a political "party." Moreover, this notion of "party" certainly does not appear before the Babeuf plot. In any case, the coalition of small employers which dominates the sections does not constitute that proletarian vanguard which D. Guérin not so long ago believed he saw.

This heterogeneity had a direct influence upon the ideology of the *sans-culottes*, their collective mental images, and their economic demands. Take for example the question of bread. According to E. Labrousse, whose conclusions Rudé repeats, bread represents an average of 58 per cent of a worker's budget. If we make an exception of the years 1790 or 1791, which were relatively favorable (bread's share in the hypothetical budget of a day laborer in construction work goes from less than 50 per cent in 1789 to less than 25 per cent in June 1791), we discover that the principal concern of the *sans-culottes* remains that of keeping the cost of bread within the means of everyone. This implied that salaries either be increased or that they resort to price fixing and requisition. The Soviet historians G. Zacker and S. Lotté write that ". . . the workers act independently, although suffering from hunger [and they] resorted to strikes and not to bread riots." To the contrary, it appears that, except in 1791 and sometimes in 1793 and 1794, the question of the price of bread led the mass of salaried workers into the *sans-culotte* movement. That seems simple enough. The coalition of the various social formations of the sans-culottery was so ill-assorted that the unreasonable demand of a higher salary would have sown discord, while the demand for controls of prices, really of wealth, was unanimously adopted by the *faubourgs* and the manufacturing quarters in the center of the city. It united the various categories of *sans-culottes* by giving the entire movement a common enemy: the *monopoleur*, the *agioteur* (speculator), that is to say the upper bourgeoisie engaged in the most modern forms of commercial capitalism. Because they did not constitute a social class, the *sans-culottes* did not achieve an exact understanding of the social function of work, reasoning like consumers rather than producers. This is why they passionately demand price controls, the Maximum, which they finally succeed in imposing on September 29, 1793.

The social aspirations of the sans-culottery were singularly contradictory and frequently vague, but at least they did not fail to be concrete. Social egalitarianism is the essential trait of their mentality. As the anonymous song of 1793 went:

Il faut racourcir les géants
Et rendre les petits plus grands;
Tout à la vraie hauteur
Voilà le vrai bonheur.

(We must shorten the giants
And make the small folk taller;
Everything at its true height
That is real happiness.)

The absolute right to ownership was countered by "the people's need" expressed in the term "equality of enjoyment." The common happiness promised by the Constitution of 1793 was for the *sans-culottes* reduced to "the right to exist," that is to say to the suppression of inequality in the consumption of foods. The *sans-culotte* went so far as to progressively claim a part of the products available to the rich. This equality of enjoyment was based on the assumption that the right to ownership was limited according to "the extent of physical needs." Inspired by the example of the price maximum, some of the more daring demanded a property maximum. However, they did not demand the suppression of private property, but its equal distribution to the advantage of each family, the basic social cell of the *sans-culotte*, that "good father and good husband." This social mythology was also that of a number of Montagnards imbued with Rousseau's ideas. We must wait until Babeuf for the notion of communal property to appear.

Nevertheless they went so far as to require legislation limiting the right to ownership, which would attack the traffickers in metallic currency, on joint stock companies, and the concentration of war supplies in the hands of a few. And, by a normal phenomenon of transfer, the social criticism of the *sans-culottes* in regard to the *monopoleurs*, who let fall upon the unfortunate people all the weight of their cupidity, led them to idealize the small independent producer, the small workshop, in opposition to the factory. Mr. Soboul also justifiably believes that the *sans-culotte* movement is both avant-garde in respect to politics, and retrograde in economics, where it remains attached to already outmoded forms of productivity. Here lies all the ambiguity of the movement. The *sans-culottes* dream of emancipating the poor, the propertyless, in conformity with the views of those philosophies derived from Rousseau. To this end they demanded progressive fiscal laws, a real burden only upon the rich and a moderate one upon the totality of property-owners, the proclamation of the right to work and to relief, but above all to "compulsory and free" instruction for the masses. But they could imagine no solution other than the "dispersion of property." In this respect the *sans-culotte* ideology is nourished by the belief in the golden age of a mythical past, and thus it includes almost all the idealism of Utopia.

Sans-culottery therefore struggled with insoluble contradictions. Hostile to the rich, it is nevertheless linked to the bourgeois order: ". . . it demands taxation and the limitation of ownership; but at the same time it lays claim to the independence of the shop . . . in this way it is a partisan of the economic liberalism dear to the capitalist bourgeoisie." These are conclusions which Rudé and Tönnesson reached by other methods.

Nevertheless, although the social aspirations of the *sans-culottes* are confused, it must be admitted that their "political tendencies" are very coherent. The very term *sans-culotte* may appear inconsistent with today's categorical sociology, but it is not so if the conditions of the time are taken into account. Rudé writes that it is solely to the members of the revolutionary committees that "the epithet *sans-culotte* in its socio-political sense, has most generally been applied." The sans-culotte group therefore appears as a concrete historical category, born of a clearly defined historical situation: the democratic phase of the Revolution.

The entire political philosophy of this group can be reduced to the Rousseauian adage that "sovereignty resides in the people" and that sovereignty is indefeasible, inalienable—an elementary principle but very representative of popular opinion. The equality of political rights becomes the principal demand of the *sans-culottes*. It, almost as much as bread, constantly mobilizes them, and in increasing numbers, until 1795. Rudé and Tönnesson see in it one of the essential motivations of the revolutionary crowd. The attachment to the principle and then to the reality of political equality is one of the aspects of *sans-culotte* egalitarianism in respect to land. The Finistère section declared on May 31, 1793, "The rich have been making laws for a long time, the poor must finally take their turn, and equality must reign between the rich and the poor." But the conception of popular sovereignty runs counter to the representative system. The law is only valid if ratified by the common people in their lower assemblies. And the common people can at any time take back their inalienable rights. In the year III, during the insurrections of Germinal and Prairial, the common people claimed they were "standing up" and putting themselves "under arms" for a "peaceful insurrection" against the representatives accused of the felony of keeping them away from political life. The tangible sign of civic dignity was the bearing of the pike, the "holy pike." The citizen, watching over the safeguard of his own civic dignity and that of his "brothers," is by definition an "armed man." (This was the name of a section.) All the above was accompanied by a real ritual with affective resonances. Thus on January 31, 1794, the Cordeliers, to protest against the arrest of Vincent and Ronsin, veiled the *Declaration of the Rights of Man* in black crepe.

From the principle of popular sovereignty, the *sans-culottes* went as far as the notion of direct government. With the same verve which made them rise against the Girondins, in the summer of 1793 certain sections demanded to keep their own civil records, to levy their own taxes, and to render justice without appeal. No limitations should be imposed upon the assembly of citizens, which decided everything. A decision by the Convention (September 9, 1793) having limited section meetings to two days a week, the *sans-culottes* got around the decree by holding a daily meeting of the "Society of the section." This assembly claimed to supervise the civil servants and magistrates, who in their eyes were merely their subordinates. Members of the *comités civiles*, revolutionary commissioners, police commissioners, or commissioners for supplies were subjected to constant surveillance by the sections, at least as long as the latter maintained their independence from the revolutionary government. Censure, "purifying" votes, and revokability of elected persons were the principal means by which this popular sovereignty was exercised, according to the Rousseauian principle of a sovereign and indivisible popular opinion.

Another political principle of the *sans-culottes* was that debates and votes be public, an indispensable condition to "foil intrigues and force the electors not to abuse their powers." Thus the vote was carried out "aloud and by open ballot." Expressing one's opinion became in a certain sense a public duty. The sections struggled energetically against absenteeism and indifference, which had quickly become grounds for suspicion. Active political participation involved the duty of denouncing lack of patriotism, for "denunciation is the safeguard of liberty in a popular republic," exclaimed Barry, of the William Tell section, on July 25, 1793, when reading aloud his *Essay on Political Denunciation*.

One final characteristic defines the political mentality of the *sans-culotte*: his attachment to the principles of "revolutionary unity" his search for unanimity. Sovereignty being one of these principles, the general will which is its extension ought to be manifest without internal discord. Hence this total absence of an individualistic spirit in the *sans-culotte*, who nevertheless remains attached to the strictest individualism in other domains, the family or society. We might almost think that the greater the diversity of social origins, the more powerful this desire for unanimity and uniformity. From the angle of political solidarity, the participants in activities of the sections saw themselves as forming a whole, a "family" of "brothers and friends," where the use of the familiar form *tu* broke down all the barriers of social or cultural origin. Outside the section this fraternal solidarity was further expressed by "fraternization," a sort of pact for mutual aid between the popular sections to resist the pressure of the aristocrats and the moderates, and then to eliminate them from the committees which they controlled. Thus on May 14, 1793, the Social Contract section, under the direction of its president, went in a body to the Lombard section to chase out the "aristocracy." In this way the sections were regenerated in the bourgeois quarters dominated by the moderates before the fall of the Girondins, and by the "new moderates" after the month of September 1793.

The social or political conceptions of the *sans-culottes* were not born in a day. They are the fruit of a rather long evolution and reflect the entire experience of the revolutionary masses in the face of food crises, the threat of a counter-revolution, and the propagation of ideas. Affirmed at the dawn of the Revolution by the theorists of the liberal Revolution, they were soon taken up by the popular masses, according to a real process of verbal dialectics. It is in year II, the period studied by Mr. Soboul, that the *sans-culotte* environment doubtlessly reaches political and ideological maturity, during those eight months when its influence upon the Convention was decisive (from May to December 1793). The popular masses previously had acted in a more episodic fashion, and, as Rudé indicates, at the origin of each uprising some sort of motivating factor always appears. In 1789 it is the fear of the "aristocratic plot" and of the "famine pact"; in 1791 and 1792, the demand for political equality; finally in 1793, hostility in regard to wholesale merchants and, as a result, to the Girondins. After 9 Thermidor, the *sans-culotte* ideology will continue for more than nine months in an aggressive form until the disarming of the *faubourgs* on 5 Prairial of year III had broken the mainspring of the revolutionary movement. Therefore the driving role of the *sans-culottes* in the political evolution of the French Revolution cannot be stressed enough.

Since Albert Mathiez we have known that the revolutionary government was a government established gradually under the pressure of events, which adapted itself to circumstances. But the nature of its relationships with the social forces caught up in the revolutionary movement were badly understood, so that the usual explanations of the "struggle of the factions" and the tragedy of 9 Thermidor remained insufficient. Soboul's thesis completely reworks these problems. For his history of the Parisian *sans-culottes* is also, by extension, the history of the revolutionary government and of the Jacobin dictatorship, seen from the point of view of the *faubourgs*. At the conclusion of his immense investigation, he distinguishes between two phases in the history of Parisian sans-culottery in year II: a period which goes from June 1793 (the fall of the Girondins) to Ventôse 1794 (the eve of the arrest of the leaders of the Cordeliers Club, the "Hébertists") marked by "the rise and stabilization of the popular movement"; a second period from Germinal in year II to 9 Thermidor, "the check and decline of the movement," when the masses cease to exert pressure on the revolutionary government, which from this time on solidly encircles the section organizations. A brief period chronologically, but rich in the multiplicity of political problems which arise daily.

The Mountain had owed its success of June 2, 1793 to the support of the Parisian *sans-culottes*. The latter made immediate use of this to press their advantage. The entire first part of Soboul's book is a very detailed description of the success of the popular movement and of the resistance it encountered in the Convention, the Committee of Public Safety, the Jacobins, and even the *Conseil général de la Commune*. Nevertheless, the force of the *sans-culotte* movement and the Mountain's need to avoid a break with it, permitted it indisputably to dominate political life in Paris during the autumn of 1793. The situation really encouraged popular demands: the food crises, the penury of meat and soap, the menace of a counter-revolution, the assassination of Marat on July 13, 1793, the fall of Mainz and then of Valenciennes. The *sans-culottes* demanded price fixing, the terror, and the *levée en masse*. On August 23, the Mountain had to grant them the *levée en masse*, for agitation did not stop. On September 4 and 5, 1793, the sections first imposed on the commune, then upon the Convention, the proclamation of "terror as the order of the day" and the organization of the general Maximum. The following weeks were marked daily by popular successes: "fraternization" with the moderate sections (the Pont-Neuf section in mid-September); the creation of permanent "Societies of the sections"; and last the extension of the notion of being *suspect* to include the moderates, the organization of price controls and of requisition, and the application of revolutionary legislation against the Girondins.

But Soboul clearly points out that each of these successes was accompanied by a parallel strengthening of the powers of the revolutionary government, which used the pressure by the *sans-culottes* to increase the extent of its powers to the detriment of the popular movement itself.

Popular pressure? Pressure by the *sans-culottes*? The author insists upon the spontaneous aspect of the popular movement. He refuses to call it "Hébertist," as Mathiez did, for Hébert was led more than he led others. In fact, it is only during the summer that Hébert, *Père Duchesne*, and the leaders of the Cordeliers took over the movement, but not without being obliged to break their ties with the "hornets of the Mountain" or those who were baptized *"endormeurs,"* like Robespierre.

Everything eventually put the Committee of Public Safety into opposition to the active elements of sans-culottery. A government adapting itself to circumstances, the revolutionary government felt compelled, in order to assure a semblance of revolutionary unanimity, to avoid the extremist measures which would have alienated the priests, the former nobles won over to the republican cause, and especially the wholesale merchants and the contractors necessary to the organization of national defense. Thus the Committee of Public Safety dealt a mortal blow to de-Christianization, ordered the dissolution of the *Société des Républicains-révolutionnaires*, forbade considering nobles, merchants, priests, or bourgeois *a priori* as suspects, and refused to call in coins from monetary circulation. Last, in the name of revolutionary centralization (decree of 14 Frimaire, year II), it went so far as to infringe upon the independence of the commune and of the section organization. The sections and the Cordeliers protested, but "reduced to the defensive," they finally accepted.

The policies of resistance of the Committee of Public Safety reinforced the authority of the "new moderates" (more or less linked with Danton). But the crisis kept worsening.

In February and March, it reached its peak. The "Maximum" was assuring the supply of bread, but bread of inferior quality. All the rest—meat, wood, and candles—reached exorbitant prices. The aggravation of the food crisis brought consumers, salaried workers, and shopkeepers into conflict. In addition, the salary Maximum had not prevented most salaries from being subjected to the law of supply and demand, and therefore to increase (for the demand for workers exceeded the supply). Thus the unity of sans-culottery, whose social composition is known to be incongruous, began to disintegrate. Division appeared everywhere, between Cordeliers and Jacobins, between the Societies of the sections and the revolutionary committees which to an increasing degree were escaping their control. The Committee of Public Safety attempted in vain to recreate a current of popular adhesion to politics, by the decrees of Ventôse which foresaw the distribution of the belongings of suspect persons. The sans-culottes on the whole were not dupes, and the maneuver, to the degree that it was one, failed. Toward the middle of Ventôse, the crisis bore fruit. The Cordeliers threatened the "aristocrats" with a new massacre, and the Convention with a new May 31. But, through their failure to increase their demands to include the question of provisions and salaries, their movement was not supported by the mass of section members. On March 14, isolated, the leaders of the Cordeliers were arrested.

"The Tragic Events of Germinal," as Soboul calls the trial of the Cordeliers and of those designated as "Hébertists," stunned popular opinion. They were condemned without arousing any reaction from the sans-culottes. Why? Aware of their impotence, having lost control within their sections of their magistrates, who from then on are salaried and under the control of the Committee of Public Safety, the Parisian sans-culottes had become frightened. In their disorder they acquiesced in what turned out to be the condemnation of their own hopes.

Four months separate the brutal rupture of Germinal from 9 Thermidor; and the latter is explained by the former. The analysis of this period is the most impressive part of Soboul's thesis.

The arrest of the sans-culotte leaders was followed by a tenacious repression of certain "prominent patriots," or extremists, who refused to sing the praises of the revolutionary government: trials of Chaumette, one of those in whom the sans-culottes "recognized themselves best," of Ronsin and of Pache, Mayor of Paris, replaced by the unconditional Robespierrist Fleuriot-Lescot. Everything which the sans-culotte movement had formerly inspired was either suppressed or put under the close control of the Committee of Public Safety: the revolutionary army was broken up, the hoarding commissioners were dismissed, the ministerial offices were suppressed and replaced by twelve commissions. The popular Societies, which had replaced the section assemblies, were accused of being so many "federalist centers." They often destroyed themselves, so strong was the pressure of the Committee of Public Safety. The revolutionary committees, made up henceforth of civil-service patriots, were subordinated to the Comité de Sûreté générale. Last, the purified Commune saw its leadership change with the addition of sixteen Robespierrists. Oscillating between fear and servility, the *sans-culottes* passed a resolution full of sycophancy on behalf of the government and the Convention. The revolutionary glow of the preceding year had turned into "conformity." "The Revolution has frozen," observed Saint-Just.

However, behind this apparent loyalism lay an "irreducible antagonism" to the Jacobin bourgeoisie. During the final weeks before Thermidor new forms of opposition reappear. Passivity, for example: the refusal to rejoin the frontier army after the dissolution of the revolutionary army, the "forgetfulness" of forty-three of the forty-eight sections to congratulate the Convention after the victory of Fleurus. Or open opposition: a rebirth of the Marat cult at the moment when Robespierre was condemning atheism and was preaching the Cult of the Supreme Being, and assemblies meeting under pretext of being "fraternal banquets." Once again, however, it was the question of bread which gave new strength to the popular movement. Under the pretext of keeping trade alive, a new salary Maximum was imposed, on 5 Thermidor, which often resulted in salaries being cut in half by official action. Strikes in arms factories and among the reapers were severely repressed, so the most humble groups of the *sans-culottes* came to protest against the Maximum. Manifestations by salaried workers were expected on 9 and 10 Thermidor.

"Between the Convention, impatient under its yoke, and an irreducibly hostile sans-culottery, the Revolutionary Government was as if suspended in a vacuum." The Committee of Public Safety, that living mirror of public opinion, was divided. The tragic ambiguity of 9 Thermidor occurred because Robespierre and his friends could not gain the support of the Convention, rendered judge of quarrels through a sort of formalist respect for legality, nor could they make an appeal to the masses. This was the result of a political program which had taken all initiative away from the popular world of Paris and which had deprived it, by repression or corruption, of its traditional framework. The call to insurrection by Robespierre's commune—but too late—the afternoon of 9 Thermidor, did not meet with a clearly asserted desire to fight. The majority of armed section members were dispersed in the tumult, when it became known that Robespierre and his companions had been outlawed.

The most truly political portion of Soboul's long inquiry reworks the ideas once held about the revolutionary government and the state of the Republic in Year II. Far from being subjected to nothing but internal necessities, the revolutionary government appears as the result of a compromise between two opposing forces: bourgeois liberalism and popular democracy. At the same time he also modifies our classic conception of the history of the French Revolution, whose unity of development appeared to be its principal trait. It was a bourgeois revolution, certainly, for in the main the bourgeoisie never stopped determining its destiny; but at the same time a popular revolution was blocked out within it and developed in an autonomous, albeit equivocal, way. It is this popular revolution whose prestige has been imposed upon the outlook of the revolutionary generations of the following era. Thus the history of the Revolution appears in its complexity, and Soboul's work, of which the "political" section is perhaps the richest, makes us feel the urgency of more profound research into the attitudes of the other social classes during the revolutionary cycle. Only then will the vast balance sheet be established which will allow us to grasp the movement of social forces in all their implications and profound reality.

Tönnesson continued Soboul's work chronologically and with an almost comparable method. He studies the defeat of the *sans-culottes,* that is to say the final victory of bourgeois reaction over the popular movement after 9 Thermidor. Georges Lefebvre, Eugène Tarlé, and G. Rudé had already worked in this period, but Tönnesson carried his analysis much farther. Relying upon a preliminary logical classification of the documents coming from the sections to avoid their dispersion according to the various collections, and using lists of the victims of repression in Year III, he undertook to reveal the deep social and economic origins of the post-Thermidor crisis. The major interest lies in the minute study he gives us of the attitude of the *sans-culotte* sections during the dismantling of the revolutionary government and the food crisis which accompanied the return to a liberal economy.

The 9 Thermidor, in itself, did not involve the defeat of the *sans-culottes.* The latter accepted with a certain amount of satisfaction Robespierre's fall and above all the end of the price Maximum which they accused of emptying the market places and also of the salary Maximum. Leaving the prisons along with the moderates were "the poor *sans-culottes* who moaned in irons." Each political or social formation hoped to profit from the collapse of the political regime of the Year II. From Fructidor to Brumaire in the Year III, a three-sided battle was waged which set against one another the "honest folk" (moderates), the Jacobins ("that tail of Robespierre's"), and the *sans-culottes.* The latter, solidly entrenched in the sections of the *faubourgs,* were regrouped into the "Electoral Club," in which the tone was set by former *enragés* like Varlet or the journalist Babeuf, fresh from prison. The *sans-culottes* often spoke out in chorus with the moderates against the Jacobins, for the gulf of hatred dug after Germinal had not been filled. In Brumaire, the Jacobin club was dissolved. The Electoral Club which had attacked it then understood that the threat would henceforth be directed against the popular movement as a whole. It attempted to resist, but too late. Besides, the *sans-culottes* no longer understood the palinodes of that three-sided struggle in which each person talked "revolutionarily," against his neighbor, "about the rights of man." The victorious reaction turned against the popular militants. The Electoral Club was outlawed, Babeuf incarcerated. A vast reactionary offensive soon began. "The proscription of sans-culottism and of all its attributes" was to be seen in popular clothing, in the struggle against popular cults (de-Pantheonizing of Marat on 20 Pluviôse), and even in the language. Under pretext of anti-terrorism, the "de-sans-culottization" of Paris was completed in the middle of the winter.

That winter was a tragic one. The Seine froze, the food crisis and the devaluation of the assignat assumed catastrophic proportions. Tönnesson mainly sees in this crisis causes of social and political origin, linked to the abandonment in practice, and then officially, of the Maximum. He stresses the monetary inflation which followed and which resulted in an extravagant rise in the prices of fuel, of bread, and more rarely of salaries, paid in paper money. Certainly, but one must also include—which he only does in passing—a harvest inadequate for a population suddenly freed from austerity and for a mass of more than a million soldiers. For, through fear of requisitions, many cultivators had done no sowing the previous year. Last, climatic conditions were disastrous. The origins of the crisis lie just as much in the classic phenomena of underproduction as in the new socio-political conditions. Its gravity, however, was accentuated by the abandonment of economic planning and by inflation. Tönnesson studies with great precision the social, moral, and more rarely the demographic consequences of famine, and he clearly shows the inability of the *agences de subsistance* to guarantee the rations promised to the poor people of Paris. With hunger, the danger of popular intervention reappeared. They laid the blame on the "gilded bellies" and on the Thermidorian Convention, accused of excluding the common people from all active political life. Trouble broke out in front of the bakeries in Gravilliers from 7 to 9 Germinal of Year III; threatening lines formed outside shops. Rudé and Soboul having already discussed at length the motives behind popular uprisings, Tönnesson limits himself to studying more precisely the political preparation and development of the insurrectional *journées* of 12 and 13 Germinal and of 1 Prairial of Year III.

Sans-culottes and Jacobins met clandestinely during the winter to urge the common people to insurrection. An agitation campaign was prepared for the 13 Germinal. They distributed widely a brochure, *Peuple reveille-toi, il est temps.* They were to demand bread and the Constitution of 1793, which had remained a dead letter since its ratification. The insurrection of the 12 and that of the 13 failed, but the defeat of the latter was rather inconclusive. The Convention was invaded by *sans-culottes* from the *faubourg* Saint-Antoine, but elsewhere in Paris a parallel movement inspired by the Jacobins attempted to liberate a few Montagnards arrested the previous day.

This defeat did not break the wave of popular emotion, and on the evening of 30 Floréal, a brochure, *Insurrection du peuple,* called upon the *sans-culottes* of the *faubourgs* to go to the Convention to demand bread and political democracy. An enormous crowd, surrounded by its gunners, completely disorganized and left leaderless, broke into the *Palais national* without any result other than compromising the last Montagnards (the *Crétois*), who had not been consulted (Tönnesson proves it, as does Eugène Tarlé), but who were willing to support the movement. Then repression began. On the 4 and 5 Prairial, the *faubourg* Saint-Antoine was disarmed and the last representatives of the section movement were arrested. From this time on the French Revolution, in the insurrectional sense of the word, was ended. "The defeat of Prairial [confirmed the evolution] which transformed a revolution of the masses into a regime supported or toppled by very small political groups."

Tönnesson raises various other questions. By other means he joins with E. Tarlé to affirm that the movement of Prairial was almost spontaneous, directed by obscure militants of popular societies, and not by the former commissioners or civil servants of Year II, who had compromised with the Committee of Public Safety. He adds this new and very important hypothesis for the understanding of the Babeuf movement: the initiative for the insurrection came from the depths of the prisons in which were incarcerated Babeuf, Buonarroti, and most of those who were involved in his conspiracy. Thus, the abortive insurrection of Prairial, a massive popular movement without firm direction, became associated with Babeuf's defeat, a partisan movement without massive support, simultaneously to mark the end of the popular movement during the Revolution and that of the egalitarian and communist ideology of the eighteenth century.

In concluding this analysis, it does not seem superfluous to recall that it was the liberal revolution which, by being used to destroy the aristocratic Old Regime, supplied the popular movement, whose origins and reflexes are much older, with the first precise notion of a political framework (section or club), a confused program but one in which egalitarian social aspirations and new political techniques were joined. So that historiography in general has perhaps benefited as much from the research inspired by the *sans-culotte* movement as has the history of the French Revolution itself.

Claude Mazauric

With *Les Sans-Culottes Parisiens en l'An II*, Albert Soboul has just put into place one of the major elements of a history of the French Revolution according to great socio-political masses, several of which, it is true, are awaiting their architect. The *Paysans du Nord pendant la Révolution Française* by Georges Lefebvre had provided the model of an historical analysis which was careful to individualize, within the French Revolution, the activity of distinct revolutionary currents sometimes allied in the assault upon the Old Regime, sometimes in opposition because of their interests and conceptions. Georges Lefebvre had called attention to the autonomy of the aspirations and the reactions of peasant society; Albert Soboul established that of the popular revolution within the Parisian revolution. A vast documentation about life in the sections, carried out with the intuition of an historian attached to his subject by a deep feeling of sympathy, casts an often definitive light upon the final phase of the development of the Revolution.

Indeed the work contains a meticulous reconstruction of the dramatic conflict which put the bourgeois Mountain into opposition with the *sans-culotte* movement, whose power was based upon the common people. Thus the final impotence of Robespierrism in finding a middle way between the sometimes utopian demands of section democracy and the undertakings of the moderate reaction, is indirectly clarified. But even more valuable is that essay in retrospective sociology which forms the central part of the book. This work is a careful delimitation of the *sans-culotte* "front" which ranges from the underpaid poor to the small property-owner, and rediscovers in political unity what it lacked in social homogeneity; a portrait of the *sans-culottes*, physically (is not one of the distinctive characteristics the way they are nourished?) and mentally (a political activity guided by a body of essential requirements and egalitarian dreams; an interpretation of the traditional structures of production and of property with an eye toward an audacious form of social progress); a discovery of external antagonisms (with the *Montagnards* over the principles of society and the methods of government) and internal antagonisms (born of those lines of social cleavage which cut through the sans-culottery); and an interpretation of the *sans-cullottes'* role in the general movement of the Revolution; in this last case for the sole reason that they attempted to give it a new social dimension— these among others, are some great contributions which can scarcely be contested.

Yet the author is nonetheless disposed to enter into controversy. He is the first to emphasize that "the methodology for the study of social and professional structures is controversial." Reacting as an analyst of crowds and revolutionary riots, George Rudé insists, for example, upon the interest, as well as upon the difficulty, of making a distinction between the leaders and the followers, the popular masses and the militant vanguard within the *sans-culotte* movement. This remark leads to another, which concerns the meaning we should give to the activity of these leaders, and consequently to the explanation—on a minor level, it is true—of the great internal conflict of the Revolution in 1793 and 1794. Between the *sans-culottes* and the *Montagnards*, there was not only the difference which separates the leveling tendency from the tendency to treat wealth with respect. There was also the gulf which quickly developed, separating the former passive citizens from the governmental elite whom Robespierre and his friends were very much aware they embodied. The leaders of the Mountain belonged to the bourgeoisie—not the very rich one, but the one of talents; several of them had frequented the best centers of culture in pre-revolutionary France and had benefited from an unquestionable intellectual prestige. Despite the experiment of 1774 and 1776, leading French *philosophes* had not realized their hopes to take over the reins of government, and the old monarchy had not evolved toward a "Republic of Philosophers." But the important thing was that the most diverse currents of philosophical and reforming thought had had the time to establish themselves—owing to a great deal of actual freedom in the sale of books and to the continuing comments about these ideas made by societies and academies—in the minds of a French *intelligentsia* which subsequently made a niche for itself in the revolutionary assemblies and administrations. The democratic sentiments of the bourgeois in power in 1793 and 1794, and especially of Robespierre, did not in the least discourage them from believing in their role as leaders, in the virtues of a strong and enlightened central authority, and in the necessity of educating the common people politically and of making the citizen more moral. An instinctive distrust undoubtedly led the *sans-culottes* to rise against these assemblies, these committees in which they found not a one of their own men; a distrust in regard to intelligence, which was suspected of serving individual ambitions in the same manner as birth or money; a fear of domination by persons set apart by their talents, who would take the places of the aristocrats or the rich; a fear of clever persons, of those who excell at justifying themselves by lofty speeches. The people felt that they would never be able to freely do what they wanted as long as they had not been freed of their political inability through instruction; they feared, in Père Duchesne's words, the monopolizing of the mind. The manual laborer saw in it a new form of tyranny.

Now the French Revolution developed in a very differentiated society, at least in a city like Paris; a society rich in elites developing at different social levels. The *sans-culottes*, most of whom were in any case absorbed with the immediate cares of existence, tended to accept more willingly as sources of inspiration or as representatives, men closer to them in speech and reactions, men from their quarter and of their social rank. They found them in the lower bourgeoisie of the merchants, artisans, and office employees who, according to K. D. Tönnesson's comment, occupied "the position of a social elite" particularly well defended in the sections where the well-to-do bourgeoisie was only slightly represented. That it is indeed a question of an elite is certainly true in Paris, where attendance at school, and sometimes *collège*, had become customary among the tradespeople; where the popular classes had become familiarized with revolutionary themes, and notably with that of equality, certainly less through books than by discussion of the ideas currently being circulated. The militant *sans-culottes* were buoyed up by a popular confidence which the members of the great committees could envy. This was owing both to their ability to defend with their pen and their speech the demands which spontaneously burst from the masses, and to the very modesty of their origins, proof of their revolutionary vigilance. Surely few of them were made of the stuff to govern. For some, it was a matter of taking advantage of an opportunity, and the guiding of popular anger was perhaps not always disinterested. This is the ambiguous impression born of a reading of Hébert's newspaper, so prized by his popular readers. We find a systematic contestation of the directing role of the bourgeoisie which is at this moment really an intellectual bourgeoisie; and we find a practice of out-bidding the men in office—who are accused of being used by those in power and of having lost their revolutionary fervor. Beyond personal enmities, on the edge of deeper conflicts, they call to mind the rivalry between the directing teams where one could have replaced the other to promote the democratic development of the Revolution; this was a rivalry which must have aggravated the dislocation of the revolutionary front in Year II. But it was because of the presence of these various groups that the *sans-culotte* movement became something more than a series of food riots or revolts over poverty. If the archives of social history permit, if they have preserved the trace of a rise, a success, it would be interesting to establish a biographical file which would permit us to trace more precisely the character of the militant *sans-culotte*.

⌘

But the mass of Parisian *sans-culottes* also remains imprecise in its general contours and its social and professional composition. Starting by noting that, for Paris, "the few statistical elements which can be assembled are characterized by their lack of accuracy and precision," Albert Soboul implicitly admits that he preferred to place himself on the "upper levels," those of the collective mentality, of revolutionary ideology and activity. The main outlines of the social and professional structure were doubtlessly sufficiently well known for it to have seemed legitimate to proceed to the more profitable process of exploiting the massive and homogeneous sources for the history of the sections. The breadth and scope of the work bear witness to this. We will, however, plead in favor of a more satisfying "statistical base" for the history of the Parisian revolution. The more traditional sources, like others more recently employed, permit us to sketch out a less impressionistic picture of the main sectors of the population, of economic activity, of the various levels of income. The levels among which are distributed the elements of *sans-culotte* society, and its demarcation in relation to the rest of urban society, could be presented more clearly.

How many people made up the labor force of the Parisian working world? We generally refer to figures compiled by F. Braesch; they come from an inquiry of 1791 which doubtlessly represents the sole attempt made in France in the eighteenth century to take a census of the salaried population, and this is its principal attraction. But these figures give a partial and distorted image of business and the Parisian salaried workers. In it we find neither the sum total of businesses (amputated from the much greater mass of very small businesses), nor the sum total of salaried workers (Braesch's tables show scarcely any trace of workers in the food industry, of porters, and of manual laborers of all kinds). Let us add that the inquiry of

1791 must have omitted a good number of those working at home independently or with materials furnished by an *entrepreneur* on a piece work basis, a dispersed body of salaried workers who, if the opportunity presented itself, also worked for themselves. Working women are scarcely more evident. The more solid documentation of the imperial administration is therefore preferable to a source of information so unreliable in so many respects. As for the commercial and artisanal employers, we know the number of licensed employers in the *I*er, *VI*e, *and* VIII*e arrondissements* in 1807: very close to 11,000, and therefore a reasonable hypothesis of 40 to 45,000 for the whole of Paris, while estimates previous to 1789 gave, at various dates, from 35 to 40,000. The 4000 odd employers of the inquiry of 1791 evidently represent the middle sized and large businesses of the time: those which employed from a few dozen to a few hundred salaried workers. The uncertainty, the margin of error are greater in the case of the salaried population, which must be reconstructed through a series of additions. In 1807, the number of male workers was estimated at 90,000 during the season of maximum employment. To this we must add nearly 7000 *"forts"* (porters in *les Halles*) and porters in the covered markets, market places, and bakeries, workers on the quays, and carriers of coal; and about 30,000 salaried female workers: nearly 15,000 women and girls in dressmaking, linen goods, and millinery; 4000 in fanmaking and fancy woodturning; several thousand in textiles and in gold work and jewellery. Thus there was an active working population of both sexes which went as high as 125 to 130,-000—a minimum, without doubt, for once again the workers at home sometimes were not included. The family population corresponding to this body of salaried workers is not easy to determine. Although we can apply the coefficient 3 to the 40,000 *entrepreneurs*, it is not valid for a working population which certainly included many unmarried persons (immigrants or youths) and households including several salaries. But in any case, it appears certain that the small businesses and the salaried workers together provided the livelihood of between 300 and 400,000 inhabitants, or more than half the total population. Domestic servants—before the emigration —would account for about 100,000 individuals. Even in the capital, a place of strong bourgeois and aristocratic concentration, the lower levels of society were very dense, both in relative and in absolute weight.

The professional distribution of employers and salaried workers is of less importance to the study of social structures than to that of economic life. The inquiry of 1791 eliminates certain trades. The figures collected by the imperial administration are from a period when the building trade and luxury or fancy articles—traditionally very important activities—suffered from the political situation or from social developments, while cotton and chemical industries prospered. We can still resort to the death records of the *Enregistrement*, but we must keep in mind that they only permit us to discover the professional structure of the population at the age of their death, and that there is often no distinction made between masters and workers.

Yet knowledge of the distribution of salaried workers among the various businesses, and therefore the sizes of the latter, is indispensable to the correct definition of social types. A very rough calculation would fix at about 1 to 3 the number of employers to salaried workers. Albert Soboul has shown that, within the framework of a section, and for a few major professions, the average number of salaried workers per business was clearly less than ten, and not above fifteen as the inquiry of 1791 would lead us to believe. Yet this inquiry has the merit of informing us about those exceptions, the large businesses; this fact is confirmed by the list of "notable" businesses drawn up under the Empire by the mayors or the Chamber of Commerce. Outside the textile industry, the big employers never controlled more than a minority of the manpower. The value of production rarely goes above a half million; it is most often under 100,000 francs for concerns of some importance. "Indeed, it is the artisans," remarks Albert Soboul, "who leave their mark upon the Parisian working world. . . . The fact that there have been some examples of purely working-class concentration does not change the problem very much. Since it is a question of social phenomena, on the scale of a large city, we must seize the general trend." We might add that the division of work is still accentuated by the predominance, in several important branches, of work at home for an *entrepreneur* or merchant. This type of structure, originating at Lyons, undoubtedly gained ground in the last years of the eighteenth century. Perhaps the proliferation of artisans working at home for "warehousekeepers," that is to say nonmanufacturing sellers, dates from this time.

This was a labor force of great fluidity and suppleness capable of adapting itself to market conditions. Work at home, we read, in a report by the Chamber of Commerce in 1807, constitutes a type of enterprise perfectly adapted to the specific activities of Parisian industry (that is: goldsmithing, jewelry, turned woodwork, fans, clocks, porcelains); the worker at home "bends to the caprices of style, to difficult circumstances; knowledge of one trade makes him fitted for five or six others closely resembling his own, and if regulations do not come to restrain him, if guild privileges do not forbid him to keep on living, the walletmaker works at buff belts for soldiers, the saddler makes boots, the painter of fans or snuffboxes tries his hand at porcelains, the manufacturer of steel becomes a gunsmith, a swordcutler, and so on. This is how, in the numerous crises of the Revolution, a multitude of workers, more than once deprived of their usual work, calmed the anxieties of the public administration by means of industrial freedom and created the resources which enabled a population with incalculable needs to live." But the home worker is in fact to be found in every Parisian industry, the newest as well as the most traditional; and the importance of work done at home for the major enterprises finally destroys the illusion of a certain progress toward the concentration of workers. In certain sections with a very great density of workers (Ponceau, Gravilliers), the worker at home becomes the very symbol of the salaried worker; for there is no quarter of Paris where he is not present. On May 17, 1798,

Widow Leroux, a fan merchant, on the rue de la Réunion, went out of business with 8000 livres in assets. This was a small business, but the pattern is a familiar one. Indeed, Widow Leroux laid in supplies, on the one hand from a Parisian commission agency and from a fan merchant in the Oise *département*, and on the other hand from two fanmakers in the rues Greneta and Saint-Martin, from two fan-embroiderers of the rue Saint-Martin, from an embellisher of the rue Ponceau, from a designer-engraver of the rue Jean-Robert, and from a shoemaker; and last she did business with a licensed artisan of the rue Saint-Martin, the only one of his kind. Thus, upon this very ordinary business depended a minimum of seven artisans awaiting payments which ranged from 48 to 900 livres for work done. In the same branch of the business world, Bénard, rue Portefoin, the largest fan shop in Paris, under the Consulate gave work to more than 200 workers as far as 6 kilometers from Paris. In the watch and clockmaking business, the big names—Bréguet, Berthoud—dealt partially or exclusively with home-based clockmakers. In mechanical constructions, Calla, of 92 Faubourg Poissonnière, employed fifty workers on the premises and fifty within the city. In the hosiery business silk stockings were almost always made at home; Coutant, of 6 rue Perrin-Gasselin, had about ten stocking-makers on the premises but gave work to eighty in the city. In 1807, Albinet the Elder, maker of woolen and cotton blankets in the *faubourg* Saint-Marcel, employed 400 workers, of whom eighty worked on the premises, the rest in Paris and in the provinces. The *sans-culotte* was a home-based worker just as often as he was a journeyman or a small employer.

The diversity and, circumstances permitting, the internal contradictions of sans-culottery cannot, however, be seen clearly enough without referring to the data in the Enregistrement: death records, with their precise professional indications; tables of inheritance payments, thanks to which the gradation of revenues, and the social stratification of the world of the salaried employees and of the tradesmen are delineated; and declarations of property transfers after decease, which inform us about the progressive increase in wealth of the various levels of income, starting at the bottom of the scale, the composition of an inheritance being perhaps as important as its sum total in defining the social thresholds. Nothing new in all that; but we simply want to indicate the particular importance of these sources for the history of Parisian social structures when we lack, for the years in question, censuses, electoral lists, and assessment rolls. Also remember that by means of the registers in *sous-séries* DQ7 and DQ8 of the *Archives de la Seine* we can come to know all the groups of the population, with only a few omissions—even as far as the most modest strata of society who never resorted to, or who to a decreasing degree resorted to notarial services. A first impression leads to the observation of the incredible pile up of salaried workers, those working at home on materials supplied them, persons of limited independent means, persons *"sans etat"* [that is, without known means of support], minor tradesmen, and servants, in the group of inheritances of personal property worth less than 300 and especially 200 francs; a great number of them do not go above the zero level of luck and leave life with a few dozen francs. The destitution of these persons (one-fifth, perhaps one-fourth of the population of Paris) is expressed by the curtness of a simple mention of the worn clothing which defies inventory. Second, we think we can observe a peculiar compactness in the group of masters and merchants between the 1000 and 10,000 franc levels, with a considerable number below 1000 francs. Their possessions are swelled by the appearance of the headings "merchandize" and "assets," but their way of life was otherwise undoubtedly very close to that of the most favored of the salaried workers. Toward the top where can we place the step up into the financially comfortable bourgeoisie, the frontier beyond which the *sans-culottes* could denounce a nefarious aggravation of inequality in the distribution of wealth? The appearance of investments in housing and in rural holdings is certainly a decisive factor just as is the transitional zone between the artisan and the shopkeeper on the one hand, and the speculative type of business on the other. This upper limit undoubtedly changes according to profession and quarter of the city; but a sufficiently detailed analysis should be able to show us the real situation.

✥

The light shed upon the vanguard of the Parisian revolution should not lead us to neglect the background, that is to say the entire Capital observed in its demographic evolution and its economic activity. As far as the latter is concerned, the study of the food problem—supply and distribution, the struggle against scarcity and high costs—seems to have overshadowed the other activities of production and distribution in Paris, which revolutionary events nevertheless visibly disturbed or temporarily stimulated. Since we lack general inquiries, or business archives, the hundreds of bankruptcy files extant in the *Archives de la Seine* enable us—despite their omissions or contents which seem too brief to the researcher—to appraise the combination of circumstances, to follow the progression of the difficulties when credit disappears, outside markets are closed, state intervention increases, and money weakens; or to notice both the perils and attractions of sharing in the profits of the war. From the most humble to the most brilliant, the Parisian business world says much in its balance sheets about its technical structure, its economic expansion, and its social rank. The explanation of political attitudes can be confirmed by them.

In regard to demography, the chronological limits of Albert Soboul's thesis place it in an unfavorable position; 1793 to 1794: it is the time of frenzied efforts by the *Comité de Division* of the Convention—a real general bureau of statistics—to determine the population of Paris for the purpose of electoral, fiscal, food supply, and police necessities. Laws, circulars, and tables of statistics overwhelmed local authorities. The word "statistical terror" has been used. But the result is deplorable. The census ordered on August 11, 1793, was for all intents and purposes never carried out; numerous sections refused to do the work or to deviate from the imposed tables (whose headings were indeed very rudimentary). In September 1795 it was decided to add the results of eleven sections, whose census had in many cases been completed for more than a year, to the totals in the bread-card registers of the thirty-seven other sections. In January, 1795, the *Agence des Subsistances* had on its own drawn up an estimate of the Parisian population. In both cases, the result was around 636,000 inhabitants. Although recalling the estimate of 640,000 inhabitants put forth by Necker in the 1780's, it is none the less very suspect. First of all, it is suspect because of the method—or the absence of method—used in reaching the figure (combination of data from different sources, chronological spread), next because the bread-card registers artificially swelled the Parisian population, either because they included inhabitants who had come from outside the city to lodge there temporarily and to benefit from the food distributions, or because the section administrations themselves were eager to turn in round numbers to increase their allocations. Now we must recall that during this very period Paris on the contrary had a tendency to empty itself of its real inhabitants, during the peak period of the voluntary or forced emigration. The census of 1793 to 1795 very likely showed an excessive increase in the Parisian population.

If we wish at any cost to show the volume of the Parisian population and its fluctuations during the Revolution, we must therefore resort to other means. The arithmetic hypothesis of old-fashioned demography is to be avoided, despite the elegance of their calculating procedures and the serious information already available to the scholars and the high officials expert at manipulating coefficients; indeed, the method remains tainted with arbitrariness and above all it implies a static conception of the capital's population, when the distinctive thing about that population, into the first half of the nineteenth century, is that it included, beyond a fixed, autochthonous element, an unstable element, that of seasonal or temporary immigration—sometimes developing into permanent immigration—which caused fluctuations in the total number of the population and which also contributed to its long-term growth. The economic role and, circumstances permitting, the political role of this unsettled population was considerable. Decisive progress toward a statistical method was achieved in July 1791, when the Constituent Assembly ordered the keeping of population registers to include names, ages, birthplaces, domiciles, and professions—and of registers of furnished lodgings to facilitate the surveillance of "nonresident" individuals. Unfortunately, only stray bits of these registers survive.

It is thus preferable to work in the period after and not before Year II, and to use the data in the census of 1797, which in the present state of documentation appears to be the true predecessor of nineteenth-century censuses. The *comités de bienfaisance* seem to have acted with a certain zeal and according to the rules of prudence and accuracy. In any case forty out of forty-eight sections completed their work between November 1796 and April 1797, thus excluding any great variations. According to this document, in 1797 Paris counted nearly 584,000 inhabitants. Starting with such a figure, can we reconstruct what the administration of the period, and even that of the Empire, calls the "normal" population of Paris, which we take to mean the population in a time of internal and external peace, on the eve of the Revolution—and draw the doubtless very irregular curve of that population under the Revolution and the Empire? That portion of the population which has gone into combat poses no problems. It was counted as being nearly 11,000, which is in keeping with the figures of 1801 (a little more than 14,000). In return, the number of "nonresident" persons is abnormally small; the census of 1797, which gives them a heading all to themselves, lists scarcely 6000. It seems that they were in some cases erroneously counted in the same columns as the resident population.

But we must take into account the time when the census was made; it was a moment of seasonal inactivity, undoubtedly aggravated by the economic crisis tied to monetary difficulties. Even in those sections with a very great working population, like that of the *Halle au Blé*, numerous vacant lodgings for rent are mentioned. At the peak season of a year of normal economic activity, Paris without any doubt would have counted thousands of supplementary workers. According to various indications we can in fact suppose that the Parisian population increased seasonally by 20 to 50,000 persons. Last, we must remember that the void created by the departure of the emigrés (and doubtless by the return of a part of their servants to their provincial homes) only began to be filled by those who first returned; that from 1790 to 1796 (principally in the last three years) deaths had outnumbered births by 13,000. Let us conclude that on the eve of the Revolution, Paris had well over 600,000 inhabitants; that from 1788 to 1791 various factors must have contributed to a temporary increase in the population (as a result of the economic crisis at first, then perhaps owing to the attraction of a free and better-paid labor market), and that after that date he natural movement of he population, the political shocks, and finally the slowing down of economic activity must have brought with it a serious regression, already noticeable in the census of 1797, and which reached its peak at the beginning of the Consulate. With 548,000 inhabitants, the Paris of 1801 shows a loss of 36,000 persons in four years owing to an accentuated economic paralysis, despite the return to a higher birth rate. After that, growth begins again, principally through immigration, but it is without doubt only toward 1811 that the population level again reaches that of 1789.

Do we digress from the classical political and social history of the Revolution in collecting in this manner the archival debris concerning the Parisian population? We feel that to the contrary the meaning of the revolutionary events becomes even richer through questioning these fragments of demographic history. The census of 1797, with its listings by street and often by building, expresses better than the most accurate maps the spatial distribution of the population and the organization of living quarters for each quarter of the city. It is a far from trifling element in a social topography of Paris, which diverse component parts of the census of 1807 enables us to complete. But it is perhaps the understanding of immigration which offers the greatest interest. Louis Chevalier was able to write that it permits us to "understand certain aspects of revolutionary violence. Indeed, in certain respects, the Revolution appears as a settling of accounts between two groups of the population: the old Parisian bourgeoisie and the others . . . , savages, barbarians, nomads." Indeed, the Parisian bourgeoisie appears to have suddenly become aware, in the first months of the Revolution, of the existence of that mass of common people accustomed to furnished lodgings, living on the edge of urban society, even though they frequented the center of the Capital. The interest in this group shown by the police bears witness to the fear it aroused. But whatever these immigrants, whose sensitivity to the least slackening of economic activity made them easily available, might have contributed to the revolutionary insurrections, the permanent, incorporated immigrants had perhaps the greatest effect upon the Parisian sans-culottery. Chance having preserved five conscription records for the former VIIIe *arrondissement*—that of the faubourg Saint-Antoine—we can see that, out of one-hundred young men whose residence in Paris appears long-standing and durable, twenty-eight originated from the neighboring departments of Seine-et-Oise and Seine-et-Marne, and forty-nine from a quadrilateral having at its extremities the departments of Calvados, Nord, Moselle, and Côte d'Or. Of course we know from other sources that at the end of the eighteenth century, about twenty departments situated north of a line Nantes-Geneva alone supplied most of the new population of Paris, and also provided a good part of the seasonal immigrants, the others coming from the Center and the South of France. But the fact that these human exchanges were frequent between Paris and a certain number of the departments of the North, the Northwest, and the Parisian basin, leads us to believe that these migrations might also have transmitted some of the elements of the revolutionary mentality. Throughout these departments we discover on the eve of the Revolution common difficulties and identical demands, whether it be a question of small property-owners, small farmers, or rural artisans. Although the common people of rural areas leave controversies about the exercise of political democracy to those of the cities, they feel, like them, the danger of an increasing concentration of fortunes and they struggle against the pressure of a capitalism which, in Paris or in the villages of the surrounding region, is often embodied in the same men. By means of its demographic attraction, Paris served, in its faubourgs and in its sections, as a crossroads for the egalitarian themes dear to the peasant as well as to the *sans-culotte*.

∽§§∾

Despite the insufficient amount of quantitative documentation concerning Paris during the Revolution, it therefore appears possible, to a certain degree, to "calculate," following Georges Lefebvre's advice to the artisans of social history. But the quantitative study takes us beyond the framework of the social group and makes us consider above all the relationships between the forces within urban society as a whole. And it is then that a negative conclusion of Albert Soboul's vast thesis appears: despite their numerical force and their effort to organize, the *sans-culottes* were not able to triumph over the resistance of the middle classes, and of the notables in power. One of the merits of social history, when it succeeds in becoming statistical, is that it helps us understand why the bourgeoisie, with the exception of its lower strata, repudiated the democratic adventure to stick to a Revolution of the happy medium.

Louis Bergeron

THE LAST POPULAR
MOVEMENT OF
THE REVOLUTION IN PARIS

The "Journées" of Germinal and of Prairial of Year III

By Richard Cobb and George Rudé

Il faut battre le fer pendant qu'il est chaud, c'est aujourd 'hui le grand coup de chien, il ne faut pas les manquer ...

> (Words attributed to a joiner of the *Quinze-Vingts* section, 1 Prairial of Year III)

(We must strike while the iron is hot, today is the big riot, we must not fail ...)

The great historians of the French Revolution, when discussing the Parisian *journées* or insurrections of Germinal and of Prairial of Year III, have not failed to stress its great importance as the last large-scale popular insurrection and the last manifestation of the *sans-culotte* movement. Crushed by the superior military strength of the Thermidorian government, the common people of Paris did not stir again until 1830, when there were popular insurrections of a rather different sort than the great revolutionary *journées* and made up of different elements of the capital's population.

It is therefore not a matter of raising once again the question of the historical significance of these events but rather of submitting them to a more detailed study than those that have been made up to the present, to search for their origins, as well as for the motivations of the participants, by following more closely the thread of the popular movement which, temporarily interrupted by the fall of Robespierre, was to be resumed, slowly at first, then at a more accelerated pace, under the incentive of Thermidorian politics and of the austerity of the times.

In order to achieve this aim, we are obliged to go beyond the framework of the sources used until now by historians, by searching for supplementary documentation in the police records. The principal sources which would aid such a fruitful exploration are the general reports of Parisian police surveillance edited by Aulard, the papers of the *Comité de sûreté genérale in série F*[7] in the National Archives, and the official reports of the police commissioners of the sections of Paris in the *Archives de la Préfecture de Police*. This documentation, based upon the daily reports of surveillance and on the personal files on the common people of the sections, enables us to see from a new angle and "from the bottom" the unfolding of the social movement during the winter and spring of 1794 and 1795, and to no longer present the insurrections of Germinal and Prairial as isolated explosions, but as the continuation of a popular movement of long duration, provoked by the economic and social policies of the Thermidorians and especially by the scarcity and high cost of basic provisions.

Georges Lefebvre has admirably summarized the political evolution of the "Thermidorian Reaction" as follows. On 11 Thermidor (July 29, 1794) the dismantling of the machinery of the revolutionary government began; a decree of 7 Fructidor (August 24) created sixteen committees to carry out the functions of the two great *Comités de Salut public et de Sûreté générale* of the Robespierrist period. The former was thereafter limited to war and to diplomacy and could not, any more than could that of *Sûreté générale*, summon armed forces except through the intermediary agent of the military committee. While breaking up the governmental machinery at its summit, the degree of 7 Fructidor dealt a mortal blow to the committees of surveillance. In the provinces, all were suppressed, with the exception of the committees of the chief towns of each district. In Paris, the revolutionary committees of the sections, after having been purged of their Jacobin and *sans-culotte* elements, were reorganized into committees for each of the twelve *arondissements*, composed of big businessmen and of men devoted to Thermidorian policies. The civil committees of the sections were also "completed" by the addition of men selected in advance by the *Comité de législation* of the Convention. Thus, while continuing to exist, the popular institutions were to undergo a total change in their composition, their truly *sans-culotte* elements—artisans, small businessmen, shopkeepers

—stepping aside for the moderates who had dominated the general assemblies of the majority of sections before June 1793. This change was to
be more or less extensive depending on the section, but in order to ac-
celerate this movement within the general assemblies, the Convention had
already suppressed, on 4 Fructidor, the payment of 40 sols granted to poor
sans-culottes who attended the meetings, and had limited them to meeting on *Décadi* only.

Even more indicative of the frame of mind of the Thermidorian government were its economic activities. The big cultivators, the *nouveaux
riches*, the wholesale merchants and ship owners—the preferred clientele
of Thermidorian officials—had always been opposed to the policies of control and constraint inaugurated in 1793 by the Mountain, to meet the
exigencies of the war and to answer popular demands, a policy whose mainspring would be the general Maximum of September 29. Having proclaimed
"political liberty" and having dismantled the revolutionary government,
the Thermidorians could delay no longer, despite war and scarcity, in also
creating economic liberty. In addition, this policy had the advantage of
harmonizing with popular desires, at least momentarily. Disillusioned by
the increasingly numerous infractions of the laws of the Maximum carried
out with impunity by cultivators and important merchants, after Fructidor
a large part of the *sans-culottes* themselves had come to desire the repeal
of the law.

The decree of 4 Nivôse (December 23, 1794) in theory abolished the general Maximum and re-established the free market for most goods. In Paris,
however, the price control of bread at 3 sols a pound and that of meat
sold in controlled markets at 21 sols a pound was continued, at least in
principle. In comparison with the provinces, Paris was therefore a privileged
city, the committees of the government trying above all to guarantee food
supplies for the capital at the expense of the other large cities and of the
rural areas, left to their own devices. The results did not, however, measure
up to the expectations of the leaders, even for the arrival of grains and
other supplies into the capital. Besides, in order to assist the big cultivators
and merchants, its new electoral supporters, the Convention allowed the
establishment in Paris, along with the controlled market for bread and
meat, of free markets in which not only eggs, butter, wood, oil, vegetables,
and other noncontrolled foods would be sold at top prices, but also that
part of the bread and meat supplies not included in the daily distribution
controlled by the government. In theory, the Parisians were assured of 1
to 1½ pounds of bread per person every day, as well as a half pound of
meat at 21 sols a pound, every 5 days. But, in practice, they received far
less. The vacillating policies of the Thermidorians, the egoism of the cultivators, the partial return to free commerce and the abandonment of the
means of constraint, the progressive dislocation of transportation by road
or by river as a result of the war, and finally the terrible winter of 1794 and
1795 together were to contribute to the very rapid decrease in arrivals of

food and to a terrible crisis over supplies, made still more acute by the progressive collapse of the paper *assignat*. This crisis, which in some areas assumed all the characteristics of a real famine, was to envelop all of France during the first half of 1795, and especially during the last months of the winter and the beginning of spring.

In Paris, essential supplies, including flour and meat, began to be rare, although to a less disastrous degree than in the chief provincial cities. Meat disappeared completely from the controlled market, where even the energetic public officials of Year II had never really succeeded in keeping it. As for bread, despite governmental promises, distributions at the fixed price was limited for months at a time—and especially during the crucial period from Ventôse to Prairial (March to May)—to 8, 6, 4, or 2 ounces a person. As a result the Parisian was forced to buy his foods, even his bread, in the free market, where the prices of all essential items frantically increased. Thus the pound of bread, fixed at 13 sols, climbed in the free market from 25 sols on March 28, to 65 sols on April 11, to 6 livres on April 21, to 9 livres on May 11, and finally to 16 livres on May 18, the eve of the events of Prairial. The increase thus stood at 1300 per cent. Likewise, a pound of meat, fixed at 21 sols, went in the free market from 36 sols in December to 7 livres, 10 sols on April 1 (12 Germinal). The index of the cost of living in Paris, based upon June 1790, is calculated to have gone from 500 in January to 900 in April.

We have less information available about the salaries and the amount of work available in this period, but it would have been quite remarkable if they had been able to keep up with the rapid increase in prices. Upon Robespierre's fall, the Thermidorians, by demagogic manipulation, had given the workers to understand that the elimination of this leader was going to result in a substantial increase in salaries, and some workers had rejoiced over the disappearance of the "triumvirate" and "their" Maximum. The Parisian salary-list of 5 Thermidor, which was to establish substantial salary reductions during the Jacobin dictatorship, was in fact revised by the new authorities, and increases of about 50 per cent were officially announced on 22 Thermidor (August 9, 1794). But these were only ephemeral gains which were quickly exceeded by the inflationary movement which followed. Judging from the rare statistics still extant, it would appear that the "real" salary of the Parisian worker in April 1795, if we calculate that he only had to buy a third of his bread in the free market, was well below that of 1793 and 1794, and had even fallen to the catastrophic level of 1789.

Historians have clearly shown the state of physical and moral collapse experienced by the Parisian *sans-culottes* in the weeks which followed the fall of Robespierre and the first proscriptions of Jacobin personnel. Deprived of their leaders, bewildered and disillusioned, they helplessly watched the "purification" of the committees of the sections and the formation of bands of "gilded youths," accepting almost without complaint the rise in the prices of supplies and the almost total disappearance of coal and wood.

Employees of workshops were the first to start agitating. In Fructidor (August and September, 1794) journeyman bakers left their shops and demanded a salary of 13 livres each *décade*. They were soon followed by a strike for a salary increase by the dock workers near the *Jardin national*, employed at handling wood floated down the river. On 1 Vendémiaire, those employed on stagecoaches refused to work until they were granted the bonus which they had been demanding for three months. In October, the 200 workers employed by the administration of military transports, supply depot of the *Pepinière*, demanded "to be paid like the workers of the stagecoaches, that is to say for the day of *décadi* and the days they mount guard," and presented the *Comité de Sûreté générale* with six petitions to this effect.

But it was in the arms works, during the period of Jacobin dictatorship, that the ferment was most active. After Brumaire (October-November), the workers had to agitate for salary increases; on 27 and 28 Brumaire, delegations from the *Réunion* workshops of the rue Avoie, and from the former Hôtel de Bretonvilliers, on the Île-de-la-Fraternité (Île Saint-Louis), appeared for this purpose before the Convention. On 1 Frimaire (November 4), under pretext of congratulating the Convention "on the fall of the tyrants," the 343 workers of the *Panthéon* workshop forced their foreman to march at their head into the very midst of the assembly to present their demands. The real aim of this manifestation, according to a report made by the supervisory authorities of this workshop,

is the decrease in salary which some workers have experienced, for it only was applied to a few sluggish and lazy workers who consider the workshops to be charitable institutions, where the Nation is supposed to give them pensions for doing nothing. . . . The vast majority were not among those who had been subjected to this decrease, an obvious proof that everything is merely the result of some intrigue.

Three days later, a delegation of workers from the Marat workshop was received before the Convention where it complained of administrators "who have made terror the order of the day in the workshops." The Convention, however, pushed by the urgent need of the economy and by the fear of more widespread working-class agitation, decided to have done with it by issuing a decree that very day that the Committee of Public Safety and the Committee of General Security would meet "to stop the disorders created by ill-willed persons in the arms works of Paris." On 21 Frimaire (December 11), therefore, the Committee of General Security had an order posted in the workshops to the effect that after 1 Pluviôse (January 20), the arms works would no longer be in the pay of the Republic. Consequently, the next day there was a general movement of the workers, who feared finding themselves unemployed in the middle of the winter; on January 23, the workers in the *Sans-culottes and Île-de-la-Fraternité* workshops joined forces to go from workshop to workshop to recruit reinforcements before appearing before the Convention where about twenty of their delegates succeeded in being received, though they were not heard; last, on January 29, these twenty "ringleaders" were arrested. Owing to the pressure by the workers, the Convention decided, however, to delay the closing of the arms works of Paris until 20 Pluviôse (February 8). From Nivôse on, no more agitation by workers movements for salary increases is cited, either in the workshops or in private industry. These movements, limited though they were, certainly contributed to preparing the insurrectionary atmosphere of the *journées* of Germinal and of Prairial. But, once the effects of inflation and scarcity were freely felt, the order of the day would be famine riots—in which the workers allied themselves with the other strata of the lower classes—rather than the "coalition" and working-class salary demands.

In the meanwhile, the popular ferment provoked by the high cost and scarcity of basic supplies gradually spread. During the course of the autumn, agitation could already be observed in the ports and in the markets, traditional points of departure for every popular "tumult" over wood, coal, oil, candles, soap, and finally the poor quality of bread. Merchants were called "hoarders" and, on 1 Frimaire (November 21), unemployed workers moved threateningly against "those who are not partisans of the Jacobins," praised the terrorist Carrier, and spoke about the Convention "with very little decency." But, until winter made itself felt with an unusual harshness, even for the eighteenth century, and until the consequences of the abolition of the Maximum had become evident to all the common people of Paris, the agitation remained on the surface and was scarcely supported. A police report dated 10 Frimaire (November 30) described the public's mood in the following terms:

The complaints and grumbling are still to be heard. The slowness with which bread is distributed, the lack of flour, the high prices of this bread, wood, wine, coal, vegetables, and potatoes in the shops and markets and their prices, which are rising daily in a terrifying manner, are throwing the common people into a state of suffering and depression which can easily be imagined. . . . Within homes, where hunger and poverty, nakedness and deprivation wreak their havoc, the ideas being formed, the conversations being carried on are certainly not moderate ones; but a bit of comfort would certainly bring these unfortunate people back to their real sentiments, those of a good government which assures everyone liberty, well being, and happiness.

During Nivôse, the Convention having abolished the Maximum and the food crisis having worsened, popular agitation took on a more menacing tone. On 7 Nivôse (December 27), three days after the revocation of the Maximum, a police informer observed: "The discontent over the excessive cost of all foodstuffs and of everything necessary to existence is at its peak; the indigent class worries the peaceful citizens about the consequences of these excessively high costs." On December 16, they complained in the markets that prices had doubled since the revocation of the Maximum and, the following day, workers gathered at the doors of the Convention are said to have claimed "that the Convention was not at all concerned with making them happy," adding "that as for the merchants, they were pigs who ought to be slaughtered." The royalist propaganda must have gained adherents: "I have just paid 70 livres for a load of wood," declared one worker, "and you come and tell me about a Republic; give me the means to live and to help my family live, and I will love the Republic." Elsewhere, others cried: "The devil take the Republic! We lack everything, and only the rich lack nothing." On 21 Nivôse, they were already spreading the news that the faubourg Antoine was preparing to come to the Convention to demand a reduction of prices, while some added that they should march upon the Convention and break it up.

This growing ferment among the lower classes of the Capital must not be attributed solely to the shortage of supplies. It also began to be influenced by clearly political events. On the one hand these elements include the repressive measures of the government—the incarceration of the patriots, the closing of the Jacobin Club, the suppression of the 40-sous payment, the destruction of the busts of Marat, the increasingly great liberty granted to the bands of Fréron's "gilded youths," whose behavior aroused popular anger; on the other hand, they include the political agitation which was kept up by the opposition and which reached the common people through the medium of the Jacobin readers of Lebois' newspaper, as well as through the clubs of the faubourgs Antoine and Marceau, and the rue du Vert-Bois in the Gravilliers section, "made up almost entirely of workers and little-educated men, very easily led astray." We find a few indications as to the spread of the mottos and of the grievances of this Jacobin opposition in the popular areas, thanks to remarks reported by the police from Vendémiaire on.

At the beginning of Frimaire, when the *Bonne-Nouvelle* section went in a body to the Convention to congratulate it for the steps taken against the Jacobin societies, "in the streets through which they passed, passers-by hooted at them, saying: 'there are the little *muscadins* (elegant royalists) of *Bonne-Nouvelle* who are going to the Convention.'" Toward the end of the winter, these political trends became more clear. All the grievances of the workers and of the lower classes are to be found in the "unpatriotic words" uttered in the place du Carrousel by a certain Jean-Louis Degré, a journeyman woodworker who had been fired from the arms works, arrested on 21 Pluviôse. According to witnesses, Degré complained because "the Convention had suppressed the workshops and had by this means put the workers into the position of dying from hunger; that the members of the Convention were plotters, who were careful to see that they received 42 livres a day, while the workers only earned 3 livres a day." Upon seeing bourgeois members of the section pass by, he is said to have cried out:

"Look at all those citizens going to the Convention; they are going to petition in the name of the mass of citizens who make up the section, though there is not a single *sans-culotte* among them; they are all plotters, merchants, sedition-mongers, a bunch of knaves, and men in warm great-coats."

Questioned on 23 Pluviôse (February 11), Degré denied having spoken unkind words about the Convention, but he admitted having said, about the demolition of the obelisk honoring Marat, "that the common people lacked character since they had allowed this destruction," and having added "that he was astonished that the Convention was not concerning itself with having the price of bread reduced." The Thermidorian majority was thus on the alert and it already expected (and perhaps desired?) a popular insurrection. Ordering Merlin de Thionville, on 14 Pluviôse, to return to Paris, his colleague, Merlin de Douai, wrote him: "The rascals are bestirring themselves and it is asserted that they are preparing a disturbance." On 24 Pluviôse, they succeeded in arresting Babeuf and the clubs of the faubourgs Antoine and Marceau were closed. Finally, on February 11, Méchin, one of the heads of the arms commission, had to suggest that the Committee of General Security "take advantage of the great deal of strength which the activities and energy of the young people of this immense commune are giving it at this moment; it is the only possible counterbalance against factionalism. This counterbalance is all the more necessary because there are no means of repression, no armed force upon which one can completely rely." These recommendations were not to fall upon deaf ears.

It is in this atmosphere of reciprocal distrust and hatred that the *journées* of Germinal were prepared. Nothing more was needed to provoke the explosion than the growing lack of price-controlled bread, which made itself felt from the beginning of Pluviôse (end of January) and which reached its peak toward the end of Ventôse (March). Already, on 26 Ventôse, assemblies of women in the *Gravilliers* section were described. From then on we can observe a mounting wave of popular activities which gradually spread to all the sections of the center, the north, the east, and even of the south, and which finally overflowed on 12 Germinal in the violent eruption of the starving masses before the Convention. On 27 Ventôse, the delegates from the faubourgs Marceau and Jacques came to state on the floor of the Convention: "We have no bread. We are on the verge of regretting all the sacrifices we have made for the Revolution." On 28 Ventôse, in the *Montagne* section, a restaurant waiter is arrested, accused of having said, "that it was awful to see the French people reduced to one pound of bread a day and to eating potatoes, which were only good for swine." On 1 Germinal (March 21), representatives of the faubourg Antoine were received before the Convention, while, near the Porte Saint-Denis, in the *Amis de la Patrie* section, there were brawls between the workers and the *muscadins*. On 2 Germinal, no bread was distributed in the *Gravilliers* and *Homme-Armé* sections. In the gardens of the Palais-Égalité, two bourgeois were insulted as *muscadins* by arms workers and, on the Pont Neuf, a worker in the paper industry was arrested for having shouted that "all the rich are rascals." On 3 Germinal, women from the workshop of the Arsenal threatened to toss into the water a group of "young folks" who had come from the faubourg Antoine to "fraternize with the workers," and in the *Gardes-Françaises* section, a wine merchant, a former member of the revolutionary committee, accused of being a "terrorist" and the "advisor and motivator of the poor workers who lodge in great numbers in that street" (rue de l'Égout), was arrested. On 4 Germinal, four individuals were arrested in the *Montreuil* section, accused of having sought "to make the faubourg rise in revolt"; in the *Droits-de-l'Homme*, *Indivisibilité*, and *Marchés* and *Lombards* sections, no bread was distributed that day, while in that of the *Théâtre-Français* one half to three-quarters of a pound per person was made available. A police report of 5 Germinal observes: "There is general discontent everywhere caused by the scarcity of bread, which has given rise to bread lines that begin forming by midnight, as well as to violent grumbling against the established authorities." In the *Amis-de-la-Patrie* section, a jeweller of rue Martin is arrested for having declared "that is was scarcely easy to live on a half pound of bread" and for having threatened the Convention ("we ought to go there and choke them"). The next day, on 6 Germinal, the women of the central sections began to organize among themselves. According to the report of an informer, "women from the rue Martin . . . said among other things that men were cowards not to show themeslves [these are just exactly the words of the Parisian women of August to October 1789!] and that it was impossible to live on such bad bread and such a small amount of it at that," while one of his colleagues notes "that the women of the *Elisabeth* flour workshop went to all the workshops to force the women there to join with them to go to the Convention and to force their foreman to follow them." The day of 7 Germinal is stormy. In the *Gravilliers* section processions of women and workers begin to form in the morning to go to the Convention to demand bread. A jeweller of the rue de la Tabletterie, accused of "having been observed in the gathering of the Gravilliers section, claimed that he had been "stopped" by workers who grabbed him by the collar and forced him to march with them "and that they stopped all the workers who passed and had them join in the march to the Convention to ask for some bread." Two deputations of women, also from *Gravilliers* section, after having enlisted reinforcements in the rue Honoré and elsewhere, appeared before the Convention where they asserted that since the bread distributed that morning had only been a half pound per person, "no one wanted to take any"; they left the assembly screaming "Bread, Bread!" Of the several women arrested during the afternoon, some were arraigned before the Committee of General Security, but others were released owing to popular intervention. The *Amis-de-las-Patrie* and *Gravilliers* sections held illegal meetings. The police claim that the agitation was the most tumultuous in the *Gravilliers* section: a man called Geoffroy, a shoemaker, is said to have put "himself and his workers at the head of the tumult, and to have forced the president to hand over to him the key to the assembly hall, so that evil-minded persons could gather there under pretext of a petition." In the *Temple* section, designated by the police as one of the principal centers of agitation, they demanded that a recent decree of the Convention be put into effect raising the workers' bread ration to a pound and a half daily, and a joiner of the rue des Fossés-du-Temple declared that three individuals came to his lumberyard and told his workers: "You will be at the Porte Saint-Martin tomorrow morning between seven and eight o'clock. There is a blow to be dealt. You are as much involved in it as we are. It is for bread." The next day, 8 Germinal, agitation did not subside, although it was less widespread than the preceding day. Toward noon, again in that effervescent *Gravilliers* section, "it was said in the groups . . . that deputations had left for the faubourgs, that the lower classes must get control of the cannons, for fear that the big merchants might have the same idea." At nine-thirty in the morning, a procession of men and women of every age passed through the rue du Temple crying out "that good citizens and citizenesses should join with them to go get bread"; it was dispersed by the National Guard when it reached the former Opera House, and eight persons were arrested, including four women workers. On 9 Germinal, the father of a family killed two of his three children through fear of famine. On 10 Germinal, in the *Droits-de-l'Homme* section, people who had not eaten for several days were reported in the lines outside the bakeries, while in the *faubourg-du-Nord* section echoed the cry: "Give us bread!" On 11 Germinal, the agitation continued in the *Droits-de-l'Homme* section, where there was still no flour. By eight o'clock that morning the president of the section was called upon to convoke the general assembly; when he refused, "individuals carrying a bell called the citizens to go immediately to the meeting place of the section to discuss the food supply." The remonstrances of the police commissioner, who tried to stand in the way of this illegal assembly, were drowned out by cries of "Bread! We want bread!" The assembly deliberated without its officers, and addressed a petition to the Convention. According to police reports, the workers left their workshops and refused to return until they got bread. It is significant that among the persons arrested in the IX arrondissement were soldiers. In the X arrondissement there were brawls between workers and the "gilded youths." In the course of the day, four deputations from the Parisian sections filed through the Convention; three of them complained about high costs and the scarcity of provisions. The orator from the *Quinze-Vingts* section expressed himself in threatening terms ("The common people finally wish to be free; they know that when they are oppressed, insurrection is one of their duties.") and demanded "the punishment or the liberation of prisoners, that everything possible be done to remedy the frightful poverty of the common people, that their rights should be restored, and that the democratic constitution of 1793 should be promptly put into force." Just so many slogans to mark the path of the popular riot which was to break out the next day.

On the morning of 12 Germinal assemblies and processions began to form in the popular quarters. Bread is still lacking; in some sections a half pound or even a pound per person was distributed but more often a quarter of a pound or nothing at all had to suffice. In the *Droits-de-l'Homme* section, women grappled with one another to grab a neighbor's bread. In the rue de Montmartre, at the corner of the rue Feydeau, construction workers meet to protest an order of the Committee of Public Safety, issued the evening before, ordering that workers lodged in furnished rooms be obliged to buy their food in the free market. A dozen of these protesters are said to have entered neighboring workshops to call upon the workers to accompany them to the Convention. On the left bank, the faubourgs Marceau and Jacques joined together to march to the Assembly, and, according to another report, the *Gravilliers* section set up a similar meeting with thirteen other sections to march to the Assembly. The members of the sections burst into the room in the middle of a speech by Boissy-d'Anglas. According to the account published in the *Moniteur*, "men, women, and children, after having taken the guards at the door by storm, entered the room in great numbers waving their caps and shouting: 'Bread! Bread!' Some of the demonstrators had written on their caps 'Bread and the Constitution of 1793,' others bore the single word 'Bread.'" But despite these labels, they do not seem to have followed any plan. While the spokesman for the *Cité* section was giving a speech in which he demanded that the Constitution of 1793 be put into effect, the orators of two other sections were applauded by the Thermidorian majority. The demonstrators were not armed and, when the National Guards of the western sections, led by Merlin de Thionville, appeared, they left without resistance. Moreover, as Mathiez pointed out, it is Gaston and Choudieu, two *Montagnard* deputies, who were the first to invite them to march out quickly and leave the room quietly.

Incidents of no great significance occurred in the city during that day and again on 13 Germinal. The *Panthéon*, *Popincourt*, and *Cité* sections declared that they would meet without interruption. In *Brutus* section, an office doy of rue Caumartin was arrested, accused of having "uttered words against the Convention concerning supplies in Paris." A gathering formed on Nicolas dock to prevent the loading of a stagecoach which they believed contained food and jewels, and at Chaillot customs-gate, workers were accused of having pillaged a wagon full of grain. Along the Boulevard du Temple, an office worker who tried to break up a group "which was talking about food supplies" was labeled a *muscadin*, while at the same place, an individual who maintained that one can live on four ounces of bread a day was arrested at the crowd's request. On 13 Germinal, the majority of sections received only a half pound of bread and some rice. Agitation continued in *Quinze-Vingts*, where an illegal assembly was held. A young worker employed at making arms in the Romain Hue workshop, *Cité* section, was arrested for having gone to see what was happening in the Tuileries (he had heard "that they were imprisoning patriots"). In the rue Richer, of the faubourg Montmartre, the gunners, notified that they should arrest Léonard Bourdon, rebelled and wanted to march to the Champs-Élysées to save the patriots. The Convention, for its part, in order to re-establish order, put Paris in a state of siege and entrusted the command of the armed forces to General Pichegru, who happened to be in the Capital, and the Committee of General Security ordered the arrest of several "ringleaders" in the *Contract-Social*, *Gravilliers*, and *Arcis* sections and in the faubourg Montmartre. The assembly would seize this opportunity to have Collot, Billaud, and Barère (Vadier, the fourth of the "great culprits" having fled) to Guiana without a trial, and to order the arrest of a dozen of the deputies of the minority, including Léonard Bourdon, Amar, and Cambon.

To solve the bread problem, the Convention merely decreed "that the Committee of Public Safety will take all steps within its power so that, should the quantity of bread be insufficient for all the good citizens, they will be supplied with rice and biscuit; that the workers, artisans, and indigents should be allowed to choose between the various distribution places and that they should be served first."

The *journée* of 12 Germinal, like the other insurrections of the Revolution, did not lack commentators who generally agreed to interpret it as the result of a conspiracy. But the agreement ceases when it comes to identifying the conspirators. Some have claimed that the insurrection was provoked by the Thermidorian government itself in order to get rid of an opposition which was regrouping both in the sections and within the Convention. The Thermidorians, to the contrary, claimed that it was the work of deputies of the Mountain and of their supporters in the clubs and popular societies— it is a question of connecting the insurrection with the old terrorist staff of Year II, as Dulac, a stoolpigeon, realized when, at the end of the month, he wrote, concerning the Jacobin prisoners in the *maison des Ortes:* "what I saw clearly is that there were ties between the prisoners and the conspirators."

Although we cannot completely reject either of these two hypotheses, it appears that we must look elsewhere for the origins of this undecisive insurrection. We must not be surprised to learn that the "gilded youths" had been summoned on the 11 Germinal to meet the following morning in the courtyard of the Louvre; the authorities had been expecting a popular explosion for a long time, and the fact that the Thermidorian majority took advantage of the situation to have its adversaries arrested does not in the least prove that it had prepared the coup which permitted it to carry out this operation. To the contrary, it is certain the same deputies of the Mountain had acted in agreement with their supporters in the sections. For example, in the *Gravilliers* section, Léonard Bourdon certainly played a decisive role, while Van Eck, an orator in the Cité section, was very closely linked with Thuriot. Moreover, certain arrested patriots are supposed to have greeted the *journée* of 12 Germinal as the announcement of a *Montagnard* insurrection, while others, more wary, smelled a police trap. These reciprocal accusations merely tend to suggest that there might have been a certain alliance between the *Montagnards* and some of the section leaders, which would undoubtedly explain the slogans of *"liberté des patriotes"* and *"la Constitution de 1793."* But the deputies, even the *Montagnards*, were on this occasion scarcely interested in anything but political problems, while the chief preoccupation of the common people was, to the contrary, food supplies. The police saw this most accurately in reporting, on 10 Germinal: "What concerns the common people at this moment is the great difficulty in obtaining bread." Likewise, at Rouen, riots having prevailed in the city during the three days of the 13, 14, and 15 Germinal, the Thermidorians attributed this movement to "royalist plots," because the riot was accompanied by the destruction of the trees of liberty and of the tricolor cockades, and because shouts of "Long live Louis XVII" were heard; but, as in Paris, the basic demands of the common people were the increase of the bread ration to 1 pound a day, and its price fixed at 3 sols a pound. In both cases, we undoubtedly have a political exploitation of popular grievances, but the true cause of these riots is the bread problem.

Though the *journée* of 12 Germinal was followed by a brief calm, the authorities would take little advantage of it to attempt a solution of the food problem which, during the 7 weeks which separate this insurrection from those of Prairial, only worsened. As in the preceding period, the bread shortage was most strongly felt, while prices climbed steeply in the free market. This bread tragedy is admirably portrayed in the cold light of the daily police reports. On 14 Germinal (April 3), a half pound of bread was distributed in most sections, but in those of the *Lombards* and *Indivisibilité*, there was scarcely a quarter pound and 3 ounces of rice; on 18 and 19 Germinal there was only a quarter of a pound throughout the city. During the month of Floréal (April and May), the same somber and monotonous portrayal of the slow increase in misery. On 7 Floréal, there were no distributions in several sections; on 14 Germinal, a distribution of 6 ounces; on 18 Germinal, of 2 to 3 ounces; on the 1 Prairial (May 20), the first day of the riot, the distributed only 2 ounces of bread in the *Finistère* and *Luxembourg* sections. During this same period, the price of bread in the free market went from 65 sols a pound on 23 Germinal, to 6 livres on 2 Floréal, to 10 livres on the 16, to 12 livres on the 20, and to 16 livres on the 29. Of course, it was not merely bread which was lacking; in the correspondence of the *Comité de Sûrêté générale* of 23 Germinal, we find the following observation:

It is no longer bread alone which arouses complaints, it is the excessively high prices of all foods especially at a time when the government, it is said, is going to stop supplying meat on the basis of ration cards. What has especially embittered people is that women from the country are announcing that they are increasing prices again, and they are threating to raise the price of butter to 50 livres.

In Ventôse of Year II, the crisis over arrival of merchandise, exploited by the Robespierrist government to overthrow its "Hébertist" critics, had already been especially concerned with foods "of the second zone"—meat, butter, eggs, vegetables. Although bread, the mainstay of the common people, was now their principal preoccupation, the lack of other foods contributed, although doubtlessly to a much less marked degree, to the physical and moral collapse of the common people of Paris. We can find multiple expressions of popular despair during these spring months; mendicity reappears, people fall dead in the streets from starvation, and suicides multiply. Royalist propaganda attempts to profit from this dispair, especially among the women in the markets, although they achieve no great results. On 26 Germinal, a policeman hears many women screaming: "Give us bread or death; kill us rather than letting us languish! Do they want to force us into asking for a king? Well! *foutre*, we don't want one." But on 12 Floréal, another tone: "Be patient, we will have a king in two weeks. Then we will not lack bread." We must remember the tone of resignation and despair heard in the complaints of these poor women, rather than their vague political desires. It is to the cry, "We will die only once, better to die now than of hunger," that the women in Norman towns will attack the storehouses of the Republic.

The popular movement, undoubtedly disoriented by the failure of the *journée* of 12 Germinal, and deprived of some of its political leaders by the accelerated repression against the former section personnel of Year II during the second half of this month, did not delay in beginning again. From 15 Germinal (April 4) on, "grumbling" began again in the markets, and on 20 Germinal, a porcelain painter was arrested at the Porte Denis and accused of having "uttered the most seditious words against the National Convention, saying that the Convention wanted to have us die of hunger, that they were scoundrels who did not want blood (a word which he pronounced in an ironic tone of voice) but who stifled children in their mother's womb, and that we should cut the throats of the National Convention." On 21 Germinal, an assembly of 400–500 women formed in the *Bonnet-de-la-Liberté* section, shouting: "Down with arms! We want no more soldiers, since there is no more bread!" On 27 Germinal, the women of the *Gravilliers* and *Lombards* sections refused to accept their bread ration. On 30 Germinal, in *Pont-Neuf* section a domestic servant was denounced because, while guarding the courtyard of the Palais, he was supposed to have declared before several women: "Eight months ago we had bread. Today we have none, we are slaves." And he is supposed to have applauded these words spoken by one woman: "Go and present a petition to the National

Convention, and they will arrest you. They closed the popular societies in order to put us back into slavery. We are c[ons, that is, asses]." An agent of the *Comité de Sûrêté générale* reported toward the end of the month of Germinal:

In the various groups which met yesterday both along the quays and on the bridges all the honest folk bewailed the terrorists who did not cease yearning for the *Montagnards*, and all their remarks concerned pillage and recrimination against the merchants and the young people whom they call *Fréronists.* . . . The stooges referred to in yesterday's declaration are still agitating and, according to them, the scarcity is only artificial . . .

On 1 Floréal (April 20), two artisans were arrested in the *Arsenal* section, and were accused of having made fun of the Convention. One of them excused his remarks by saying that "he believed that it was because of bread." The following day, the same agent reported having seen several intoxicated persons who were running along the quays shouting: "Bread! Bread! to the bread manufacture!" and who collected all the women who happened to be in the streets as they went along. On the same day, dock workers, busy unloading about forty sacks of oats from a boat along the Quai de la Rapée, tried to get possession of this cargo, "saying that they wanted it for themselves, to mill it and make bread, since they did not have a sufficient quantity of bread." On 6 Floréal, in *Piques* section, women refused their bread ration, proposing to march upon the Convention; the following day they behaved in the same manner in *Popincourt* section. On 7 Floréal, women from the *Bonnet-de-la-Liberté* section, having received only 3 ounces of bread that day (while the neighboring *Invalides* section received 10 ounces), stopped a cart loaded with sacks of flour, and insisted that the flour be distributed to the eighteen bakers of the section.

It is from this moment that agitation was resumed on the section level and that the movement, which until then had been a series of isolated incidents without much linking them together beyond scarcity and need, assumed a more menacing character by becoming more organized. Thus, on 10 Floréal, the *Montreuil* section declared that it would be meeting constantly and invited the other sections to follow its example to discuss the food problem. In the *Jardin-des-Plantes* section, a similar show of iniative was nipped in the bud when the principal "ringleaders" were arrested. On 16 Floréal, a police agent reported that on the Pont-Neuf and the Pont-au-Change, extremely seditious groups were forming, made up "of all classes of people, even soldiers." On the following day, near the Pont-Neuf, a woman was arrested for having said to the crowd: "The men must march against the Convention, which is the seat of all crimes." Even the trial and execution of Fouquier-Tinville on 18 Floréal (measures "approved by everyone," claims a policeman) did not long serve to divert popular discontent. The same day, in the *Poissonnière* section, 2 quarter-pounds of flour per person were distributed:

It was explained to the citizens that this small quantity . . . resulted from a delayed shipment into the city, that the goverment committees and the supply administration had taken steps to avoid such annoyances in the future. The reply was that they wanted to make the people die of poverty . . . and that that would soon come to an end and that they would believe nothing, because they were always being taken in; and that they were constantly being told that supplies were coming, yet their daily ration was always being diminished.

On the following day, in the same section the 2 quarter-pounds provided were refused, it being said: "How can you keep children alive on such a small amount of bread," and the committee of the III arrondissement observed sadly: "The explanations which are offered them increase their anger, the voice of persuasion can no longer make itself heard." On 21 Floréal, women were accused of having incited the men to fight for bread and, in the rue Martin, a gathering of men and women hurled invectives at the Convention. On 23 Floréal, "agitators" are said to have shouted: "The workers must stand up against the merchants, the hoarders, and the egoists"; while construction workers threatened "to rebel at the first opportunity," if they were not supplied with bread and if speculation did not end. On the same day, Alamion, a policeman, observed sadly that it is not easy to arrest everyone who curses the government," because it would be necessary to arrest more than half the Parisians." On 24 Floréal, agitation was reported in the *Muséum*, *Lombards*, and *Marchés* sections, where women flocked to the bakeries to prevent the distribution of bread; and the *Committee of General Security* judged the situation dangerous enough to warn the military committee and ask it to patrol the area. "The *Committees of Public Safety* and *General Security*," wrote the Committee, "are now meeting to tend to the needs of the common people." On 26 Floréal (May 16), a day when the bread ration fell to 2 ounces per person, there was already talk of a new popular insurrection. The governmental news sheet, *Le Messager du soir*, related that "all the good citizens are persuaded that a riot would be completely to the advantage of the terrorists" (from there it is only one step further to insinuate beforehand that it will also be the doings of the latter), "and, far from procuring bread, it would create new obstacles to the arrival of supplies."

On 29 Floréal, women in the *Arcis* section forced a carter to sell them the bread he was carrying for from 5 to 6 francs a pound; and Inspector Leroy reported that there was a rumor that the *gendarmes* and *carabiniers* will be replaced by German regiments (as in 1789!), that the salary of members of the Convention will be increased to 84 francs a day, and that if the bread ration was not increased the faubourg Antoine will rebel on 1 Prairial and "urge the rest of Paris to follow its example." On 28 and 29 Floréal, the government showed concern about the state of shipments into the city, and the *Committee of General Security* called a meeting in Paris, for 1 Prairial, of the municipal authorities of Francanville and Épernon, where the population had just stopped grain wagons heading for Paris. The brutal and unusual intervention of the Committee shows the anxiety of the authorities in the last days of Floréal. On 30 Floréal (May 19), the threat of a march upon the Convention was heard everywhere. Women from the *Mutius-Scevola* section, having that morning refused their 3-ounce ration, came to ask the Committee of Public Safety for bread; and the police pointed out that in the *Invalides* section, "workers are preparing to meet in the faubourg Antoine." In the *Droits-de-l'Homme* and *Quinze-Vingts* sections, general assemblies were called, during which they are said to have preached "the system of pillage" and claimed "that we must march in a group and in arms to ask the Convention for bread or death." That evening and the following morning, an anonymous manifesto entitled *"Insurrection du peuple pour obtenir du pain et reconquérir ses droits"* was distributed openly.

On 1 Prairial (May 20), the tocsin sounded early in the faubourg Antoine and in the *Jardin des Plantes*. As on 7 Germinal and during the insurrections of October 1789, the women were the first to go into action; through their own initiative they won the men over. By seven o'clock in the morning, in the *faubourg-du-Nord* section, they were flocking into the workshops to rally the workers. In *Popincourt* section, they carried off a supply of biscuits by force from the former Bon-Secours convent where it had been stored away. In *Gravilliers* section, citizenesses fixed the price of barley bread at 4 francs a pound, and in *Droits-de-l'Hommes* section the movement was begun by groups of women who formed at the bakery doors, while, in *Tuileries* section, women dragged along the housewives who were in the bakeries to lead them to the Convention. On the left bank, in *Mutius-Scevola, Jardin-des-Plantes*, and *Finistère* sections (where the bread ration had been only 2 ounces), they broke into the *comités civils* to ask them to let them march on the Convention. In *Fidélité* section, the women demanded a drum in order to beat to arms, "so that they could march upon the Convention." In faubourg Antoine, they had the shops closed and began to march at about one-thirty in the afternoon, followed by groups of armed men, "several of whom had on their hats the motto 'bread or death' "; an eye witness reports "that they pulled women out of shops and houses, that they made them get out of carriages, when they had them, and that they forced them to follow." Bearing the seditious inscription, "Bread and the Constitution of 1793" on their hats or pinned to their jackets, they marched to the Tuileries.

Reaching the Place du Carrousel at about two o'clock, they invited a woolscourer from the *Muséum* section to be their leader, and they overran the Convention hall. Chased from the precincts by whips, they broke in again an hour later accompanied by men. Meanwhile, the alarm was sounded in the faubourg Antoine, and men armed themselves, preparing to follow the feminine contingents. Among the most violent they later listed Olivier, a joiner of the rue Trouvée in *Quinze-Vingts* and a former soldier in Ronsin's army, who is said to have shouted: "Let's go cut the throats of those rascals. We must strike while the iron is hot. Today is the big riot, we must not fail." The movement rapidly spread to the sections of central Paris and of the faubourg Marceau, everywhere taking a similar course—the doors of the *corps de garde*, were forced open and weapons were confiscated. In *Finistère* section, they had been distributed to un-armed "terrorists" since 21 Germinal. In certain sections of the center, as the partisans of order still had the upper hand, violent struggles were some-times needed to convince the commanders to start marching. And other battalions, where the insurgents apparently were only a small minority, marched just the same—but to answer the call of the Convention which had beat the alarm at about twelve-thirty. It would therefore be erroneous to conclude that the greater part of the battalions which at about three-thirty formed around the Tuileries had come to participate in the insurrec-tion. In any case very few of these battalions entered the assembly room *en masse*; most of them were unarmed citizens and a few individuals from the various sections who had broken away from their fellows in arms. Nevertheless, the demonstrators, who burst into the meeting room after having broken down the doors, were numerous enough to intimidate the Thermidorian majority and to encourage the *Montagnard* deputies to have their principal demands approved, and an extraordinary commission created to carry them out. Representative Féraud, officer in charge of incoming shipments, who had opposed the entrance of the demonstrators, was mas-sacred and his head was carried about on a pike. But, despite its extensive-ness, despite its important results, the insurrection lacked leaders to see that its program was carried out. After seven hours of speeches and extraordinary uproar, the leaders of the majority, after having let the *Montagnards* com-promise themselves, were able to rally the loyal sections—with those of *Butte-des-Moulins*, *Muséum*, and *Lepeletier* at their head—and to chase the insurgents from the Tuileries.

Early the next morning, the alarm was sounded in the *Quinze-Vingts* section. The tocsin sounded at nine-forty-five in *Fidélité* section, and at ten o'clock in *Droits-de-l'Homme*. In *Arcis*, *Gravilliers*, *Droits-de-l'Homme*, *Popincourt*, and *Fidélité* sections, illegal assemblies were held. In *Poisson-nière* section, the rearming of those "disarmed" in Germinal was demanded. At *Franciade* (Saint-Denis), a crowd of 150 to 200 women met in the square before the *Hôtel de Ville* at about eleven o'clock, after they had had wagons of grain unloaded. The three sections of faubourg Antoine took up arms and once again marched upon the Convention, under the leadership of a Negro, Guillaume Delorme, wheelwright and captain of the gunners of *Popincourt* section. Supported by certain sections of central Paris, they emerged into the Place du Carrousel at about three o'clock in the afternoon; they loaded their cannons and aimed them at the Convention . . . . General Dubois, Commander of the Convention cavalry, had about 40,000 men at his command; the insurgents numbered perhaps 20,000, including about ten companies of gunners. "Paris," wrote the *Courrier républicain*, "resembled a vast camp . . . . Neither July 14, nor August 10, nor May 31 saw such extraordinary military preparations." The gunners and *gendarmes* of the Convention defected, but the insurgents did not take advantage of this opportunity to put the National Guards of the bourgeois quarters to flight. Toward eight o'clock in the evening, representatives came to parley with them; petitioners were admitted before the Convention and received the accolade of the President, after having once more demanded bread and the Constitution of 1793. Deluded by vain hopes, the demonstrators returned to their quarters, allowing their last chance to slip through their fingers.

Now, the Convention decided to end the matter. On the morning of 3 Prairial, it beat the call to arms for the "gilded youths" and the sections of western Paris, and made military preparations to surround the faubourg Antoine. The "youths" ventured in at noon but were forced to withdraw. That evening, workers of the faubourg freed one of Féraud's murderers, whom the police were leading to the scaffold. But, during the night the government took control of a great number of the sections. On 4 Prairial, it required the faubourg to surrender Féraud's "murderers" at once, as well as the cannons and the arms they possessed. In the event of a refusal, the faubourg would be declared in a state of rebellion and all the sections would be requested to march "in order to subdue the rebels by force; from then on all food distributions in the three rebel sections will cease." At the same time, an army under command of General Menou was advancing upon the faubourg. In the other sections, however, we encounter several attempts by revolutionary elements to aid the three besieged sections, and consequently in *Poissonnière* section Étienne Chefson, cobbler and gunner, former soldier in the Parisian revolutionary army in the detachment at Brest, was arrested and accused of having "stirred up the construction workers of rue Hauteville and of rue de l'Échiquier in order to lead them to the faubourg Antoine"; and in this same section a woodworker attempted to turn back the gunners marching against the faubourg and to convince them to attack the Convention instead. In the *Arcis* section, a similar attempt also occurred, and several individuals who had come from other sections, either through simple curiosity, or in order to aid the inhabitants of the *faubourg* were subsequently arrested. Women screamed in the streets: "We must support our brothers of the faubourg Antoine, overcome the representatives, and have no mercy for the merchants and *muscadins*"; and at eight o'clock in the evening the cry, "To arms to support the faubourg Antoine," was heard in the faubourg section of *Finistère*. At that hour, it was already too late. But at five-thirty that evening, the faubourg was still resisting and there was no question of surrender. This is made clear in a very detailed report made by the police concerning *the situation within the faubourg Antoine* at that hour.

The cannons are trained upon the city at the aforesaid Porte Antoine, the wide rue Antoine is filled with platoons of citizens armed with pikes and a few sorry rifles. The rues Charonne, Nicolas, Montreuil, Traversière, and so on, have no picket of armed citizens. It appears that the citizens are very determined not to allow themselves to be disarmed. The women have gathered noisily on every corner and are creating an uproar. *Bread is the basic cause of their insurrection, physically speaking,* but the Constitution of 1793 is its soul, this they admit. It appears that the *Panthéon, Sans-Culottes, Finistere, Cité,* and *Gravilliers* sections, and a great part of the *Thermes de Julien* section have declared themselves supporters.

These were only vain hopes. In the end arms, victuals, and reinforcements were lacking—the policeman, author of this report, remarks that "in general they are very poorly armed and are a very sorry sight." To the bitterness of defeat was added the regret of having allowed the young *muscadins* whom they had easily detained that morning go free. The *faubourg* surrendered without a shot that evening. "My friend, we are lost," Dauphinot, a café-keeper of *Bonconseil* section is supposed to have said to a young gunner. "The patriots have gone under, the faubourg Antoine is lost, but I hope that with our cannons we will *foutre* a cannonball at all those d . . . aristocrats and *muscadins* of the *Butte-des-Moulins* and *Lepeletier* sections and at other blessed rogues." But these whims about resisting, surely largely verbal, led to nothing. All was lost.

⋘⋙

The impetus of the popular movement had been broken, and on 6 Prairial a policeman had only to observe: "The reports of this day," he wrote, "present the state of Paris yesterday as the calmest possible. Not only was no bread refused, as in recent days, but its distribution even took place in a very orderly fashion . . . the men watched, the women were quiet."

The government lost no time in putting repressive measures into force. On 1 Prairial the Convention had already ordered the arrest of the six *Montagnard* deputies who had been compromised, as well as six others. On 4 Prairial (May 23) it created a military commission presided over by a brigadier general to which any individual carrying weapons or bearing "seditious signs" would be handed over, "to be judged and shot immediately." The commission sat for 10 weeks and judged 132 persons, including eleven representatives and thirty-three *gendarmes*; nineteen persons, including the six *Montagnard* deputies, were condemned to death. The sections were ordered to meet on 5 Prairial to see to the disarming of the "terrorists," but the majority of them did not need official encouragement to abandon themselves to an orgy of denunciations. The result was a massive outlawing of all the former Jacobin and *sans-culotte* leaders, which included thousands of persons. By 9 Prairial the *Gazette française* already estimated the number outlawed at 10,000, but the sum total of arrests and disarmings certainly far exceeded that figure for, in many sections, they *automatically* disarmed all the members of the old popular governments of Year II, including the companies of fusiliers and gunners of the revolutionary army, the gunners having been especially attacked for the role which they had played in the recent insurrections.

This proscription, carried out by the reactionary majorities of the section administrations of Year III, gave rise to an unfurling of personal emotions and to settlings of personal grievances which far exceeded the intentions of the Thermidorian Convention. Thus we must not be too surprised to observe that, in many cases, the *Committee of General Security* attempted to restrain the repressive zeal of the section authorities by freeing persons prominent in the popular institutions of Year II.

⋙⋘

How can we explain the origins of the *journées* of Prairial and, subsequently, the crushing and decisive defeat which the Parisian *sans-culottes* experienced? The Convention majority did not hesitate, of course, to attribute the popular insurrection to a Jacobin conspiracy, prepared over a long period and supported by distributions of money. A police report of 1 Prairial expressed this convenient and reassuring theory as follows:

We have grounds to believe [wrote the inspectors] that food scarcity was the *pretext*, unfortunately all too plausible, which agitators used to lead credulous citizens astray, but that the cause of the popular movement, organized long ago, arises from the faction of oldtime ringleaders, who today are making the common people demand, along with bread, the re-establishment of the Commune, the Constitution of 1793, and the liberation of all the *Montagnard* deputies and of all the members of the old revolutionary committees.

A report sent by the committee of the II arrondissement to the *Committee of General Security* on 3 Prairial claimed "that the men designated by the various sections of Paris as terrorists . . . greatly contributed to swelling the battalions of faubourg Antoine. . . . This presumption . . . is all the more founded since citizens of the faubourg Marceau were heard to say upon returning home: *They have tricked us; we only wanted to ask for bread.* Last, on the 4, the police pointed out "that they said that *assignats* had been distributed in the faubourg Antoine to promote the rebellion."

Political agitation, supported by the old Jacobin leaders and swelled by the arrival in Paris of a great number of provincial "terrorists," unquestionably played a certain part in the origin of the events of Prairial, as it had previously done in Germinal. It would be impossible to explain in any other way the junction made, as on 12 Germinal, between the popular movement, inspired over a long period by high prices and the lack of bread, and the clearly political demands of the Jacobin members of the societies—a junction symbolized by the very motto of the insurrection: "Bread and the Constitution of 1793." The police correctly described the Constitution of 1793 as "the soul of the movement," and there is nothing to indicate that it had been necessary to distribute money to win the common people over to the political program of the Jacobin opposition. It is indisputable that the role of the *Montagnard* deputies was minimal. They only ratified, and at the eleventh hour at that, the program sanctioned by the *sans-culottes*, under the direction of the section rangleaders.

But, everything considered, political motives were only of secondary importance. The real "base" of the insurrection (to use the police's expression) was scarcity, primarily caused by the return—although incomplete and hesitant—to a free economy. The word most frequently repeated in these pages is "bread." Moreover, the role played by the women in the *journées* of Germinal and Prairial was more important than in any popular movement since the *journées* of October 1789—additional proof that scarcity was more important than any other motive.

What do we know about the other participants? Among the several hundred persons arrested for having directly participated in the riots of 1 and 2 Prairial, we have found the names of fifty-eight salaried workers, out of the 168 whose occupations are given. The other names are those of small businessmen, masters of workshops (some of whom employ a relatively large number of workers whom they were able to involve in the movement —at least the police records reproach them for having done so), artisans, and office workers—the usual elements making up the lower classes of the faubourgs and the center who rose up, more or less spontaneously, as they did on so many occasions during the course of the Revolution, against the government or the municipality, when they had no bread.

Mathiez tried to explain the defeat of the *sans-culottes* in Prairial by the weakness of the *Montagnard* deputies, who "did not assume their responsibilities boldly and soon enough." His explanation is valid to the degree that the movement, provoked by hunger, lacked leaders and a plan of action . . . . But more important than the hesitations of the *Montagnard* deputies is the fact that, for the first time since 1789, the common people felt isolated and could find no part of the bourgeoisie with whom they could ally socially and politically. Lacking an alliance with a part of the bourgeoisie, the common people reverted to their political position of 1775 or of 1778 when, despite the extent of their activity, the popular riots produced no results.

The popular action of Prairial had no sequel. "For the first time since 1789, the government had repressed by force the popular insurrection and had thus broken the mainspring of the Revolution . . . . The common people would not budge again until 1830." If the defeat of the insurrection is explained by its very spontaneity, by its being a "famine riot" provoked by despair, to what cause can we attribute this long slumber of the common people of Paris? Short-term economic factors will not provide the answer.

Far from improving, scarcity and the high costs of victuals worsened even more during the winter of 1795 and the summer of 1796. The bread ration remained at between 4 and 8 ounces, and then the price increase continued without respite. In November 1795 bread sold on the free market at 24 francs a pound, in December for between 45 and 50 francs, and in May 1796 for 80 francs a pound; and the price of meat increased from 75 francs a pound in January 1796 to 97 francs in March. But popular movements do not always correspond to the automatic movement of prices, and to explain their creation or their absence, we must take into account factors which to a great measure often escape the historian's grasp, for example the state of mind of the common people. Now, the common people of Paris had experienced three severe defeats in the course of a single year, which, when combined with poverty and hard times, constituted a powerful element of discouragement and resignation. Revolutionary enthusiasm could only survive such a combination of defeats with great difficulty, and the common people no longer believed themselves to be invincible. In addition to these psychological factors, we must take into account the practical measures adopted without delay by the Thermidorian leaders who, although hesitant, vacillating, and incompetent in many matters, demonstrated a formidable efficiency in handling the repression. Their first step, of a military nature, deprived any future insurrection of its principal weapon by having the companies of gunners broken up; and, without cannon, the common people of Paris were powerless in the face of the army and the forces of order. The Thermidorians and their successors were to make considerable progress in the realm of police techniques. The repression which followed closely on the heels of the *journées* of Prairial inaugurated a whole series of proscriptions which recur from the year III until the year IX, and even beyond, and which always strike the same groups of former members of the popular institutions of the year II. By thus subjugating the old revolutionary leaders through repeated detentions, the firing squad, and deportation, and also through the economic ruin resulting from these long periods of detention, they succeeded in depriving any future movement of its chosen leaders and isolated this nucleus of old revolutionaries.

Discouragement, disarming, perfected police techniques, the progressive elimination of the revolutionary leaders, and finally changes occurring in the meanwhile in the Parisian population—these are a few explanations for the absence of any extensive popular movement between 1795 and 1830. A more detailed study of the social movement in Paris during the Consulate and the Empire would certainly reveal others even more conclusive.

ஒ§ The Rural Movement

THE MURDER OF
THE COMTE DE DAMPIERRE
June 22, 1791
ஒ§ **By Georges Lefebvre**

I

At about three o'clock in the afternoon of June 22, 1791, as the coach bringing the royal family back from Varennes was leaving Sainte-Menehould, the Comte de Dampierre, a nobleman of the region, was massacred by the peasants when he came to salute Louis XVI as he passed.

The Comte de Dampierre was on horseback, at the corner of the rue de l'Abreuvoir, at the very moment when the royal coach was leaving the city. He was wearing a grey redingote, a lace-trimmed hat, top boots, and he had "allowed his cross of the Order of Saint Louis to be seen attached to the buttonhole of his coat." He was armed with a rifle and had passed two pistols through his belt. When the King passed, he presented arms. Then via the rue des Capucines he met the coach a second time near the place de la Halle and, drawing near this time, he saluted, stated his titles, and reminded the King that he had married a relative of the Maréchal de Ségur and of the Comte d'Allonville. Well-meaning bystanders advised him to refrain from saying anything more and to go away, but he obstinately continued to escort the sovereigns and rode along without incident for a kilometer as far as carp pond of the Ru, a spot marked by a solitary willow tree beyond Griverie hill, on Chaude-fontaine land. At this spot he was taken to task by the peasants, who pushed him far away from the coach and forced him off the road.

Instead of quietly retiring and allowing the crowd of people on the road to disperse, he cried, "Long live the King!" fired a rifle shot into the air to salute their Majesties, and sent his horse galloping along the levee [which bordered the meadow and sloped into the Auve River.] Immediately, the National Guard on horse and on foot ran after him and fired without hitting him. But his horse, slipping into the ditch, fell, giving those in pursuit time to catch up. However, he got up again and was continuing on his way when a new volley knocked him off his horse. The assassins shot him again point-blank and, with an unimaginable ferocity, threw themselves upon his body, which they pierced once more with their bayonets.

So goes a contemporary account. Thoury (another contemporary, who wrote long after the fact) denies the shots, claiming that the loaded pistols were found; but Buirette, who also reports this last fact, speaks of a rifle shot and adds that the weapon was carried off by the murderers. His story seems more plausible than Thoury's, which differs slightly: The Count was

mounted on a horse capable of going two leagues in an hour, but he was merely proceeding at a walk and seemed to be leaving regretfully. He had scarcely gone two hundred paces into the fields when he heard rifle shots fired at him from all sides, but he did not fall and did not go any faster. Then I saw a young man named Gallois and several others run after him, sabers in hand, This Gallois attacked him first and gave him a sword wound in the head. The Count pulled out a white handkerchief, which he held up to his wound with both hands to his head, and then I saw him fall over near a ditch. . . . Those wretches sent more than twenty rifle shots into his dead body.

According to Neveu-Lemaire (who wrote under the July Monarchy), Gallois was also on horseback; the evening before, near Varennes, he had appropriated a hussar's horse for himself. Excited by his comrades' cries, he dashed in pursuit of the fugitive and shot him in the back with his rifle. The wounded man collapsed just as his horse reared. The peasant dashed forward, sabre raised, and unhorsed the Count, who on bended knee begged in vain for mercy.

The murderers abandoned the cadaver without looting it, merely taking away the horse and the rifle. At the first village, Dommartin-la-Planche, they almost began to fight over the loot, adds Buirette. Onlookers told them they had no right to claim these spoils. The murderers had cause to regret their looting, and they only avoided the worst by hiding in a farm.

The dead man's servants came to bury him in the cemetery of Chaude-fontaine. Besides the pistols, they found on him a case containing 50 louis. In 1821 the Count's son, a *maréchal de camp* and commander of the guards of the Comte d'Artois, had the body exhumed. They found several fractures, caused by the shots, in the left parietal and in the occiput, in the lower jaw, the breastbone, the shoulder blades, and the ribs.

The police had made an inquiry and discovered the guilty parties. Thoury was among the witnesses for the prosecution. The amnesty of September 15, 1791 stopped the proceedings. In 1791, an inhabitant of Passavant came and asked Buirette, the President of the Tribunal, to hand over the records to him. The request was refused, but the Revolutionary Committee of the district ultimately forced him to do so, and the records were burned.

II

The murder of the Comte de Dampierre is reported by the narrators of the events at Varennes as an illustration of the dangers to which the royal family was exposed while returning to Paris. In reality, the murder only assumes its full historical significance if it is included among the episodes of the "Great Fear" provoked in France by the flight of Louis XVI. On hearing the news everyone had the feeling, which they either rejoiced over or became alarmed about, that the counter-revolution was beginning, and the revolutionaries consequently prepared themselves for war. The fortified cities, principally along the frontiers, closed their gates, guarded their ramparts, and mounted cannons and munitions on them; the frontier troops were alerted and the National Guard activated. From one end of the kingdom to the other public officials met around the clock, and when they did not seem reliable, a permanent committee was organized, as for example in le Puy in 1789. A vast network of surveillance was spontaneously created to hinder the comings and goings and supposed plots of the aristocrats; passport control, inspection of stage coaches and inns, searches of châteaux, arrests of suspects, and confinement of nobles and refractory priests to their domiciles.

The "fears" (properly so-called), panics caused by false news, were not missing from the picture. Buirette reports that at Sainte-Menehould, on June 23 at about six o'clock in the morning,

an unknown man, without a coat, bathed in sweat and accompanied by a *gendarme*, arrived on horseback. He announced in a frightened manner that Varennes has been pillaged and that the Austrians are wreaking horrible carnage on its inhabitants. This news plunged the town into terror. The National Guard assembled. The alarm was sounded, a large number of National Guardsmen came running from neighboring villages. Courriers left for Clermont and Varennes.

The news reached Châlons toward noon, at the moment when the royal coach had just left the city. Since the authorities in Sainte-Menehould had also written to those in Verdun, the district officials of that city hurriedly sent a copy of their letter in every direction. At Châlons, the courier arrived about five in the evening, and messengers were at once sent toward Rheims, Sézanne, and Vitry. Sézanne was alerted during the night, Rethel only on the evening of June 24. The effect was everywhere the same, and the reaction as vigorous as at Sainte-Menehould. The National Guards started out from Rheims toward Châlons and Sainte-Menehould, from Sézanne toward Châlons and Epernay; the districts of Sézanne and Rethel called for help for the villages in their jurisdiction, and peasants came running from everywhere. At Vouziers, the battalion which the district had sent on June 22 to camp at Autry and Grand-Pré, and which had returned on June 23, was sent back to the same places on June 24 upon the announcement of the invasion. But in the course of the day of June 23, the municipality of Verdun found itself able to reassure that of Sainte-Menehould by announcing that Bouillé had fled to Luxembourg and that they could be at peace "about the arrival of enemy troops of which there is no trace at all." At Epernay, the National Guard of Sézanne arrived just after the King had passed through, and it was advised to return peaceably; on the return trip they noticed columns of peasants advancing as reinforcements. The National Guard of Vouziers also turned back on the evening of June 24, after having ascertained that everything was calm at Varennes.

The fear of "brigands" cropped up from time to time. At Trappes, to the south of Paris, on June 22, upon learning of the King's flight the municipal government forbade the National Guard to take up arms and urged the *département* to authorize a request for gunpowder for the Corbeil district, which it did the following day, because of the commune's location "which is between two roads, consequently it is more exposed to pillage by brigands than others." We are therefore not too surprised to learn that the region around Dreux experienced on June 24 an "emotion" exactly like that of July 1789. On that day the city learned that brigands were advancing through the countryside cutting down the wheat; they were at Bu, to the north of the road from Houdan to Paris along which the news had probably spread. Yet brigands do not seem to have played a major role in 1791, and they caused no problem in Champagne. The reason is that there was no great scarcity of goods, and troops of beggars and vagabonds had not assumed the same frightening character that year as in 1789.

Whether or not these alarms were caused by the rumored approach of the enemy or of brigands, they did not degenerate into pointless flight because in 1791 the public authorities, made up of revolutionaries, inspired confidence and because the Third Estate was, if not well armed, at least organized for better or for worse into national militias who had been on their guard for a long time and who were solidly anchored in their resolve to defend themselves.

However, in spite of the differences which can also be observed between the popular movement of 1789 and that of 1791, a fundamental identity none the less betrayed itself. What was the basic cause of the Great Fear of 1789? It was the fear inspired by the "aristocratic plot," which was born in the minds of the Third Estate—bourgeois and lower classes—when the election for the Estates General were announced, and which continued to grow in the course of the spring and summer. The Third Estate was conscious of the sacrifices it wanted to impose on the nobility and of the blow it was dealing them; it was considered inevitable that the nobility would defend itself and seek vengeance. This fear was premature, because no attempt to rise in arms against the claims of the Third Estate materialized within the nobility, and because even at Court a forceful attack was not envisaged before the end of June. It was, however, not chimerical. Certain remarks indicated that there was no lack of privileged persons willing to resort to extreme methods, and in fact the Court finally decided to resort to them. In any case, by autumn the "plot" began to gradually become a reality. We need only recall the attempt by Favras, the disorders stirred up at Nîmes by Froment in agreement with enemy princes, the camp at Jalès, and the conspiracy of Lyons. Besides, after the spring of 1789, the collusion of the aristocracy with foreigners was regarded as certain, which explains why during the course of the Great Fear, the English, Germans, Spanish and others were mentioned almost as often as the brigands in the hire of nobles. This charge, also erroneous at the beginning, subsequently became only too well founded, and the emigration convinced even the most incredulous.

The King's departure therefore appeared as proof that Louis XVI had gone over to the counter-revolution and that invasion was imminent. As in 1789, the revolutionaries credited their adversaries with a union, a determination, and a competence which they themselves lacked; but they won out because they were wise enough to foresee the worst. No region was as well prepared to react in this regard as the east, precisely where Louis XVI had fled, because it was the most exposed and because in 1790 the movements of the Austrian troops, sent to put down the Brabantines, had aroused suspicion and spread alarm several times. In July and August 1790, and once again in February 1791, the easterners had taken up arms at the news that the Emperor's soldiers had entered France. The revolutionaries had acted on their own initiative without waiting for orders from the National Assembly. In his excellent work on the events at Varennes, Monseigneur Aimond shows to what degree public distrust was aroused, and he elucidates the essential role of the successive mobilizations of the crowds and of the spirit of initiative among its leaders.

It is true that historians have often presented the facts in a different way. Aulard himself described the reaction provoked by the King's flight in terms which nevertheless present some ambiguities: "France felt abandoned, orphaned. It appeared to her that the King had carried off with him a preservative talisman. France became aware of terrible dangers. She felt invaded and lost without a leader." As we see, Aulard clearly perceived the alarm, the anguish, the feeling of an imminent invasion. He nevertheless seemed persuaded that the revolutionary common people felt lost because they no longer had a king. It is certain that at this date the vast majority of Frenchmen did not imagine a government which was not monarchical. But one must not conclude that in dashing off in pursuit of Louis XVI, they were preoccupied with keeping him for themselves at any cost as an indispensable leader, without whom their defeat would have been certain! They had distrusted this leader since July 14; their real leader was the National Assembly. For them it was a question of spoiling the aristocratic plot by arresting the King and either taking him hostage or punishing him for complicity.

The defensive reaction has always been associated with a punitive reaction, inspired by the thirst for vengeance, but also by the deliberate desire to prevent new plots by discouraging their possible supporters, or by imprisoning suspects. This repressive zeal, a basic cause of the Terror, is inseparable from the popular Revolution; its first bloody manifestations accompany or immediately follow the first uprising, such as the agrarian revolt in Provence at the end of March 1789, the July days and the fall of the Bastille, the Great Fear. The popular mobilization which resulted from the flight of Louis XVI was also marked by acts of violence. For example, on June 26, near Lyons, the Seigneur de Poleymieux was put to death and his château burned; in the province of Maine, the châteaux of Martigné-Ferchaud and Bois-de-Cuillé were put to the torch. The Comte de Dampierre was merely the first victim. His noble rank and his audacious bearing might lead us to suppose that he was looked upon as an accomplice to the "aristocratic plot." But an incidental detail reported by Buirette allows us to exclude this hypothesis. To attenuate the horror of the murder, he says, they spread the rumor that the rifle shot fired by Dampierre at the moment he rode off was a "planned signal given to troops hidden in the Planches woods, near the main road, and to armed men who appeared from the opposite direction, coming down through the fields to reach the coaches." There was no ambush in the woods, he objected, and the men in question were the National Guard and the peasants. But the very form of the story shows that the rumor was not made up after the event, and that it expresses the psychological reaction of the crowd at the very moment that the rifle shot was fired.

Even if the crowd was mistaken in believing the Count to be accessory to a conspiracy, it did not err in attributing counter-revolutionary feelings to him. That much is certain. The attitude of his widow provided further proof when Prussians and emigrés invaded the region in 1792. The King of Prussia settled down in the Count's château of Hans, while the Duke of Brunswick took possession of his house. Then, when it came time to retreat, Madame de Dampierre followed the King and the emigrés, among whom, says Buirette, were several of her relatives. She only decided to return home when she realized she was being abandoned at Buzancy.

Moreover, we would not have returned to the subject of Dampierre's death if it had appeared to be solely determined by political events. As in the case of the Seigneur de Poleymieux, the true situation is more complex. The Comte de Dampierre was not unknown to the inhabitants of the region. Buirette writes that he had lived in Sainte-Menehould for some years and "had become known for his gentle manners and amiable qualities, for his loyal and truly chivalrous character." His brash behavior bears witness to this last trait. But what Buirette does not add, and what he nevertheless undoubtedly knew very well, a fact which no historian has yet reported, is that the Comte de Dampierre was detested by his peasants, with whom he had long been on bad terms.

III

The du Valk family, whom local historians also call Duval, traced its origin, according to Brouillon, to Etienne Duval, a bourgeois of Caen, ennobled in 1548, and had included among its members Duval de Mondreville, Governor of Sainte-Menehould in 1580.

The father of the person who interests us, Henri du Valk, Comte de Dampierre, according to the record of his death, was a brigadier and former *mestre de camp* in the cavalry regiment bearing his name. In 1750 he received a pension of 3000 livres. Death came to him on February 17, 1785, at about 85 years of age.

His elder son, who is our Dampierre, born on April 5, 1745, was christened Anne-Elzéar. He chose a military career; in 1779 we find him a Captain attached to the cavalry regiment of Artois, which was also that of his younger brother; in 1785 a captain in the Quercy regiment and Knight of the Order of Saint Louis; in 1790, lieutenant-colonel. After 1779 he received a third of his father's pension to use during his father's lifetime.

On May 23, 1785, he had married Aglae-Rosalie de Ségur-Chabanac, a relative of Maréchal de Ségur, then Minister of War. To facilitate the marriage, he himself says, the Maréchal increased his pension to 2000 livres, an annual income which was eventually to revert upon his death to the fiancée, as a dowry.

Unfortunately, we know nothing of the du Valks' patrimony. At Dampierre-le-Château, formerly Dampierre-en-Astenois, they had replaced the feudal family either by purchase or through marriage. The acquisition may go back as far as that Duval de Mondreville who seems to have transferred his family from Caen to Sainte-Menehould. They also owned the seigniory of Hans, which is the first village one encounters to the northwest of Valmy; it was there that they lived. Dampierre and Hans are in a barren area called *Champagne pouilleuse*. They must not have been productive seigniories, and the circumstances described above concerning Anne-Elzéar's marriage do not create an impression of wealth.

This is therefore a question of members of the bourgeoisie who had become prosperous enough during the sixteenth century to secure a sudden rise in social status and, transforming themselves into gentlemen, they had taken the place of the vanished feudal lords. Condemned to live from then on as nobles, no longer willing or able to have any careers other than the sword or the Church, they saw the relative importance of their fortune dwindle, because it was no longer kept up by work, and because it was divided by inheritance. War had ceased to be profitable, and declining purchasing power decreased the real value of part of their income. By 1789, they had become very much a part of those country gentlemen portrayed so well by Monsieur de Vaissière, the majority of whom resisted the abolition of privileges and seignorial rights, as much because what possessions they still had thus risked being dispersed, as from concern for maintaining their social authority. Consequently they contributed as best they could to transforming the peaceful bourgeois Revolution into a popular and violent revolution. This situation is quite noticeable in the surviving documents concerning the disputes between the Comte de Dampierre and the peasants.

Complaints made by the peasants to the *Comité des rapports* of the National Assembly, in May 1790, indicate that their principal concerns were the rights to the hunt, the warren and the dovecot on the one hand, and the ownership of communal property on the other. They indicate that in about 1778, the community had the Count condemned to suppressing all but one of his warrens, but he had preserved them. He had taken possession of Mount Ivron, which figures in accounts of the battle of Valmy and on which the inhabitants claimed the right to graze their livestock in complete freedom. In 1789, their *cahier de doléances* asked the suppression of the rights to the hunt and the dovecot.

If we believe the peasants, the Count was visibly irritated. He was supposed to have offered 6 livres to whoever would thrash the deputy appointed to represent the parish at the Assembly of the *bailliage*, so that he would not be able to attend the meeting. And on April 13, 1789, he is said to have appeared armed at the door of the church threatening his vassals about the *cahier de doléances* which they had drawn up. These details must be accepted with caution, but the spite and anger of the seigneur are probable; and, let us say in passing, this example indicates that if the peasants were encouraged to express their wishes upon more than one occasion by the members of the bourgeoisie or by their parish priests, the fear of their seigneur and of his retainers must have prevented them on more than one occasion, and probably much more often, from speaking out or, in any case, saying everything they had on their minds.

When the time for the agrarian revolt had arrived, in July 1789, the peasants of Hans went into action. This time the Count himself tells of a complaint addressed to the same *Comité des rapports* on December 31, 1789. It is easy to believe, for the violence in the villages is an accurate measure of their grievances. On July 26, 1789, an anonymous letter threatened the Count with arson if he did not shut up his pigeons. Then his rabbit warrens were destroyed, and the community admitted the deed in 1790. They began to hunt in groups on the Seigneur's land to exterminate his game. They laid waste to his property, that is to say (he gives the details himself) that they "destroyed all his fences, broke down the floodgates of his moats and the barriers of the fish pond." This means that they suppressed the enclosures which had deprived the peasants of free grazing in the Count's fields and prairies, and which had also, perhaps, annexed portions of the communal land to his domain. They also went to work on his ponds. In the days when ocean fish could not be transported a long distance, they provided an income which was far superior to that of farming; but in a time of trouble they were easy prey. Moreover, the creation of such ponds restricted free grazing and justified recriminations.

As we know, the agrarian revolt was never completely quelled during the months which followed; but it has been less frequently noted that the nobles attempted to regain those of their rights which had been respected by the decree of August 5 and 11, 1789, and that they often sued the peasants. This is what the Comte de Dampierre did. On the basis of his complaint of November 5, the *maîtrise des eaux et des forêts* of Sainte-Menehould condemned the community of Hans to pay almost 18,000 livres in damages. Upon appeal, the *Table de Marbre* reduced the sentence, on May 6, 1790, to 1000 livres fine and 1000 livres damages.

The Count's forcefulness had not intimidated the peasants. On the contrary, when they saw they were being prosecuted, "they acted like madmen," wrote Dampierre. The destruction continued, and they tumbled one of his bridges into the river. That is why, on December 31, he decided to ask the *Comité des rapports* for help. This step seems to have had no effect, and when the day came to notify the peasants of the decision of the *Table de Marbre*, a riot broke out.

On June 28, 1790, the *huissier* appeared, escorted by the *maréchaussée*. The peasants, gathering quickly, put them to flight. Dampierre entrenched himself in his chateau which, it is said, was "very well built." The insurgents went to attack it, put the barriers to the torch, and tried to scale the outer wall in order to lower the drawbridge. The Count's resolute manner prevented them, but they left sentinels and watched for a favorable moment. Thus the chateau narrowly missed being put to the torch, and if it had been, it is highly probable that the murder of June 22, 1791, would have been committed a year earlier. But the municipality of Sainte-Menehould, warned of the danger, immediately sent 150 National Guardsmen, who reached Hans at three-thirty in the afternoon. According to the official report of the municipal government and that of the detachment's leader, the village's National Guard advanced peacefully to meet the new arrivals, crying, "Long live the Nation!" and presented the commander with a petition. The National Guard of Sainte-Menehould does not seem to have been animated by any great sympathy for the Count. They did not admonish the peasants; they opened no inquiries and made no arrests. Their leader installed protective pickets and led the guardsmen off. Calm having apparently been re-established, the pickets also withdrew on June 29.

Then what happened? We do not know; but it can be considered certain that the affair had no judicial sequels, and that the peasants' animosity was not calmed. It is true that in July the Count, in a new complaint to the *Comité des rapports*, assured them that out of eighty homes in the village, only thirty-three were on the rebel side. But, he admitted, they were those belonging to the members of the municipal government and the National Guard.

Now, the relationship between these facts and the murder of June 22 is established by Thoury's testimony. "A crowd of peasants who, it is said, were his and with whom he had been in litigation, insulted him, prevented him from approaching the King's coach, and forced him to leave the road." Buirette also testifies that the inhabitants of Hans figured among the accused. The others were from Laneuville-au-Pont, Somme-Yèvre, Braux, and Passavant, but they must have felt the same, for they surely knew about the riot at Hans. Moreover, on August 18, 1791, the municipality of Laneuville-au-Pont, telling the *Comité des rapports* about the events of June 22, called the Comte de Dampierre a "notorious aristocrat" and expressed the unanimous solidarity of the peasants concerning the matter under investigation:

We have just been assured that the people of this district and its vicinity, informed about this inquiry, announce and declaim that, if one of its citizens were to be involved in this inquiry, and if everyone wanted to arrest him, they would assemble and revolt. All this worries us, because if this inquiry were to be carried out, we fear that it would have a bad effect and that we would not, despite our remonstrances, be able to prevent the effervescence of a large group of irritated and emotional people.

The murder of the Comte de Dampierre was therefore not solely the result of his imprudent behavior. He had long been hated by those who surrounded him on June 22, 1791, and who considered his attitude provocative. It is undoubtedly an episode in the Great Fear which followed the King's flight, but through the political event can be seen, as always during the course of the popular Revolution, the social agitation which was its basic driving force.

FROM BEGGARY
TO BRIGANDAGE

The Wanderers in the Beauce
During the French Revolution

∽§ **By M. Vovelle**

[Numerous works, most of them popular, have been written about the brigands in the Beauce between the years III and VI. This brigandage has come to symbolize the crisis of the authority of the state during this period. On the other hand, the picturesqueness of the theme made a place for it in the local almanachs of the nineteenth century, where the images of Beau François and Rouge d'Auneau were often evoked.]

Old or new, none of these works has up to now sought to pose the problem of the content and social explanation of brigandage in the epoch of the Directory. All of them, especially the old ones, remain slaves to the myth of the "brigand" judged in reference to a moral system or exploited as a picturesque theme. Has present-day history nothing more to learn about this matter? A few lines of the accepted description have led us to reopen the debate.

All the authors, in order to swell the importance of the affair, emphasize the number of accused persons sent to the prisons of Chartres. Seven hundred, says one; 760, another precises; about a thousand, says a third. A thousand prisoners—for about a hundred crimes and offenses spread out over five years? There is a mystery here that needs to be cleared up.

The documents relative to the investigation of the Orgères affair in the archives of the Eure-et-Loir represent a considerable volume: interrogations of prisoners, procedural documents, the public prosecutor's charges, lists of physical descriptions, final judgments constitute a mass of documents so much the easier to use as most of them were printed at the time. This documentation has been completed by going through the imprisonment registers of the four prisons in Chartres during the Revolution. The archives of the Loiret have also furnished a certain number of unprinted documents.

The results of these researches? No doubt the numbers cited by our authors, like the armies of antiquity, diminish under investigation. We must count on fewer than five hundred individuals. The figure remains sufficient for this study to bring forth certain new facts.

Much more than brigandage itself, the documents of the Orgères affair permit us to study the wandering population of beggars who moved about in the Beauce at this time, as in all areas where large scale farming was the rule.

Let us imagine a kind of "rounding-up" by the police of all beggars without passports or means of making a living in the three departments of Eure-et-Loir, Seine-et-Oise, or beyond. They are sent for identity checks to the Chartres prisons. Most of them are released immediately because they have no connection with the current investigation. For the present-day historian, a census of them is nonetheless precious for that.

In this society of the end of the eighteenth century, indigence is a difficult thing to get hold of: absent from the notarial sources as well as from the political sources, it appears only occasionally in the fiscal sources. Attempts to count the number of indigents carried out by the Constituent Assembly reached only those who were domiciled. In order to find out about the wanderer, we must have recourse to the judicial sources: and even then the small fry imprisoned and then let go, often without being judged, is found only on the imprisonment registers. And they are often discontinuous and neglected in this period.

It is on this account that we begin to realize the importance of the documentation revealed by the Orgères affair, an importance which is due first of all to its concentration: at the time when lists of the 500 most highly taxed individuals were being drawn up in each department, there is the list of the 500 most indigent persons in the area of the Beauce.

For some, we will have to be content with a simple statement of imprisonment, reduced to essential information and often lacking in detail. But for many others, on the contrary, the documents give us the possibility of reconstituting in detail their odyssey and the history of their uprooting.

It is with these elements that we have tried to analyze, on the basis of a local example, the formation of this wandering population, and its life. At the end of this typology of the beggar, we will come back to the brigands with which we have started, and the analysis of them will perhaps benefit from being put back into the context of this rather special society.

❦

The population we are going to study is made up of about 400 units, 375 more precisely if we exclude the twenty or so very young children on whom we have no information.

There are 150 women and 225 men. The majority of men among the uprooted is significant, but not so great as might be imagined. In reality, the society under investigation is more or less in equilibrium, as is shown by the pyramid of ages. While the beggar whom we have a tendency to picture when we think of our literary reminiscences is most of the time an old man, we have here a young population, the illustration of the official term "ablebodied beggar": two-thirds of them (67 per cent) are less than 40 years old, two-fifths (39 per cent) are less than 30 years of age. The male population, showing a significant upsurge in the group between 15 and 20 years of age, shows a marked weakening between the ages of 20 and 25 and especially 25 to 30, only to show a new upsurge in the group aged 30 to 40. It is natural, it seems, to attribute this decline (age group 20 to 30) to the departure for the army of volunteers, which creates a sort of puncture in the group. However that may be, a single criterion, division according to age and sex, is already sufficient to pose the problem of the formation of this wandering population of "ablebodied beggars."

❦

How did one become a beggar? However imperfect our maps and investigations may be, they propose a double answer by informing us, in some of the cases, about the geographical and social origins of the beggars of the Beauce.

The geographical origin, in this case the place of birth, is known in more than one-half the cases—246 out of 345. The study of maps that have been made shows the greatest proportion in the three departments of the Eure-et-Loir, Loiret, and Seine-et-Oise, which were touched as much by the operations of the gang as by the operations of the police, in a word the departments of the Beauce: 110 beggars, almost half, were born there. Sometimes born in urban centers—Orléans, Versailles, Chartres—they are more often natives of the plain and its forest borders. If we are not astonished by this proportion of natives, the very large area of recruitment throughout France is more striking, since about 100 of these beggars, two-fifths of the total, were born outside the limits of the three departments of the Beauce. There were very few natives of the south of France, about 15 in all; the main part came from the plains and plateaus of the Parisian Bassin (about thirty from Champagne, Lorraine, and Picardy) and especially from western France: the wooded districts, the Breton borderlands, and Lower Normandy, the traditional reservoirs of manpower for harvest work: more than fifty beggars are of this origin. The presence of beggars who came from just about everywhere thus appears to be an illustration of the vast uprooting of populations, of the social and geographical mobility of the end of the eighteenth century, a mobility all the more astonishing as it was in contradiction with the legal dispositions which regulated travel very strictly by making the passport obligatory.

A document on geographical mobility, this statistic informs us also on country-town relationships, and especially on the crisis of the urban milieux. A part of these people who "ran about the plain" came not from the countryside, but from the cities. Paris and the towns of the Seine immediately surrounding it furnished thirty-four, Versailles on the one side and Orléans on the other each supplied a dozen, and Chartres, half a dozen: in the last analysis, at least a quarter of these beggars came not from the countryside but from Paris and from urban regional centers. This figure is itself too small. Interrogations of the accused as to their identity in the Orgères affair reconstitute the stages and the tramping that led them to beg in the Beauce: in numerous cases, Paris appears as the obligatory stage, the transit center from which provincials who were not assimilated by the urban milieu were sent forth into the plain. More than twenty-five cases of this type have been noted; and if we can be permitted a rather rough approximation, we can say that two-thirds of the beggars are people of the countryside, a third come from the city, which bears witness to the urban exodus that is mentioned by so many contemporary sources.

In fact, if we possess for many cases the point of arrival, the Beauce, and the place of origin, their simple comparison seems rather a poor means to account for the extent of the movements which the interrogations about identity often reveal. Not that we ought to have perfect confidence in them, for persons suspected of brigandage or even simple beggars often reconstruct for themselves a past that is, to say the least, subject to doubt. For the present-day historian, it is enough if their stories are likely. Thanks to these interrogations, itineraries begin to show up. One of the simplest and most often met with is the one that the man of the wooded areas of the Manche and the Orne followed toward the plains of large-scale agriculture of the Ile de France: for example, the case of Gervais Morel, called the Norman of Rambouillet, from the region he frequented: born in a village of the Orne, he left it at the age of 17, stayed at Sées until 1789, then reached the plains of the Beauce, worked in the winter in the saltpeter manufacture at Rambouillet, in the spring on the hay harvest, then at the harvest between Longjumeau, Arpajon, and Palaiseau, and then went down, in time for the wine harvest, to the Valley of the Loire between Beaugency and Mer.

This type of case is the simplest: very often the rural person, the man from the wooded districts, tried his luck in Paris before coming to wander in the Beauce.

The most typical example, among many others, is that of Michel Paris, called Father Paris. He was 60 years old, but had left his native village, in the Manche near Domfront, when he was 10 or 11. Alençon, where he settled, kept him for 10 years. Then he went up to Paris: a laborer, he worked there for roofers and masons, and then became a watercarrier. He left the city at the beginning of the Revolution to begin his wandering existence in the plain: working, he said, as much as he could, he participated in the hay and grain harvests near Palaiseau, the wine harvest at Beaugency, and then no longer able to work, he traveled about the plain as a beggar. Father Paris, it is hardly necessary to add, lied without shame and his chronology often becomes imprecise. It is sufficient for us that his account be true in its main outlines.

For women beggars, there exist symmetrical processes of integration into wandering society: here is the example of Agnès Nibault, one of the concubines of the "Borgne du Mans" [the One-Eyed Man from Le Mans], 37 years of age, born in the Cher at Châteauneuf-en-Berry: an orphan, she became a domestic at the age of 11, watched over the ewes and the cows "until the year of the great winter," then came to Paris at the beginning of the Revolution, where she was first of all placed at a domestic and then worked in the manufacture of military uniforms "until the bread shortage," when, she said, "I came to the Beauce and the Brie asking for bread."

Isolated, perhaps, in the middle of these often stereotyped accounts, those of the journeymen of the *Tour de France* [1] or of ex-soldiers bear witness to movements of a still greater extent; such is the case, to take only one example, of Simphorien Joulin, a hatmaker, born at Segre in the Maine-et-Loire, suspected of being the proprietor of an iron-weighted cane, who declared that he had come directly from Sedan, immediately after having finished his *Tour de France*, although he admitted having begged in the meantime "the work of my trade not being much available."

We see at this stage that the problem of uprooting and geographic origin leads directly to the problem of social origin which conditioned it and explains it.

Where do these beggars come from? What milieux sent them forth? These are so many problems which our statistics allow us to resolve partially, since we know the social origin of two-thirds of the 332 (wandering) beggars (the domiciled prisoners were classified separately). There is, to be sure, the great unknown of 120 individuals, whose origin escapes us; if we leave aside the uncertainty of the sources, they are those whose quasi-professional status as beggars goes back so far, more than 10 years and

---

[1] The *Tour de France* was the tour of a number of cities made by journeymen in certain trades. Having finished his apprenticeship, the journeyman took this means to perfect his technique and to gain experience. Only upon completion of the tour might he become a candidate to mastership. The tour was organized and controlled by the extra-legal secret societies of journeymen known as *compagnonnages*. These organizations have never been properly studied, but some information is available in Coornaert, *Les Corporations En France avant* 1789, Paris, 1941.

perhaps as many as 50, that their original status was forgotten. They are those as well who never knew any other "profession": women or children less than 15 years old, who had often been beggars since their earliest years. Those who had always been beggars account for half of those whom, for lack of further knowledge, we are forced to put in the category of indeterminate social origin.

But where do the others come from? The answer to this problem at the statistical level presupposes a considerable effort of schematisation in so far as, at the lowest levels of salaried workers, social mobility is as great as geographical mobility: in the occupations of unskilled laborers, migration from one trade to another was an easy matter, and the simultaneous exercise of several activities was very frequent. For example the man who is a weaver in the winter, becomes an agricultural day laborer for the hay or grain harvest, thresher or wine harvester in the autumn, and is ready to beg when times are hard. We must be ready to accept for what it is worth the inevitable simplification.

Of 130 men whose original profession is known, rural salaried workers make up about one-third: forty-one persons, a very few small holders, some gardeners, much more often agricultural day laborers, or what is almost the same in the language of the time, farm attendants, threshers, harvesters, or haymowers. There is a nuance in that these denominations correspond to the difference between seasonal activities and that the thresher generally had a personal domicile that the farm attendant did not have. The youngest called themselves shepherds or cowherds. None of them belonged to that rural aristocracy made up of plowboys, who were better paid, better thought of, and more stable as well in so far as they represented a group of specialized and skilled salaried workers in the rural society of the Beauce.

There is nothing astonishing in the fact that the lowest fringe of this rural proletariat, its most poverty stricken and easily uprootable part should participate in the formation of the wandering population.

What is more astonishing, no doubt, is the strong percentage of artisan journeymen and textile workers, for they constitute one-half of the persons about whom we have information. Forty-five journeymen can be divided into two approximately equal groups. On the one hand, we have the very heterogeneous group of journeymen from various trades: the food industries (five bakers), the clothing industries (nine shoemakers, tailors, wigmakers, or hatmakers), the iron and wood trades (five locksmiths, farriers, or coopers), and, on the other hand, the massive group of twenty-three worker masons, roadworkers, and carpenter roofers, who represent, no doubt, the least skilled part of this journeyman labor force. Many of them had worked, according to their own expressions, "on the road," or "serving masons," principally in Paris or Versailles on the public works projects of the last years of the Old Regime.

It is a question here of unskilled workers, much more than of journeymen. Very few of them, two or three at most, had done their *Tour de*

France: but it remains to be seen whether the very common practice of adopting a pseudonym was not a result of a certain mixing with the milieux of the *compagnonnage*, rather than a simple convergence.

Another element, and numerically one of the most notable, was made up of weavers, wool workers, workers in flax, workers in (textile) manufactures, who furnish fifteen examples among the men and as many among the women.

From the Parisian manufacturers of military uniforms, from Rouen and Louviers, and still more from the manufacture of Jouy as from Meudon or Claire-Fontaine to the south of Paris, came cotton mechanics, drawers, and textile printers.

From the rural milieux of the Beauce, to the south of Paris and north of Orléans, came the weavers, women cotton spinners, and knitters of stockings, who were very numerous at that time and were engaged in domestic work for the manufacturers of Paris, Orléans, and Chartres.

The last notable category in this census of poverty is made up of professional wanderers such as peddlars, merchants of religious images, of needles and gun flints, basketmakers, makers of whips, birchrods and strawhats, tin casters, hide merchants or dealers in second-hand clothing . . . in a word all the small wandering trades of the plain. For them, the passage to beggary was scarcely a change in status: if they find themselves reduced to poverty, they will continue to follow the same roads, sleeping in the farms instead of at the inns, and at most they would lack the commercial authorization and passport that bore witness to their status as traders.

The ex-soldier "who had served" represents a characteristic figure in this society. He is a personage such as we find in the drawings of Jacques Callot; very often crippled, he had left the army as a result of his wounds, or else he had deserted, which was a less avowable motive. Often he came from far away, like "Father Provenchère," born in Briançon, who ran about the Beauce earning a living as a strawhat maker, accompanied by his daughter, born, as she said, "in a caisson."

In reality, if these often highly colorful characters are out of the ordinary, that is not to say that they were very numerous. There were four or five, at most ten, even if we add the beggars who had served in the army briefly at one time or another; in any case there were relatively few deserters from the revolutionary armies. Perhaps this is a result of the region we are studying: there were no doubt more in Picardy, Champagne, or Lorraine. It is even more likely that this small proportion is characteristic of the period under consideration: before the Jourdan law and the conscription of the year VII, very few deserters or young draftdodgers were running about the plain. We would have to wait for the year VIII to find young conscripts absent without leave. Our wandering gangs still owed nothing to the influx of draftees.

Two studies, one of the geographical origin and the other of the social origin of the wanderers, have furnished us with the point of departure for the majority of them; it would be necessary to follow the progress that brought them from their original position to the status of beggar, as we have tried to do in the case of geographical origins. When we follow the interrogations and record cards, we are tempted to think that there were as many kinds of cases as there were individuals. Nonetheless, repetition leads to sketching out a certain number of schemes.

First of all, there are the individual cataclysms: infirmity, illness, the death of a spouse or abandonment appear among the most frequently mentioned causes.

The crippled and the infirm are not lacking in the crowd of wanderers, and they make of the group a true *Cour des Miracles*.[2] Their miseries are evoked by the pseudonyms they took: "Toeless," "the one-eyed man of Jouy," "the one-eyed man from Le Mans," "Julien the one-armed," and "Julien the ringworm," and "thumbless." In more than one case, the indication "begs since he has been crippled" reminds us cruelly of the precariousness of the destiny of this group of salaried workers without resources. Certain registers of imprisonment in their dryness evoke rather bizarre trains of events, such as the case of Guillaume-Pierre Poulain

who says that he was a journeyman founder, then a peddler and a newspaper salesman, and presently handler of a blind woman's cart and fortune teller, and Charlotte Malet, who says she is a merchant of bouquets and fruits, and who live together in Paris, rue Christophe; given that they have no passport although they have been traveling, they appear to be persons with no visible means of support and who live together in an irregular liaison.

Sickness, even when it did not involve permanent invalidity, was often sufficient to cause the uprooting of salaried workers living on a day to day basis; and we see, for example, a family of weavers from Bullion, near Rambouillet, go off to beg collectively, mother, father, and three children, because the illness of the father and the oldest son had reduced them to poverty.

In this gallery of the disinherited, we are not astonished to find side by side with the infirm a number of abandoned children, raised at Bicêtre or at the Foundling Hospital in Paris: the example of Belle Agnès, a beggar at 18 years of age, who had been raised at the Foundling Hospital until the age of 10, had been put out to work, had stayed at her job for 2 years to become an apple seller, had turned prostitute—the example is the classic image of these seemingly prefabricated vocations. Many were widows, left without resources at the death of their husbands; many were abandoned women as well, most often because their husbands had gone off to the armies. We see arrive in the prisons of Chartres the abandoned wife of a

[2] The *Cour de Miracles* was the name given to certain areas, and especially one such in the Halles District of Paris, frequented by beggars. Returning to these quarters at night, they would shed their false infirmities, hence the idea of a miracle.

lieutenant of the sixty-fourth *demi-brigade* "wandering without a passport and furnished with insufficient papers."

But apart from these different cases, uprooting seems to have been most often the sanction of a social failure. It is in this context that social and geographical mobility takes on all its meaning. The provincial person who left for Paris to try his luck, hangs around there for a few years, a part of the unskilled and floating labor force working on road building. This does not mean that he had lost all contact with the countryside, and often if he worked in Paris during the winter, he went to work in the Beauce for the harvest. Then, the city that had never assimilated him rejects him. He becomes a wanderer, first an agricultural worker, a thresher or harvester according to the season; little by little he gets into the habit of begging when there is no work. Then work becomes occasional, a facade, a pretext. From that time on he is integrated into the gangs of beggars of the Beauce.

This is only one of the patterns, one of the most frequent it is true, by which one could become a beggar, but, beside the individual miseries that justify the uprooting in each particular case, the examination of all these cases persuades us that collective factors of uprooting were at work in this period, and that it would be impossible to understand this astonishing concentration of beggars without placing it in the context of the revolutionary social crisis.

This social crisis, whose culminating point was the year III and partially the year IV, is constantly evoked by our sources, the interrogations striving to find out in the case of each individual "how long he had been wandering about the plain." We are struck by the frequency with which the year III appears in the declarations. The statistics based on eighty-one conclusive cases that we have drawn up are, in this regard, very clear: there exist in this wandering population elements firmly implanted from years gone by; some, rare it is true, had been wandering for more than 50 years, others for 20 years. But the greatest majority is of revolutionary age: and more precisely goes back to the year III, because it was then that, out of a total of eighty-one, thirty-three cases of uprooting had taken place, a rather spectacular upsurge after the calm of the year II (three cases!) and even in comparison to more comparable periods such as the year IV and the year V. It was then that the massive exodus from the city toward the country and the mobilization of part of the rural working force had taken place. The alleged causes? The difficulty, especially for artisanal and industrial salaried workers, of getting paid "in the time of paper." The lack of work was also particularly noted among the weavers and textile workers as well as among the journeymen. The major theme that dominated all the others was "the dearness of grains," "the shortage of bread," to the point that frequently, in the uncertain chronology of persons who refer to "the great winter" rather more than to the calendar, even the old-style calendar, the expression "left his domicile at the time of the dearness of grains" became the perfect synonym of the year III.

Much contemporary testimony confirms this collective uprooting which individual investigations have verified for us on a semistatistical level. For instance, citizen Durand Claye of an old family of Chartres notables, who was the remarkable public prosecutor in the Orgères affair, several times emphasized in his charge to the court the extent of this migration:

Whatever may have been the number of brigands assembled in these places long time since, one can not hide the fact that it has singularly augmented in recent years. We can only recall with sorrow the unhappy time when a real or artificial shortage came to afflict our area. Bread was lacking . . . and it was particularly in the most populous cities that the famine exercised its greatest ravages. How many entire families did we not see at that time—men, women, and children—leave the Capital and the surrounding cities to spread out over the countryside and implore the commisseration of the cultivators. The farms were filled with strangers . . . .

Behind the extreme diversity of causes and modalities of the uprooting, the wandering population thus seems susceptible to being classified in two major categories: on the one hand, the old nucleus of chronic beggars, already implanted a long time back; on the other hand, the massive influx of those whom the revolutionary social crisis threw out on the plain. Is the phenomenon specifically revolutionary? Or was it not rather one of the constants of the wandering society of the Old Regime that it be enlarged periodically by famine and crisis?

We have not the evidence with which to confirm the second thesis, although it seems most likely.

In the case analyzed, it is all the more remarkable to see all the elements mix together, the oldest members providing the education of those who had just arrived, into a single style of life and even a true wandering society.

◄§§►

Beggary, such as we have been able to picture on the basis of the enormous documentation of interrogations, appears in these plains of large-scale agriculture to be a true institution: it has its rites, its code of conduct. On the fringes of established society, a veritable society of wanderers had been constituted.

First of all, the status of beggar had become a quasi-profession.

No doubt, there existed many transitional states between the initial professional activity and total beggary: occasional beggary, seasonal beggary, beggary while exercising a subsidiary profession.

In a first stage, uprooting had not yet taken place, and the beggar maintained as his point of departure a domicile to which he returned periodically: Pierre Bouilly called "Father Lapierre," a weaver at Rochefort-en-Yveline, after having been at Versailles, working in company with his oldest son; but he sent his wife and two children to beg in the environs at the same time. They came back periodically, every week, they said, to the family domicile. In this first form, we see, beggary was still only a complementary, subsidiary form of income. Only part of the family engaged in it, and it did not suppose the abandonment of the domicile. Then again, it remained almost legitimate in so far as the beggars, hardly ever leaving their own canton, were not subject to the passport and were not considered to be "wanderers without visible means of support, traveling without passport outside their own canton." This first form of beggary was above all feminine and juvenile, although it sometimes happened when the mother was sick that the father himself took his young children on his back to go beg —we meet with this more than once in our sources. This form of beggary was certainly much more widespread, but because it was not punished by the law or was at least tolerated, it cannot easily be detected in our judicial sources.

In order for it to leave traces, it was necessary for the search for subsistence to lead the indigent and hungry a little too far from their points of departure. This was in particular the case of most of the Paris or Versailles beggars running about the Beauce and whom we see end up in the prisons of Chartres.

At a later stage, beggary, having been occasional, became at the very least seasonal. The beggar lost the surety that his domicile represented, but he still kept at least the facade of a professional activity. He took a job when the opportunity presented itself for one or several months, even for a year as a farm attendant. More frequently, he participated in seasonal work in the region where he was active, cutting hay in the spring, harvesting in summer, haycutting once again, and grape gathering in the Loire Valley in the autumn, unless he had succeeded in getting a job as a thresher which would keep him occupied until the very heart of the winter.

It was at that moment above all that it would become necessary, in order to survive, to ask for bread in the farms. This second form of beggary was practiced especially by young men or men in the prime of life. Children aged 10 to 16 years took work more often as shepherds and cowherds. Cleaning out wells or working for masons supplied some of them with the beginning of a skill. At the most, there was no fundamental difference between this existence and that of a harvest worker or the August migrant who generally came then from Normandy rather than from Brittany to work on a seasonal basis in the plains of large-scale agriculture. At least, the harvest worker returned home periodically. Without a fixed base, the wanderer, on the contrary, underwent a generally irreversible evolution: work occupies less and less of a place in his movements, to the benefit of beggary.

The complete beggar drawing his subsistence from public charity remained one of the most frequent cases. A part of the men, especially above 50 or 60 years of age, and the greatest part of the women were in this situation. They sometimes kept up the pretence of some wandering activity, basketmaking or strawhat making, manufacturing birchrods or whips. But most of them no longer had even this pretext.

Henceforth, their life was divided between the road and places of shelter.

Each beggar had an area of habitual displacement: according to the official expression, "he ran about the plain," and it was in fact usually a matter of the plain. The greatest part of them, according to their own declarations, traveled about the Beauce and the Gâtinais between Paris to the north and Orléans to the south, Chartres to the west, Montargis or Nemours to the east. Part of them were habitués also of the Brie and a few event went down as far as Berry. Only a few frequented Eastern Normandy or the Vexin, and almost none went into the wooded areas. It was thus the country of the plain or of champagne that attracted the beggars who were, however, used to long trips: the difficulty of finding shelter or a refuge other than in the peripheral forests was compensated for by the greater ease of life, by the wealth of the farms.

During the day, it was on the road that one met them. They rarely traveled alone, whatever they may have claimed. The association, the group being by definition suspect, almost all of the interrogations show them as being isolated. They traveled alone, they say, or "with people they do not know." The prosecution witnesses, the farmers, gave the lie to this picture: in their stories we always see the beggars arriving at the farms in groups. "Beggary in association" was the rule. For the beginning beggar, it was a matter of necessity: "I was traveling," they said, "with other beggars who showed me the shelters." Associations formed: two or three, rarely more than six beggars, such are the figures most often found. These associations were often precarious, sometimes more durable, and were constituted in several different forms. Certain families traveled together—father, mother, three or four children. This family-type beggary was rare, for most often uprooting distends family ties and numerous were the married men and abandoned women who knew nothing about their families. Their husbands? They do not know. "It is said that he debauched the wife of an innkeeper of Ponchartrain and that he went away with her . . . . They say that he hanged himself at Orléans."

New associations were formed on the plain. What most struck the witnesses, both farmers and villagers, were the gangs of children. Young people less than 20 years old, sometimes less than 15 years, were denounced: beggars, said one cultivator of Rouvray en Beauce, "solid and in the best of health," "who have circulated almost all winter in this canton and sometimes slept in his stable."

Confirmation of the existence of these gangs of young people was provided by several "*mioches*," as they were called, who swore that they "never traveled except with young people of their own age." The public prosecutor got some rather easy effects from the presence of these "children without experience."

Most often, however, associations were developed, between both men and women, between young people and older beggars who had more experience: for instance, a man of 41 years of age and another about 60 years who carried with them a companion of 10 or 12 years. Then again, the example of three girls aged 9, 16, and 19 years who traveled about the plain under the leadership of an older woman.

Between men and women, couples were formed, most of the time illegitimate ones: the oldest and most respected beggars chose one or even two women companions among the gangs of women and girls traveling about the plain. These associations were sometimes stable, more often temporary, contracted and broken on the chance of a meeting in the shelters. Thérèse d'Orléans, who was accused of being the concubine of Gros Normand, one of the principal suspects, agreed that she had lived with him "but not more with him than with the first comer."

If these more or less stable associations formed thus on the roads and if the most common form of beggary seems to be beggary "in association," it was above all in the shelter that the beggars met and assembled.

There was no farm, however isolated, that was sheltered from their gangs. Detested, feared, they were received everywhere. It is true that they had some arguments: the "summoner," the beggar who imperatively solicited charity by threatening the farmer with the burning of his farm or crops, was a common type: one sees a farmer of Richerolles, near Audouville, denounce a group of six men and two women who demanded, by threats of setting a fire, a sum of 400 francs.

Public rumor accused them of other misdeeds: they poisoned cows in the farms where they were not welcomed, and any epizooty could be more or less blamed on them.

To speak the truth, it was hardly necessary to invoke fear in order to understand why they were welcomed, so much does it seem that in this rural society their arrival was an admitted fact that had become part of the mores of the community. If all farmers gave them charity, not all of them could give them asylum; the experience of the beggar "in the know" made him recognize the shelters where he was sure of being lodged. One was certain of being received at the Poly farm near Outarville, as at the Spuis farm near Chaussy or the Chauffeton farm at Loigny, whose master defined his farm as "a great shelter for the beggars."

How many went to meet there for the night? Six or seven at least, more often twenty or so, sometimes still more, since one farmer declared that he was in the "habit of giving lodgings to a great quantity every day and sometimes as many as thirty-four at a time."

Here, we see, it was a matter of a true institution, recognized, codified even: the farmer lodged the beggars for the night in a barn or stable; the large farms even had an out building more or less specialized in the lodging of beggars: the *Taudion*.

The farmer owed not only lodgings but also food to those whom he sheltered: "It was necessary when they arrived to give them bread and soup. And woe unto him who showed the least lack of desire to pay this contribution; he would have been sure to pay it a hundred times over."

The prosecution's documents describe this rite: it was the mistress of the house or the chief servant who brought the collective pot of soup to the beggars in the barn. The soup contained at the very least a milk base and bread, and it was brought together with the spoons the beggars would use and would sometimes forget to return.

By chance meetings in these shelters, beggars got to know one another, frequented one another. The new arrivals discovered the older members and little by little a true marginal society was born, whose points of encounter and centers of initiation were the shelters of the plain, the forests, and even the prisons of Etampes, Orléans, and even more of Neuville aux bois.

In order for the new arrival to be accepted by his confrères, he had to pass through a period of observation: certain of them were never admitted and terrible squarings of accounts eliminated those whom the others rejected. In this world where the struggle for life was present in its most degraded forms, the beggar "nude in a nightshirt" whom the farmers found in the morning, beaten and fleeced by his neighbors of a night, could count himself happy, for many did not get off so cheaply.

Finally admitted into this society which was, paradoxically, so open and so closed at the same time, the beggar saw his accession to the rank of a habitué sanctioned by the attribution of a pseudonym. Beggars recognized one another by these nicknames: in general it was only the new beggars arrested for the first time who did not have them; the pseudonym sometimes recalled the origin of its bearer, the *limousin de Méréville*, the *Gros Normand*, *breton cul sec*, *Thérèse d'Orléans* . . . sometimes a physical peculiarity or an object of clothing: the one-eyed man from Le Mans, the Belle Agnès, Julien the ringworm, Green Suit; sometimes past or present activities: the sailor, the needle seller, the whore of Saclas.

A hierarchical society was born; constantly churned about, added to by newly uprooted persons, it nonetheless took on its own rites, organization, and jargon.

Between beggars, as between beggars and farmers, a kind of ritual existed. Completely illegal, periodically imprisoned for vagabondage or for lack of a passport, these beggars nonetheless became a quasi-official part of the society of these plains of large-scale agriculture.

It is conceivable, then, that brigandage found among them a terrain particularly favorable for its development.

≈§≈

From beggary to brigandage, the passage was logical. The wandering gangs were, by their very situation, outside all legality, since they were made up of persons "without means of support," begging without authorization, and without passports outside their own canton.

In the legislation then in force, this occupation was liable to 1 year of prison and 2 years for a second offense. In fact, there were few beggars who had no police records: we find among them numbers of habitual criminals, condemned for vagabondage now in Etampes, now in Neuville aux bois, well placed on the fringe of the forest of Orléans to filter the beggars who traditionally assembled there.

Outside the law by his situation, the beggar soon went outside the law by necessity, theft being the obligatory complement to beggary. Everything began by minor thefts: theft of linen drying on a hedge, an old shirt traded for a new one, food stolen in the shelters, both poultry and cheese, very often the farmers not daring to complain.

The true brigands would appear as a kind of aristocracy of these beggars, hidden in the mass of wanderers who furnished them with accomplices and informers and among whom they could lose themselves in anonymity.

We do not intend to retell in detail all the events of the history of the Orgères gang; the story has already been told many times. But we would at least like to show how this spectacular upsurge of brigandage in the period of the Directory was the result of a long tradition of brigandage and at the same time of the revolutionary social crisis.

The tradition of brigandage in the Beauce, the long line of crimes of which the Orgères gang was only the end, all these facts were exploited at the time they took place. The accusation, the stories of Leclair recall the letters of nobility of the brigands of Orgères, whose ancestry is made to go back as far as the *Grandes Compagnies*.[3] Without going back that far, they invoke the first activities of the gangs of the forest of Orléans between 1750 and 1760, then their migration into the forest of Dourdan under the direction of Renard between 1760 and 1770, the reorganization of the troop installed in the woods of Montargis by Robillard, who was broken on the wheel in Montargis in 1783, and finally the return to the place of origin in the forest of Orléans after 1783 under the conduct of Fleur d'Epine, massacred in the prisons of Versailles where he was being held at the time of the September Massacres of 1792. Jean Anger, called Beau François, and his second in command Ringette, called Rouge d'Auneau, took up under their orders; especially from the year III onward this was the gang that a murder committed at Millouard near Orgères would cause to be known as the Orgères gang.

To this long tradition, to the innovations which, it was said, Fleur d'Epine had brought about at the beginning of the Revolution, was due that organization that the One-eyed Man of Jouy, one of the confederates who denounced his accomplices, described minutely and which is in fact a separate society modeled on civil society. It had a very strict organization, founded on the division of labor between the "*francs de maison*," domiciled accomplices, generally tavernkeepers, horseskinners, or simple day laborers,

[3] The *Grandes Compagnies* were troops of adventurers in feudal Europe. Paid by princes in time of war, they lived by pillage and the taking of ransom in time of peace. Known in France as early as the twelfth century, they were particularly active in The Hundred Years War. They were dissolved, not without some difficulty, by Charles VII, after the reconquest of his domains in the 1440's.

who had as their mission to harbor, hide, and liquidate stolen merchandise, and the *"francs de plaine,"* who mixed into the crowd of wanderers and executed the plans prepared and decided upon in the periodic meetings held in the woods of Cercottes, Lifferemeau or Sainte-Escobille, to the north of the forest of Orléans.

Beyond this discipline, the gang had taken on a semblance of administrative organization with divisions into districts or cantons, according to the zones of operation, and a caricature of family organization, since a false priest celebrated a kind of marriage ceremony between the beggars, while a surgeon operated on the wounded in the basements of a house belonging to a domiciled accomplice, and a teacher of the *"mioches,"* Father Louis, indoctrinated the children of the gang with the rudiments of the trade.

A technique of theft and murder completed this system: operations knowingly prepared by the reconnaissances of the *mioches* and the women, breaking-in *"à la bombe,"* that is, thanks to a battering ram or a plow coulter, the frequent use of the disguise of a national guard charged with making a search, and, to get the farmers to talk, the procedure of burning the bottom of their feet that gave the brigands both their name (*chauffeurs*) and their sinister reputation.

If we add to this the practice of a slang of which Leclair, the curious recordkeeper, kept a register and made a dictionary, we will keep the impression of a sort of aristocracy within the world of wanderers, where it recruited its members, which were its accomplices through ties of fear and interest, but which remained subordinate to it: all beggars do not understand or speak the slang which remains the privilege of this elite of crime.

To an initial nucleus of survivors of the old gangs of Robillard or Fleur d'Epine, the guardians of traditions and ancient practices, the revolutionary crisis added an influx of uprooted persons who found themselves surrounded and taken in charge quite naturally by these old wanderers of the plain. There is then nothing astonishing in the fact that the curve of the influx of the uprooted coincides almost exactly with that of the activities of the gang, ninety-five misdemeanors and crimes, among which there were twenty-five murders from 1791 to the year VII; fifty-six misdeeds less directly ascribable to the gang, including nine murders, were not included in the accusation. No doubt, the growth that started in the year III and asserted itself especially in the year IV was so spectacular only because prescription, oversight, and fear had caused more distant misdeeds to be forgotten. It remains nonetheless true that it was from the years III and IV that dates the upsurge properly so called of brigandage.

By causing a spectacular growth in the reserve of wanderers among whom brigandage recruited its personnel, the crisis of the year III and the following years gave brigandage a means of development. We will not insist on the degradation of the local authorities which so many authors have recognized as an essential cause of the plague; it seems more interesting to us to emphasize an element noted by the public prosecutor in his charge to the court: the installation of a barter economy in the plains of large-scale agriculture around Paris.

> That moment [he said] when the Beauce and the Gâtinais saw themselves covered so to speak by numerous associates of that criminal horde is the moment when the shortage of bread was felt in all the cities and almost all the rural areas.

> It was then that children without experience and debauched girls swelled the ranks of the first nucleus of brigands, it was at that time that thefts and murders were multiplied and that their authors were able to rid themselves more easily of the fruit of their plundering.

> Everyone recalls those frightful moments. The action of the police was then slowed down, hunger, that terrible need, led urbanites to seek their subsistence in the countryside, money was without value, bread could be had only by exchanging landed property or non-real property for it. Farms were transformed into shops; beds, linen, furniture, silverware, and jewellery were continually offered to the proprietors of grains and flour, and it was by profiting from this unhappy circumstance that the thieves peddled the product of their brigandage without becoming suspect.

If we have wanted to quote the above *in extenso,* it is because it seems to us to be revelatory of the conditions of life, both social and economic, in the plains of large-scale agriculture to the south of Paris. On the one hand, we have the crowd of uprooted, hungry urbanites and, on the other, the farmers, distrustful of paper money, rich in stocks of grain. Between the two, a current of exchanges by means of barter grew up. Beggars and brigands appear in this economic system as two essential cogs, necessary to these exchanges of which they make themselves, on the one hand, the intermediaries and agents, but parasites as well in so far as they practiced direct recovery by beggary or theft. They enriched the farmer until he was "ready to do." Leclair, who was very sententious, gives some moral illustrations of this curious system, on the theme of the avaricious miller who sold flour to the brigands at a huge price, at the risk of being stolen from a little time afterward. Dirty money . . . .

Shall we try to draw a partial conclusion from this last development?

The Revolution certainly did not create brigandage in the Beauce. Constantly undergoing a rebirth in the course of the eighteenth century, brigandage corresponded to the special conditions of the plains near Paris, whose outlet they were, while at the same time by their very sharp social antagonisms, they juxtaposed the wandering bands in which brigandage made its recruits and the rich peasantry isolated in its farms.

But if the French Revolution is in continuity with this tradition, it illustrates at the very least with a special amplitude the part played by the social and economic crisis in the recurrent upsurges of brigandage.

At the end of this study, the dossiers of the Orgères affair reveal their richness, even beyond the romantic history that seemed to be their proper vocation. Perhaps we may complain that we have not seen enough of Rouge d'Auneau, Beau Francois, Gros Normand, or Grande Marie. To evoke them as have done other authors has not been our purpose.

We wanted to show that these dossiers represent an important contribution to the study of the structure of this rural society, by enabling us to see how the wanderers who were one of its essential elements lived.

Beyond the study of structure, we have wanted to emphasize the enrichment they represent for the study of that special conjuncture of the revolutionary crisis, especially after the year III.

It would be necessary and desirable to compare this local study to other aspects of brigandage in the period of the Directory, too often evoked in a uniform way.

To this brigandage of the plains that went to the wealth invested in the farms, the brigandage of southern regions would contrast the search for "circulating" wealth by means of attacking stagecoaches.

The regions of the west would contrast with this brigandage directly tied to the revolutionary situation but very curiously abstracted from any political consideration a brigandage of the wooded regions which willingly flowed into the mold of insurrectionary action.

Who knows what might be the results of a comparison with contemporary forms of Rhenish brigandage of a Schinderhannes, or the eternal insecurity of the latifundia societies of the Mediterranean.

If comparative studies are necessary in various geographical areas, what might an evolutionary study of the nineteenth century bring forth? By the analysis of the recruitment of the poorhouses of the Restoration we would no doubt see the image of the wanderer that we have attempted to sketch change. The Norman in the Beauce would become the Breton. After the last great agricultural crises, the able-bodied beggars and the associated beggars would no doubt give way to the isolated and peaceful beggar whose image we still bear in mind. The myth of the vagabond and the brigand would no doubt appear to be more durable, and was perpetuated by Rouge d'Auneau at his trial when he distributed his own portrait and the plaintive ballad he had himself composed. From the Marquis de Sade to the Comtesse de Ségur, from the literature that plays up complexes to that which exorcises them, the wanderers of these forests of the Beauce borderlands have furnished the portrait of the man who inspires fear. It would no doubt be interesting to study the transformations and survival of this myth.

All these suggestions go way beyond the limited framework of what we have tried to do in this study: to make of brigandage a social phenomenon by putting it back into the framework of the wandering society that fed it and gave rise to it.

SOME ASPECTS OF THE REVOLUTIONARY MENTALITY

April 1793—Thermidor, Year II

≈§ **By Richard Cobb**

What sort of person was "the average revolutionary," the typical "man of the Revolution"? Did he in fact exist, or was he merely an abstraction, a point of view, a pointillist portrait, a pure fabrication lacking any historical basis in reality? These are valid questions. Accordingly, we must begin by defining the sources which have been utilized in fashioning this Seurat-style portrait and then define the man we have tried to sketch, indicating those characteristics that seem to us to distinguish him from men living in less turbulent periods than the time of the *Grande Terreur*, the Reign of Terror.

Existing documentation imposes from the outset an extremely important limitation on our choice. We are confronted above all with documents of a collective nature: legal proceedings of political assemblies, reports of popular societies, of committees of surveillance, of general assemblies and regional groups. Even in those rarer instances when we have access to private correspondence, this correspondence is still addressed to collective groups, committees, or societies. Consequently, we are dealing with the public man, with the collective man. Now the collective man is also the

305

orthodox man, and our documentation places a premium on conformity rather than sincerity.

There exists, of course, another source of information—the records of the police and the judiciary: interrogations, accusations, the testimony of witnesses, the reports of observers, in short, all the gossip of informers and writers of anonymous letters. Undoubtedly, one distinguishing mark of this hypothetical "revolutionary" was his fondness for talking. These men talked too much and in too many places. They thus provided their enemies with a fearful weapon and furnished historians with sources based on their verbal fecundity. Indeed, a great deal of the anti-terrorist proceedings initiated in the criminal tribunals during the Republican year III consisted of "selected quotations," of bits and snatches of speeches given at popular assemblies, or even casual remarks uttered at the wine merchant's shop or spoken in the streets by these loquacious revolutionaries. The criminal court of the Bouches-du-Rhône indicted twenty-six inhabitants of the commune of Mallemort on charges "of having constantly advocated plunder and assassination *in the galleries of the popular society, in taverns, in the streets, and on the highways . . . .*" That is the price they paid for talking too much.

If the "revolutionary" thereby enriched historical documentation and greatly facilitated the task of the courts by his imprudent eloquence, he was not so thoughtful as to leave us his "intimate notes," and we are therefore compelled to see him as he wished to be seen by the public, with all the trappings of revolutionary orthodoxy, with all the ardor of his patriotic enthusiasm, or, on the other hand, to view him as his worst enemies wished to depict him (among whom we must include—and in the first rank—the judges of the year III). Yet in every instance we are still dealing with a portrait of the public man. We must resign ourselves to the fact that the private individual almost completely eludes us, a fact that spares us the difficult task of trying to separate the public image of the revolutionary man from the one he presented to intimate friends and associates. We are obliged to be content with a documentation necessarily deceptive in nature which consists partly of public and quasi-official declarations, partly of remarks knowingly lifted out of context, and partly of denunciations inspired in many cases by deliberate malevolence.

The public man tends naturally toward orthodoxy. It is not merely a matter of simple prudence. The collective ambience affects him in a very real manner. It is obviously extremely difficult to distinguish sincere revolutionary convictions from momentary enthusiasms and simple conformity among men who seem to have been turned out of the same uniform mold even to the point of making the same common pronouncements in exactly the same phraseology. But by drawing our illustrations from widely varied sources, we can at least discern what appears to have been characteristic and what represents, on the other hand, individual reactions seldom repeated or emulated by others.

We must consider another kind of objection. Do not collective documentation and information obtained from the police or judiciary attach great importance not only to orthodoxy but also to revolutionary extremism? Those whose voices are the most audible, are they not precisely those who shout the loudest, the super-revolutionaries, the professional revolutionaries, the "inciters to action"? Now those who make the most noise are sometimes those who have a political or private past they would like to have forgiven or forgotten. Such men were not lacking at the time of the Terror, and we encounter them in all the popular societies and all the committees of exception. It was not too difficult to acquire a shining reputation for revolutionary ardor (especially because of the numerous committees which could remove the *révolutionnaire* from his home town where he was too well known) by indulging in the excessive and scurrilous language of such strident newspapers as *Le Père Duchesne*. Indeed editor Jacques-René Hébert had imitators in almost all the large cities of the Republic. There were *Pères Duchesne* in Lyons, Toulouse, Lille, Limoges, Perpignan, and Bayonne, just as there was a "Marat of Compiègne" and a whole company of "Marats" in Nantes. There were often rather dubious individuals like Marc Dolle, a one-time bankrupt Grenoblese who had squandered a fortune in gambling and who succeeded in establishing a great reputation for revolutionary patriotism. He was to be found enjoying life in his new residence at La Guillotière thanks to generous donations on behalf of the poor and the volunteers, thanks also to his "preachments" of unusual violence during his tours of the district of La Tour-du-Pin. Or again, there were men like Groslay who, in Lyons, echoed the vituperative blasts of *Père Duchesne* before later becoming a writer of defamations in the royalist cause. This species flourished for a while especially during the great waves of repression and in the revolutionary committees they spawned to carry out their directives. As long as there was a job to be done with guillotine and rifle, with counting heads and demanding blood, such individuals could give the full measure of their capacities. But they rarely survived the hours of extremism. People eventually came to distrust these men in whom the rank and file detected the spirit of demagoguery and professional blood letting. In the long run the majority of these dubious individuals, who indulged in excesses, were to be unmasked, thanks in large measure to the correspondence maintained throughout France by the different *sociétés populaires* which acquired a sort of "central filing system" concerning the revolutionary record of all their members, especially those associated with the Jacobins.

But here is another more serious objection. Did the "revolutionary man" really exist? Was he so very different from the ordinary man? What distinguished the little shopkeeper in the Rue Saint-Denis from the repressor of Lyons or the rioter during the days of Prairial? Often it was the same man. Now if the sans-culotte of the year II had something in common with the little businessman who took up arms in July 1789 or again in the year III, he disappeared, insofar as he was a *révolutionnaire*, after the year IV to become once more the anonymous little artisan in Paris. The same might be said of a certain umbrella merchant in Nantes who, after having taken part in the repression, won a respite from revolutionary life thanks to the trial of Carrier. But when this trial was over, he disappeared from sight as if he had fallen through a trap door. A few of the breed could still be found in Grenelle,[1] but already the revolutionary was giving way to the conspirator. By 1796 the reign of the *révolutionnaire* had ended. The public man rejoined the private man. But this public man had indeed existed and had played his rôle on the revolutionary stage. His contemporaries, moreover, were the first to become aware of a certain *"ambiance"* that characterized the revolutionary period, one we can discern only in vague manner through the memoirs of the day and the writings of the great historians and novelists of the last century. How often do we encounter that familiar remark of the sans-culottes: "We are living in a time of Revolution." That meant, presumably, that revolutionary times were different from other times, that one could and was expected to act differently than one did in ordinary times, that the Revolution had its own laws and its own *raison d'état*, conceptions expressed in that overworked verb: *révolutionner*, and in that very evocative phrase: *dans le sens de la Révolution*, "in the direction of the Revolution." And whenever they recalled that period in retrospect, they meant to say that one must take into account its very special atmosphere, its peculiar *ambiance* composed of enthusiasms, dangers, fears, and credulity before passing judgment on the actions they took. Politically speaking, the revolutionary was, moreover, always very conscious of his importance and of his "revolutionary" rights, rights to which he was entitled as a member and representative of the Sovereign People, especially if he was a Parisian, an inhabitant of "the cradle of liberty." The Parisian revolutionary was even so thoroughly imbued with the part he was assigned to play in the Revolution that very often he succeeded in making himself perfectly obnoxious to Frenchmen from the provinces by giving himself the airs of a "Ph.D. in Revolution" and affecting an attitude of scorn, condescension, and distrust toward his "provincial brothers." The Parisian not only regarded himself as the revolutionary man par excellence, he was only too inclined to think he held a monopoly on this title. However, he had many imitators among the inhabitants of the other large cities who, in turn, behaved in the same patronizing manner toward "ignorant country folk." The "revolutionary man" truly existed if only because countless city dwellers believed in him, in his rôle, and in the rights he exercised beginning with that of *"Revolutionizing,"* whatever form it might take.

We may be accused, perhaps, of having ridiculed revolutionaries by

[1] Grenelle was the location of a barracks in Paris, whose soldiers Babeuf, Buonarotti, and their fellow conspirators tried to win over to their cause on the night of September 9–10, 1796. Carnot knew of their plans in advance, and they were arrested before they could carry them out. Babeuf and his accomplice, Darthe, were guillotined on May 27, 1797.

drawing up a list of their follies, consisting of *morceaux choisis*, specially selected texts which, however amusing, may be nothing more than caricatures. This is a charge to be especially fearful of. Now it is a fact that humor and revolutionary fervor are never congenial bedfellows. The lack of a sense of humor is doubtless one of the most salient characteristics of the revolutionary. Wit and humor appeared as counter-revolutionary vices. Sadet, a shopkeeper in Lyons, is reported to have said that one should mistrust above all people "who have wit." The remark is perhaps apocryphal, but it reveals a state of mind that the revolutionaries of the year II would not have denied, for they took life very seriously and attached a quasi-religious significance to words. They could not have been further removed from the good-natured tradition of jokes and pleasantries of army life, so dear to Frenchmen as a rule. A joke was simply not appreciated. It might offend the delicate ears of young citizens and citizenesses. It was found necessary to dismiss a member of a Parisian revolutionary committee for having used improper language while questioning the wife of an *émigré*.

It was not merely a question of avoiding "dirty" jokes. Words had a literal sense and often baleful consequences. At a time when the concierge was *queen* and when an anonymous letter could have fearful repercussions in matters other than marital infidelities, people had to be careful of their remarks. But they rarely practiced discretion, as a matter of fact. Revolutionaries were as careless and loose with their tongues as the most loquacious enemies of the régime. For example, Vincent, the General Secretary of War, had allowed himself, at the end of a fine banquet, to poke fun at the new costume of the Representatives of the people by referring to them as *"mannequins habillés,"* (mannequins in costumes). That remark was not to be forgotten by the meticulous Fouquier-Tinville. Had not Vincent's quip "vilified the national representation," the counter-revolutionary crime par excellence? Many people were to take the road to prison, nay, to the guillotine or firing squad, for having "vilified" the Convention, the Revolution, the Republic, the city of Paris, and the French People. Some residents of Lyons were prosecuted for having made fun of the Parisians. Austrian, Spanish, and English prisoners of war were punished for having indulged, while drunk, in speculations as to the military and amorous capacities of French Republicans. The country was at war.

There were also crimes of omission. The abbé Sicard, director of the Institute for Deaf Mutes, was rebuked for not having taught his pupils the Rights of Man. When questioned on the matter, a pupil had declared—or rather, had written—that he did not know what an aristocrat was, or even a patriot. He did not know that France had become a Republic!

It would, of course, be unseemly to exploit such easy opportunities to laugh at people who took themselves so seriously and who exposed themselves to combat and danger at a time when words were fraught with peril and when France, surrounded by enemies and subverted by traitors, was living through a period of high drama. Indeed it was not a time to make jokes. Nevertheless, we can not help being amused by the fact, for instance, that certain people called themselves Absinthe Jalabert, Endive Pagès, and Haricot Vidal. These were the names of three revolutionaries from Perpignan. And it does not seem disrespectful to the revolutionaries to smile at that Parisian, Aristide Lyon, who changed his name to Aristide Lille because "the name of Lyons filled him with horror" or to chuckle for a moment over that citizen of Lyons named Février (February) who took as his first name Janvier (January), or to be amused by a member of the *Société Révolutionnaire de Lille* who, arguing from the premise that there are no wolves in England, proposed that two shiploads be sent there and let loose on the coast of Kent to devour the flocks of that tyrant, George III. At least we find that more amusing than the sinister, macabre humor of an Hébert whose ever-recurring subject was "the little window, the *linotte*, the national razor, the republican head-shorteners, and the little basket." When the time came for Hébert to put his own head in "the republican window," the little people of Paris may be forgiven for laughing their heads off at the humorist who was shaved by "the national razor." People have always enjoyed jibing at an *arroseur arrosé* [a sprinkler (of blood) who gets sprinkled in turn].

But it is for the purpose of emphasizing the serious side of the revolutionaries, the great importance they attached to words and symbols, that we have chosen these random examples of their lack of humor, a characteristic that went with their sincerity, their conformity, or their desire to excel one another in revolutionary zeal.

We have spoken elsewhere of the revolutionary sans-culotte during the period of his greatest activity, between April 1793 and Germinal, year II, with particular attention to describing his personal and affective attitudes. These men were puritans for whom vice was associated with counter-revolution. They condemned celibacy, gastronomy, gambling, prostitution, obscenity, personal adornment, and luxury, but they showed themselves, on the other hand, altogether indulgent toward drunkenness. So much then for the essential features of their private attitudes. Certain outward postures, certain external attitudes, remain to be described, in particular their political gullibility, their attitude toward the Terror and toward the revolutionary measures of repression, their conception of France and of the outside world. Finally, we shall try to explain the reasons for the disappearance of the "revolutionary man" after the last great fireworks during Prairial. As for the remote origins of revolutionary ideology, the dissemination among the masses of the writings of Rousseau, Mably, and the *philosophes,* as for the influence on a certain revolutionary mentality of *Emile* or *The Social Contract,* decrees of the *Parlements,* and American writings—all that is too vast a subject and one that goes beyond our present intentions. We prefer to leave those topics to historians who have made thorough studies of the dissemination of the printed word during the final years of the Old Regime. Accordingly, we shift the center of attention from the inner life of the revolutionary man toward external objects and their immediate impact upon him. What was his reaction to the sudden changes continually taking place on the Parisian political scene, changes which transformed a former "man of the hour" or a "revolutionary athlete" into a traitor and a conspirator? Did he join in the worship of important men who managed to stay alive, and did he willingly and uncritically accept the explanations offered him in high places? Did he approve of extreme measures of repression, and if so, was that proof of a predilection for blood and a natural taste for violence? How did he regard his country, the French Republic, the land of Revolution? And since, in spite of everything, there still existed an outside world and other peoples, all less free, the majority still slaves—how did he feel with respect to them, in public and in private? And last, what set apart our "revolutionary man" from the shopkeeper, the urban artisan, at the close of the eighteenth century? What was the true character of the individual *révolutionnaire*? We have only certain indications, a number of hints and suggestions suitable for a composite portrait in the impressionistic manner, not the sharply defined details of a "realistic" likeness.

POLITICAL CREDULITY

The revolutionary man was gullible. He believed what he was told, especially in matters of public affairs. This class of men were novices in political life. In spite of the astonishing political sophistication of Parisians in particular, it was not within a period of just two or three years that they learned to acquire a critical attitude in the discussion of public affairs. And as for the sans-culottes, the institutions that constituted the *forum* for such discussions—the popular societies of town and country—were creatures that had only recently come into existence. They emerged largely from the popular victories of May 31 and June 2. In the provinces the sans-culottes joined these societies in large numbers only during the summer and especially in September of 1793. The societies and district assemblies were already functioning in Paris before May, but it was only from July on that they underwent "internal revolutions" which drove out the moderates. In the rural areas they were organized in the fall and winter of the same year after the harvest and field work were over and there was a respite from farm labor. Then country people had time to devote to affairs of state and long nights to be filled with some kind of activity. These societies were as much recreation and social centers as they were classrooms in civics. But when planting time returned in March, they were neglected again only to drag painfully along until the beginning of the harvest season when they stopped altogether.

This credulity which, as we shall see, had its roots in a distant past, also concealed peoples' indifference and especially their ignorance. In matters concerning the development of political indifference among the revolutionaries, it is very important to keep in mind the movements of the political barometer. From September 1793 to February and March 1794, discussions were very lively within the Parisian and provincial societies. They discussed everything with great vivacity and often in utter confusion amid shouts and cries from the spectators' galleries. They were a long way yet from true freedom of discussion. The speed with which orators hastened to abandon opinions or motions found to be unpopular is proof of this fact. It was a situation that permitted *noisy and militant minority groups* to stampede the assembly into voting, for instance, for the closing of churches and to take the first steps in disestablishing Christianity, while a majority had sat by in embarrassed silence or offered a few timid protests that were quickly withdrawn. In certain rural societies members who dared speak out in favor of retaining religious worship, when confronted with the reactions of officials and agitators, were quick to say that they had been *mistaken* and that they wished to withdraw their objections. Nevertheless, all the great problems of the day were discussed at that time with special emphasis on questions of subsistence and the means of combating scarcities and hoarding. They took the liberty of denouncing higher authorities and even their own representatives.

In February and March of 1794 the great spring political crisis broke out. The *hébertistes* were arrested. The Committees turned against the popular movement. Popular institutions were dismantled or emasculated. Popular societies dwindled along with attendance. Meetings were largely given over to making platitudinous speeches and eulogies in stereotyped language. People sensed the lassitude, indifference, and dull conformity that permeated these bodies like the termites of every revolutionary régime. The Supreme Being aroused no popular enthusiasm. People conformed. That was all. They no longer had the right to discuss living costs and questions of subsistence. They hastened to congratulate Robespierre and Collot for having escaped the assassination attempt by Admiral, but Robespierre enjoyed very little genuine popularity. Moreover, at least in revolutionary circles, popularity seldom assumes a human form, and when it does, it is generally a dead one: Marat, Lepeletier, and Châlier. People accepted with discipline and a certain weariness the official version of the crimes of Hébert, Chaumette, Danton, and Robespierre by making dutiful speeches all turned out of the same sad mold, grandiloquent and vacuous. They asked no questions. So far as the *révolutionnaire* was concerned, these men were guilty since the Convention and the Committee of Public Safety had said so. They had been traitors, for the proofs were there. They deserved a thousand deaths. . . . Now let us proceed to the next order of business! It is unfortunate that we misjudged this or that *athlète en révolution,* but after all, *men* are unimportant, and leaders who are hungry for power, *les ambitieux,* deserve to be punished for their crimes.

There were at the same time indifference, conformity, even perhaps cynicism, but above all *credulity* and *confusion*. Besides, how could any-one make any sense out of it? Let us listen to a sans-culotte from Aix-en-Provence as he expressed what must have been the feelings of so many average revolutionaries after the events of Thermidor: "The Majority," he wrote, "in order to take refuge . . . in their good faith and in themselves, admit that they are weary of being constantly *buffeted about* by the Bris-sots, the Orléans, the Robespierres, the Pitts, the Royalists, etc." This suc-cession of names, this series of pictures, was an unreal as a theatrical performance in the eyes of the provincial revolutionaries who watched the procession of impressive names and understood only one thing: the cost of living was going up; most basic commodities were not to be found; the bread ration was inadequate; military expenditures were becoming unbearable; and there was a shortage of labor and horses. People were credulous, but they were convinced by the evidence presented to them. Now whose fault was it? Who was to blame? The blame was placed on *ill will, conspiracies, foreigners, exports, hoarding,* and *egotism.*

For there was widespread belief in conspiracies. That was what made Fouquier-Tinville's task so easy, as it did for Saint-Just. For the revolu-tionary mind everything could be explained in terms of plots and conspira-cies, especially the causes of shortages and economic difficulties, military failures and soaring prices—everything that had a political explanation. The chief villains were: conspiracies, active ill will, and English gold. More-over, belief in conspiracies was not something new. It was not a product of the revolutionary period. It went far back into the history of this people who were suspicious and gullible at the same time. It was at the base of all actions of popular life, and there is no doubt that the malevolence found therein a fertile soil which yielded an implausible but persistent harvest of falsehoods. We find a flourishing output during the entire Revo-lution and even during the Terror. At one moment a rumor is planted to terrify all villagers by making them believe their entire wheat crop will be requisitioned. On another occasion they are told that all their cows and sheep will be taken from them. The rumors were believed and precaution-ary measures were taken. In Marseilles there was incipient panic among divorcés in the wake of a report that the divorce law had been revoked, and they would all be obliged to return to their former spouses. But it was especially in Lot, Averyron, and Cantal, breeding grounds par excel-lence for false reports, that the most fantastic rumors circulated among rural groups. The city of Rodez is aflame! The soldiers of Lot have all been massacred in Aveyron! Eye witnesses have reported it. "Swarthy men," probably from Bordeaux, encountered on the highways had said so. At the same time this impoverished region was overrun by witches and sor-cerers, and "golden letters" rained down from heaven, "written in the hand of God." The dissemination of newspapers and of the *Bulletin des Lois* (the Law Bulletin) did not in the least halt these absurd reports to which the rural population, and even the residents of a large city like Marseilles, gave unqualified credence. We find strong evidence of this readiness to believe any and all rumors in the continually recurring instances of fear and panic, some of which prompted outbursts of popular brutality. For example, the persistent belief in "a prison plot" provoked the September massacres in Paris, the drownings (*noyades*) in Nantes, and the great slaughters in Lyons and southern cities in the year III. This legend was the basic ingredient for preparing every dish in the revolutionary cookbook, and was used by the government itself when the decision was made to eliminate the unpalatable *hébertistes*. It was used to foment the murder of recalcitrant priests, the *chouans* [insurgent Royalists in Brittany, La Vendée, and so on], terrorists, and "*mathevons*."[2] It is not hard to imagine the countless opportunities there were for malevolent groups to exploit such popular gullibility especially by striking that "most sensitive nerve," public fear of food shortages.

In revolutionary times this human tendency to accept rumors and hearsay at face value was infinitely more dangerous since immense powers were concentrated in the hands of credulous individuals, unlike normal times under a less popular but more stable form of government. Most of the victims of the Terror and of the Counter-Terror can testify to its power. Aided and abetted by peddlers of slander and by secret informers, the force of credulity gives us the key to understanding the public's acceptance of the Reign of Terror and all the rapid, inexplicable shifts in policy among top revolutionary figures. Who knows if Committee members themselves were not dupes of their own imaginings? By dint of talking continually about Pitt and Cobourg they ended up believing in the "foreign plot," and it is a known fact that they thought themselves constantly in danger of assassination.

But such credulity was not without some foundation in fact. These plots they believed in so much did indeed exist. The history of the Terror is sown with obscure and impenetrable plots. Certain Royalists indulged in playing "the policy of the worst" by encouraging excesses and circulating exaggerated reports. The conclusions of Fouquier-Tinville and Saint-Just to the effect that "extremes come together" and ultimately behave in the same manner, were not without justification. There existed an intermediate ground on the edge of Royalism and of a certain strident *hébertisme*. Counter-revolutionaries were by no means deprived of a magnificent opportunity to fish in troubled waters by meddling in anti-religious activities and by goading extremists into committing excesses. And there were also "foreign plots," schemes envisaged by Pitt and Wickham, all of them, it might be added, singularly inept. But that did not prevent the revolutionary from believing in them as one believes in Satan. And as the most incompetent of English military chieftains committed one blunder

[2] Mathevon—the name of a character in a popular farce of the day, and during the White Terror used to designate revolutionaries hunted down by the Royalists.

after the other, his sinister prestige loomed larger than ever in the land of the Revolution.

The discussion methods favored by the revolutionaries not only put a premium on credulity, as long as they were dealing with political problems of national interest (they were far more sensible in discussing questions of local and regional interest), they also encouraged the most insipid kind of blind conformity. The discussions were conducted publicly before galleries crowded with spectators who ignored house rules to express their approval or disapproval in the noisiest possible manner. Votes were taken by acclamation or a show of hands. The political ideal of the *sans-culottes* was "the unanimous decision" as often as possible. Failure to achieve unanimity of opinion seemed to them a public confession of disunity, hence a sign of weakness. Speeches and decrees were endorsed unanimously to let the enemy or the neutral observer know that the French people were united behind the Convention and the Committees. This unanimity of agreement was all the easier to achieve in political matters because, by the month of September, the majority of the moderates had been eliminated from most of the societies or accused of "federalism," and the threat of being placed on the list of those slated to be purged acted as a restraining influence on the would-be dissident. Societies issued certificates of good citizenship. Anyone deprived of this political passport was sentenced to civic and economic death. He could not hold a public job or obtain foodstuffs at the official market.

Still, we must include some shadings and nuances in the colors of our picture which may otherwise look too crude and oversimplified. Orthodoxy and conformity were not entirely the result of fear or caution or always prompted by selfish motives, ignorance, or credulity. While unanimity no doubt remained the *summum bonum* in decisions concerning public affairs, the great questions of the day affecting the entire nation which were, for that reason, the primary concern of the Convention, when it came to local affairs and local personalities, there were many genuine and passionate debates. Far from reaching unanimous agreement in these matters, members of the revolutionary societies often devoted entire sessions to the struggles and differences among rival cliques. Local societies reproduced on the local level the same kind of conflicts to be found in Paris on the national level. Local personalities clashed among themselves as, in Paris, *hébertistes* fought *indulgents*, as Jacobins fought Cordeliers. Local disputants were not by definition Jacobins or *hébertistes*, but these great political questions became unintelligible as soon as they were presented by a recognizable face, and, just as in Paris, groups took sides with this or that individual in keeping with their personal animosities as much as their individual temperaments. Obviously, we cannot evaluate with accuracy the role played by private grudges and prejudices in these short-lived allegiances which were made and broken from one day to the next during stormy sessions, notable above all for their displays of personal feelings and passions. But it is clear that the Revolution was a remarkable catalyst for age-old rancors and bitter hatreds which Revolutionary conditions brought out into the open by affording them an opportunity for public expression. Neither orthodoxy nor conformity, ignorance nor indifference, could resist the needling pressure of repressed animosities and jealousies. A certain individual would adopt an anti-religious stand simply because his neighbor and enemy had taken a pro-religious stand. Another would be opposed to the Revolution merely because his personal antagonist was making a career of it. Personal matters and local interests took priority over everything else. It was useless to call the "brothers" back to order and remind them of the original subject, the important subject, under discussion; members inevitably returned to their private feuds and unending complaints about inefficient business production and the scarcity of commodities on the legal markets. Those were the problems that meant the most to them and their families. They were far more interested in such immediate concerns than with idle explanations offered them regarding the ever-recurrent changes on the Parisian political scene.

THE JUSTIFICATION FOR THE TERROR

No opportunity was overlooked to remind the revolutionary that his first duty was to be vigilant. The famous *Instruction*, published in the name of the Temporary Commission of Lyons, was a veritable manual for the perfect revolutionary. It devoted an entire section to the subject of denunciations which it held to be the first civic responsibility of every good sans-culotte. In circulars addressed to the provincial popular societies, the Committee of General Security reminded members that their societies (which were to become intelligence centers for police informants during the Revolution) were duty bound to be constantly alert for counter-revolutionary activities and even unpatriotic remarks or conduct of any kind. The same Committee insisted that Committees of Surveillance should keep a watchful eye on all inns and hotels, paying particular attention to any passing "strangers" or "foreigners." A member of the society of Vaison-la-Romaine brought back from a mission he had fulfilled in Paris a brochure given him by "a Parisian brother." It was entitled *The Sixteen Commandments of the Patriot*. The president of the society read it aloud to an assembly which sat as still and hushed as though listening to words of divine revelation. The *Twelfth Commandment* admonished: "Be not an unjust informer, but maintain constant vigilance over the enemies of liberty. Fear not to denounce conspirators, for failure to do so will make you as guilty as they are . . . ." Young Mazuel, a former silk weaver of La Croix Rousse and a squadron leader of the Revolutionary Army, was to be accused of not having denounced certain Royalist remarks uttered in his presence, according to several witnesses, by a colonel of the Hussars. Mazuel's dereliction was an instance of "guilt by silence," which could only be regarded as a form of complicity.

There was, moreover, no need to remind the revolutionaries so often of their obligations and responsibilities as vigilant and militant patriots. If members of surveillance committees were so very meticulous about inspecting passports in all centers of travel, even to the point of blocking traffic, delaying government mails, and greatly inconveniencing representatives on official business, they were just as conscientious about making denunciations to the police. Also they were inclined to show far less leniency toward anyone suspected of hoarding or committing economic crimes than toward anyone merely making unpatriotic remarks, for economic problems touched them personally. Books of "denunciations" kept by most of the urban popular societies, are full of charges leveled against wine merchants alleged to have sold their glasses or bottles at prices above the legal maximum, or against farmers reported to have fed their pigs with wheat. Urban revolutionaries, motivated no doubt by traditional popular beliefs, revealed a veritable obsession with *caches*. They were convinced that hidden treasures and hidden *émigrés* were all around them—in open fields, in caves, in walls of adjoining properties, behind fireplaces, in vegetable gardens and orchards. No sooner had they arrived in some unfamiliar locality than they began digging, digging everywhere in spite of the protests of property owners and tenants, so certain were they of finding a *magot* (a hoard of money), or some refractory priest, or a concealed supply of grain. In an era when farmers often buried their coin, the searchers occasionally uncovered something, but for the most part they succeeded only in laying bare the ruins of ancient canal works or fortifications built during the Middle Ages or the troubled period of the religious wars. A belief in hidden treasure was obviously inherited from popular legends along with the notion of artificially planned scarcities, "famine agreements," and prison conspiracies.

Of course unpatriotic opinions were also denounced. The revolutionary élite, members of revolutionary armies, and especially committees of exception, were always vigilant for such unguarded remarks, especially when they were "in foreign territory," that is to say, a long way from Paris, in regions supposed to be unfavorably disposed toward the Revolution. In Lyons in particular they displayed the most obdurate attitude of suspicion and distrust to the point where they seemed to regard every man and woman in Lyons as a sworn enemy of the Revolution.

But if Parisians, Nivernais, and people of the Allier, carrying out repressive measures in Lyons, were quick to report to committees of exception the "dangerous remarks" uttered in public by the inhabitants of France's second city, the really dangerous denunciator was not the *révolutionnaire* on a mission far from home. Rather it was a person's own neighbor, someone who knew a lot, whose allegations could prove fatal. He was also the most assiduous informer. In Lyons the "books of denunciations," kept by the Committees, teemed with so many secret denunciations of one citizen of Lyons against another that the informers must have been well known by those they informed on. And indeed they were to be revealed and identified as such during the assassinations and violence of the year III. And it was the same story elsewhere. One had to fear his own neighbor far more than the gullible Parisian who went about uncritically gathering every bit of malicious gossip and idle chatter to be heard in the shops and cafés and who, more often than not, was merely an unconscious instrument of the pent-up irritations of disgruntled innkeepers and wine merchants. What an open invitation for gossip and calumny! What a golden opportunity for giving vent to ancient grudges and prejudices was offered by a régime of terror, whether that terror was revolutionary or royalist, blue or white! The professional informer, the slanderer, the writer of anonymous letters, was devoid of political scruples. He simply made up for lost time, for years of silence, by denouncing one after the other: federalists, *hébertistes*, *dantonistes*, partisans of the agrarian law, foreign agents, fanatics, atheists, Jews, Robespierristes, *les buveurs de sang* (the blood-drinkers), the septembriseurs (those responsible for the September Massacres of 1792), and, beginning with *Vendémiaire*, year IV, the "enemy" was once again "the Royalists." Every revolutionary régime, like every government in time of war or of counter-revolution, attaches great importance to secret intelligence and reports by informants. When we are told that during the Terror the *concierge* and the woman janitor ruled like queens, the remark is not to be taken as an expression of contempt for the revolutionary regime. We need only to note the position these women occupied in the incredible testimony given at the trial of the *hébertistes*, as well as all the other great political trials that took place during the Terror. The golden age of calumny was to flourish *after* Thermidor in the year III during the ensuing search for the Terrorists. "Why were there so many prisoners?" a woman of Toulon inquired at the close of this year of sad renown (and Toulon was, of all cities, the one in which skilled practitioners in the art of slander had given stunning evidence of their virtuosity). Why were there so many prisoners? It was because of the ease and impunity with which denunciators operated. Why did the Revolution claim so many victims? For the very same reason. And why were there so many secret denunciations? Because the informer risked nothing and was applauded at the time by those incapable of knowing whether the informer was motivated by a concern for public interest or by personal animosity. The secret informer is not a creation of revolutionary regimes. He exists, alas, at all times and in all places. But in times of national trouble he finds unexpected and unusual opportunities to display his talents. We must not confuse the denunciator with the revolutionary. The latter made denunciations on occasion, but the virtuosos of the profession were those anonymous individuals who wrote letters indiscriminately to all the authorities, one after the other.

As for the *révolutionnaire*, he was not a malicious person, still less a professional in the art of denouncing others or in writing anonymous letters. If he did occasionally make secret denunciations, it was primarily because of his political naïveté (a fact we have alluded to more than once), because of his readiness to believe in plots and perils of every conceivable nature. Enemies of the régime, it should be noted, made it their practice to keep him convinced that his life was in constant danger from "the sword of the assassin." As a matter of fact, the government's adversaries were incredibly indiscreet, and their indiscretion was not due entirely to their fondness of alcoholic beverages. The evidence is clear and unmistakable. In spite of the Terror, in spite of the guillotine, so prominently displayed in the busiest public squares, in spite of the secret informers who might be anywhere, especially in the cafés and crowded public places, Frenchmen who disliked the revolutionary régime had no qualms about expressing their dissatisfaction as loudly and publicly as possible, excoriating the Revolution and all its works in the crudest terms of popular speech. They were the *Pères Duchesne* in reverse, as vociferous as street vendors. Even young women of Lyons, who worked as waitresses in cafés patronized by the troops stationed in that recalcitrant city, did not hesitate to defend the events of May 29 in front of the government soldiers, adding that they would have been proud to aid the federalist troops by bringing them food and ammunition, and if the situation arose again, they would once more be at the side of "our brave men of Lyons." Whether common people or members of high society, they were not content to grumble quietly among themselves, and if one judged the situation simply by the comments to be heard, Parisians would have no trouble convincing themselves they were living in a completely royalist country. It was not only in Lyons that people were so unguarded in their remarks. The same propensity to verbalize their feelings was noted among the enemies of the regime and the malcontents of Nantes, Brest, and Rouen, and especially in the country, where farmers were outspoken in declaring what they thought about a Revolution which, to them, meant price controls, requisitions, and the closing down of churches. Verbal counter-revolution marched in the open. Royalism raised its banners publicly, and federalism still sought converts even at the height of the Terror, particularly in places like Lyons where it identified itself with local patriotism.

A denunciator on occasion, and a denunciator in spite of everything, the average revolutionary approved the great repressive measures which were taken and which, moreover, he had insistently called for in the meetings of the popular assemblies during the autumn of 1793. At least in his public utterances and collective decisions, he dealt more harshly with internal enemies than did the government itself from which the revolutionary demanded above all a legalization of the Terror. The repression carried out in year II was supposed to follow the rules of "revolutionary legality," while the events of year III were largely uncontrolled violence, outright murder, banishing or doing away with the individual, and inflicting vengeance out of class hatred, even when the decisions were handed down by the criminal tribunals. The revolutionary of 1793 wanted to punish internal enemies of the régime according to summary rules of justice, a justice to be administered, of course, by the sans-culottes, hence a political justice, but a form of justice, notwithstanding, that permitted some rights for the defendant. The year III was a return to September 1792, but with this difference—it was the terrorists this time who were its victims. Even in the tribunals it was a question of class justice, justice of a social nature. In 1795, in the south of France, people claimed to recognize the *"buveurs de sang"* (the blood drinkers) by the clothes they wore. They were dressed as artisans and workers. The repressive justice of the year III assumed a character of class distinction scarcely known during the revolutionary repression a year earlier. A goldsmith from Salon was to be accused in the year III of having "invoked Death upon the heads of those wearing wigs and cuffs," which is also a way of imposing a justice based on class. But make no mistake; it was mostly idle talk. People blustered about certain sartorial frivolities, but the bewigged members of society did not resolve for that reason to outlaw the sans-culottes.

These *buveurs de sang*, these *mathevons*, were they really so ferocious? There is no question about the ferocity of their language. Let us listen, for example, to what they were saying and writing about Lyons and its citizens. A former *curé* (parish priest) of Jaligny in Allier by the name of Marcillat, who was a member of the temporary commission, wrote to his colleagues on the committee of Moulins: ". . . Our commission has sworn to regenerate the public spirit. I am in error, my comrades. There is no public spirit. It is lost. Ville-affranchie [Lyons] is composed of aristocrats and egotists. As for the former, we will send them to the guillotine. The latter will pay for their follies and be forced to recognize the poor and unfortunate as their equals." Let us note, in passing, this didactic side of the repression, which was also known at the time as a "regeneration." "There must be blood shed," the former priest added, "in order to cement the Republic and make it the acknowledged government in the city where we live." And he ended his letter with this unexpected comment: "The Lyonnese are fools." A member of the society of Valence even proposed to drive out all the federalists from Commune-affranchie [Lyons] and from the city without a name [Marseilles], that is to say, virtually the entire population, and replace them with sans-culottes who would be given the homes vacated by the federalists. This proposal was frequently put in writing by Parisian revolutionaries when referring to Lyons, a city whose inhabitants were accused of being both counter-revolutionary and "crassly mercantile." In public, and, what is more important, in private, they approved, like Marcillat, a rigorous repression which fell, with little regard for social status, on humble silk workers and noblemen or wealthy members of the bourgeoisie alike. A dealer in chessboards in the Rue Saint-Denis, a staunch Republican who was to be banished in the aftermath of the Grenelle affair and banished again in the year IX, wrote to his section: "In my previous letter I told you that the guillotine was doing a daily job with several *dozen* rebels and that the rifle was accounting for an equal number each day. Today I can tell you that from now on several *hundred* will face the firing squad every day. In this manner we will soon be rid of those scoundrels who dare to defy the Republic even when put to torture . . . ." Officers coming from Montpellier, who were also garrisoned in Lyons at that time, expressed the same kind of unqualified approval in letters addressed to personal friends—hence all the more reason for believing in their sincerity: "Every day," one of the soldiers wrote, "Saint-Guillotine purges the land of liberty of all the federalists in the Department of Rhône and Loire. It is always the same business, and *ça ira*, it will continue." "Everything is going fine here. All the rebels are being shot or guillotined," another officer from Montpellier wrote to a compatriot in an almost blithe and light-hearted manner.

And yet these men were not professional executioners, nor were they bloodthirsty by nature. But they felt no pity for the people of Lyons. The Lyonnese were federalists who threatened the indivisibility of the Republic, an unpardonable crime which deserved the supreme punishment. Their hatred for the Lyonnese population was already strongly conditioned by the Parisian press which formed a unanimous chorus demanding summary vengeance on the heads of all federalists. Their animosity was doubtless reinforced on the spot by the state of isolation imposed on them by a silent and hostile citizenry. To be stationed in Lyons in the year II was by no means a pleasant assignment, and the military complained bitterly about the cold and unfriendly inhabitants. The Lyonnese disliked them, those Parisians, Nivernese, and people of the Allier. And yet these citizens, so disliked by the Lyonnese, were the good sans-culottes, the true revolutionaries. Consequently, it was just one more proof of indifference to republicanism among "the stupid Lyonnese." A few soldiers, it is true, were moved by pity at the sight of the great poverty and wretchedness among ordinary people, and there was even a revolutionary officer who, talking to women of the working class, dared to denounce the repression by declaring "no group in a Republic should ever be singled out for the violent measures of proscription." But these were isolated instances. The majority did not mix with a population they distrusted (soldiers were sometimes fished out of the Rhône), and the local imitators of *Père Duchesne*, Dorfeuille and Millet, made it their business to keep the occupying forces in a feverish state of repressive ardor by constantly trumpeting their strident blasts calling for revolutionary retribution.

It is of course easy to condemn, from the beginning, the Lyonnese repression not only as an atrocious crime, but as a supremely unwise political measure which succeeded only in antagonizing and unifying the entire population of Lyons in its opposition to a Republic which, to them, was symbolized by the guillotine and the firing squad—a fact Couthon understood quite well. But we must also remember the conditions that existed in the year II and not lose sight of the fact that the great federalist insurrections during the summer had almost plunged the Republic into a dreadful civil war. Not too much effort was made to understand the causes of these revolts, but memories were vivid of the critical situation they had precipitated in June and July of 1793. That is why the revolutionary, whether he was a small shopkeeper, a military man, a former priest, a doctor, or a laborer, approved the measures of repression directed against Lyons, Marseilles, the Vendée, or Toulon. He approved the measures taken against recalcitrant priests and more generally against those accused of being "fanatics," for the *révolutionnaire* could not forgive the latter for having created "little Vendées" in various parts of the country. In addition, the military, who had contributed everywhere to the development of a specifically revolutionary mentality, was especially antagonistic to rural Catholic populations in which it saw potential allies of the *chouans* [insurgent Breton Royalists] and other avowed enemies of the régime. In its hatred of the "fanatic," there was also a more personal element. Many of the military had had experience with atrocities committed against Republicans by the peasants, both men and women, in the Vendée.

But the revolutionary demanded even stronger measures against the hoarder, the economic offender, the rebellious farmer, and the *"égoïste,"* the selfish individual, by seeking to justify the repression in terms of economic necessity. If Parisians and the little people of Moulins and Nevers approved wholeheartedly the violent repression in Lyons, it was above all because they regarded Lyons as "a great mercantile capital" where even the workers were unworthy of freedom. For comparable reasons Hébert, and certain section leaders in Paris, demanded that the instrument of terror and committees of popular justice should be sent to that other business capital, Rouen. The revolutionaries took an equally dim view of its inhabitants. There was even a desire to extend repressive operations throughout the rural areas to terrorize the farmers, but this time government policy fell short of the measures advocated by the city-dwelling *sans-culottes*.

This general approval of repression and the Terror was the result of a common attitude among very diverse elements in French society. With respect to the violent measures applied to Lyons and Marseilles, there was a mixture of economic prejudices on the part of small shopkeepers and little businessmen toward big businessmen, ship owners, and large industrial enterprises, as well as a condemnation of "special groups" who interposed themselves between the ordinary citizen and the Sovereign People and who had dared to raise a sinister and sacrilegious hand against the Convention. And there was, of course, the desire to conform to popular attitudes, and a vivid recollection of the dangerous threats the federalist crises had posed for the Republic. The press, moreover, was resorting to every journalistic technique to keep public opinion in a state of near-hysteria, so favorable to the enactment of repressive measures. The revolutionaries themselves, living like soldiers, like occupying troops, and like strangers in the midst of hostile populations, were easily persuaded that only terror and violence could save them from retaliatory acts by their enemies. They *had* to strike first. Otherwise, *they* would be struck by "the sword of the assassin." Such, in short, was the role played by fear and credulity, generously nourished by the incredible verbal imprudence of enemies of the regime who did not hesitate to shout in the faces of Parisians their hatred of the Republic and of the French capital.

A taste for blood or a desire for revenge do not seem to have been important considerations, although it is very difficult to separate what may have been a purely political and collective attitude from evidence suggesting a personal predilection for violence and brutality. In the affair of the *noyades* [collective execution by drowning carried out by Carrier at Nantes in 1793], certain members of the Marat Company, and of the revolutionary committee of Nantes, displayed extreme cruelty in harassing prisoners, in pursuing the wives of the *chouans*, striking them with the butts of their rifles, pulling young women by the hair, and roughing up everyone in general, not to mention their indiscriminate use of abusive language. Yet according to witnesses, inebriation accounted for this especially odious instance of brutality, as it had played a part in stimulating the murderers at the *Carmes* prison in Septembr 1792. It is true that there was a witness at Carrier's trial, a 20-year-old youth, who not only admitted taking part in the *noyades*, but who added that he had no regrets, and that if he had it to do over, he would gladly carry out again the execution of such violent measures. But he was a young soldier from the first battalion of Nantes who had seen some of his own comrades, who had fallen into the hands of the *chouans*, tortured by the wives and daughters of Breton peasants in the country around Nantes, and who only escaped being knifed and tortured himself because of a wound he had received that was more ghastly in appearance than serious in nature.

At the time of the trial, most of the witnesses became ill when they recalled the scenes of horror that had taken place in the boats when the trap doors, installed in the holds, were opened. If men of the eighteenth century were rather accustomed to brutality, they had not become sadists. The revolutionary regime undoubtedly permitted some of the latter to exercise their deplorable talents under particularly favorable conditions, and everyone has heard of Jourdan [Coupe-Tête] and other bloody executioners of his species, but they were, we may be sure, exceptional monsters. Revolutionaries were often a violent lot, especially in their language, excitable and hot-headed, and when under the influence of drink, they sometimes took on a frightening appearance and committed repulsive acts worthy of *Père Duchesne*. Certain civil commissioners were highly emotional individuals, capable of violent outbursts, whose tempestuous natures were particularly in evidence during the years of proscription following Thermidor. No one would dare to maintain that a Collot-d'Herbois and a Javogues were normal, rational individuals, and they had a number of emulators. But even this state of violence was to be temporary and attributable to the recent dangers provoked by the federalist crisis. The Revolution had its professional hangmen, its murderers, and its sadists, and in the cities of southern France, certain assassins of the years II and III were to be found later on among the perpetrators of bloody deeds in 1814 and 1815. But the average revolutionary was neither brutal nor sadistic.

Finally, there was the educational objective. A program of "regeneration" was in order and repression was an integral part of the overall program in civic education. A revolutionary from Yonne insisted on the need "to bring together all children, age seven to ten, to witness all acts of punishment, the public executions." Now this *Emile* of the repression was not a *"buveur de sang,"* a bloodthirsty fanatic, no more than the revolutionaries of the year II, despite the efforts of Thermidorean propaganda to identify them with the murderers. On this score it was more fitting to pin the "bloodthirsty" label on certain youths of the year III who went about attacking isolated terrorists, men of humble appearance and modest attire, who did not even have time to invoke fear. It would be just as inaccurate to try to identify the revolutionary with the habitual murderer as to equate him with the professional denunciator. No doubt, under certain circumstances, he could on occasion be both the one and the other, but the revolutionaries we are familiar with—shopkeepers, small businessmen, doctors, ex-priests, and lawyers—in no way resembled those "sanguinary brutes" of Thermidorian and royalist imaginations.

It would be equally wrong, it seems, to try to look for the origins of the Terror and the approval with which the revolutionaries accepted its extreme measures, in certain obscure psychological motives peculiar to the traditional popular mind, the mind, for instance, in which a fear of the plague can create an atmosphere of panic and mutual alarm among bourgeois and artisans. The revolutionary of the year II had no need to fall back on ancient memories in order to demand the pitiless elimination of all who, at that moment, threatened the existence and survival of the Republic. It was not a question of class proscription or even of a tradition of violence. The danger was there. It was apparent. And once it had passed, there was the need to prevent its recurrence by "striking a great blow." Indeed, all of that seemed quite unreal to the revolutionaries themselves when, from the year III on, they had occasion to recall the crisis. Already the political and social climate had changed, and the period of emergency had passed. The justification for the Terror lay in certain circumstantial facts. It did not reflect a permanent state of mind or a natural disposition to violence. It was as impermanent and evanescent as the revolutionary man himself.

FRANCE AND THE WORLD

Surrounded by inaccessible hills and mountains, and situated in the most temperate of climates, producing an abundance of everything needed to sustain life, France can and must remain isolated, forever separated from all enslaved and corrupted nations. But at the same time, all her parts must be unified and so constitute an impenetrable whole. The French people must cultivate the soil and cultivate the social virtues. Liberty is irrevocably predicated on these four conditions. . . .

It was a program in four stages that represented the views of the future as envisaged by a rural Society in the Basque country, but it was a program to which every Parisian revolutionary could readily subscribe by adding to the virtues of farming those of small business. The entire philosophy of the *sans-culottes* was, in fact, epitomized in this abbreviated view of France and the world in general. The first task was to isolate France, the land of the Revolution, from any contamination by enslaved nations. Certain zealots, like Hébert, were to go so far as to maintain the necessity of avoiding any foreign contacts whatever, even with neutrals who are either "crudely mercantile," or *républiques d'argent* (money-minded republics), "dedicated to trafficking in public goods," or else "fanaticized" lands. It was not an entirely baseless charge that the Committees and Fouquier-Tinville brought against the newspaper, *Père Duchesne*, and its disciples, accusing them of having compromised French supplies of foreign grains by inveighing against the merchants of Genoa, Denmark, and Hamburg, and by alienating neutral sympathizers with a policy directed against the Roman Catholic Church. The men in government were not to go quite that far, but most revolutionaries would probably have preferred to keep all contacts with the outside world at a bare minimum.

France was to be isolated from a world as yet unworthy of liberty and which must therefore be placed under quarantine. So much for the world outside. Within the country, within France, there were to be no intermediary groups, no particularisms, no regionalisms, but only an enforced centralization in all domains in the name of the indivisibility of the Republic and under the aegis of Paris, "the cradle of liberty," "the capital of the Revolution." Whence there was to be a gradual elimination of all patois and dialects, vestigial remains of federalism and vehicles for Catholicism, ignorance, and superstition. Everywhere it was to be the primacy of the French language, *la langue de la liberté*, the only language worthy of free men and republicans.

This insistence upon unity was due in large measure no doubt to the fact that the most active revolutionaries in the provincial Societies, and precisely those who had other means than mere powers of eloquence to insure a respectful hearing, were very often Parisian commissioners who had fanned out over the entire country and especially in the military zones on the frontiers. Now the Parisian artisan or shopkeeper had no trouble visualizing the unity of the Republic with Paris in command. Paris was the city that had "made the Revolution" and to which all France owed an enormous debt of gratitude. If Paris was the capital of the Revolution and of the free world, the people of Paris were the official guardians of its holy shrines. We can understand the attachment of the Parisian revolutionary to a centralized system which, by preventing the recurrence of federalist crises, consecrated the formula: *Paris-capitale-de-la-Révolution.* As for the revolutionaries from other cities, needled and pressured and under constant surveillance by their "Parisian brothers" who meddled in everything, they marched, more or less willingly, in the footsteps of the Parisians. More willingly among the inhabitants of large cities like Toulouse or Lille, who saw in the process of centralization a means of obliging the rural areas to replenish their markets and food supplies; less willingly among people in the small towns and villages, who were afraid of being subjected to the whims of the large population centers.

The revolutionary, as we have seen, believed firmly in the virtues of education, and even repression was thought of as a "regenerative" measure. He therefore counted on the organizing of elementary schools in a manner to insure the rightful pre-eminence of the French language as the language of free men. But until that happy day arrived, the popular societies, doubt-less encouraged in part by the reports of the abbé Grégoire, in addition to the exhortations of their own leaders, converted their societies into schools for the study of civics, to lead the fight against regional languages regarded, with good reason, as strongholds of federalism, local particularism, reaction, ignorance, and superstition. To learn French, and to make the rural populations do the same, was also a way to prove one's revolutionary patriotism and to hasten the people's advance toward freedom. At Roque-laure in Gers, a member of the society

insisted that everyone should speak French, whether he spoke it well or badly, since he had observed that popular assemblies were, strictly speaking, only schools for educating our young people . . . and since daily drills, as well as all other military manuevers, were commanded in French, it was decided that all should speak French, but because everyone might not be able to understand it, citizen Mayor agreed to read publicly all the decrees and edicts of the representatives both in French and in Gascon, so that no one could plead ignorance of the law. . . .

One of the purposes of *La Propagande* (a group of "civic preachers" selected by nearly all the popular societies throughout France to go to Strasbourg to enlighten the city and regenerate public spirit) was to find bilingual professors whose civic virtues were above reproach and who would carry out the mission of teaching Alsatians to speak French. For, they ar-gued, Alsatians will become republicans only when they learn to speak the language of liberty. Candidates for *La Propagande* were therefore required to have some knowledge of German. At the other end of France, authori-ties in the Department of *Pyrénées-Orientales* were to insist on the urgency of organizing elementary schools as the most effective means of winning peasants of Rousillon away from the Catholic religion and from its official protector, His Most Catholic Majesty, Charles IV of Spain. They were convinced that when the day came that men in Alsace, Brittany, the Basque country, and the Catalan provinces could all speak French, the only task remaining would be to "de-fanaticize" the women. This effort to extend the use of French was therefore regarded as part of the campaign to combat Christianity as well as federalism and royalism.

In the same manner it opposed regionalism, revolutionary opinion proscribed "cosmopolitanism" and especially the Anglomania that prevailed in certain affluent segments of French society at the end of the eighteenth century. The revolutionary committee of the Section of the Armed Man in Paris refused a certificate of good citizenship to a certain Revel, a ventriloquist and "magician," pondering "whether a man who claims to have been successively in the employ of Cagliostro, and Rousseau, who betakes himself from country to country, first in Europe and then in the East Indies, should not be regarded as a *Cosmopolite*, which is to say, a man, strictly speaking, without a country, unable to identify himself with any government . . . ." Among the offenses attributed to a well-to-do notary, who had retired in Choisy-le-Roi, was that of having built a *jardin à l'angloise*, an English-style garden, in his park. Likewise, revolutionary committees in the small towns of the Midi refused to make any distinction between those who had emigrated in 1791 or 1792 for political reasons and those who, having gone to Italy to study and visit museums, had remained abroad beyond the legal time limit set by laws determining at what point an individual was to be regarded as an *émigré*. Republicans, they decreed, had no need to go visit foreign museums since there was no shortage of allegorical subjects in a revolutionary France dedicated to all the virtues. The committee of Dax was even to argue that one of its inhabitants, who was an artist and had remained for a long time in Rome, could scarcely be a good citizen since he was clearly more interested in paintings than in questions of public concern. And the society of Auch issued a decree denying the admission of those who had received a higher education on the grounds that such persons could not be regarded as good sans-culottes. The Grand Tour, in short, was good only for members of the Old Regime and in this hostility toward "cosmopolitanism" we can detect overtones of class jealousy, heightened no doubt by the existence of a revolutionary war.

This xenophobia was reserved only for the governments of enslaved nations. For the common people of other lands there were expressions of pity, tinged with condescension, impatience, and distrust. Since France had opened the gates of freedom, other peoples had only to demonstrate their valor by imitating the French and by accepting, for their part, the French lesson in civic responsibility. Until such time, they were hardly worthy of esteem, and French republicans could not be advised or expected to associate with them. When the deputy Chabot announced his marriage to Leopoldine Frey, the daughter of a wealthy Jewish banker in Moravia, hence a subject of the Emperor and a member of that much-detested nation, Austria-Hungary, there were cries of indignation among Parisian *sectionnaires*. Young Leopoldine, a rich foreigner with a large dowry, became a target of criticisms crystallizing all the popular resentment felt toward a person of wealth and a subject of the Hapsburgs. How could such a thing happen! A member of the Convention, a representative of the people, marrying the daughter of a slave! What an example! A true patriot should marry only a good French republican, and only in the event all French republican women were already provided for might a patriot even consider marrying a woman of Genoa, Switzerland, America, Poland, or perhaps Belgium, although the inhabitants of the "Belgian provinces" were viewed with deep suspicion in matters of citizenship, a suspicion nourished in part by the polemics of *Père Duchesne* leveled against those "fanatical" subjects of the Emperor, a people who had already rejected on one occasion the precious gift of freedom. If a free Frenchman were to marry a slave, the results of this unnatural union might well be tainted with moral and political blemishes.

Every revolutionary felt extremely proud of belonging to the nation that had been the first to carry out its revolution, for he scarcely acknowledged any American claim to have preceded him in that course of action. He drew confidence also from the extremely favorable demographic conditions in France, another source of satisfaction and promise for the future. In every document originating in the popular assemblies, there were allusions to this large population which accounted for the wealth of France and betokened a secure future for the Republic. From this demographic concept came a condemnation of any proposals to combine existing farms or shops, to authorize any concentration of wealth or industry, or to place agriculture on a scientific basis that might involve a reduction in cultivation by creating artificial grasslands. In short, it was the entire economic program of the sans-culottes. But the political nationalism was accompanied by very little personal hatred of foreigners, taken individually, in spite of the propaganda war waged by *Père Duchesne* and the government press against the ferocious slaves of tyrants and their unholy alliances, in spite of reports exposing the many crimes of the British people.

On all levels of French society during the last years of the eighteenth century, people had become accustomed to working side by side with foreigners. In almost every urban popular society the membership included Prussians, Englishmen, Genevese, Sardinians, Genoese, and Greeks. In the revolutionary committees of the two sections of the old faubourg Saint-Germain, almost half the members of the Commission were former employees of foreign embassies and literary men from Naples, Turin, and Milan. The mayor of Cahors in the year II was a Swede who could scarcely speak French. Swedish, too, was the *hébertiste* Lindberg, a very active member of Marat's section and a friend of Vincent and Momoro. An outstanding revolutionary figure of the neighboring section, Unity, was the Genevese printer Sandoz. The Commissioner of Subsistence in the commune of Franciade (Saint-Denis) was the Englishman Devonshire, while the most inveterate denouncer of Mme Dubarry, the president of the Committee of Surveillance of Louveciennes, was an American, born in Newcastle, England. We could go on multiplying the examples of foreigners who proliferated in the popular societies of many French cities and who sometimes held confidential positions in the hierarchy of revolutionary authorities. At the same time in the cities of Normandy, weavers, spinners, textile workers from Yorkshire, English manufacturers and mill owners, who made up a number of small colonies in Ingouville and Graville, as well as in Le Havre, Harfleur, Bolbec, and Honfleur, worked, for the most part, in complete tranquility during the Reign of Terror. Local authorities protected them by invoking the laws which excluded from internment those foreigners who were "artists" and whose work was profitable to the Republic. Sometimes they even violated the law to insure the freedom of foreigners who were well thought of by the inhabitants of localities in Haute-Normandie. In Le Havre the society dutifully read the reports on the *Crimes of the English Government*. But we are tempted to see in such actions more evidence of conformity than conviction. The fact remains, Englishmen in the district of Montvilliers were well treated throughout the Terror.

It was the same with prisoners of war, who were well treated everywhere and everywhere accepted almost as friends, always as human beings. In most places within the interior of the country, they were permitted to walk about freely in the cities to which they were assigned. Consequently, they could be seen frequenting the cafés where they often created a scandal or an uproar or else they were proving to the women of the French Republic that even the subjects of despots, slaves though they were, were nevertheless men in all other respects. The Committee of Surveillance in Moulins granted an indemnity and expressed its thanks to a group of Prussian prisoners for having played in an orchestra which performed at patriotic dances. On the other hand, authorities in Montpellier were worried about the influence of Spanish prisoners, quite numerous in the city, who were reported to have imbued the women of Montpellier with an *esprit fanatique*, by denouncing the *décadi* and the closing of the churches, and by acting as agents of the clergy. Certain women in Montpellier were believed to have been led astray by these Spaniards. The very nature of these anxieties is proof of the large measure of freedom granted to foreign prisoners and of the liberal attitudes of French authorities and the French population with respect to military enemies of their country. A member of the surveillance committee of Corbigny in Nièvre declared

that he had learned with astonishment that Prussian prisoners were giving nightly performances of plays in that city at the home of the aforementioned Bierge and particularly on evenings regularly scheduled for meetings of the *société populaire* . . . with the result that these theatrical performances were drawing citizens away from going to the polls to vote and that he felt he was compelled to remind his fellow citizens that the Prussians referred to are our enemies . . . .

But in spite of such warnings, in spite of a momentary reaction of panic in the early spring (Ventôse-Germinal) of the year II on the outskirts of Paris, which was provoked by the transfer of a large contingent of Austrian prisoners, easily recognized by their white uniforms—a movement that seemed to the inhabitants to presage some *coup* against the capital, and despite the ineradicable belief in "foreign conspiracies," only in rare instances was there any interference with the freedom of movement accorded foreign military personnel, some of whom even ventured into rural areas and farm houses in search of food.

This liberalism, a holdover from eighteenth-century "civility," yet so unexpected in time of revolution, and in such marked contrast to the attitude of English authorities and English citizens toward unfortunate French sailors, who were treated abominably—this liberalism of the French was attributed to an eagerness to win over to the armies of the Republic foreigners who had deserted the armies of the enemy. A Hungarian hussar addressed the committee of Versailles in a Latin of sorts: *Natus bonus respublicanus,* he declared. He wanted to leave the Imperial Army, in which the ordinary soldier could be struck twenty, thirty, or fifty blows at the slightest provocation, to join the cavalry of the revolutionary army in the cause of liberty. There was nothing unusual in his request, and this hussar, named Georgius Kenessey, had many imitators among Spaniards, Prussians (including the famous Laukhard), and, above all, the Belgians. It is obviously impossible to estimate the numerical importance of these enlistments by foreign deserters, but it is clear that the republican armies, with their very relaxed discipline, exerted a strong appeal upon Prussian and Austrian soldiers. Moreover, such enlistments represented a fine propaganda victory for revolutionary France even if the military value of such undisciplined deserters as pastor Laukhard left much to be desired. As a matter of fact, it was finally found necessary to disband the *Légion germanique,* while the Belgian units provoked innumerable complaints from residents in the localities where they were stationed, because of their lack of discipline and their frequent state of inebriation.

Revolutionary confidence in the conversion of enslaved peoples often took the form of a naïve readiness to believe the most fantastic reports about imminent popular uprisings against the crowned tyrants of Madrid, London, and Saint Petersburg. Almost every month, in every Society, they announced the fall of William Pitt, nay, even the fall of *George Dandin,*[3]

[3] George Dandin is here meant to refer to George III of England. In reality, George Dandin is the title character of a play by Molière. He married a woman above his station and was forever after regretting it. His oft-repeated self-recrimination is "Tu l'as voulu, George Dandin, tu l'as voulu!" (You asked for it, George Dandin, you asked for it!) In applying this name to the King of England, the revolutionaries no doubt meant that he would come to regret his entrance into the war against the French Republic.

and the establishment of a new ministry instructed to negotiate a peace treaty with France. And they hastened to congratulate the compatriots of Algernon Sidney for having emulated the French example by recovering their freedom. Great hopes were aroused over the insurrection in Warsaw. In the southwest of France the fall of Charles IV was expected momentarily. It was another example of that popular credulity so invaluable to the committees in their difficult task of guiding France in time of war. It was further evidence also of an unshakable confidence in the destiny of the Revolution. Moreover, Englishmen and other foreigners living in France were only too glad to keep the *sociétaires* believing these rather naïve illusions. But this credulity proved to be a double-edged sword. When, following the great victories of the summer of 1794, French frontiers were no longer menaced and the long-anticipated insurrections did not occur, a segment of French revolutionary opinion lost interest in the war and in all the arduous efforts it demanded. The evidence was inescapable. No general uprisings could be expected in the near future, and a disenchantment set in which was to contribute greatly to a pervasive feeling of lassitude and indifference.

The public and private attitude of French revolutionaires toward foreigners varied from one region to another, depending on local interests. Englishmen, as we have noted, were well regarded in the Pays de Caux and in Honfleur, but less so in Rouen. Yet it was in Rouen at the time of the popular insurrection in Germinal, year III, that working-class women invaded the district seat of government, demanding bread, and shouting: *Long live peace! The English offer us a helping hand. We shall have food!* At Lorient it was quite another story. The Society of Lorient nourished great hopes of driving the English out of India by means of republican propaganda alone: "Not in the English manner, with sabres and cannons, will we subjugate the Indians, a generous, gentle, and philanthropic people. Not at all. We shall say to them quite simply: *Let us be friends. You produce beautiful cloth for us; here is what we give you in exchange.*" The citizens of Lorient were not content with fine words. A *sociétaire*, back from Martinique, "outlined great objectives to be accomplished on the South American continent whose enslaved peoples are but waiting for the moment to break free of their shackles. He envisaged great commercial possibilities for the Republic." However revolutionary they might be, the sans-culottes never lost sight of the private interests of their cities, and popular societies were as much *Syndicats d'Initiative* (Chambers of Commerce) as they were schools for political studies. In Givet, the Thermidorian *sociétaires* (who, it is true, had emerged from a very different social level than the sans-culottes) drew up ambitious plans for the eventual reopening of Belgian markets following Fleurus [the battle in which Jourdan defeated the Austrians, 1794]. In the Midi, the ever-greater hold on coastwise shipping by the Genoese, a consequence of the English blockade, and the demands of Italian shippers who knew how to exploit the dependency of the coastal cities, and the arrivals of Italian or Adriatic grain shipments, aroused strong resentment among the *sociétaires* of Nice and Monaco against "those leeches," "those monopolists," whom they accused of taking advantage of the needs of the Mediterranean departments to indulge in highly profitable grain speculations. In the Alpine departments, the sans-culottes of Savoy did not fail to complain about Swiss selfishness, and local committees denounced in particular the cantonal authorities of Berne, well known for their hostility to the principles of the Revolution. But these were exceptional cases reflecting old local prejudices and ancient rivalries among neighbors more than any general attitude with respect to foreigners.

The city-dwelling sans-culottes were accustomed to the presence of foreign workers, so numerous in the larger cities of France. But what accounted as much for this tolerance and understanding of strangers was the extreme mobility of the French population itself, notably, the revolutionary cadres. The latter included a substantial number of servants, artisans, businessmen, dancing teachers, and French goldsmiths and jewelers, who had returned from London, Madrid, Berlin, St. Petersburg, and especially Cadiz after the war. As the first victims of their revolutionary principles, they were likewise often the first to find employment under the new revolutionary administration. They brought to their new positions a strong hatred of tyrants who had caused them so much suffering and hardship by depriving them of their sometimes flourishing businesses abroad. But they also brought with them a deep knowledge of foreigners and a spirit which, if not cosmopolitan (which would have been frowned on) was at least comprehensive in its attitudes and awareness of problems confronting foreigners. French refugees, victims of their republicanism, were to be found in choice posts within the new para-revolutionary government agencies, such as the Parisian Revolutionary Army and the Temporary Commission for Commune-affranchie.

The revolutionary sans-culotte thus brought to his concept of France, and of the world in general, the prejudices of the city artisan, the small tradesman. In this revolutionary France they would cultivate the soil and the social virtues, and the economy would be based on small-property holdings, on little independent farms and shops. The indivisibility of this Republic of virtues was to be insured by a relentless war on surviving regionalisms and on dialects and patois, the last strongholds of "superstition" and federalism.

While awaiting the arrival of the universal reign of liberty and freedom, it was deemed necessary to preserve France from any contact with subjugated peoples by isolating her from the rest of the world even at the cost of curtailing trade with neutral nations, for the logical conclusion of the system preached by Hébert in his newspaper would have been to cut France off completely from the outside world. It was precisely the threat of such total isolation that prompted members of the Committee of Public Safety to accuse *Père Duchesne* [Hébert's newspaper] of playing into the hands of the counter-revolution by embroiling France with Switzerland

and the Republic of Genoa, and by making the eventual task of French occupying forces in the Belgian provinces infinitely more difficult.

As for the private attitude of the revolutionaries, a certain popular xenophobia found additional support in the war and in the revolutionary pride of the average Frenchman, convinced he had freed himself from the chains of repression. A distrust of foreigners was heightened further by the atrocities Englishmen committed in Toulon. But this xenophobia did not carry over where individual foreigners were concerned. In spite of a few exceptional decrees, ordering that every British prisoner of war be put to death, such prisoners were, in truth, quite well treated. As for the rest, the private attitudes of the sans-culottes varied on this subject in accordance with local considerations from one region to the next, and on other problems of the day such as the campaign against Christianity. Once again we must emphasize the great diversity of attitudes and opinions which make it so difficult to offer any hasty generalization on the popular mentality and daily life during the Terror. In all likelihood the revolutionaries, who were more representative of the shopkeeper than the businessman, were much less interested in international trade than those who replaced them in the Thermidorian administrations. But the examples of Lorient and the cities in the south of France suggest that they were not wholly indifferent to the subject.

And finally, there does not appear to have been any spontaneous or virulent Anglophobia among Frenchmen generally, such as would correspond to the deeply rooted Francophobia of the people of London. Among the common people, the Piedmontese seem to have been the most detested and disdained, with the Austrians next in line as objects of scorn. The Anglophobia of the year II seems rather to have been an artificial product of Robespierrist orthodoxy, one more way in which to prove one's revolutionary conformity. No doubt the cascade of petitions addressed to the Convention after the assassination attempts on the lives of Collot d'Herbois and Robespierre, will be cited as evidence of a popular and spontaneous Anglophobia. These petitions, demanding the most dire punishment for the government and people of Britain, prepared the way for promulgating the law of 22 Prairial. Yet it would be difficult to prove that petitions, dating from the period of Robsepierre's dictatorship, could represent anything other than a reflection of official government propaganda. The sameness of these petitions, a uniformity even in the choice of language used to denounce the English people, indicates a common origin other than popular spontaneity. It was a question of a "command performance" in Anglophobia, inspired by a *chef d'orchestre* whose presence, while not visible, was nonetheless real. What seems more indicative of popular feeling than these petitions was the testimony of local authorities, in Normandy and elsewhere, in favor of individual British subjects.

The war began in a burst of popular enthusiasm. This revolutionary nationalism lasted until the period of the great victories in the summer of

1794. But already the "maximums," the requisitions, and the needs of recruitment had begun to dull the keen edge of popular fervor. Its reverse side was reflected in the steady stream of desertions that never ceased to plague the local authorities. During the final months of Robespierre's regime, collective enthusiasm itself—with all the attempts made by the different popular societies to raise funds to build ships called *vengeurs* (avengers)—reflected orders from above, just as everything else did that concerned the societies at that time. In spite of an unmistakable wave of enthusiasm during the great crisis of 1793, revolutionary nationalism could hardly resist the lassitude and discontent provoked by a war economy, the weight of which fell most heavily on the small consumer and the wage earner, on the workers, in short, rather than on those who produced or controlled commodities. If popular opinion turned more and more away from the revolutionary government, it was because the burdens of war generated increasingly stronger desires for peace and compromise among popular elements. The strident tone of official propaganda, in describing the crimes of Pitt and the English government, was in itself a confession of weakness. If popular credulity had no trouble in placing the blame on Pitt for all the misfortunes besetting France in the year II, and especially the food crisis, this ingenuous explanation did not, by the same token, bring about complete popular adherence to a propaganda of war. Rather do we find a personal attitude of moderation on the part of the revolutionaries toward the external enemies of their country, an attitude all the more striking in contrast not only with the tone of official propaganda—which preached murder and revenge—but also with the almost universal attitude of agreement, among rank and file revolutionaries, with the stringent measures directed against internal enemies —"federalists," "fanatics," and others. We must distinguish here between the popular readiness to accept any and all political explanations for the country's economic conditions—foreign plots, famine pacts, and so on—and that inherent kindness, tolerance, and generosity toward foreigners which many travelers have indicated as characteristic of the French people even at the height of a revolutionary crisis. It was the hallmark, no doubt, of a mature and highly developed people, a people conscious of its strength and confident of its future, thanks to an awareness of the demographic situation especially favorable in France during the last quarter of the eighteenth century.

THE DISAPPEARANCE OF THE REVOLUTIONARY MAN

Let us return now to our point of departure. Our "revolutionary man," if he existed at all, finds his existence only in an historical documentation belonging to the revolutionary period, a documentation revealing at least the public attitudes of an entire social group, a slice of life on the popular level in towns and villages, one that in more normal times remains completely obscured. It is difficult for us to make a sharp distinction between the public person and the private individual in view of the fact that we are acquainted with him only at this particular moment in history, a period of a year or a year-and-a-half, which, in private life as in the life of France, was quite definitely an exceptional moment.

But let us try, notwithstanding, to bring our picture into focus. We are dealing above all, it seems, with a question of temperament, and it appears that the study of social structures by itself will not provide the basis for a satisfactory answer, for the revolutionary man seldom acted in terms of social struggles except to the extent that he represented the small-property owner, the small tradesman, or the operator of a small business. His predominant traits were an undeniable political and physical courage, strongly held convictions, also, no doubt, a certain pleasure in wielding power, and finally, an unmistakable penchant for pomp and oratory. Collective life in the year II, a fact we must not forget, was to offer many of these tradesmen the opportunity to play the rôle of important persons, "politicians," Roman Senators, and to become involved in the affairs of their neighbors. And the rewards? Well, they were not to be scoffed at. There was, first of all, the presidential chair or else, less spectacular but far more influential, a position in the executive body of a popular society. A conspicuous seat in one of these assemblies could sometimes provide excellent free advertising for one's business. We recall, for example, a *sociétaire* in Vaison, a painter by trade, who, when asked to paint the tree of liberty in three colors, refused the honor (there was no idea of paying him for the painting). But when the society then addressed itself to another painter in Vaison, the former had second thoughts on the matter and announced he was flattered by the confidence placed in him by the popular society. These positions and honors were the object of bitter personal struggles and rivalries which often had little to do with republican propriety but which proved they were well worth the effort and skill expended in acquiring them. The revolutionary was all the more fond of honors, sashes, and gold braid as they were to compensate him for his years of obscurity and unimportance.

But in the last analysis, despite the appeal of material motives, the revolutionary temperament was compounded primarily of faith, enthusiasm, and generous impulses. The poet Coleridge was not the only one to recall the enthusiams of his youth and to say how good it was to be alive in those days. How many men, reaching maturity in professions as obscure as they were honorable, would also remember, in their old age, *Le Grand Soleil de 93* (The radiant days of 1793)! For the men of the revolution were, for the most part, young or in the prime of life, and their enthusiasm was no doubt part of the exuberance of youth.

We must emphasize as well the role the war played in giving birth to a certain mentality of struggle and crisis. The revolutionaires always imagined themselves as men forever standing in the breach. Nor was it always purely imaginary. Those in Nantes knew they were surrounded by almost universal hatred. Those in Lyons, still more isolated, lived with the picture of Châlier's head constantly before their eyes, and most of the *"mathe-*

vons" were to perish in the terrible massacres of the year III. Like the chiefs of the great committees, they were firmly convinced that Pitt had written their names on the lists of those to be murdered. In general, it is true, nothing happened to them in the year II, but the Thermidorian proscription because of its desire for revenge was blindly directed toward any and all personnel who had held power a year earlier, and surely contributed greatly to a certain survival of the revolutionary temperament. A society in Vaucluse put this question to candidates in its "weeding out" process: *What have you done for which you would be hanged if the counter-revolution should gain the upper hand?* It was not mere rhetoric. The revolutionaries had to contemplate such a possibility, especially in a region like the former Comtat, where they were but a tiny minority cut off from the population. They were, in every sense of the word, *combattants*.

But to keep alive the spirit of combat, danger must be constantly lurking. Now beginning with Floréal, year II, the feeling of danger lessened continually in a France that had been under siege and threatened with invasion up to that time. The great victories of the summer of 1794 brought about a definite relaxation as the threat of invasion and the fear of military success by the counter-revolution gradually subsided. The sense of urgency was disappearing, and it was just at this moment that the government of Robespierre decided to attack popular institutions. Moreover, with the coming of summer, current affairs were demanding attention, all the more so for having been neglected so long. That was not only the case among rural populations whose revolutionary zeal seldom resisted the down-to-earth call of agricultural duties. The city-dwelling *sans-culotte* also had to live and to give some thought to his business, as his wife was forever reminding him. Now popular societies met, as a rule, nearly every evening, and the sessions lasted from five to ten o'clock, sometimes until midnight. These meetings, coupled with many other obligations imposed on the revolutionary, including security watches and guard duty, not only encroached upon what little free time he had for pleasure and relaxation, they entailed long absences from his shop which, nevertheless, had to be kept open sixteen hours a day. They also cut in on his billiard game. And so, little by little, almost imperceptibly, normal life, the banal routine of ordinary living, regained the upper hand. We can see clearly the drama of their lives. A protester from Anduze summed it up thus: *À force de trop tendre l'arc, il se casse* (If you bend the bow too much, it will snap). And indeed the bow snapped for most of the *sociétaires*. They were short-term politicians. In general their wives and billiard tables had the last word.

And also there was nothing very amusing or agreeable in Robespierre's Republic. It exuded ennui and virtue just like the insipid and didactic speeches of the Incorruptible himself. We have only to think of those dull, interminable celebrations of the *Être Suprême* at the end of which they sat down to partake of the *plat républicain,* "the Republican dish," the only one that was available, and sometimes served *sans vin!* It was useless to try to exhort these listeners with oratorical bombast: *Attention! Don't let go! Above all, don't neglect your regular meetings! You are still needed. The hidden enemy has not been vanquished. The victory is not yet ours!* If they were needed only to vote congratulatory speeches and extravagant eulogies in weary, hackneyed platitudes, there was no need to pretend any sense of urgency. The revolutionaries had finally grown tired. For proof we have the records of the sharp drop-off in attendance at provincial society meetings, beginning in Germinal, year II. The picture of the revolutionary man begins to blur and grow dim. He has begun to recover his anonymity long before Thermidor. The time to *révolutionner* had already passed.

To sum up, the revolutionary man was only a temporary phenomenon, incapable of resisting wear and tear, destined to succumb to lassitude, a creature produced by unusual circumstances. He was not a professional in conducting Revolutions. And what is a professional Revolutionary if not a bureaucrat like the rest, a bureaucrat solidly intrenched in a frozen Revolution, or else a would-be conspirator, a *romantique*, or again *un révolutionnaire en peau de lapin* (a revolutionary in a rabbit's skin). People like Babeuf had little in common with the revolutionaries of the year II except in the imagination of the police and their informers. Our men of 1793 were not "revolutionaires in rabbit skin," nor were they professors of revolutionary theory. When they got home and put on their slippers, their political and revolutionary activity was over and done with. Once the great hopes and perils had passed, they returned to their familiar, everyday way of life. The year III, by accentuating social inequality and the overriding problem of a bread shortage, took care of the rest. The revolutionaries were less victimized by young *muscadins*, youthful murderers in fine footwear, than by economic crises and food scarcities which were to affect their families and, in many cases, reduce them to poverty, anonymity, and public charity.

There was doubtless a certain survival of the revolutionary mentality, especially in the military, where it took the form of violent anti-clericalism. It was also to manifest itself on the political plane after the elections of the year IV, which witnessed numerous attempts to regroup old terrorist cadres. But these efforts were confined to a handful of political leaders. As for conspirators, they made up a very small minority of "hard-boiled" individuals, stubborn revolutionaries, and perhaps also some persons of violent propensities, for the revolutionary temperament certainly included a measure of violence. For the remainder, it was silence once more as it had been before 1789. The revolutionaries were swallowed up along with the extraordinary events that had given them a fleeting but passionate moment on the stage of world history. They disappeared with the institutions whose recorded proceedings have permitted us to bring to light a few months in the submerged history of the little people, the attitudes and prejudices of a world of shops and workshops, whose voice would no longer be heard thereafter save through the distorted media of police reports.

RELIGIOUS SENTIMENT AND POPULAR CULTS DURING THE REVOLUTION

Patriot Saints and Martyrs of Liberty

~§ **By Albert Soboul**

For a long time, historians of the French Revolution have viewed the revolutionary cults as nothing but pragmatic political attempts. Reacting against this tendency, Albert Mathiez wished to point out the specifically religious nature of these cults. Yet we must still reach an agreement on the nature of the religious act. On this matter, Mathiez closely followed Durkheim, when the latter asserted that these religious phenomena were essentially distinguished by their form. Like his predecessors, Mathiez seems to have been little concerned with studying the religious sentiment manifested by those who took part in the ceremonies of the revolutionary cults; yet it is here that their nature could be clarified. Were they political expedients or a true religion?

The difficulty of this undertaking cannot be concealed. The documents certainly permit us to observe the creation of new ceremonial groups. To what degree do they inform us about the exact beliefs of the followers of

338

these new rituals? Here we can see the difficulty of studies in historical psychology. The relative abundance of popular documents concerning in particular the cult of the martyrs of liberty seems to us, however, to authorize this first attempt.

I

Catholic writers have naturally denied the revolutionary cults anything of a religious nature, in order to look upon them as nothing but a war machine against the Church. In his *Histoire des Sectes*, Grégoire above all stressed the dogmas of this *civil religion* which the revolutionaries, according to him, were trying to establish; but although he described the symbols, the rites, and the ceremonies, he too only considered it as a political creation without any real religious spirit.

Michelet was the first to have a presentiment of the religious nature of the great manifestations of the Revolution, of the Federations in particular, which he justly considered to be the first steps in the formation of the revolutionary cults. But in the end he criticized these various attempts for having been merely political forms devoid of dogma. "Fertile in laws, sterile in dogmas [the Revolution] did not satisfy the eternal hunger of the human soul, still starved, still thirsting after God . . . . The two reasoning parties, the Girondins and the Jacobins, did not bear this in mind. The Girondins completely dismissed the question, the Jacobins avoided it. They thought God would be content with lip service."

Aulard attached enough importance to the revolutionary cults to devote a special study to the cult of Reason and to that of the Supreme Being. But he emptied them of all religious content. He saw in them

the necessary and rather political results of the state of war into which the resistance of the Old Regime to the new spirit had thrown the Revolution. [The men of the year II] by enthroning the Goddess of Reason at Notre-Dame, or by glorifying the God of Rousseau on the Champ-de-Mars, had an essentially *political* aim and, for the most part, in these measures taken against the hereditary religion, or in their other violent attitudes or words, they were not looking for anything but an expedient for national defense.

Mathiez, although asserting his agreement with Aulard to see in these religious attempts not only the struggle against the Church, but essentially the defense of the new France, went even further: the revolutionary cults were a true religion. To isolate the religious aspect, Mathiez followed the analyses of Durkheim, for whom, we know, the religious act was above all distinguished by its form. Obligatory belief and obligatory worship and external observances; these are the two essential characteristics distinguished by Durkheim and Mathiez after him. Starting with these premises, Mathiez was less interested in the study of the common creed of the revolutionaries, than in the manifestations of the new faith, in the observances and ceremonies, in the revolutionary symbolism.

If I show all this, will I not have the right to conclude that there was a revolutionary religion, analogous in its essence to all other religions? [And Mathiez affirmed at the end of his study:] There is a revolutionary religion whose object is the social institution itself. This religion has its obligatory dogmas (the Declaration of the Rights of Man, and the Constitution), its symbols surrounded by mystical veneration (the three colors, the trees of Liberty, the altar of the Fatherland, etc. . . .), its ceremonies (civic festivals), its prayers, and its chants.

Mathiez's study, however, remained on the surface of things. Not that he can be reproached for having followed a purely historical plan: such a method is also appropriate for the history of religions. But Mathiez poorly characterized the religious reality, by identifying the religious with the collective. He applied to the eighteenth century an identification which was justified in Durkheim's context. The latter described archaic societies in which a diffuse religiosity impregnated everything; the social and the religious were mingled to a rather great degree. Can this be asserted for the end of the eighteenth century? With the development of rationalism during the previous century, religion became specialized and then occupied merely one part of collective life. It is therefore necessary to describe it by itself and to consider both the religious beliefs and the specifically religious ceremonies, as distinct from civil ceremonies. It is doubtless not incorrect to assert with Mathiez that the religious act is distinguished by its form. Yet this form must be stated precisely and the religious act considered as a whole: rites, symbols, dogmas, and beliefs, the latter approachable only indirectly like every mental activity.

The problem of the revolutionary cults appears to have been badly stated by the two most important historians who both misunderstood the specificity of the religious act, the political preoccupation of Aulard and the sociological deformation of Mathiez creating a false perspective. They both were more interested in official creations of the governing bourgeoisie than in the popular cults. Not that any given cult in that period belonged to any one class; but the popular cults allow us to form a realistic picture of the manifestations of religious spontaneity of the revolutionary masses. Aulard and Mathiez both stressed the break between the traditional religion and the new religion, agreeing in this way, as well as for other reasons, with the Catholic historians of the revolutionary cults. This break is scarcely to be contested and this innovation is precisely the interesting fact; again it is a question of knowing how to characterize it and what factors were involved.

However, whatever the importance of the political upheaval from 1789 to 1794, the Revolution could not destroy the traditional religion in the soul of the common people. The Revolution made its mark upon the people to a certain degree and used certain aspects of the evolution of Catholicism in a new popular religion. There is no doubt that, once the revolutionary crisis had passed, the men and women who, through some need within their soul, had embraced the new cult, went back to the traditional one. Although the momentary abandonment of Catholicism had constituted a break, we must nevertheless use the viewpoint of the traditional religion in order to study the revolutionary cults.

Without doubt, the study of the new rituals upon which Mathiez based his demonstration, is important. Yet we must state precisely how the syncretism with the old forms occurred, and what the new ceremonies borrowed from the Catholic service. In addition, what were the beliefs and to what degree were they related to the traditional beliefs? A religious cult implies on the part of the believer (especially from the viewpoint of eighteenth-century Catholicism) a veneration for its object—a transcendant, supernatural object—which to him appears endowed with an efficacious virtue, here below and in the great beyond. Thanks to the cult, the believer participates in the efficacy, which in a certain sense constitutes an exchange of oaths between man and the supernatural. Last, the religious act implies participation in the personal life of each individual. These are the characteristic features of the traditional religion; to what degree do they apply to the revolutionary cults?

II

The cult of the patriot saints permits us to state precisely one aspect of the shift from the Catholic religion to the revolutionary cults. To the old religious context this cult brings new political aspects which become a part of traditional worship.

Perrine Dugué belonged to a family of small farmers in Thorigné, a village in the Mayenne department, along the banks of the Sarthe. The entire family (Perrine had five brothers) was strongly partisan to the Revolution and opposed as best it could the *Chouans*. At Sainte-Suzanne, a market town to the north of Thorigné, two of the brothers had become members of the volunteer companies which protected it from the "brigands." On March 22, 1796, Perrine, who was soon to be nineteen, disregarding the threats which she had received, set out for the fair at Sainte-Suzanne and also to see her brothers, for whom she was accused of acting as an informer. Midway on her journey, she was killed by three *Chouans*; she was found the next day, and three days later was buried in a nearby field. Both sides accused one another of the murder, and perhaps these reciprocal accusations drew together all the elements of the population, the murder having strongly affected the popular imagination. Three tragic ballads of the period made no mention of Perrine's republican ideas and saw in her only a good Christian who had preferred death to rape. But it is none the less true that, since her feelings were known, Perrine generally came to be looked upon as a republican saint. She had been seen, according to abbé Coutard, "mounting into heaven with tri-colored wings"; the crowd ran to her tomb, where cures took place. As the rumor of these miracles spread, pilgrims came from as far away as the neighboring departments of Orne,

Sarthe, and Maine-et-Loire. In 1797, a chapel was constructed. Although the restoration of Catholic worship put an end to the cult of the Republican saint, whose miracles were not recognized, it did not completely erase the memory of her which persisted for a long time.

Perrine Dugué is not a unique example. The forest of Taillay, on the borders of the departments of Loire-Inférieure and Ille-et-Vilaine, conceals a famous tomb, called "the tomb of the girl." It is that of Marie Martin, originally from Tresboeuf. Either because she had shown the "blues" (republican soldiers) where a band of royalists was hiding, or because she did not wish to reveal the hiding place of her masters, she was abused and massacred by the *Chouans*. She was buried on the spot. According to an account of 1950, two crosses are at the head of the grave; to the surrounding oaks are nailed little niches containing statuettes. One of these niches serves as a collection box for pecuniary offerings, which a woman came and pocketed, until the war of 1914, every Sunday and on pilgrimage days. Today there are still pilgrimages to this tomb from all the neighboring communes, especially on Midsummer, Easter Monday, and Whitsunday. Sainte Pataude (as the local residents call her, after the nickname given to the republicans by the *Chouans*) is said to grant all favors which are asked of her. Mothers bring their small children to her so that they will walk early, and make them go around the tomb three times forcing them to take normal steps. The tomb is still kept up by the persons who leave ex-votos there. Woodcutters say that no ax has been able to cut into the trunk of the tree where the saint was tied and martyred.

These two examples show how the syncretism with old forms of worship is established. We observe a broadening of the traditional cult by the integration of republican and patriot saints. The old religious forms still clearly outweigh the new political aspects. Religious belief, although condemned here by the Church, could not be denied. The patriot saints appear endowed with an efficacious virtue, they perform miracles. The revolutionary cult still remains very close to Catholicism.

III

The cult of the martyrs of liberty seems to mark the end of an evolution in revolutionary religious sentiment based upon the traditional cult. Here new forms and political aspects, which are secondary in the cult of the patriot saints, clearly outweigh the old religious context.

By being primarily interested in the Cult of Reason and in the Cult of the Supreme Being, artificial creations of the governing revolutionary elements, the historians of the revolutionary cults have neglected the spontaneous development of the popular cult of the martyrs of liberty, especially of Marat. Yet it would have permitted them to form a precise picture of the development of religious sentiment during the Terror. This popular cult developed after July 1793, in the Parisian sections, the basic organizations of sans-culottery. It had for an object the veneration of three illustrious victims of the counter-revolution: first, Marat, assassinated on July 13, 1793; to whom was added Lepeletier de Saint-Fargeau, assassinated on January 20, 1793, by the *Garde de corps* Paris; and last Châlier, condemned by the reactionaries and guillotined at Lyons on July 17, 1793.

Marat, as a result of the role he had played since the beginning of the Revolution, enjoyed an immense prestige among the Parisian sans-culottes. His assassination (we will say nothing of its political consequences) caused the awakening of a popular veneration which remains one of the most original characteristics of the sans-culotte mentality. The formation of the new cult was marked, in the days which followed the assassination, by a veritable competition over the body of the Friend of the People. Who would keep these "precious remains"? The *Théâtre-Français* section, which was that of Marat and which would soon take his name, claimed them. Jacobins and Cordeliers fought over his heart, which finally remained with the Cordeliers. The women of the *Société des Républicains-Révolutionnaires* took an oath on July 17 to raise their children in the *cult* of Marat and to put in their hands no other *Holy Scriptures* but his collected works. On July 26, the Cordeliers decided to "raise an altar to the heart of the incorruptible Marat." The ceremony took place at the beginning of August. In reality, Marat's heart was put in a vase and these "precious remains of a god," as the invocation of a patriot called them, were suspended from the archway of the meeting hall: an imitation of an old rite, or the creation of a new one? .... A few days before, a popular brochure had at great lengths compared Marat to Jesus, who had also fallen "under the blows of fanaticism, while working with all his strength to bring about the salvation of mankind." It was undoubtedly a question of making Jesus a revolutionary; but as a result, Marat shared some of Jesus' divine nature.

We must emphasize here that ambiguity which lies so heavily on numerous words, transposed directly from the religious vocabulary, and the mental contagion which results. When the authorities declared that Marat was immortal, they meant that he was alive in their memories; but for the sans-culottes who had been brought up in Catholicism, the word *immortal* was inseparable from the immortality of the soul. For the same sans-culottes, *saint* applied to Marat could only mean he was *sacred*. Among the saints commonly invoked, the martyrs held a lofty place; to say that Marat was a martyr, for the sans-culottes assuredly meant to elevate him to sainthood. While the militant expected to receive comfort for his actions from the Friend of the People, living in his memory, the sans-culottes hoped that Marat, elevated into the ranks of the saints, would grant the success of the Revolution. The Revolution had been a *gospel*, a holy scripture, which would assure the salvation of humanity. For the sans-culottes, brought up in the Catholic religion, salvation also could be understood in a temporal sense; the ex-votos in churches bear witness to this. Doubtless we have found no ex-votos dedicated to the Friend of the People; but to call upon Marat, a martyr of liberty because he had offered his life for the Revolution, and therefore for the salvation of humanity, must have had the same result in the popular mentality.

During the month of August, several sections and popular societies held funeral services in honor of Marat or installed his bust and that of Lepeletier—ceremonies in which the characteristics of the new cult began to become clear.

On August 4, the fraternal society of the patriots for both sexes placed the busts of the martyrs in their meeting room. On August 8, the *Contrat-Social* section exposed in the church of Saint-Eustache, its meeting place, "the effigy of this representative of the people lying on his deathbed": a spectacle which borrowed the framework of the traditional religion and which was well made to strike the popular imagination. The *Société des Hommes-du-Dix-Août* listened to the funeral oration for Marat on August 16 in the Filles-Dieu where they met.

How can we characterize these ceremonies? The mere inauguration of a bust accompanied by speeches doubtless does not constitute a religious rite. The sans-culottes found new energy in these manifestations which generally ended with a civic oath. Here it was not a question of supernatural aid, but of the normal comfort which a group provides. We can assume, however, that for many of those present these funeral ceremonies in honor of Marat, which usually took place in churches, served as masses for the repose of his soul.

At the same time, the external characteristics of the new cult were becoming established. Here is the description of the funeral service in honor of Marat held on August 18, 1793, in Bonne-Nouvelle Church.

The effigy of Marat was exposed in the nave in a sarcophagus decorated with blue drapery spangled with stars. At each end were two candelabra in a classical style; before it, on another sarcophagus at a different level was the bust of Lepeletier. The afore-said sarcophagi, decorated with garlands of cypress, with inscriptions containing the virtues of these great men. Behind Marat was a representation of the bathtub . . . . The principal altar of the church served as a throne for the figure of Liberty. The periphery of the church was decorated with great draperies in the national colors and with branched candelabra. Above the principal door of the church was a transparency in the national colors on which were these words: entrance of the *Temple of Liberty*.

Here we are witnessing the creation of a new ceremonial ensemble, and we can see the syncretism with the old forms of the Catholic service taking shape. Draperies, candelabra, and sarcophagi come from the traditional ceremony; but the national colors replace the funereal black. The cypress garlands and the inscriptions are more evocative of memories of Antiquity. To strike the imagination of the faithful, an appeal is made to the resources of the plastic arts, painting, and sculpture. The representation of Marat's bathtub calls to mind the portrayal of the instruments of the passion; the statue of liberty replaces that of the Virgin. Thus, elements borrowed from

Catholic worship or from antiquity and revolutionary elements are gradually formed into a ceremony. A symbolism takes shape. But the new cult remains essentially revolutionary; although the documents permit us to show precisely what these new ceremonies borrow from Catholic ceremony, nothing permits us to indicate the influence of Catholic beliefs themselves. The new ritual tends above all to exalt the civic sentiment of the sans-culottes: sermons, invocations, prayers—the contents of the oral rite are basically political.

❦

Toward the end of the month of August 1793, the popular thrust became stronger. During September the sans-culottes definitively won out in those sections which were still not under their control. The cult of the martyrs of liberty then became widespread and more precisely outlined at the same time. Lepeletier was then always associated with Marat. The ceremonial ensemble was enlarged; choirs (but patriotic choirs) and soon processions came to give the new cult a truly religious pomp.

On September 1, the *Fontaine-de-Grenelle* section proceeded to inaugurate the busts of Marat and Lepeletier. On September 15, the *Molière-et-Lafontaine* section, now placed under the patronage of Brutus, held a ceremony in their honor in the Church of Saint Joseph, of rue Montmartre. That same day, in the "regenerated" *Montagne* section (regenerated, that is to say sans-culottized) the "apotheosis" of Lepeletier and Marat took place. These ceremonies usually took place on Sunday, in the churches where the general assemblies met. Thus the new cult gradually supplanted the old, but not without borrowing many of its external elements. On September 22, the *Panthéon-Français* section made an innovation through the creation of a veritable republican trinity, by joining Brutus to Marat and Lepeletier. On subsequent Sundays, September 29 and October 6, these ceremonies multiplied and without a doubt a part of those attending were church-goers. To the now customary speeches and choirs, the *Halle-au-Blé* and *Guillaume-Tell* sections on October 6 added a procession through the streets of their quarters. Here Brutus again preceded Lepeletier and Marat. The addition of Brutus, like the consecration of a stone from the Bastille with the Declaration of the Rights of Man engraved upon it, emphasized the civic nature of the ceremony. On September 9, in the *Piques* section, a true procession was held. Thus a new element in the cult of the martyrs was confirmed.

The processions of Catholic worship had taken place in the various quarters of Paris until the spring of 1793, especially the Corpus Christi Day procession, which had, however, been marked by incidents here and there. The corteges of the cult of martyrs unobtrusively replaced them. As religious processions formed an important part of traditional popular life, the militants of the sections and of the clubs adapted them to their own points of view. But to what degree was there among the faithful a transfer of

Catholic beliefs to the new ceremonies? The documents remain silent on this important point, or are difficult to interpret. To the traditional procession with chants and stations before the street-altars and the images of the saints, the sans-culottes added, in addition to the republican theme and symbols, elements borrowed from the national celebrations which since 1790 had marked the great revolutionary anniversaries, especially the military paraphernalia. Thus, in honor of the martyrs of liberty, there developed a popular art form of the cortege inspired both by religion and patriotism, which in the autumn of 1793 contributed to the growth of civic feeling. But how can we establish exactly what proportion of the feelings of the followers of the new religion were really religious?

The first processions, still brief, were inspired by the *Halle-au-Blé* and *Guillaume-Tell* sections of October 6, and by the *Piques* section on October 9. On Sunday, October 13, the *Révolutionnaire* section, formerly the *Pont-Neuf* section, formed a long cortege through the streets of its quarter with banners and statues of the martyrs, patriotic choirs and military bands. On the afternoon of October 16, the procession of the *Muséum* section (David's section) went through the streets surrounding the Louvre, then entered the central courtyard by the Perrault colonnade. At their head, drums and gunners in two rows abreast; then the popular societies with their emblems, the Parisian sections preceded by their banners, and the members of the administration and of the tribunals; an armed detachment followed them, a flag and drums at their head, then the section as a whole. A band preceded a deputation from the Convention, which was followed by the young men from the first troop levy, an oak branch in their hands, surrounding the citizenesses of the section, dressed in white, leading their children by the hand, and carrying flowers. A detachment of the armed forces concluded the parade. In the courtyard of the Louvre, they had placed sarcophagi over which rose original paintings by David of Lepeletier and Marat assassinated; a funeral service was held there with hymns and civic speeches tinted with a vague religiosity. As in the ceremonies of Catholic worship, all the arts added their prestige to the exaltation of the faithful. The sans-culottes received a sort of communion in the memory of their martyrs. But to what degree did these ceremonies imply an attitude of veneration in regard to the object being commemorated? In other words, to what degree did religious sentiment come to exalt the civic spirit? In reading the documents one senses a religious fervor; but precise manifestations of it cannot, however, be found.

The new cult gradually spread to all the sections, finally becoming formal. On 9 Brumaire, the *Bonne-Nouvelle* section put new forges to work at manufacturing arms; once work was begun, they dedicated the busts of Marat and Lepeletier. Patriotic effort and civic enthusiasm went together. The same day the *Temple* section celebrated "that festival which patriotism has created. The benefactors of the common people should receive altars [. . .] Paris raises temples to the martyrs of liberty [. . .] The priests and all the enemies of the Republic are daring to vilify the solemn worship which we pay them. May the representatives of the people avenge them this calumny." Here for the first time appears the clearly stated opposition to Catholicism and the specific role of the new cult in the de-Christianization. Although the new ceremonial ensemble borrowed certain aspects from the Catholic religion, there does not seem to have been, at least in the minds of its promoters, a syncretism with the old beliefs. Here a reference is made not to the saints of the Catholic Church (although Marat and Lepeletier were styled as *apostles*), but to the heroes of antiquity placed among the gods: "the inventor of the plow and the courageous mortal who dared to avenge humanity for the outrages of tyrants." Likewise, the syncretism appeared to be purely formal, when the *Champs-Élysées* section asked the Convention of 10 Brumaire, "whether the first two days of the republican era should not bear the names of its first two martyrs."

The organization of the cult of the martyrs of liberty was, however, reaching completion when Châlier, guillotined by the counter-revolution on July 17, 1793, at Lyons, was added to Lepeletier and Marat. Thus was formed the revolutionary triad or trinity, depending upon whether reference was made to Antiquity or to Catholicism. But here it is a question of a political initiative involving no popular spontaneity, from which all feelings of religious veneration seem excluded from the very first. The addition of Châlier represents one step further toward the nonreligious and, despite his being associated with two other martyrs, he represents a third stage in the evolution, beyond the cult of patriot saints and beyond the cult of Marat, toward unbelief.

The initiative for the cult of Châlier came from Chaumette, *Procureur général* of the Commune of Paris. Was this a political maneuver on his part? Undoubtedly. The cult of the martyrs had developed spontaneously in the sections, without intervention by the municipal authorities. It expressed in religious forms the revolutionary enthusiasm of the sans-culottes whom the ceremonies exalted. It is significant that during the summer of 1793, while the new cult was forming, the commune organized no ceremonies. It was only toward the middle of Brumaire, once the cult of the martyrs had become widespread, that the authorities did anything to support it. Chaumette intervened in order to link to Marat and Lepeletier a martyr more in keeping with his political aims. On 11 Brumaire (November 1, 1793), Chaumette gave a funeral oration for Châlier before the General Council of the commune. In it the Jacobin from Lyons appeared more as a hero from Antiquity than as a saint of a new religion. The praise of Chalier's republican virtues, the *simple and true account* of his last moments, and his final, rather Socratic words, all contributed to creating an image of the new martyr which was very apt to strike the popular imagination, to make him worthy of entering the republican Pantheon. But nothing in it encouraged the veneration and exaltation of the religious sentiment.

Here we can see the difference in behavior between the sans-culottes themselves and the militants coming from the lower and middle bourgeoisie. The latter, possessing a certain classical culture, referred to memories of Antiquity; the former borrowed the elements of a new cult from the Catholicism in which they had been raised. But, once again, to what extent does the syncretism go beyond the ceremonial aspects and affect belief itself? No document provides evidence of the cult of Marat as a saint. His tomb did not become an efficacious place where miracles took place. Herein lies the difference between it and the cult of the patriot saints and the evolution of belief in them.

However, it appears that the manifestations in honor of Marat must be considered as more than mere evidence of esteem for a statesman. Undoubtedly, the militant members of the sections who officiated over the new cult, stressed its civic aspect. Although they preserved the external forms of the traditional litany, the invocation, and the prayer, its new contents were essentially political. But we must clearly point out that there was a continuity in worshippers between the traditional cult and the revolutionary one. Was there also, in their minds, a transfer of the old beliefs concerning the saints to the new martyrs? . . . The reports of police observers most often stressed the great numbers attending the ceremonies of the *culte décadaire* with which the cult of the martyrs had become integrated. For example, on 10 Ventôse (February 28, 1794), in the *Bonne-Nouvelle* section, "there was a considerable number of people, and especially women" present in the Temple of Reason, formerly the Bonne-Nouvelle Church. On the same day, in the *Gravilliers* section, "the former Church of Saint-Nicolas des Champs was almost completely full, and with many young people." On 30 Ventôse (March 20, 1794), a police observer noted in his report that: "In the past we used to see many more women than men in church; this is also true in the Temples of Reason. Few men and many women." Did these women consider the martyrs of the new trinity to be saints enthroned in heaven? We might assume so, although no document permits us to assert that such was the case. The framework of the religious manifestations had not changed; the pomp of the new cult could be compared with that of the traditional cult. It is not implausible that for these women from the common people who formed the main body of the faithful, the adoration of the Catholic saints had simply been replaced by that of the republican martyrs.

The de-Christianization movement which developed in Brumaire of year II (autumn 1793) and whose origins were far from being popular, gave a new impetus to the cult of the martyrs. Those sections, lagging behind, hurriedly established it. The cult now appeared as one of the elements of the republican cult which the militants of the sections intended to establish on the ruins of the traditional religion. The devotion to the republican trinity became a part of the Cult of Reason, a divinity which was too abstract, even though she had borrowed the features of a chorus girl in the opera.

The continuity of religious sentiment under new forms did not, however, proceed without arousing opposition. The Catholic believers accused the new cult of idolatry. On 26 Brumaire (November 16, 1793), the revolutionary committee of the *Arcis* section arrested a candlemaker's shopboy and accused him of fanaticism. He had refused to attend a ceremony in honor of Marat, saying "that he would prefer to die a thousand times rather than to attend a celebration like that." Yet this man was a good sans-culotte who had taken up arms in all the great revolutionary insurrections. His case was not an isolated one.

The cult of the martyrs also aroused attacks from the atheists, where political reasons were combined with ideological motives. On 8 Frimaire (November 28, 1793), Hébert attacked the cult of Marat before the Jacobins: "It has already been said that the Parisians had substituted Marat for Jesus." And in Volume 315 of his *Père Duchesne*: they would like to make us believe that "the Parisians no longer wish to recognize any god other than Marat." On 12 Frimaire, Danton chided a petitioner who was beginning to read a litany to the glory of Marat before the Convention. Was there political or personal hostility in this reaction, or a conviction that the new cult, because it was religious, was on the whole still too close to the traditional religion? All these motives doubtlessly explain the mortal blow dealt to the cult.

The cult of the martyrs, integrated into the Cult of Reason, nevertheless persisted until the spring of 1794, and the ceremonies held each *décadi* attracted large crowds, especially women and children. The reaction which set in with the trial and execution of Hébert (March 24, 1794), dealt it a mortal blow. Marat was to a certain extent involved in the discredit attached to Père Duchesne, for the moderates taxed their ingenuity in order to create confusion in the popular mind. As early as 27 Ventôse (March 17, 1794), a police observer heard someone say that "if Marat were still alive at this moment, he would have been indicted and perhaps guillotined." On 5 Germinal (March 25, 1794) the news was spread that the *Marat* section, not hesitating to disavow him, had veiled the portrait of the Friend of the People. According to the testimony of a police observer on 8 Germinal, the inhabitants of the villages around Paris had been perturbed about the rumors circulating about Marat: "If it is possible that Marat deceived them, they will no longer be able to trust anyone."

This campaign was brutally stopped by the authorities of the commune of Paris who, on 9 Germinal (March 29, 1794) threatened to declare suspect all those who attempted to alter the esteem "justly due" the martyrs of liberty. But esteem is far from veneration. The Robespierrist authorities of the commune thus marked the narrow limits within which it intended to allow the cult of Marat to continue. It was no longer a question of religious fervor, but simply of civic spirit. Germinal of the year II forshadowed the reaction of the Year III. Counter-revolutionaries and Catholics would then be able to defenestrate at their ease the statues of the martyrs of liberty. On 30 Thermidor of the year III (August 17, 1795), in the *Nord* section, "the statues established by terrorism and placed in the choir of the Church of Saint-Laurent" were destroyed. It was the same in all the sections.

Thus at the end of this study, and without wishing to touch upon the political aspect of the popular cults here, we can observe that the political and social crisis in 1793 had profound repercussions upon the religious sentiment of the revolutionary masses. But how are we to interpret the position of the popular cults expressing these repercussions within the general evolution of religious sentiment at the end of the eighteenth century? Are we to believe that there was on the whole a de-Christianization during the ten years of revolution and that the popular cults studied here represent the steps in this de-Christianization? Or else should these cults be considered as new forms of sects, through which the traditional religion was regenerated? This implies a broader problem: when the Christian faith is lost, is unbelief attained by means of a sect? These questions can only be asked. Undoubtedly, for a better approach to the truth, we would have to consider the social groups which created these cults or which simply participated in them: some, the lower or middle bourgeoisie, appear to have been rather on the side of unbelief,—the others, the sans-culottes themselves, apparently remained within the traditional religious context.

Here we can see the fatal obstacle to the popular cults. Although we can sense in these cults the factors which through the ages have contributed to the germination of religions, these religions had theologians. The popular cults did not. The militants who organized these cults were undoubtedly rationalists; but the common people transposed their ideas within the framework of the religious education they had received. Were the orators of the ceremonies in honor of the martyrs of liberty aware of this transposition? If such were the case, they would doubtless have turned against this survival of the education by the clergy which was precisely what they were trying to annihilate by de-Christianization. It goes without saying that the common people were incapable of formulating the theology of new cults; and their leaders were no less incapable of so doing.

The ephemeral character of the revolutionary cults explains why we have encountered no critical and independent mind which observed this popular transposition and left us a written record of it. Thus, owing to the lack of documents, we can only indicate these problems and establish a few landmarks.

Bibliography

N.B. For the most part this bibliography is limited to books and articles that treat the subjects dealt with in this volume. The citations that appear in the footnotes to the introduction will not be repeated here. Unless otherwise noted, the place of publication is Paris.

Any student approaching the history of the French Revolution should know the major bibliographical tools. We cite here only those devoted wholly or in part to printed materials. Consultation of these works will lead directly to the manuscript sources and to tools available for their utilization. Pierre Caron, *Manuel pratique pour l'étude de la Révolution française* (1947) is indispensable. Louis Villat, *La Révolution et l'empire (1789–1815), I—Les assemblées révolutionnaires (1789–1799),* in the Collection Clio (1947) is now somewhat out of date but is still useful as an introduction to the state of our knowledge. It should be supplemented by Jacques Godechot, *Les Révolutions (1770–1799)* (1963), in the Collection Nouvelle Clio. The last-named volume has the distinction of providing bibliographical references on revolutions outside France, as might be expected from the co-author of the "atlantic revolution" thesis. More advanced students will want to consult A. Martin et G. Walter, *Catalogue de l'histoire de la Révolution française* (1936–1955, five volumes), which lists contemporary publications, and G. Walter, *Répertoire de l'histoire de la Révolution française* (1914–1945, two volumes), which catalogues later work. Most notable among bibliographies of local history is Maurice Tourneux, *Bibliographie de l'histoire de Paris pendant la Révolution française* (1890–1913, five volumes), which actually covers more than its title indicates. But once again it is limited to the writings of contemporaries.

To keep up to date, the student ought to consult the quarterly issues of the *Annales Historiques de la Révolution Française,* published since 1924 by the Société des Etudes Robespierristes (hereafter cited as *AHRF*). It is the principal journal in the field. Other important periodicals for our purposes are the *Revue Historique,* the *Revue d'Histoire Moderne et Contemporaine* (hereafter *RHMC*), and especially its supplementary bulletin, obtained only through membership in the Société d'histoire moderne. In the United States, *French Historical Studies* has been publishing regular bibliographical lists since 1960. In England, *Past and Present* publishes many articles on the Revolution.

To the major general works already cited, we ought to add Georges Lefebvre, *Etudes sur la Révolution française* (1954, new edition, 1963). Albert Soboul, *Précis de l'histoire de la Révolution française* (1962) is an authoritative new summary. In English, Norman Hampson, *Social History of the French Revolution* (London, 1962) is not quite so social as the title would have us believe, but it is well written and up to date. R.R. Palmer, *The Age of the Democratic Revolution* (Princeton, 1959–1964, two volumes), and Jacques Godechot, *La Grande nation, l'expansion révolutionnaire de la France dans le monde, 1789– 1799* (1956, two volumes) argue the world or Atlantic revolution thesis they first developed in "Le problème de l'atlantique," a report presented to the Tenth World Historical Congress in Rome in 1955 and published in its *Relazioni,* V (Florence, 1955). Finally, E.J. Hobsbawm, *The Age of Revolution, 1789–1848* (New York, 1962, now in a Mentor paperback) is a remarkable synthesis that goes far beyond the French Revolution to show its effects on the formation of the nineteenth-century world.

For the problem of method in the study of social structure, consult F. Furet, "Structures sociales parisiennes au XVIIIe siècle, l'apport d'une série fiscale," *Annales: Economies, Sociétés, Civilisations,* XVI (1961), pp. 939–958, and *idem.,* "Pour une définition des classes inférieures à l'époque moderne," *A:ESC,* XVIII(1963), pp. 459–474. Preliminary results of the research on Paris being carried out under the guidance of Professor Labrousse are contained in A. Daumard and F. Furet, *Structures et relations sociales à Paris au milieu du XVIIIe* (1961). This has been strongly and cogently criticized by Jean-Yves Tirat, "Problèmes de méthode en histoire sociale," *RHMC,* X (1963), pp. 211– 218. Finally, two books that treat the early nineteenth century ought to be read for their methodological contributions: A. Daumard, *La Bourgeoisie Parisienne de 1815 à 1848* (1963), and Louis Chevalier, *Classes laborieuses et classes dangereuses* (1958).

Specific studies on social classes are still relatively few in number. Elinor G. Barber, *The Bourgeoisie in XVIIIth Century France* (Princeton, 1955) is based on literary sources and is superficial. There are some good articles in Commission d'histoire économique et sociale de la Révolution française, *Assemblée Générale de 1939,* I (Besançon, 1942). George Lefebvre's magnificent *Etudes Orléanaises* have been published posthumously (1963, two volumes). An excerpt in English, "Urban society in the Orléanais in the late eighteenth century," was published in *Past and Present,* no. 19 (1961), pp. 46–71. See also

J. Kaplow, *Elbeuf during the Revolutionary Period: History and Social Structure* (Baltimore, 1964).

For the nobility, see R. Forster, *The Nobility of Toulouse in the Eighteenth Century* (Baltimore, 1960). Also M. Reinhard, "Elite et noblesse dans la seconde moitié du XVIIIe siècle," *RHMC*, III (1956), pp. 5–37. A very short introduction by J. McManners in English is contained in A. Goodwin (ed.), *The European Nobility in the Eighteenth Century* (London, 1953).

The peasants are treated by Lefebvre, "Les Paysans et la Révoution française," in his *Etudes*, already cited, as well as in his thesis. Paul Bois, *Les Paysans de l'ouest* (1960) is excellent. P. de Saint-Jacob, *Les Paysans de la Bourgogne du Nord au XVIIIe siècle* (1961) is also important.

There have been few works dealing directly with the urban poor in the period before the Revolution. For the moment, we must be content to approach them from several diverse angles. For instance, the role of the guild is treated by Fr. Olivier-Martin, *L'Organisation corporative de la France d'ancien régime* (1938). Demographic studies may teach us something about urban class structure. To begin with, there is M. Reinhard and A. Armengaud, *Histoire générale de la population mondiale* (1961). See also the studies in Commission d'histoire économique et sociale de la Révolution, *Mémoires et Documents*, XIV—*Contributions à l'histoire démographique de la Révolution française* (1962). The publications of the Institut National des Etudes Démographiques and its journal, *Population*, are prime sources for the study of French population on the eve of the Revolution and after.

The problem of subsistence (*subsistances*) has been better worked. Among the important studies are L. Cahen, "L'approvisionnement en pain de Paris au XVIIIe siècle et la question de la boulangerie," *Revue d'histoire économique et sociale*, XIV (1926), pp. 458–472, and the same author's "La question du pain à Paris à la fin du XVIIIe siècle," *Cahiers de la Révolution française*, I (1934), pp. 50–76. J. Vidalenc, "L'approvisionnement de Paris en viande à la fin de l'ancien régime," *RHES*, XXX (1952), pp. 116–132 deals with the luxury commodity of meat. Most suggestive as to the possible biological consequences of malnutrition are A. Poitrineau, "L'alimentation populaire en Auvergne au XVIIIe siècle," *A:ESC*, XVII (1962), pp. 323–331; see also J. Meuvret, "Les crises de subsistances et la démographie de la France d'ancien régime," *Population* (1946), pp. 643–650; and J. Bourgeois-Pichat, "L'evolution de la population française depuis le XVIIIe siècle," *Population* (1951), pp. 635–662.

For the beginnings of the Revolution, see George Rudé, "The Outbreak of the French Revolution," *Past and Present*, no. 8 (1955), pp. 28–42. Also F. Braesch, *1789: L'année cruciale* (1941), G. Lefebvre, *Quatre-Vingt-Neuf* (1939), translated as *The Coming of the French Revolution* (Princeton, 1947) by R.R. Palmer and now available in a Vintage paperback. J. Egret has recently added a general treatise to his massive output on the period 1787–1789, *La Prérévolution française* (1962).

For an introduction to the ideology of the Revolution, consult Daniel Mornet, *Les origines intellectuelles de la Révolution française* (1933), which contains a wide-ranging bibliography. Ph. Sagnac, *La formation de la société française moderne, II—la révolution des idées et des moeurs et le déclin de l'ancien régime* (1946) is also worthwhile. On a more specific subject, see Ph. Ariès, *Histoire des populations françaises et leur attitude devant la vie depuis le XVIIIe siècle* (1948). For the popular mentality, see R. Baehrel, "Epidémie et terreur," *AHRF* (1951), pp. 113–146, and R. Cobb, "The revolutionary mentality in France," *History*, XLII (1957), pp. 181–196. The study of criminality undertaken by B. Boutelet, "Etudes par sondage de la criminalité dans la bailliage du Pont de l'Arche (XVIIe–XVIIe siècles)," *Annales de Normandie*, XII (1962), pp. 235–262, promises to prove fruitful in bringing us closer to the popular mind, but the results are as yet very limited.

The literature on the *sans-culottes* is now growing to immense proportions. In addition to the several titles cited in the introduction, consult R.B. Rose, "The Revolutionary Committees of the Paris Sections in 1793," *Bulletin of the John Rylands Library*, XXXV (1952), pp. 88–110, and the same author's "Eighteenth century price riots, the French Revolution and the Jacobin maximum," *International Review of Social History* (1959), pp. 432–445. The second volume of Lefebvre's *Etudes Orléanaises* deals entirely with the disintegration of the sans-culotte movement in the face of the maximum. A. Soboul, "Robespierre and the Popular Movement of 1793–1794," *Past and Present*, no. 5 (1954), pp. 54–70 is a good essay in English by the authority in the field. Also in English is W. Finley Shepard, *Price Control and the Reign of Terror* (Berkeley, 1953), but it relies almost entirely on Mathiez and adds little or nothing to what is already known. R. Cobb's thesis, *Les armées révolutionnaires* (1962, two volumes) is of fundamental importance. The articles in W. Markov (ed.), *Jakobiner und Sansculotten, Beiträge zur Geschichte der französischen Revolutionsregierung, 1793–1794* (Berlin, 1956) are useful, as is the collection of documents he edited with Soboul, *Die Sans-culotten von Paris* (Berlin, 1957).

The basic work on the peasants during the Revolution is G. Lefebvre, *Questions agraires au temps de la Terreur* (second edition, 1954). A. Soboul, "La communauté rurale (XVIIIe–XIXe siècles)," *Revue de Synthèse*, 3rd series, VII (1957), pp. 283–315, is a good introduction to long term problems, while Marc Bloch, *Les caractères originaux de l'histoire rurale française* (new edition, 1953–1956, two volumes) is a classic that must be read by anyone who wishes to study the agriculture of the old regime. A comprehensive bibliography will be found in H. Sée, *Histoire économique de la France, II: de 1789 à 1914* (new edition by Robert Schnerb, 1951).